WORLD FOOTBALL RECORDS 2024

Published in 2023 by Welbeck

An imprint of Welbeck Non-Fiction Limited, part of Welbeck Publishing Group.

Offices in: London - 20 Mortimer Street, London W1T 3JW &
Sydney - Level 17, 207 Kent St, Sydney NSW 2000 Australia

www.welbeckpublishing.com

Text & Design © Welbeck Non-Fiction Limited, part of Welbeck Publishing Group

A CIP catalogue record for this book is available from the British Library.

ISBN: 978-1-80279-657-5

Editor: Conor Kilgallon
Design: Tall Tree
Picture research: Tall Tree
Production: Rachel Burgess

All stats, facts and figures are correct up to 21 June 2023.

Printed in Dubai

10 9 8 7 6 5 4 3 2 1

WORLD FOOTBALL RECORDS

2024

FIFTEENTH EDITION

KEIR RADNEDGE

WELBECK

CONTENTS

INTRODUCTION

World football is on the move. The FIFA World Cup in Qatar in November and December 2022 drew a line between eras in the international game. This was the first World Cup held in the Arab sphere and the first in the northern hemisphere winter. From Argentina's opening defeat to Saudi Arabia to their ultimate shootout triumph over France, the drama proved magnetic, with record broadcast and internet ratings around the planet. Yet this was also the end of an era as Qatar marked the last FIFA World Cup in its traditional form. In 2026, the finals will expand from 32 to 48 teams, which demands staging across three neighbouring countries. Only a handful of nations will now be capable of hosting the World Cup within their territory alone.

Once upon a time the governing bodies, from world federation FIFA to Europe's UEFA and the other continental confederations, worried that national team football was losing the battle for popularity with international club competitions. Complex negotiations to find a balance resulted in the vision presented by FIFA president Gianni Infantino in March 2023 on his re-election for a further four-year term of office.

As a result of its growing popularity, the FIFA World Cup is being expanded. This expansion acknowledges the improving standards of national team football in Africa and Asia. Saudi Arabia and Japan achieved major upsets in Qatar, while Morocco became the first African – and Arab – national team to reach the semi-finals.

The various confederations are also celebrating the increasing popularity and success of their regional championships and adopting their own versions of Europe's UEFA Nations League. In addition, FIFA will launch its rebuilt 32-team Club World Cup in 2025 and explore the creation of a World Series to offer new opportunities for inter-continental competitive experience.

This is the future for women's football, too. The FIFA Women's World Cup in Australia and New Zealand broke records of its own and finally helped encourage all of the world federation's member associations to invest seriously in girls' and women's football. A FIFA Women's Club World Cup is not far off.

All aspects of this grand football landscape are featured in this latest, 15th edition of *World Football Records*. Read on to follow the achievements and stars, old and new, from all of football's major international tournaments for men and women at all levels of the global game.

Keir Radnedge
London 2023

THE COUNTRIES

The founding fathers of association football back in the mid-19th century would be amazed to see how the game has swept the globe. Today's players and fans dare not envisage where football will be in 10 years' time, let alone another 170.

Association football dominates the world of sport around the planet. The small seed sown by the creation of the Football Association in London in 1863 has grown into a mighty sporting empire.

At the head of the global football pyramid is FIFA, the world governing body. Supporting FIFA's work are national associations in 211 countries, across the six regional geographical confederations: Africa, Asia, Europe, Oceania, South America, and the Caribbean, Central and North America. These associations not only field the national teams who have built sporting history, but they also oversee the growth of football in their countries, from professional leagues to grassroots.

It was England and Scotland that played the first international football in the late 19th century; the British Home Championship followed, laying the foundations for international tournaments to come, with the *Copa América* of South America and FIFA World Cup following in 1916 and 1930 respectively.

The FIFA World Cup is merely the peak of a competitive pyramid that extends down through the six regional confederations for men, women and youngsters. The age-group competitions at both under-17 and under-20 level will be converted into annual events so that no rising generation feels at a disadvantage in scaling for football ladder.

CONCACAF
Founded: 1961
Associations: 35 (+6 non-FIFA members)
Headquarters: Miami, United States

CONMEBOL
Founded: 1916
Associations: 10
Headquarters: Luque, Paraguay

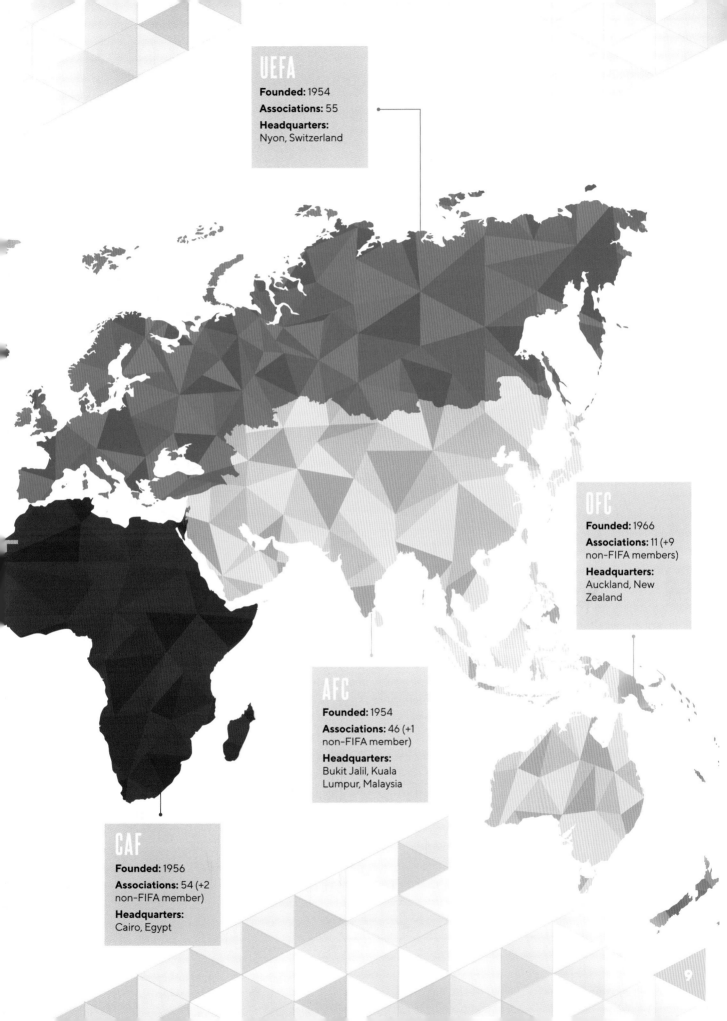

UEFA

Founded: 1954
Associations: 55
Headquarters:
Nyon, Switzerland

OFC

Founded: 1966
Associations: 11 (+9
non-FIFA members)
Headquarters:
Auckland, New
Zealand

AFC

Founded: 1954
Associations: 46 (+1
non-FIFA member)
Headquarters:
Bukit Jalil, Kuala
Lumpur, Malaysia

CAF

Founded: 1956
Associations: 54 (+2
non-FIFA member)
Headquarters:
Cairo, Egypt

EUROPE

Europe has dominated the world game at both national team and club levels over the past 25 years.

UEFA

Confederation founded: 1954

Number of associations: 55

Headquarters: Nyon, Switzerland

Most continental championship wins: Germany, Spain (three)

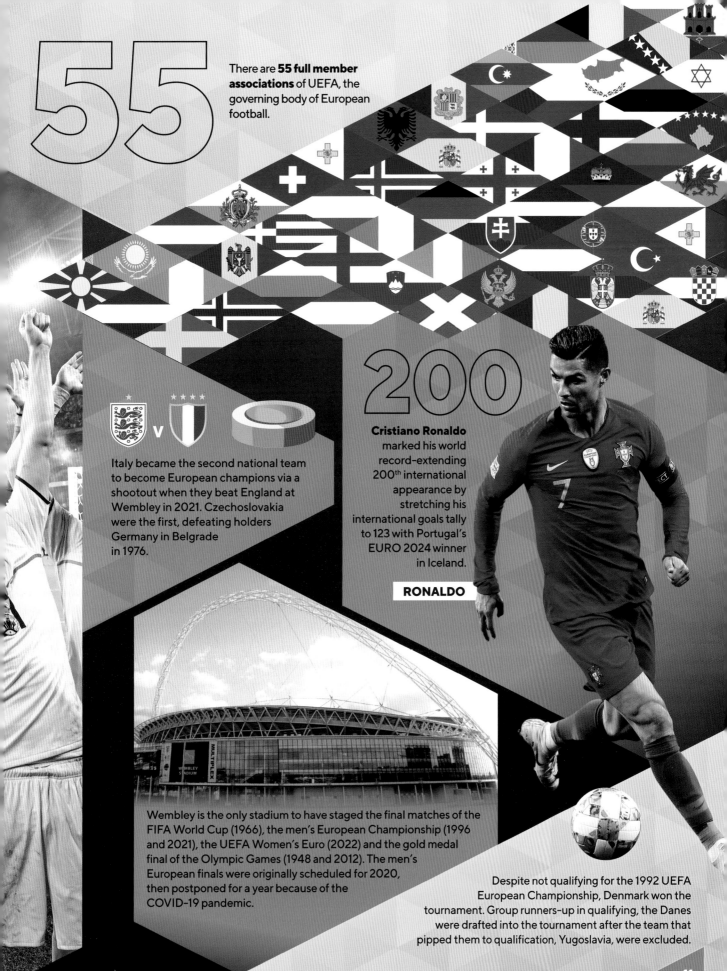

55

There are **55 full member associations** of UEFA, the governing body of European football.

Italy became the second national team to become European champions via a shootout when they beat England at Wembley in 2021. Czechoslovakia were the first, defeating holders Germany in Belgrade in 1976.

200

Cristiano Ronaldo marked his world record-extending 200th international appearance by stretching his international goals tally to 123 with Portugal's EURO 2024 winner in Iceland.

RONALDO

Wembley is the only stadium to have staged the final matches of the FIFA World Cup (1966), the men's European Championship (1996 and 2021), the UEFA Women's Euro (2022) and the gold medal final of the Olympic Games (1948 and 2012). The men's European finals were originally scheduled for 2020, then postponed for a year because of the COVID-19 pandemic.

Despite not qualifying for the 1992 UEFA European Championship, Denmark won the tournament. Group runners-up in qualifying, the Danes were drafted into the tournament after the team that pipped them to qualification, Yugoslavia, were excluded.

ENGLAND

England is where football began; the country where the game was first developed, which saw the creation of the game's first football association and the first organised league, and which now plays host to the richest domestic league in the world.

Joined FIFA: 1905

Biggest win:
13-0 v. Ireland, 1882

Highest FIFA ranking: 3rd

Home stadium: Wembley Stadium, London

Honours: 1 FIFA World Cup (1966)

SOUTHGATE

41

The oldest player to make his debut for England remains Alexander Morten, who was 41 years and 114 days old when he captained England against Scotland on 8 March 1873 in their first home game.

MOORE

NATIONAL LEGEND
NEW SOUTHGATE, NEW HOPE

Former England centre-back **Gareth Southgate** was the manager when England reached their first FIFA World Cup semi-final for 28 years, at the 2018 finals in Russia – only to lose 2-1 to Croatia. Three years later, at UEFA EURO 2020, he and his players went even further, reaching a first major tournament final since Sir Alf Ramsey's side beat West Germany in the 1966 FIFA World Cup final. Yet 55 years of hurt go on, after Italy prevailed 3-2 on penalties after a 1-1 draw at Wembley Stadium in London. England's run to the final included a 2-0 second round victory over Germany, also at Wembley, 25 years after Southgate had missed the decisive spot-kick in a semi-final penalty shoot-out defeat to Germany at the 1996 UEFA European Championship. Southgate won 57 caps, and the UEFA EURO 2020 final was his 61st game in charge – he is the first man to reach a half-century of England internationals both as a player and as manager.

1872
The first official England international took place on 30 November 1872. It was a goalless draw away to the "Auld Enemy", Scotland.

NATIONAL LEGEND
CAPTAINS COURAGEOUS

The international careers of Billy Wright and **Bobby Moore**, who both captained England a record 90 times, very nearly overlapped. Wright, of Wolverhampton Wanderers, played for England between 1946 and 1959, and West Ham United's Moore from 1962 to 1973. Moore remains England's youngest captain, having been 22 years and 47 days old when appointed against Czechoslovakia on 29 May 1963. He also remains the only man to have lifted the FIFA World Cup for England, after West Germany were beaten 4-2 at Wembley on 30 July 1966.

TEAM TRIVIA
FREE SCORING

Not counting the UEFA EURO final defeat on penalties to Italy in July 2021 after a 1–1 draw, England went a national record 22 matches unbeaten between beating the Republic of Ireland 3-0 in November 2020 and a 3–0 victory over Côte d'Ivoire in March 2022. They were Europe's top scorers in qualifying for the 2022 FIFA World Cup with 39, ahead of Germany's 36 and the Netherlands' 33. Their campaign concluded with a 10–0 away win against San Marino in November 2021, including four goals by captain Harry Kane. The 22-match unbeaten run ended with a 1–0 loss away to Hungary in a June 2022 UEFA Nations League match in Budapest.

7
England's 2–1 defeat to France at the 2022 FIFA World Cup in Qatar was the seventh time they have been eliminated from the tournament at the quarter-final stage – more than any other nation.

MOST APPEARANCES:

1 Peter Shilton, 125
2 Wayne Rooney, 120
3 David Beckham, 115
4 Steven Gerrard, 114
5 Bobby Moore, 108

DISCIPLINARY
SEEING RED

Alan Mullery became the first man to be sent off playing for England against Yugoslavia in June 1968, in a UEFA European Championship semi-final defeat. Some 19 more expulsions have followed. The 20th was Luke Shaw's red card in a 2–1 victory over Italy in a March 2023 UEFA European Championship qualifier. Two apiece have been shown to **David Beckham** and Wayne Rooney. Beckham's included a shootout defeat to Argentina in the second round of the 1998 FIFA World Cup. Rooney was dismissed in a quarter-final loss to Portugal at the FIFA World Cup eight years later.

BECKHAM

1:57

Left-back Luke Shaw's first goal for England, in his 16th international, was also the fastest ever in a UEFA European Championship final – just one minute and 57 seconds into the UEFA EURO 2020 showdown with Italy.

SCORING RECORD
SPURRED ON TO GLORY

Many England fans felt their team was cursed when it came to penalty shoot-outs, following spot-kick defeats to Germany in the 1990 FIFA World Cup and 1996 UEFA European Championship semi-finals, and to Portugal in the 2004 UEFA European Championship and 2006 FIFA World Cup quarter-finals. Yet they turned the tide by beating Colombia on penalties in the round of 16 at Russia 2018, en route to finishing fourth – they then repeated the trick against Switzerland to clinch third place in the following summer's inaugural UEFA Nations League. Everton goalkeeper Jordan Pickford was among the heroes on each occasion, not only saving a penalty each time but also scoring one against the Swiss. Midfielder Eric Dier struck England's decisive final spot kick on both occasions. Dier's club Tottenham Hotspur have provided England with more players than any other side, with fellow midfielder Harry Winks becoming the 78th in October 2017. Three of England's top five leading scorers are Tottenham legends: current player Harry Kane, Sixties hero Jimmy Greaves, whose goals included a national record six hat-tricks, and Gary Lineker, the nation's top FIFA World Cup goalscorer with ten across the 1986 and 1990 tournaments.

STAR PLAYER
FAST STARTS

Bryan Robson holds records for England's fastest goal in the FIFA World Cup – after 27 seconds in a 3–1 win against France in 1982 – and at the old Wembley Stadium, netting after 38 seconds in a 2–1 friendly victory over Yugoslavia in 1989. Robson scored three of England's 12 quickest goals. Tottenham Hotspur striker Teddy Sheringham scored England's quickest goal after coming on as a substitute. His first touch, a header 15 seconds into a substitute appearance, brought England level with Greece in a 2002 FIFA World Cup qualifier at Old Trafford, in October 2001.

LINEKER

TOURNAMENT TRIVIA
YOUNG AND OLD

Tom Finney is England's oldest scorer at a FIFA World Cup, aged 36 years and 64 days against the Soviet Union in 1958. Jordan Henderson became the second-oldest at 32 years and 170 days in a 3–0 second round victory over Senegal at the 2022 finals. Michael Owen is the youngest. He was 18 years and 190 days old when scoring as a sub in a 2–1 defeat to Romania in 1998. **Jude Bellingham** became the second-youngest in opening England's account at the 2022 finals, aged 19 years and 145 days, in a 6–2 victory against Iran. Midfielder Bellingham previously became England's youngest player at an international tournament, aged 17 years and 349 days, when coming on in a 1–0 triumph over Croatia at EURO 2020.

BELLINGHAM

NATIONAL LEGEND
GRAND OLD MAN

Stanley Matthews became England's oldest-ever player when he lined up at outside-right against Denmark on 15 May 1957 at the age of 42 years 104 days. That was 22 years and 229 days after his first appearance. Matthews was also England's oldest marksman. He was 41 years eight months old when he scored against Northern Ireland on 10 October 1956. In stark contrast to Matthews's longest England career, full-back Martin Kelly holds the record for the shortest – a two-minute substitute appearance in a 1–0 friendly win over Norway in 2012.

STAR PLAYER
PICK OF THE STOPS

After he was the penalty-saving hero in shoot-outs against Colombia at the 2018 FIFA World Cup and Switzerland in a UEFA Nations League third-place play-off the following year, goalkeeper **Jordan Pickford** achieved another landmark at UEFA EURO 2020. He went the longest time without conceding for any England goalkeeper at a tournament. He beat Gordon Banks's previous best of 720 minutes at the 1966 FIFA World Cup by going 726 minutes before Denmark's Mikkel Damsgaard scored in a semi-final England went on to win 2–1.

TOP SCORERS:

1 Harry Kane, 55
2 Wayne Rooney, 53
3 Bobby Charlton, 49
4 Gary Lineker, 48
5 Jimmy Greaves, 44

17

Theo Walcott remains England's youngest-ever international, aged 17 years and 75 days when facing Hungary in a friendly on 30 May 2006. The winger was called up for that summer's FIFA World Cup squad but did not make it on to the pitch during the finals in Germany.

TOURNAMENT TRIVIA
ROON AT THE TOP

When **Wayne Rooney** scored against Macedonia in September 2003, he became England's youngest goalscorer at the age of 17 years and 317 days – and it long seemed only a matter of time before he broke Sir Bobby Charlton's record 49-goal haul. He drew level thanks to a penalty against San Marino in September 2015, and then reached his half-century with another spot kick, against Switzerland, three days later. Rooney's 100th cap in November 2014, at the age of 29 years and 22 days, made him the youngest man to rack up a century of appearances for England. He retired from international football in August 2017 but made a brief return as a substitute on 15 November 2018, against the United States, for a farewell 120th appearance.

ROONEY

⚑ STAR PLAYER
NEW KING KANE

Harry Kane's international career got off to the perfect start in March 2015, when he scored 79 seconds after coming on as a substitute for his England debut against Lithuania. Almost precisely eight years later, he became his country's all-time leading scorer with a penalty in a 2–1 win against Italy. That spot-kick took him to 54 goals, ahead of former international strike partner Wayne Rooney. England captain Kane had equalled the record with a spot-kick against France at the 2022 FIFA World Cup, but missed a second penalty that day as England were knocked out 2–1. His 12 goals for England at international tournaments – a national record, two ahead of Gary Lineker – include six at the 2018 FIFA World Cup, which earned him the Golden Boot for tournament top scorer.

🏆 TOURNAMENT TRIVIA
ROLL UP, ROLL UP

The highest attendance for an England game came at Hampden Park in Glasgow on 17 April 1937, when 149,547 spectators saw Scotland win 3–1 in the British Home Championship. By contrast, only 2,378 turned up in Bologna, Italy, to see San Marino stun England and take the lead after just seven seconds on 17 November 1993. A 7–1 victory for Graham Taylor's side was not enough to secure England a place at the 1994 FIFA World Cup.

7–1
England's biggest defeat came against Hungary in 1954. They lost 7–1.

SCORING RECORD
STERLING'S VALUE

Chelsea forward **Raheem Sterling** scored just twice in his first 45 England appearances. He then netted 15 in his next 23 – with three at UEFA EURO 2020, including first-round winners against Croatia and the Czech Republic at Wembley Stadium, just a mile from where he grew up in Brent, north-west London. He also opened the scoring in England's 2–0 victory over Germany in the second round, also at Wembley, before Harry Kane added the second. Sterling's goal against Côte d'Ivoire in March 2022 meant England had won all 15 matches in which he had found the net. The previous record of ten had been held by 1970s forward Martin Chivers.

STERLING

KANE

66

England's most-capped player Peter Shilton also holds the goalkeeping record of 66 clean sheets between 1970 and 1990. He could well have won more caps, but manager Ron Greenwood alternated him and Ray Clemence between 1972 and 1982.

35

Striker Jermain Defoe came on as a substitute 35 times for England – more often than any other player in England's history – between his debut in 2004 and his final appearance in 2017.

🌍 NATIONAL LEGEND
WONDERFUL WALTER

Walter Winterbottom was England's first full-time manager and he remains both the longest-serving (with 138 games in charge) and the youngest, aged just 33 when he took the job in 1946. The former teacher and Manchester United player led his country to four FIFA World Cups, from their first appearance in 1950, to the 1962 tournament in Chile.

WINTERBOTTOM

FRANCE

With two world titles and a rich history of helping to develop the game, *Les Bleus* are footballing heavyweights, most recently becoming world champions in 2018.

Joined FIFA: 1907

Biggest win:
10-0 v. Azerbaijan, 1995

Highest FIFA ranking: 1st

Home stadium:
Stade de France, Saint Denis

Honours:
2 FIFA World Cups (1998, 2018), 2 UEFA European Championships (1984, 2000)

MBAPPÉ

FRANCE AND FIFA

Jules Rimet – FIFA president from 1921 to 1954 – was the driving force behind the creation of the FIFA World Cup and the first version of the trophy was named in his honour.

STAR PLAYER
IN FOR THE KYL

France won their second FIFA World Cup in July 2018, 20 years after their first. Nineteen-year-old **Kylian Mbappé** scored their last goal in the 4-2 final triumph over Croatia, and was named the best young player of the tournament. Mbappé also became the second teenager to score in the final of the FIFA World Cup, following Pelé against Sweden in 1958, and with his strike against Peru in the group stage, he also became France's youngest scorer at a major tournament at the age of just 19 years and 183 days. Four years later he became only the second man, after England's Sir Geoff Hurst in 1966, to score a FIFA World Cup final hat-trick. Mbappé also scored from the spot in the shoot-out against Argentina after the match ended 3-3, but Kingsley Coman and Aurélien Tchouaméni missed as France fell to defeat 4-2.

7

Seven French players have won the FIFA World Cup, UEFA European Championship and UEFA Champions League: Didier Deschamps, Marcel Desailly, Christian Karembeu, Bixente Lizarazu, Fabien Barthez Thierry Henry and Zinédine Zidane.

STAR PLAYER
BENZEMA'S BACK

Karim Benzema's France career has stretched longer than any other player's, from his debut as a substitute scoring the winning goal against Austria in March 2007 all the way into 2022. This includes a lengthy absence from the side from October 2015 until returning in June 2021 as part of his country's squad for UEFA EURO 2020, where he scored four times despite France losing to Switzerland in the second round. That October, he scored in the 2021 UEFA Nations League final to equalise in a 2-1 triumph over Spain.

BENZEMA

STAR PLAYER
GRIEZ LIGHTNING

Striker **Antoine Griezmann** won the 2016 UEFA European Championship Golden Boot as the six-goal top scorer, plus the Golden Ball as the best player. France lost the final 1-0 to Portugal, but two years later Griezmann's four goals helped France win the 2018 FIFA World Cup. His tally included three penalties, with one in the final to give his team a 2-1 lead over Croatia. Griezmann shared the record for most assists at the 2022 FIFA World Cup, with three, and was named Man of the Match in France's 2-0 semi-final victory over Morocco.

GRIEZMANN

NATIONAL LEGEND
KOPA – FRANCE'S FIRST SUPERSTAR

Raymond Kopa was France's first international superstar. Born into a family of Polish immigrants (his family name was Kopaszewski) on 13 October 1931, he was instrumental in Reims's championship successes of the mid-1950s. He later joined Real Madrid and, in 1956, became the first French player to claim a European Cup winner's medal. He was also the playmaker of the France team that finished third at the 1958 FIFA World Cup, his performances for his country that year earning him the European Footballer of the Year award. Kopa's death, aged 85, on 3 March 2017 was met with sadness around the world.

KOPA

ZIDANE

2
Playmaker **Zinedine Zidane** scored twice with his head to help France win their first FIFA World Cup, 3–0 in the 1998 final against Brazil. He was also sent off twice at FIFA World Cups – against Saudi Arabia in the first round in 1998, and for an extra-time headbutt against Italy in the final eight years later.

TOP SCORERS:
1. Olivier Giroud, 53
2. Thierry Henry, 51
3. Antoine Griezmann, 43
4. Michel Platini, 41
5. Kylian Mbappé, 38

MOST APPEARANCES:
1. Hugo Lloris, 145
2. Lilian Thuram, 142
3. Thierry Henry, 123
4. Olivier Giroud, 122
5. Antoine Griezmann, 119

LLORIS

PLATINI

HIDALGO

MANAGER RECORD
MICHEL, MICHEL

Michel Hidalgo, who died aged 87 in March 2020, was the first coach to lead France to glory at a major tournament when the hosts won the UEFA European Championship in 1984, helped in no small part by captain **Michel Platini**'s haul of nine goals. Platini would later coach France at UEFA EURO 1992, help to organise the 1998 FIFA World Cup in his home country, and serve as UEFA President between 2007 and 2015. Hidalgo was the first man to reach 75 games in charge of France, though his record was later surpassed by Raymond Domenech, whose 79 matches included a run to the 2006 FIFA World Cup final, and Didier Deschamps, who ended June 2022 on 130.

STAR PLAYER
VICTOR HUGO

Goalkeeper **Hugo Lloris** became France's most-capped player at the 2022 World Cup, passing Lilian Thuram's 142 appearances in a 2–1 quarter-final victory over England. His 145th and last match for France before retiring from international football was their penalty shoot-out loss to Argentina in the final, four years after Lloris had lifted the trophy as captain in Russia with a 4–2 triumph over Croatia.

NATIONAL LEGEND
DESAILLY: JE SUIS UN ROCK STAR

Despite having been born in the Ghanaian capital of Accra, **Marcel Desailly** always insisted he only ever wanted to play for France – the country he moved to as a four-year-old – and he duly became the nation's most-capped player in 2003. He retired the following year with a then-record of 116 international appearances, although this was later passed by frequent team-mate Lilian Thuram. Desailly, a commanding presence at either centre-back or in midfield that saw him dubbed "The Rock", not only won both the 1998 FIFA World Cup and 2000 UEFA European Championship with France, but he was also the first player to win the UEFA Champions League in successive seasons with different clubs – with Marseille in 1993, and then with AC Milan the following year.

THURAM

DESCHAMPS

NATIONAL LEGEND
DESCHAMPS THE MULTIPLE CHAMP

Didier Deschamps is one of only three men to have won the FIFA World Cup as a player and manager, together with Brazil's Mário Zagallo in 1958 and 1970 and Franz Beckenbauer with West Germany in 1974 and 1990. Defensive midfielder Deschamps captained France in 1998 and in 2000 for their UEFA European Championship triumph, and retired after winning 103 caps – 55 as captain. He became national team head coach in 2012, leading his side to the UEFA EURO 2016 final on home soil, where they lost 1–0 to Portugal, before lifting the 2018 FIFA World Cup with a 4–2 victory over Croatia in Moscow. The run to the final of the 2022 FIFA World Cup took him to 139 matches in charge, including 89 wins, followed in 2023 by victories over the Netherlands and the Republic of Ireland in two qualifiers for the UEFA EURO 2024.

17

Fabien Barthez holds his country's record for the most FIFA World Cup finals appearances, 17 between 1998 and 2006.

EARNING THEIR STRIPES

France are the only country to play at a FIFA World Cup while wearing another team's kit. At Argentina 1978, *Les Bleus* were forced to wear the green-and-white stripes of a local club side, Atlético Kimberley, after a colours mix-up with Hungary.

THURAM

NATIONAL LEGEND
LILIAN IN THE PINK

Lilian Thuram made his 142nd and final appearance for France in their defeat by Italy at UEFA EURO 2008. The defender's international career had spanned nearly 14 years since his debut against the Czech Republic in August 1994. Thuram played his club football for Monaco, Parma, Juventus and Barcelona before retiring in the summer of 2008 because of a heart problem. He was also one of the stars of France's 1998 FIFA World Cup-winning side, scoring both goals in their semi-final victory over Croatia: the only international goals of his career. His Parma, Italy-born son Marcel Thuram, a forward who signed for Borussia Mönchengladbach in Germany in 2019, helped France win the 2016 UEFA U-19 European Championship. Marcel made his senior international debut against Finland in November 2020.

STAR PLAYER
GIROUD AWAKENING

Striker **Olivier Giroud**, once at home in London with Arsenal and Chelsea, knocked England out of the 2022 FIFA World Cup with a late goal for France in their 2–1 quarter-final victory in Qatar. It was his 53rd strike for his country. Giroud had become France's all-time top scorer in the group stage against Poland after he equalled Thierry Henry's record with two goals in the opening 4–1 victory over Australia. His first 40 strikes for France were all from inside the area but on his 100th international appearance he swept in his 41st from outside the box, in a 7–1 win against Ukraine in October 2020. With this goal, he equalled Michel Platini's mark of international goals.

GIROUD

Against Austria in June 2022, centre-back Ibrahima Konaté became the 65th man to make his France debut under coach Didier Deschamps. This broke the previous record of 64 players given their international bows by Michel Hidalgo.

HENRY

NATIONAL LEGEND
HENRY BENCHED

Thierry Henry did not play in the 1998 FIFA World Cup final because of Marcel Desailly's red card. Henry, France's leading goalscorer in the finals with three, was a substitute and coach Aimé Jacquet planned to use him late in the game. But Desailly's sending-off forced a re-think: Jacquet instead reinforced his midfield with future Arsenal team-mate Patrick Vieira going on instead, leaving Henry as an unused substitute. But Henry does have the distinction of being the only Frenchman to play at four different FIFA World Cups (1998, 2002, 2006 and 2010). He also passed Michel Platini's all-time goal-scoring record for France with a brace against Lithuania in October 2007.

STAR PLAYER
CAMAVINGA THE COMING MAN

Attacking midfielder **Eduardo Camavinga** was born in a refugee camp in Cabinda in Angola, but his family moved to Fougères north-western France when he was two. He became the Rennes' youngest ever player in April 2019 as a 16-year-old, and later became France's second-youngest international and second-youngest scorer. He made his debut against Croatia in September 2020 aged 17 years and 303 days, and opened his account with an overhead kick in a 7–1 win over Ukraine 29 days later. Camavinga came on for the final minutes of Real Madrid's 2022 UEFA Champions League final triumph in May 2022, having repeatedly proved a valuable "super-sub" in earlier knock-out rounds.

CAMAVINGA

SO NEAR YET SO VAR
Antoine Griezmann became the first man to have an international goal disallowed by the intervention of a video assistant referee when he was judged to be offside after finding the net against Spain in March 2017, a match Spain won 2–0.

NATIONAL LEGEND
FONTAINE UP-FRONT

Just Fontaine, who died aged 89 in February 2023, scored more goals in one FIFA World Cup than any other man – 13 across the six games he played for France at the 1958 tournament, including four in a 6–3 victory over West Germany to finish third. He later spent the shortest amount of time as France manager, taking over on 22 March 1967 and leaving on 3 June that year after two defeats in friendlies. Before Kylian Mbappé's treble in the 2022 FIFA World Cup final, Fontaine was the only Frenchman to score a FIFA World Cup hat-trick.

GERMANY

13
Serge Gnabry's hat-trick against Northern Ireland in November 2019 made him the first man to score 13 goals in his first 13 Germany internationals since Gerd Müller hit 16 in 13 in 1969. Both men managed ten in their initial ten.

Germany are almost ever-presents in the closing stages of major tournaments. Their 2014 success ended an 18-year trophy drought and was their first FIFA World Cup success as a reunified nation after winning in 1954, 1974 and 1990 as West Germany.

Joined FIFA: 1908

Biggest win:
16-0 v. Russia, 1912

Highest FIFA ranking: 1st

Home stadium:
(rotation)

Honours:
4 FIFA World Cups (1954, 1974, 1990, 2014),
3 UEFA European Championships (1972, 1980, 1996)

100

Ulf Kirsten is one of eight players who played for both the old East Germany and the reunified Germany after 1990. He managed 100 appearances: 49 for East Germany and 51 for Germany.

SCORING RECORD
KLOSE ENCOUNTERS

In 2014, **Miroslav Klose** became the third player, after Uwe Seeler and Pelé, to score in four FIFA World Cup final competitions. After strikes in 2002, 2006 and 2010, his first goal in 2014 – an equaliser against Ghana – put him alongside former Brazil star Ronaldo at the top of the all-time FIFA World Cup scoring charts. And it was against the Brazilians that Klose would later push out ahead on his own. His 24 appearances left him behind only compatriot Lothar Matthäus (25), but Klose's 17 wins were one more than previous record-holder Cafu, of Brazil. Klose retired in 2014 as Germany's all-time leading scorer, with 71 goals in 137 matches – and his team-mates never lost an international in which he found the net.

KLOSE

TOP SCORERS:

1 **Miroslav Klose**, 71

2 **Gerd Müller**, 68

3 **Lukas Podolski**, 49

4 **Jürgen Klinsmann**, 47
= **Rudi Völler**, 47

BECKENBAUER

NATIONAL LEGEND
DER KAISER

Franz Beckenbauer is widely regarded as the greatest player in German football history. He defined the role of attacking sweeper, first in the 1970 FIFA World Cup finals, and then as West Germany won the 1972 UEFA European Championship and the 1974 FIFA World Cup. Beckenbauer later delivered a FIFA World Cup final appearance in 1986 as an inexperienced coach, and the 1990 trophy in his final game in charge. He later became President of Bayern Munich, the club he captained to three consecutive European Cup victories between 1974 and 1976. He also led Germany's successful bid for the 2006 FIFA World Cup finals and headed the organising committee.

TOURNAMENT TRIVIA
SAMBA SILENCED

Germany's 1-0 win over Argentina in 2014 came in their record eighth FIFA World Cup Final, this coming after they were the first side to reach four consecutive semi-finals. But their 7-1 semi-final humiliation of Brazil may well live longest in the memory – and the record books. Germany led 5-0 at half-time in what became the biggest FIFA World Cup semi-final win and the hosts' heaviest defeat. Other FIFA World Cup finals records include: Germany were the first team to score four goals in six minutes, and Toni Kroos, whose two goals in 69 seconds is the fastest brace, is the only FIFA World Cup winner born in East Germany. Thomas Müller's opening goal was also Germany's 2,000th in full internationals.

NATIONAL LEGEND
KEEPING A LÖW PROFILE

Joachim Löw bowed out as Germany manager after a 2-0 second round defeat to England at UEFA EURO 2020 in 2021, ending a 15-year reign of 194 games, which took him beyond Sepp Herberger's 162. The highlight of Löw's time in charge was lifting the FIFA World Cup in Brazil in 2014, making him the first German to do so without having played for his country. After a mid-ranking playing and coaching career, he was appointed as new Germany manager Jürgen Klinsmann's assistant in 2004 before taking the top job in 2006. As well as 2014's glory, his German side finished runners-up at the 2008 UEFA European Championship before reaching the semi-finals four years later, with third place at the 2010 FIFA World Cup in between.

LÖW

10
Joachim Löw's successor as Germany manager, Hansi Flick, became the first man to go unbeaten in his first ten games, following in the footsteps of Sepp Herberger Josef Derwall. This was followed by him overseeing a new German record of four consecutive draws.

NATIONAL LEGEND
"DER BOMBER" BOWS OUT

German club Bayern Munich said they were "standing still today" when announcing the death of former strike **Gerd Müller** aged 75 in August 2021, while the national team mourned "one of the greatest German footballers of all time". Müller, nicknamed "Der Bomber", struck 68 times in just 62 internationals between 1966 and 1974, including a brace against the Soviet Union in the final to help win the 1972 UEFA European Championship and the winner versus the Netherlands to clinch the FIFA World Cup title two years later. His 365 goals in 427 league games for Bayern remains a Bundesliga record. On his death, club president Herbert Hainer said: "Without Gerd Müller, FC Bayern would not be the club we all love today."

5
Gerd Müller scored a record eight hat-tricks for West Germany between 1967 and 1972, including four four-goal hauls. But Otto Stiffling remains the only German man to score five times in one international, when Denmark were beaten 8-0 in May 1937.

TEAM TRIVIA
OK, MOUKOKO

After winning the FIFA World Cup in 2014, Germany failed to make it past the first round in the two subsequent tournaments in Russia in 2018 and Qatar in 2022. The latter tournament saw Youssoufa Moukoko become the youngest German international to appear at a FIFA World Cup. He came on as a 90th-minute substitute in a 2-1 defeat to Japan at the age of 18 years and three days. The Borussia Dortmund striker's international debut seven days earlier, in a friendly versus Oman, had made him Germany's fourth-youngest ever player. The record is held by forward Willy Baumgärtner. He was 17 years and 104 days old on facing Switzerland in April 1908.

MÜLLER

NEUER

F FOR FAILURE

Germany went into the 2018 FIFA World Cup as defending champions – and FIFA Confederations Cup holders, which they had won in Russia a year earlier. Yet Joachim Löw's side finished bottom of Group F, ensuring their first first-round exit for 80 years – they did not compete in 1950 – and only their second ever. Germany were eliminated in 1938, a straight knock-out tournament, after losing 4-2 to Switzerland in a first-round replay following a 1-1 draw. That German team featured several Austrian players following the *Anschluss* (German annexation of Austria) earlier in the year.

1-0
East and West Germany met only once at senior national team level, in the FIFA World Cup finals on 22 June 1974. After the teams were drawn into the same group, East Germany produced a shock 1-0 win in Hamburg, but both teams advanced.

STAR PLAYER
NEUER RECORD

Manuel Neuer holds the German record for the longest run between conceding international tournament goals. There were 557 minutes between Brazil's late consolation in the 7-1 2014 FIFA World Cup semi-final rout and a goal from Italy's Leonardo Bonucci in the 2016 UEFA European Championship quarter-final. Germany won that game 6-5 on penalties, helped by two spot-kick saves by Neuer. The previous best run had been Sepp Maier's 481-minute shutout in the 1970s. Neuer – renowned for his ease with the ball at his feet as a "sweeper keeper" – was appointed Germany captain in September 2016 after Bastian Schweinsteiger retired.

GÖTZE

SCHÜRRLE

NATIONAL LEGEND
FABULOUS PHIL

Four German men have lifted the FIFA World Cup as captain: Fritz Walter in 1954, Franz Beckenbauer in 1974, Lothar Matthäus in 1990, and **Philipp Lahm** in 2014. Lahm, a full-back comfortable on either flank, was Germany's youngest FIFA World Cup captain when they finished third in 2010, and he later retired from international football aged just 30 after the Germans defeated Argentina in the 2014 final. A Bayern Munich ballboy as a teenager, Lahm also wore the armband as they won the UEFA Champions League in 2013. Lahm's only other club was VfB Stuttgart, for a brief loan spell.

NEW BOYS REUNION

Bayern Munich's **Mario Götze** was the hero when Germany finally overcame Argentina's resistance in the 2014 FIFA World Cup final. His 113th-minute volley was the first winner hit by a substitute. It seemed apt that Germany's first FIFA World Cup triumph since the reunification of East and West Germany in 1990 was secured by Götze, set up by **André Schürrle**. They had jointly become the first German football internationals born post-reunification, when making their debuts as 79th-minute substitutes against Sweden in November 2010.

6
Werder Bremen striker Niclas Füllkrug made his Germany debut aged 29, scoring in a friendly against Oman in November 2022. He followed up with five more in his next five internationals, including goals against Spain in a 1-1 draw and Costa Rica in a 4-2 victory at the 2022 FIFA World Cup. Despite his efforts, Germany missed out on the knock-out stages.

LAHM

STAR PLAYER
JAMAL'S A GERMAN

Jamal Musiala was voted Germany's player of the year for 2022, a rare bright spot in their second successive first-round elimination at that winter's FIFA World Cup in Qatar. Germany had become the first country other than the hosts to qualify for the tournament, with Musiala scoring the final goal in their decisive 4-0 victory over North Macedonia in October 2021. That also made him the youngest man to find the net for Germany in a competitive game, aged 18 years and 227 days. Musiala was born in Stuttgart but moved with his family to England aged seven and represented that country at U-15, U-16, U-17 and U-21 levels before switching international allegiance to the land of his birth in February 2021. He made his senior debut as a substitute against Iceland a month later.

MUSIALA

22

Sepp Herberger (1897-1977) was Germany's longest-serving coach (22 years at the helm) and his legendary status was assured after West Germany surprised odds-on favourites Hungary to win the 1954 FIFA World Cup final – a result credited with dragging the country out of a post-war slump.

NATIONAL LEGEND
WHOLE LOTTA LOTHAR

Lothar Matthäus was dubbed "Der Panzer", or the panther, during his playing days as a combative defensive midfield presence. He enjoyed a 20-year international career, winning 87 caps for West Germany and 63 for post-reunification Germany to make a national record tally of 150. He was the captain who lifted the 1990 FIFA World Cup trophy after taming Diego Maradona and Argentina in the final, four years after a 3-2 defeat to the same opponents in the Mexico 86 climax. Matthäus – who could operate as a defensive midfielder, attacking midfielder or sweeper – played in five FIFA World Cups (1982, 1986, 1990, 1994 and 1998), a record matched only by Mexico's Antonio Carbajal and Rafael Márquez.

MÜLLER

200

Thomas Müller's third-minute goal for Germany against Argentina in their 2010 FIFA World Cup quarter-final, setting his side on the way to a 4-0 victory, made Germany the second country after Brazil to complete a double century of FIFA World Cup goals. The game came four months after Müller's international debut, a 1-0 defeat to the same opposition after which Argentina manager Diego Maradona mistook him for a ballboy in a post-match press conference.

STAR PLAYER
GOLDEN BOY JULIAN

World champions Germany won their first FIFA Confederations Cup title in Russia in 2017, despite coach Joachim Löw resting many of his senior stars, including Thomas Müller, Mesut Özil and Toni Kroos. Lars Stindl scored the only goal of the final, against Chile, while goalkeeper Marc-André ter Stegen was named man of the match. The Golden Ball for the tournament's best player went to 23-year-old captain **Julian Draxler** – Germany's youngest skipper at a tournament since Max Breunig at the 1912 Summer Olympics – and the Golden Boot went to three-goal team-mate Timo Werner. Germany also had the youngest average age of any FIFA Confederations Cup-winning squad: 24 years and four months.

NATIONAL LEGEND
GRAND SAMMER

Matthias Sammer is not only one of eight men to play for both East Germany and the reunified Germany, but he also holds the honour of captaining the side and scoring both goals in East Germany's final game, a 2-0 away win over Belgium on 12 September 1990, 21 days before the official reunification. His powerhouse midfield performances later drove Germany to glory at the 1996 UEFA European Championship, where he was voted the player of the tournament.

ITALY

Only Brazil (with five victories) have won the FIFA World Cup more times than Italy. The *Azzurri*, however, were the first nation to retain the trophy (winning in 1934 and 1938), were surprise champions in Spain in 1982, and collected football's most coveted trophy for a fourth time in 2006.

Joined FIFA: 1910

Biggest win:
9-0 v. USA, 1948

Highest FIFA ranking: 1st

Home stadium:
Stadio Olimpico, Rome

Honours:
4 FIFA World Cups (1934, 1938, 1982, 2006), 2 UEFA European Championships (1968, 2020)

MANCINI

NATIONAL LEGEND
ON THE REBOUND

Roberto Mancini's rebuilding of Italian football after their failure to qualify for the 2018 FIFA World Cup reached a peak when winning UEFA EURO 2020, just three years after his appointment. The former Sampdoria and Lazio playmaker oversaw a new national record 34 consecutive internationals unbeaten – including penalty shoot-out victories against Spain in the semi-final and England in the final. That record run included an unprecedented 11 successive Italy victories. Mancini had previously been part of Italy's squad when finishing third as hosts of the 1990 FIFA World Cup, but failed to make it on the pitch that tournament. At UEFA EURO 2020, he brought on back-up goalkeeper Salvatore Sirigu for the closing minutes of Italy's 1-0 first round victory over Wales to give him a taste of the action.

18

Wilfried Gnonto became Italy's youngest ever goalscorer on 14 June 2022, in a 5–2 UEFA Nations League away defeat to Germany, aged just 18 years and 222 days. Ten days earlier he had made his international debut in a 1–1 home draw with Germany. The record was previously held by Bruno Nicolè, who was 18 years and 258 days old when scoring both goals in a 2–2 draw against France on 9 November 1958.

TOURNAMENT TRIVIA
BACK WITH A BUMP

Roberto Mancini's Italy quickly went from joy to despair after winning UEFA EURO 2020 in July 2021. Eight months later, they failed to qualify for a second consecutive FIFA World Cup, despite their campaign forming part of a new national record of 27 successive internationals without defeat stretching back to October 2018. That run ended when Spain came to Milan's San Siro stadium in October 2021 and won 2-1 in their UEFA Nations League semi-final. Disaster struck the following month, when a disappointing goalless draw with Northern Ireland in their final FIFA World Cup qualifier left them second behind group winners Switzerland. Italy then did not even reach the final of their play-off round, losing in Palermo to a stoppage-time strike by North Macedonia in their March 2022 semi-final.

NATIONAL LEGEND
ZOFF THE SCALE

Goalkeeper **Dino Zoff** set an international record by going 1,142 minutes without conceding a goal between September 1972 and June 1974. Zoff was Italy's captain when they won the 1982 FIFA World Cup – emulating the feat of another Juventus goalkeeper, Gianpiero Combi, who had been the victorious skipper in 1934. Zoff later coached Italy to the final of the 2000 UEFA European Championship, which they lost 2-1 to France thanks to an extra-time "golden goal" – then quit a few days later, unhappy following the criticism levelled at him by Italy's then Prime Minister, Silvio Berlusconi.

ZOFF

DONNARUMMA

TOP SCORERS:

1 **Luigi Riva**, 35

2 **Giuseppe Meazza**, 33

3 **Silvio Piola**, 30

4 **Roberto Baggio**, 27
= **Alessandro Del Piero**, 27

STAR PLAYER
THE YOUNG ONE

Goalkeeper **Gianluigi Donnarumma** began UEFA EURO 2020 by becoming the youngest Italy goalkeeper ever to play at a major tournament, aged 22 years and 106 days, in their 3-0 victory over Turkey in the opening game. He ended it by being named the player of the tournament – the first goalkeeper to win the award - having just saved penalties from England's Jadon Sancho and Bukayo Saka to give Italy victory on spot-kicks in the final. It was his fifth penalty shoot-out – three for AC Milan and two for Italy – and the fifth he has won, including saving from Spain's Álvaro Morata in their UEFA EURO 2020 semi-final. He had made his senior international bow in September 2016, aged just 17 years and 189 days, in a 3-1 defeat to France.

60
Italy's play-off defeat by North Macedonia in March 2022 was the first time they had lost at home in FIFA World Cup qualifier, after 48 wins and 11 draws beforehand. They also became the fourth country – after Czechoslovakia, Denmark and Greece – to miss the next FIFA World Cup after becoming European champions.

NATIONAL LEGEND
HAPPY CENTENARY

After captaining Italy to the 2006 FIFA World Cup title, **Fabio Cannavaro** was named FIFA World Player of the Year – at 33, the oldest winner of the prize, as well as the first defender. Cannavaro, born in Naples in 1973, played every minute of the 2006 tournament, and the final triumph against France was the ideal way to celebrate his 100th international appearance. Cannavaro is widely considered to be one of the greatest defenders of the modern-day game and played for clubs including Juventus, Internazionale and Real Madrid.

NATIONAL LEGEND
APPETITE FOR SUCCESS

The stadium shared by AC Milan and Internazionale is popularly known as the San Siro, after the district in which it is located. Its official title is the Stadio **Giuseppe Meazza**, named after the star inside-forward who played for both clubs, as well as Italy's 1934 and 1938 FIFA World Cup-winning sides. Meazza, born in Milan on 23 August 1910, was spotted by an Inter scout while playing keepy-uppy in the street with a ball made of rags. He was so thin he had to be fattened up with a diet of steaks. His last goal for Italy was a penalty in the 1938 FIFA World Cup semi-final against Brazil – taken while using one hand to hold up his shorts, whose elastic had broken.

MEAZZA

Vittorio Pozzo is the only man to have won the FIFA World Cup twice as manager – both times with Italy, in 1934 and 1938. Only two players, Giuseppe Meazza and Giovanni Ferrari, played in both finals.

CANNAVARO

25

117

Giorgio Chiellini played his 117th and final international at Wembley in June 2022, equalling the tally of 2006 FIFA World Cup-winning midfielder Daniele De Rossi. Chiellini came off at half-time in a 3-0 "Finalissima" defeat to Argentina, a match that revived after 29 years an intercontinental showdown between the reigning European and South American champions.

MOST APPEARANCES:
1 **Gianluigi Buffon**, 176
2 **Fabio Cannavaro**, 136
3 **Paolo Maldini**, 126
4 **Leonardo Bonucci**, 120
5 **Giorgio Chiellini**, 117
= **Daniele De Rossi**, 117

NATIONAL LEGEND
KEEPING IT IN THE FAMILY

Cesare and **Paolo Maldini** are the only father and son to have hoisted the European Cup/Champions League as captains – both with AC Milan and both for the first time in England. Cesare lifted the trophy after his team beat Benfica at Wembley Stadium in 1963. Paolo repeated the feat 40 years later when Milan defeated Juventus at Old Trafford, Manchester. Although he retired as Italy's second most-capped player, Paolo never managed to win an international tournament – he played for Italy sides that finished third and runners-up at the FIFA World Cup and runners-up in the UEFA European Championship. Paolo's son Daniel, a midfielder, became the third member of the family to play for AC Milan in February 2020, and the following year played his first games and scored his first goal for Italy's U-20s.

MALDINI

TOURNAMENT TRIVIA
IN SAFE KEEPING

During World War Two, the Jules Rimet Trophy – won by Italy at the 1938 FIFA World Cup – was hidden in a shoebox under the bed of football official Ottorino Barassi. He preferred to keep it there, rather than at its previous home – a bank in Rome. The trophy was only handed back to FIFA, safe and untouched, when the FIFA World Cup resumed in 1950. Barassi also helped to organise the 1934 FIFA World Cup, which was played in his native Italy.

NATIONAL LEGEND
WHEN THE GOING GETS BUFF

Gianluigi Buffon has not only been one of the finest modern-day goalkeepers in the world but he has also even surpassed some of the achievements of legendary Italian predecessor Dino Zoff. Buffon emulated 1982 world champion Zoff by being part of Italy's 2006 FIFA World Cup-winning side – only conceding two goals during the tournament, one an own goal and the other a penalty. Buffon also became only the third player to be selected for five different FIFA World Cups when he made two appearances in Brazil in 2014, only missing one of Italy's three matches – their opener against England – due to a late ankle injury.

BUFFON

ROSSI

NO. 3

Italy captain Giacinto Fachetti called the toss of the coin correctly to beat the Soviet Union in their 1968 UEFA European Championship semi-final. Fachetti spent his entire career with Internazionale, who retired the No. 3 shirt he wore when he died in 2006.

NATIONAL LEGEND
COMEBACK KID

Paolo Rossi was the unlikely hero of Italy's 1982 FIFA World Cup triumph, winning the Golden Boot with six goals – including a memorable hat-trick against Brazil in the second round, and the first of Italy's three goals in their final win over West Germany. But he only just made it to the tournament at all, having completed a two-year ban for his alleged involvement in a betting scandal only six weeks before the start of the tournament. Thousands attended Rossi's funeral in Vicenza in December 2020 after his death from lung cancer aged 64.

19

Midfielder Emmanuele Giaccherini's first international goal was the fastest in Italy's history, 19 seconds into their June 2013 friendly against Haiti, which ended 2–2. This was one second faster than the previous record.

7

Roberto Baggio has scored the most penalties for Italy during matches – seven. Yet he was also involved in all three of his country's FIFA World Cup shoot-out defeats, including firing his spot-kick over the bar in defeat to Brazil in the 1994 final.

NATIONAL LEGEND
ROLLING RIVA

Italy's all-time leading scorer is Luigi "Gigi" Riva, with 35 goals in just 42 appearances. Perhaps the most important was the opener when Yugoslavia were beaten 2–0 in the replay final of the 1968 UEFA European Championship in Rome's Stadio Olimpico. It was Riva's first game of the tournament after a leg injury. Unlucky Riva had broken his left leg playing for his country in March 1967 and broke his right one, again on international duty, in 1970, months after his three goals had helped Italy to the runners-up place at the 1970 FIFA World Cup in Mexico.

1000

Christian Vieri's first goal for Italy in 1997 not only came on his debut, it also marked the *Azzurri*'s 1,000th goal scored in all internationals.

NATIONAL LEGEND
CHIESA'S KEY

Enrico Chiesa's seven goals in 22 appearances for Italy included one at the 1996 UEFA European Championship, in a 2-1 defeat by eventual runners-up the Czech Republic. His son Federico did better at UEFA EURO 2020, scoring twice – in a 2-1 victory over Austria in the second round and the 1-1 semi-final draw with Spain, which Italy won on penalties – before starting in the final victory over England. However, Enrico still shares with Alessandro Del Piero the record for goals as a substitute for Italy: five. The Austria win in June 2021 was Italy's 14th in a row in UEFA European Championship matches, including qualifiers, equalling a record held by Belgium – and the Italians would set a new record in their next match, defeating Belgium 2-1 in their UEFA EURO 2020 quarter-final.

NATIONAL LEGEND
THE OLD GUARD

With a combined age of 70, veteran centre-backs **Giorgio Chiellini** and **Leonardo Bonucci** were seen by some as potential weak links in Italy's armour at UEFA EURO 2020, but they had the last laugh. Chiellini, 36, had announced his international retirement after Italy failed to make the 2018 FIFA World Cup, but was called up nevertheless by caretaker boss Luigi Di Biago for friendlies in March 2018, and new permanent manager Roberto Mancini appointed him as captain. He lifted the UEFA EURO 2020 trophy at Wembley on 11 July 2021, after Italy beat England 3-2 on penalties following a 1-1 draw. Italy's equaliser was a goalmouth scramble finished by Bonucci – at 34 years and 71 days old, the oldest man to find the net in a UEFA European Championship final. The previous record-holder was West Germany's Bernd Hölzenbein, 30 years and 103 days old when scoring for West Germany against Czechoslovakia in 1976. Bonucci's appearance in the final also took him to 18 UEFA European Championship matches, one more than the Italian record formerly held by Gianluigi Buffon.

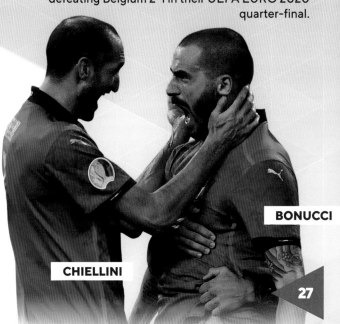

BONUCCI

CHIELLINI

NETHERLANDS

Patrick Kluivert's son Justin made his international debut as a 78th-minute substitute against Portugal in March 2018, aged 18 – the same age at which Patrick first appeared for his country.

Banks of orange-shirted Dutch fans have become a regular sight at the world's major football tournaments, not least thanks to Johan Cruijff and his team's spectacular brand of "Total Football".

CRUIJFF

Joined FIFA: 1905

Biggest win:
11-0 v. San Marino, 2011

Highest FIFA ranking: 1st

Home stadium: Johann Cruijff Arena, Amsterdam

Honours: 1 UEFA European Championship (1988)

9
The Netherlands became the first team to be shown as many as nine cards during a single FIFA World Cup finals match. In the final in 2010, they picked up eight bookings and then a second yellow for defender John Heitinga in a 1–0 extra-time defeat to Spain.

NATIONAL LEGEND
CRUIJFF THE MAGICIAN

Johan Cruijff was not only a genius with the ball at his feet but also an inspirational football philosopher, who spread the concept of "Total Football" not only with Ajax and the Netherlands in the 1970s but also in Spain where he played for and managed FC Barcelona and acted as a mentor to those who followed him there, such as Pep Guardiola and Xavi Hernández. He also gave the world the much-imitated "Cruijff turn", after pushing the ball with the inside of his foot behind his standing leg before swivelling and surging past bemused Swedish defender Jan Olsson.

NATIONAL LEGEND
HERO HAPPEL

Ernst Happel is maybe second only to Rinus Michels for his coaching achievements with Dutch teams. The former Austria defender made history by steering Feyenoord to the European Cup in 1970 – the first Dutch side to win the trophy – and was drafted in to coach the Netherlands at the 1978 FIFA World Cup after guiding Belgian club Brugge to the European Cup final. In Johan Cruijff's absence, Happel drew the best from stars such as Ruud Krol, Johan Neeskens and Arie Haan as the Netherlands reached the final, where they lost 3–1 after extra-time to hosts Argentina in Buenos Aires.

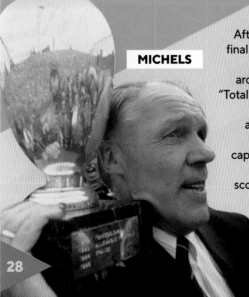

MICHELS

NATIONAL LEGEND
MICHELS THE MASTER

After FIFA World Cup heartache not only in the 1974 final against West Germany but also at the same stage four years later versus hosts Argentina, one of the architects of the country's – and leading club Ajax's – "Total Football" approaching to playing the game finally led the Netherlands to a first tournament victory at the 1988 UEFA European Championship. **Rinus Michels** was known as "The General", though his captain on the field that summer was the flamboyant, dreadlocks-flying all-rounder Ruud Gullit, who scored the opening goal in the final, helping beat the Soviet Union 2–0. Gullit was voted European Footballer of the Year in 1987 and 1989, and Michels was named FIFA's Coach of the Century in 1999 for his achievements with the Netherlands and Ajax.

NATIONAL LEGEND
DIFFERENT SIDES OF SNEIJDER

In 2017, **Wesley Sneijder** not only became his country's most-capped footballer but also marked his 131st international appearance with his 31st goal. He enjoyed an almost perfect 2010 as he won the treble with Italy's Internazionale – a domestic league and cup double and the UEFA Champions League – but just missed out on adding the FIFA World Cup as the Netherlands lost 1-0 to Spain in the final. Sneijder almost won the tournament's Golden Boot too – his five goals left him level with Diego Forlán, Thomas Müller and David Villa, but it was Müller who claimed the award by virtue of registering more assists.

38

Abe Lenstra is still the Netherlands' oldest goalscorer. He was 38 years and 144 days old when he netted in his final game, a 2-2 draw with Belgium, on 19 April 1959.

SNEIJDER

MOST APPEARANCES:

1 Wesley Sneijder, 134

2 Edwin van der Sar, 130

3 Frank de Boer, 112

4 Rafael van der Vaart, 109

5 Giovanni van Bronckhorst, 106

STAR PLAYER
STARTING MAARTEN

Goalkeeper Maarten Stekelenburg became the oldest Netherlands international at a major tournament at UEFA EURO 2020 – a 3-2 victory over Ukraine. He was 38 years and 278 days old when his side were knocked out in the round of 16 by the Czech Republic. He had taken over in goal after first-choice Jasper Cillessen tested positive for COVID-19 on the eve of the tournament. Stekelenburg, who is deaf in one ear, was the first goalkeeper to be sent off while playing for the Netherlands – shown a red card in a 2-1 friendly defeat against Australia in September 2008 – but was one of the key performers when the Dutch reached the 2010 FIFA World Cup final. Another goalkeeper remains the Netherlands' oldest international and oldest debutant: Sander Boschker was 39 years and 256 days old when winning his first and only cap, as a second-half substitute against Ghana in a June 2010 friendly.

NATIONAL LEGEND
BACK FOR BATTLE

Having taken Netherlands to third place at the 2014 FIFA World Cup then seen his country fail to make the finals four years later, Louis van Gaal emerged from retirement to begin a third spell in charge in August 2021. He guided the Oranje to the quarter-finals of the 2022 FIFA World Cup in Qatar. His side were knocked out by eventual champions Argentina, amid high drama in Lusail, on penalties after recovering from 2-0 down. The Dutch had been given a lifeline by two late strikes from substitute **Wout Weghorst**, the second 11 minutes into stoppage-time. Goalkeeper Andries Noppert saved from Enzo Fernández, but Virgil van Dijk and Steven Berghuis missed for the Dutch. Eight Argentina players and seven Dutch were shown yellow cards, including two for Netherlands right-back Denzel Dumfries, who saw red for his angry reaction to Argentina's winning strike.

WEGHORST

STAR PLAYER
VIRGIL RECORD

Virgil van Dijk became the world's most expensive defender in January 2018 after joining Liverpool from Premier League rivals Southampton for a reported GBP 75 million. Two months later, he was named as the Netherlands' new captain, replacing Arjen Robben, who had retired from international football the previous October. Van Dijk scored a stoppage-time equaliser in a 2-2 draw with Germany in November 2018 that clinched his country's place at the inaugural UEFA Nations League final tournament the following year. He wore the armband in a 3-1 semi-final victory over England and the 1-0 defeat in the final to European champions Portugal. However, he missed out on UEFA Euro 2020 because of a serious knee injury suffered in a Merseyside derby against Liverpool's arch rivals Everton in October 2020. The national captaincy went to midfielder Georginio Wijnaldum.

VAN DIJK

★ STAR PLAYER
DE LIGT AND DARKNESS

Centre-back Matthijs de Ligt has long seemed full of youthful promise for the Netherlands. His debut against Bulgaria in March 2017, aged 17 years and 225 days, made him his country's youngest player since Mauk Weber in 1931 (17 years and 92 days). Yet his UEFA EURO 2020 ended unhappily – sent off for deliberate handball in the Netherlands' 2–0 second round defeat by the Czech Republic. He became the fourth Dutch player to be sent off in the UEFA European Championships, all against Czech opposition: midfielders Johan Neeskens and Wim van Hanegem in when losing a quarter-final 3–1 in 1976 and defender John Heitinga when beaten 3–2 in Group D in 2004.

RONALD KOEMAN

NATIONAL LEGEND
DE BOER BOYS SET RECORD

Twins Ronald and **Frank de Boer** hold the record for the most games played by brothers for the Netherlands. Frank won 112 caps, while Ronald won 67. Ronald missed a crucial spot-kick as the Dutch lost to Brazil in the semi-finals of the 1998 FIFA World Cup, while Frank suffered a similar unfortunate fate at the same stage of the UEFA European Championship two years later. Frank served as assistant to manager Bert van Marwijk as the Netherlands reached the 2010 FIFA World Cup final, and took the top job in September 2020 after Ronald Koeman's departure for Barcelona. He became the first Netherlands manager to fail to win in his first four matches in charge, and they could not go further than the second round of the following summer's UEFA European Championship.

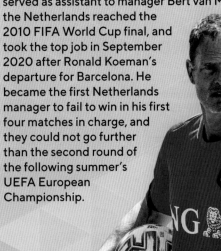

FRANK
DE BOER

NATIONAL LEGENDS
KOEMAN PEOPLE

Brothers Erwin and **Ronald Koeman** were Netherlands team-mates when they won the 1988 UEFA European Championship and they later teamed up in management. Elder brother Erwin served as Ronald's assistant at English clubs Everton and Southampton, but when Ronald was appointed the Netherlands' head coach in February 2018, Erwin opted not to join him. After the Dutch had missed out on both UEFA EURO 2016 and the 2018 FIFA World Cup, Ronald led them to the top of their UEFA Nations League group above France and Germany and the final in 2019, before securing qualification for UEFA EURO 2020. When the tournament was postponed for a year, he quit to become Barcelona manager in August 2020, returning to the Spanish club for whom he scored a UEFA European Cup-winning goal back in 1992. After he was fired by Barcelona, it was announced in April 2022 that Koeman would take over again as national coach once Frank de Boer's replacement Louis Van Gaal had taken the side to Qatar the following winter for the FIFA World Cup.

🏆 TOURNAMENT TRIVIA
KRUL TO BE KIND

Louis van Gaal pulled off a masterstroke when he replaced goalkeeper Jasper Cillessen with Tim Krul in the 119th minute of the Netherlands' quarter-final against Costa Rica at the 2014 FIFA World Cup. He reasoned that the Dutch stood a better chance of winning the resulting shoot-out with Krul as he was two inches taller than Cillessen. Sure enough, Krul saved two penalties and the Dutch went through. Van Gaal could not repeat the trick against Argentina in the semi-final though, but third-choice goalkeeper Michel Vorm also replaced Cillessen during stoppage time of the third-place play-off against Brazil, making the Netherlands the first country to field all 23 squad members at a FIFA World Cup.

9 Nine Netherlands players were on the losing side in both the 1974 (2–1 to West Germany) and 1978 (3–1 to Argentina) FIFA World Cup finals.

VAN PERSIE

Four players have scored five goals in a game for the Netherlands: Jan Vos, Leen Vente, John Bosman and Marco van Basten.

5

NATIONAL LEGEND
ROCKIN' ROBIN

In 2014, **Robin van Persie** became the first Dutchman to score at three different FIFA World Cups when he planted a spectacular looping header over Iker Casillas in the Dutchmen's 5-1 victory over holders Spain. The Netherlands eventually finished third, beating hosts Brazil in the third-place play-off, making them the first country to enjoy three World Cup wins over Brazil. Van Persie had become his country's leading scorer in a pre-tournament friendly against Ghana, but his final international goals came in a 3-2 defeat to the Czech Republic that denied the Dutch a 2016 UEFA European Championship slot. Unfortunately for him, goal no. 50 came after his own goal had put the Czechs 3-1 up.

STAR PLAYER
MEMPHIS STYLE

When he scored to help beat Australia in a 2014 Group B clash in Port Alegre in Brazil, **Memphis Depay** became the youngest Dutch scorer at a FIFA World Cup – aged 20 years and 125 days. He would go on to reach further landmarks for his country. His prolific scoring form in the years ahead included seven braces before finally hitting his first hat-trick, as Turkey were beaten 6-1 in Amsterdam in September 2021 in a FIFA World Cup qualifier. Another brace in another six-goal spree the following month versus Gibraltar made him the first Dutchman to find the net for the nation 13 times in a calendar year. A last-minute winner against Wales in June 2022 in the UEFA Nations League put him level-second in the Dutch goal rankings, and he moved ahead of Klaas-Jan Huntelaar with the first goal in a 3-1 win over the USA at the 2022 FIFA World Cup.

TOP SCORERS:

1 **Robin van Persie**, 50

2 **Memphis Depay**, 43

3 **Klaas-Jan Huntelaar**, 42

4 **Patrick Kluivert**, 40

5 **Dennis Bergkamp**, 37
= **Arjen Robben**, 37

DEPAY

3

Netherlands forward Cody Gakpo scored the opening goal in all three Group A games at the 2022 FIFA World Cup, including 2-0 victories over Senegal and hosts Qatar either side of a 1-1 draw with Ecuador. He made his international debut at UEFA EURO 2020, as a substitute against North Macedonia.

NATIONAL LEGEND
SENIOR ADVOCAAT

Dick Advocaat holds two records as Dutch national team coach. When he was re-appointed for his third spell in May 2017, he became, at 69, his country's oldest national coach – one year older than Guus Hiddick had been when he was fired in 2015. Advocaat also boasts the most wins as national coach, victories in November 2017 friendlies over Scotland and Romania taking him to 37, one more than Englishman Bob Glendenning, who was in charge between 1925 and his death in 1940. After the Romania victory, however, Advocaat stood down as national coach and former player Ronald Koeman was appointed to replace him.

ADVOCAAT

31

SPAIN

Spanish clubs have won a record number of European Cup/UEFA Champions League titles between them and the country has produced some of world football's finest players. Spain won their first FIFA World Cup in 2010.

Joined FIFA: 1920

Biggest win:
13-0 v. Bulgaria, 1933

Highest FIFA ranking: 1st

Home stadium:
(rotation)

Honours:
1 FIFA World Cup (2010),
3 UEFA European
Championships (1964,
2008, 2012)

4-3
When Spain came back from 2-0 and then 3-2 down to win 4-3 in Madrid in May 1929, they became the first non-British team to beat England.

INIESTA

NATIONAL PLAYER
ANDRÉS THE GIANT

Andrés Iniesta left Barcelona in 2018, having won nine *La Liga* titles, six *Copa del Rey* trophies and four UEFA Champions League titles in his 17 years at the club. He also bade farewell to international football after the 2018 FIFA World Cup, aged 34, having played 131 times for Spain and scored 13 goals – the most important of which won the 2010 FIFA World Cup. Uniquely, Iniesta picked up man-of-the-match awards in a UEFA Champions League final (2015), a UEFA European Championship final (2012) and a FIFA World Cup final (2010).

58

Centre-back Pau Torres needed just 58 seconds to score his first goal for Spain, finding the net almost instantly as a substitute for Sergio Ramos in a 7-0 victory over Malta in November 2019. In the same game, fellow debutant Dani Olmo found the net three minutes into his appearance from the bench.

TOURNAMENT TRIVIA
TRIPLING UP

Spain's 2010 FIFA World Cup triumph in Johannesburg, South Africa, made them the first country since West Germany in 1974 to lift the trophy as the reigning European champions. When France combined the two titles, they did it the other way round, winning the world crown in 1998 then the continental showpiece two years later. No nation had won three major international tournaments in a row until Spain won the UEFA European Championship in 2012, trouncing Italy 4-0 in the final and making them the first European champions to retain the cup. Since then, glory has been scarce. They exited in the first round of the 2014 FIFA World Cup and the second in 2018, and the second round of the 2016 UEFA European Championship. They lost penalty shoot-outs to eventual champions Italy in the semi-finals of UEFA EURO 2020 and to Morocco in the second round of the 2022 FIFA World Cup.

NATIONAL LEGEND
HAPPY XAVI

When Spain's second most-capped outfield player, with 133, retired from international football after the 2014 FIFA World Cup – and when he left Spanish club football a year later – he was recognised as his country's most-decorated player. Curiously, both the first and final appearances of **Xavi Hernández**'s international career were defeats to Netherlands sides coached by Louis van Gaal, 2-1 in 2000 and 5-1 in 2014. Triumph was far more familiar to the midfield playmaker, a mainstay of Spain's 2010 FIFA World Cup-winning side as well as the teams that lifted the UEFA European Championship trophy in 2008 and 2012.

XAVI

TOURNEMENT TRIVIA
RED ALERT

Spain refused to play in the first UEFA European Championship in 1960, in protest at having to travel to the Soviet Union, a Communist country. But they played ball four years later, not only hosting the tournament but also winning it, and beating the visiting Soviets 2-1 in the final for good measure. Marcelino scoring the winner with six minutes left. Spain were captained by Fernando Olivella, spearheaded up-front by striker Luis Suárez and managed by José Villalonga, who had been the first manager to win the European Cup, with Real Madrid in 1956.

TORRES

7

Spain enjoyed their biggest-ever FIFA World Cup win beating Costa Rica 7-0 in their opening match of the 2022 FIFA World Cup. **Ferrán Torres** scored twice in the Group E meeting in Doha, with Dani Olmo, Marco Asensio, Gavi, Carlos Soler and Álvaro Morata also on the scoresheet.

TEAM TRIVIA
FIT FOR PURPOSE

Luis Suárez remains the only Spanish-born player to be named European Footballer of the Year, in 1960. That same year, his country refused to play in the first UEFA European Championship in protest at having to travel to hosts the Soviet Union. He helped spearhead Spain to their first trophy at the same competition four years later, however, beating the visiting Soviets 2-1 in the final in Madrid's Bernabéu stadium. Team-mate Marcelino hit the winner with six minutes left. Suárez had played on despite fitness doubts. Watching from home, ruled out by injury, was Atlético Madrid forward Luis Aragonés, who was Spain manager for their next UEFA European Championship triumph in 2008, a month short of his 70th birthday, making him the oldest coach to win the tournament.

NATIONAL LEGEND
BEST CAS SCENARIO

Goalkeeper **Iker Casillas** has long been known to devotees back home as "Saint Iker" – an anointment richly supported by his haul of trophies and medals, both for team and individual. He is one of only three men to lift the FIFA World Cup, the UEFA European Championship and the UEFA Champions League/European Cup trophies as captain, emulating Germany's Franz Beckenbauer and France's Didier Deschamps. As well as winning the 2008 and 2012 UEFA European Championships and the 2010 FIFA World Cup, Casillas also became the first goalkeeper to reach 100 international clean sheets in a 2-0 friendly win over England in November 2015.

CASILLAS

MOST APPEARANCES:
1 **Sergio Ramos**, 180
2 **Iker Casillas**, 167
3 **Sergio Busquets**, 137
4 **Xavi Hernández**, 133
5 **Andrés Iniesta**, 131

18
At UEFA EURO 2020, Barcelona midfielder Pedri became the first man aged 18 or under to start six consecutive games at a FIFA World Cup or UEFA European Championship.

4
Spain became the first country to lose four FIFA World Cup penalty shoot-outs when they were knocked out by Morocco in the Round of 16 at the 2022 FIFA World Cup – beaten 3-0 on spot-kicks after a goalless draw. Spain missed all three of their kicks, by Pablo Sarabia, Carlos Soler and captain Sergio Busquets. Spain's only FIFA World Cup penalty shoot-out victory came in the second round in 2002, against the Republic of Ireland.

SCORING RECORD
VILLA FILLS HIS BOOTS

David Villa became Spain's all-time FIFA World Cup top scorer with his first-round goal against Chile in 2010, his sixth across the 2006 and 2010 tournaments. Villa became Spain's all-time leading scorer with a brace against the Czech Republic in March 2011, but a broken leg ruled him out of the 2012 UEFA European Championship, so he missed out on adding to his UEFA EURO 2008 and 2010 FIFA World Cup winner's medals. Villa and Fernando Torres share Spain's record for most hat-tricks – three each, including one apiece when Tahiti were crushed 10-0 at the 2013 FIFA Confederations Cup.

0
The UEFA EURO 2020 squad picked by manager Luis Enrique, who played for both Real Madrid and Barcelona, did not feature any players from Real Madrid – the first time that has happened for Spain at a major tournament.

TOP SCORERS:

1 **David Villa**, 59
2 **Raúl**, 44
3 **Fernando Torres**, 38
4 **David Silva**, 35
5 **Álvaro Morata**, 30

VILLA

TOURNAMENT TRIVIA
HARD TO BEAT

Spain share with Brazil the record for the longest international unbeaten run – the Brazilians went 35 games without defeat between 1993 and 1996, a tally matched by the Spanish between 2007 and 2009, when they lost 2-0 to the United States in the semi-finals of the FIFA Confederations Cup. That vintage Spain side also became the first country to take maximum points, 30 out of 30, in a FIFA World Cup qualification campaign, and they duly went on to lift the trophy in South Africa in 2010.

RAMOS

STAR PLAYER
MORATA OUT OF LUCK

Álvaro Morata suffered mixed fortunes when UEFA EURO 2020 finally came around in summer 2021. He was booed by his own home fans when Spain opened with a goalless draw against Sweden in Seville, but ended the tournament with three goals, taking him to six overall in the UEFA European Championship. One of these was a late equaliser in the semi-final against Italy. That took him past Fernando Torres' Spanish record of five at UEFA EUROs. Morata then missed during the penalty shoot-out to deny Spain a place in the final. Morata scored once in each of Spain's group games at the 2022 FIFA World Cup, but he and his team-mates fired a blank in their second-round defeat to Morocco.

STAR PLAYER
SURGING SERGIO

In March 2013, **Sergio Ramos** became the youngest-ever European player to reach 100 international caps at the age of 26 years and 358 days. He marked the occasion by scoring Spain's goal in a 1-1 draw with Finland. Korea Republic's Cha Bum-kun, who was 24 years and 139 days old when he achieved the landmark, holds the global record. Ramos, a right-back or central defender who has 2010 FIFA World Cup and 2008 and 2012 UEFA European Championships to his name, not only became Spain's most-capped player when he won his 168th cap in October 2019 but also the most-capped outfield player in European men's football. He later overtook Italy goalkeeper Gianluigi Buffon for the overall European record. Ramos was left out of Spain's UEFA EURO 2020 squad, ending a run of ten straight tournaments.

NATIONAL LEGEND
TORRES! TORRES!

As a child, **Fernando Torres** wanted to be a goalkeeper, but he made the wise decision to become a striker instead. He had a penchant for scoring the only goal in the final of a tournament, doing so for Spain in the 2008 UEFA European Championship against Germany in Vienna, having done the same in the U-16 UEFA European Championship in 2001 and for the Under-19s the following year. Torres became the most expensive Spanish footballer ever when Chelsea paid GBP 50 million to sign him from fellow English club Liverpool in January 2011. After stints in Italy and back home in Spain, he moved to play in Japan in July 2018 and retired 11 months later.

TORRES

NATIONAL LEGEND
THE RAÚL THING

Raúl González Blanco – known as Raúl – remains a Spain and Real Madrid icon, despite his record goal tallies being passed, respectively, by David Villa and Cristiano Ronaldo. He was an Atlético Madrid youth-teamer before signing for city rivals Real, where he scored 228 goals in 550 games and captained them from 2003 to 2010. But despite playing for Spain at five tournaments between the 1998 and 2006 FIFA World Cups, he was left out of Spain's UEFA EURO 2008 squad – and they promptly won the trophy. After leaving Real, Raúl enjoyed further success at Schalke 04 in Germany, Al Sadd in Qatar and New York Cosmos in the United States.

50
Centre-back Carlos Marchena became the first footballer to go 50 internationals in a row unbeaten when he played in Spain's 3-2 victory over Saudi Arabia in May 2009.

GAVI

STAR PLAYER
GAVI GOALS

Barcelona midfielder **Gavi** became Spain's youngest ever international, aged 17 years and 62 days, in their 2-1 UEFA Nations League semi-final victory over Italy in October 2021, then their youngest ever scorer, at 17 years and 304 days, against the Czech Republic the following June. The previous scoring record had been set by his Barcelona team-mate Ansu Fati, seven days older when he scored against Ukraine in September 2020. Gavi's goal in the 7-0 victory over Costa Rica in Qatar made him the third-youngest man to score at a FIFA World Cup, aged 18 years and 110 days – behind Brazil's Pelé (17 years and 249 days) in 1958 and Mexico's Manuel Rosas (18 years and 93 days) in 1930.

STAR PLAYER
MAGIC BUSQ

Vicente del Bosque, who managed Spain to glory at the 2010 FIFA World Cup and the UEFA European Championship two years later, once said: "If I were a player, I would like to be like Busquets." Del Bosque did actually play hundreds of times in midfield for Real Madrid and won 18 caps for his country. He is among the many to appreciate the tidy and essential work done by Sergio Busquets either as a defensive midfielder or emergency centre-back. Busquets – whose father Carles previously played occasionally in goal for Barcelona – was key to Spain winning the 2010 FIFA World Cup and the 2012 UEFA European Championship and, aged 33, was still influential enough to be named best player of the tournament at the 2021 UEFA Nations League despite Spain losing 2-1 to France in the final.

35
Aritz Aduriz became Spain's oldest goalscorer when he found the net in a 4-0 win over FYR Macedonia on 13 November 2016 in a 2018 FIFA World Cup qualifier. He was 35 years and 275 days old – 50 days older than the previous record-holder José Maria Peña, who scored the only goal in 30 November 1930 friendly against Portugal.

BUSQUETS

BELGIUM

Belgium's golden generation has risen: they reached the 2014 FIFA World Cup quarter-finals, and the *Red Devils* surpassed any previous achievements by finishing third at the 2018 FIFA World Cup.

Joined FIFA: 1904

Biggest win: 10–1 v. San Marino, 2001

Highest FIFA ranking: 1st

Home stadium: (rotation)

Honours: -

COURTOIS

STAR PLAYER
LUK'S GOOD

Romelu Lukaku, Belgium's all-time leading scorer, had to wait 24 internationals before completing 90 minutes for his country. He was hampered by injury during the 2022 FIFA World Cup, going goalless in Belgium's three games as they departed in the first round. He scored all three in their next match, a convincing UEFA European Championship qualifier away to Sweden in March 2023, four days before taking his international goal tally to 72 in a 3–2 victory in Germany. He had previously found the net four times at both the 2018 FIFA World Cup and UEFA EURO 2020. Lukaku made his first-team debut for Belgian club Anderlecht aged just 16 years and 11 days in May 2009, before playing for Chelsea, Everton and Manchester United in England and Internazionale in Italy.

LUKAKU

TEAM TRIVIA
BELGIUM'S PERSONAL BEST

Under Spanish manager Roberto Martínez, Belgium enjoyed their most successful FIFA World Cup in Russia in 2018, losing 1–0 to eventual champions France in the semi-finals then beating England 2–0 in the third-place play-off. They were the tournament's top scorers with 16 goals. Belgium's so-called "Golden Generation" went into UEFA EURO 2020 among the favourites, having spent almost three years top of FIFA's world rankings, but fell 2–1 to Italy in the quarter-finals. They then failed to make it out of the first round at the 2022 FIFA World Cup, beating Canada 1–0 but losing 2–0 to Morocco and drawing 0–0 with Croatia. Martínez was succeeded by Domenico Tedesco as head coach.

9

Belgium have won by nine goals on four occasions, most recently a 9–0 defeat of San Marino on 10 October 2019, when they also set a new national record by having seven of their own men on the scoresheet – including a brace by Romelu Lukaku – as well as an own goal by the visitors' Cristian Brolli.

STAR PLAYER
KEEPING COR

Thibaut Courtois became Belgium's youngest goalkeeper on his debut in a goalless friendly draw away to France in November 2011, aged 19 years and 189 days. He has gone on to play between the sticks for the country more often than any other man, reaching a century of caps in Belgium's last match at the 2022 FIFA World Cup in Qatar – another 0–0, this time against Croatia. Courtois had made 27 saves at the FIFA World Cup in Russia four years earlier on his way to claiming the Golden Gloves as the tournament's best goalkeeper. He was also named Player of the Match in Real Madrid's 1–0 win in the 2022 UEFA Champions League final against Liverpool, making nine saves, including spectacular stops to deny Mohamed Salah and Sadio Mané.

TOP SCORERS:

1 Romelu Lukaku, 72

2 Eden Hazard, 33

3 Paul Van Himst, 30
  = Bernard Voorhoof, 30

5 Marc Wilmots, 28

TOURNAMENT TRIVIA
COMEBACK KINGS

Belgium's 3-2 victory over Japan in Rostov-on-Don at the 2018 FIFA World Cup was the first time since 1970 that a team had come back from two goals down to win a knockout game – when West Germany had needed extra time to beat England 3-2 in a quarter-final tie. Jan Vertonghen scored Belgium's first goal after 69 minutes, followed by Marouane Fellaini's equaliser five minutes later. Fellow substitute Nacer Chadli got the winner four minutes into stoppage time. Belgium's ten different goalscorers in Russia equalled the FIFA World Cup record held by France (1982) and Italy (2006).

MOST APPEARANCES:

1. **Jan Vertonghen**, 147
2. **Axel Witsel**, 139
3. **Toby Alderweireld**, 127
4. **Eden Hazard**, 126
5. **Dries Mertens**, 109

11

Belgium's most-capped footballer, defender **Jan Vertonghen** made his 100th appearance on 2 June 2018 against Portugal – 11 years to the day after his first cap, against the same country. His mother Ria Mattheeuws handed over a commemorative cap to celebrate the 100-match landmark.

VERTONGHEN

19

In 2014, striker Divock Origi became Belgium's youngest FIFA World Cup finals scorer – aged 19 years and 65 days – when he hit the only goal as a late substitute against Russia. He scored Liverpool's second in a 2-0 victory over Tottenham Hotspur in the 2019 UEFA Champions League final.

THYS

NATIONAL LEGEND
HE'S OUR GUY

Unquestionably Belgium's greatest manager – as well as their longest-serving – was **Guy Thys**. He led them to the final of the 1980 UEFA European Championship and – with a team featuring the likes of Enzo Scifo and Nico Claesen – the semi-finals of the FIFA World Cup six years later. He spent 13 years in the job from 1976 to 1989, then returned for a second spell just eight months after quitting. He stepped down again after managing Belgium at the 1990 FIFA World Cup. During his playing days in the 1940s and 1950s, he was a striker and won two caps for Belgium.

39

Belgium's tenth most-capped player, Timmy Simons, became his country's oldest international when he faced Estonia 2018 FIFA World Cup qualifier in November 2016, aged 39 years and 338 days.

STAR PLAYERS
HAZ A GO HEROES

Eden and Thorgan **Hazard** became the third pair of brothers to score at the UEFA European Championships, with younger sibling Thorgan finding the net at UEFA EURO 2020 five years after Eden had done so in France. The two brotherly duos to precede them were Frank and Ronald De Boer for the Netherlands and Denmark's Michael and Brian Laudrup. Thorgan scored twice at EURO 2020, in a 2-1 victory over Denmark and the only goal of their second round win over defending holders Portugal – making him the first Belgian to score in consecutive UEFA European Championship appearances. Their parents are both former footballers – father Thierry spent most of his career at semi-professional level with Belgian second division club La Louvière, while mother Carine only retired from the women's game when pregnant with Eden. Eden retired from international football after the 2022 FIFA World Cup having captained Belgium a record 59 times. He was replaced as skipper by Manchester City's **Kevin De Bruyne**.

EDEN HAZARD

DE BRUYNE

BULGARIA

Regular qualifiers for the game's major competitions, and the birthplace of some of the sport's biggest names, Bulgaria have too often failed to deliver on the big occasions and make a mark on world football.

63

Bulgaria visited Qatar in March 2022. They lost 2–1 twice, to their hosts and to Croatia. Captain Kiril Despodov, a three-time Bulgarian Footballer of the Year, opened the scoring against Croatia after 63 minutes, but instantly received a second yellow and a red card for removing his shirt while celebrating.

STOICHKOV

Joined FIFA: 1922

Biggest win: 15–0 v. Ghana, 1968

Highest FIFA ranking: 3rd

Home stadium: Vasil Levski National Stadium, Sofia

Honours: -

NATIONAL LEGEND
HRISTO'S HISTORY

Hristo Stoichkov, born in Plovdiv, Bulgaria, on 8 February 1968, shared the 1994 FIFA World Cup Golden Boot, awarded to the tournament's top scorer, with Russia's Oleg Salenko. Both scored six times, though Stoichkov became the sole winner of that year's European Footballer of the Year award. Earlier the same year, he had combined up-front with Brazilian Romario to help Barcelona reach the final of the UEFA Champions League.

1994
Yordan Letchkov headed the winning goal against holders and defending champions Germany in the 1994 FIFA World Cup quarter-final in the United States. At the time, he played for German club Hamburg. He later became mayor of Sliven, the Bulgarian town he was born in.

NATIONAL LEGEND
MOB RULES

Much-travelled Bulgaria centre-forward **Dimitar Berbatov** claims to have learned English by watching the *Godfather* movies. Berbatov joined Manchester United from Tottenham in 2008 for a club and Bulgarian record fee of GBP 30.75m. Before joining Spurs, he had been a member of the Bayer Leverkusen side who narrowly missed out on a treble in 2002. They lost in the final of both the UEFA Champions League and the German cup and finished runners-up in the German *Bundesliga*. Berbatov surprised and disappointed fans back home when he announced his international retirement aged just 29, in May 2010, having scored a national-record 48 goals in his 78 appearances for Bulgaria.

BERBATOV

TOP SCORERS:

NATIONAL LEGEND
BOSSMAN BONEV

Hristo Bonev was out on his own as Bulgaria's leading man both for appearances and goals – and a national hero for his stylish flair on the field. A mainstay of the side at the 1970 and 1974 FIFA World Cups, Bonev scored in Bulgaria's opening game at the 1970 tournament, a 3–2 defeat to Peru, and again four years later in a 1–1 draw against Uruguay. His 48th and final goal came on his last game (his 96th) for his country, a 2–1 loss to Argentina in April 1979. Bonev coached Bulgaria at the 1998 FIFA World Cup in France, the last manager to lead them at the finals, but they were knocked out in the first round.

BONEV

3

Three of Bulgaria's 1994 FIFA World Cup semi-finalists later coached the national team: Hristo Stoichkov between 2004 and 2007, Petar Hubchev, 2016–19, followed immediately by Krasimir Balakov, but only for six games.

NATIONAL LEGEND
A NATION MOURNS

Bulgaria lost two of its most popular footballing talents when a June 1971 car crash claimed the lives of strikers Georgi Asparukhov and Nikola Kotkov; Asparukhov was only 28 years old at the time, while Kotkov was 32. Asparukhov scored 19 goals in 50 internationals, including Bulgaria's only goal of the 1966 FIFA World Cup finals in a 3–1 defeat to Hungary. Asparuhov was nominated for the 1965 Ballon d'Or award and finished eighth: over 500,000 people attended his funeral in Sofia.

7

Dimitar Berbatov has been named Bulgarian Footballer of the Year a record seven times, followed by Hristo Stoichkov on five and Hristo Bonev, Ivelin Popov and **Kiril Despodov** on three wins apiece. Despodov took the prize in 2018, 2021 and 2022.

DESPODOV

NATIONAL HERO
STAN THE BURGER VAN MAN

Stiliyan Petrov – "Stan" to fans of his English club Aston Villa – was applauded onto the field when he became Bulgaria's first outfield player to reach 100 caps, against Switzerland in March 2011. The elegant midfielder received far more acclaim after recovering from a March 2012 diagnosis of acute leukaemia – Villa fans stood and clapped for 60 seconds in the 19th-minute of every game for the rest of the season, 19 being his squad number. He previously fought homesickness when playing for Scottish club Celtic but improved his English skills by working behind the counter of a friend's burger van. Petrov became Bulgaria's most-capped player in a 3–1 defeat to Switzerland in September 2011 and bowed out of international football a month later.

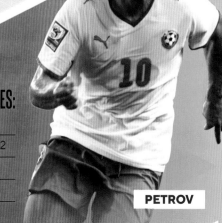

PETROV

NATIONAL HERO
HEAD BOY

Bulgaria's second most-capped player is goalkeeper **Borislav Mihaylov**. He captained the side for their surge to the FIFA World Cup semi-finals in 1994. saving two penalties when beating Mexico in a second-round shoot-out. He sometimes wore a wig while playing, and later had a hair transplant. After retiring in 2005, he became president of the Bulgarian Football Union for 14 years. His father Bisev had played five times in goal for Bulgaria between 1962 and 1971 and his son Nikolay, once on the books of Liverpool, won the first of 38 caps for the country between the sticks in a May 2006 5–1 defeat to Scotland.

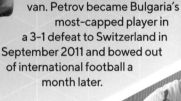

MOST APPEARANCES:

CROATIA

ŠUKER

Croatia's distinctive red-and-white chequered jersey has become one of the most recognised in world football. They hit a new peak in 2018 when they reached their first FIFA World Cup final.

Joined FIFA: 1992
Biggest win: 10-0 v. San Marino, 2014
Highest FIFA Ranking: 3rd
Home stadium: (rotation)
Honours: -

NATIONAL LEGEND
SUPER ŠUKER

Striker **Davor Šuker** won the Golden Boot for top scorer at the FIFA World Cup in 1998, scoring six goals in seven games as Croatia finished third. His strikes included the opening goal in Croatia's 2-1 semi-final defeat to eventual champions France, and the winner in a 2-1 triumph over the Netherlands in the third-place play-off. Šuker, by far his country's leading scorer of all time, had hit three goals at the 1996 UEFA European Championship – including an audacious long-distance lob over Denmark goalkeeper Peter Schmeichel. Šuker was named president of the Croatian FA in July 2012.

TOP SCORERS:

1. **Davor Šuker**, 45
2. **Mario Mandžukić**, 33
   = **Ivan Perišić**, 33
4. **Eduardo da Silva**, 29
5. **Andrej Kramarić**, 23
   = **Luka Modrić**, 23

MODRIĆ

37
Luka Modrić became Croatia's oldest international on 25 March 2023 in a UEFA European Championship qualifier against Wales – a 1-1 draw – aged 37 years and 197 days. He extended the record three days later in a 2-0 away win against Turkey. The previous record-holder was goalkeeper Dražen Ladić, 37 years and 149 days old for his 59th appearance in 2000.

STAR PLAYER
MAGICAL MODRIĆ

Croatia made history by reaching their first FIFA World Cup final in 2018 – and star of the show was captain and playmaker **Luka Modrić**, who won the Golden Ball for the tournament's best player despite their 4-2 final defeat to France. Modrić began his career with Dinamo Zagreb before moving to Tottenham Hotspur in England and then winning four UEFA Champions League titles with Spain's Real Madrid. In Russia, Croatia became the first country since Argentina in 1990 to win two penalty shoot-outs at the same FIFA World Cup – beating Denmark in the round of 16 as well as hosts Russia in the quarter-finals. Modrić, a five-time UEFA Champions League winner with Real Madrid, became his country's most-capped player with his 135th appearance in a 1-0 FIFA World Cup qualifier victory over Cyprus in March 2021.

GVARDIOL

Centre-back **Joško Gvardiol**, who played the 2022 FIFA World Cup in a face mask after breaking his nose playing for German club RB Leipzig, scored Croatia's opener in their 2-1 win over Morocco in the third-place play-off. That made him Croatia's youngest goal-scorer at a major tournament, aged 20 years and 328 days.

TEAM TRIVIA
RUNNING RIO

Croatia clinched their place at the 2022 FIFA World Cup thanks to a late own goal by Russia's Fedor Kudryashov in their decisive Group D qualifier in November 2021 in Split. Three days earlier, Croatia had equalled their biggest ever away victory, winning 7-1 in Malta, including a first two international goals for Lovro Majer. Croatia had previously triumphed 6-0 in Andorra in September 2007 in a UEFA European Championship qualifier and by the same scoreline away to Kosovo in a FIFA World Cup qualifier in October 2016, with Mario Mandžukić hitting a hat-trick. The country's biggest win remains a 10-0 trouncing of San Marino in June 2016.

STAR PLAYER
UNLUCKY MANDS

Striker **Mario Mandžukić** was Croatia's hero in their 2018 FIFA World Cup semi-final – only to unwittingly turn villain in the final four days later. In the semi, his goal, 19 minutes into extra time, beat England 2-1 and sent Croatia to their first-ever FIFA World Cup final. In the final, however, he headed into his own net after 18 minutes to give France the lead. Mandžukić did pull a goal back to make the score 4-2 to France with 21 minutes left. He thus became the first man to score for both sides in a FIFA World Cup final. Mandžukić was assistant coach to Zlatko Dalić as Croatia finished third at the 2022 FIFA World Cup.

MANDŽUKIĆ

22

Croatia competed in the 2018 FIFA World Cup with only 22 squad players for the majority of the tournament. Coach Zlatko Dalić sent Nikola Kalinić home after the striker allegedly refused to come on as a substitute in their opening game against Nigeria.

117

Only three minutes of extra-time remained when Bruno Petković equalised for Croatia in the 2022 FIFA World Cup quarter-final against Brazil, which his team won on penalties. The left-foot finish was the striker's seventh goal for his country.

2

Croatia's 4-0 victory over Cameroon in the 2014 FIFA World Cup saw striker Ivica Olić become the first player to score for Croatia at two separate FIFA World Cups, having previously found the net in 2002.

NATIONAL LEGEND
PERIŠIĆ THE THOUGHT

In 2018, winger **Ivan Perišić** became the first Croat to score at the right end in a FIFA World Cup final, levelling up in first-half stoppage-time after team-mate Mario Mandžukić had inadvertently given France the lead. Perišić had previously equalised against England in the semi-finals. His ten goals at international tournaments are a Croatia record, the latest being an equaliser against Japan in the second round of the 2022 FIFA World Cup before his side won on penalties, as they did again in the quarter-finals against Brazil. Perišić had previously provided two goals and an assist in the first round of UEFA EURO 2020, against the Czech Republic and Scotland.

MOST APPEARANCES:

1. **Luka Modrić**, 164
2. **Darijo Srna**, 134
3. **Ivan Perišić**, 125
4. **Stipe Pletikosa**, 114
5. **Ivan Rakitić**, 106

TOURNAMENT TRIVIA
DOUBLE IDENTITY

Robert Jarni and **Robert Prosinečki** share the rare distinction of playing for two different countries at different FIFA World Cup tournaments. They both represented Yugoslavia in Italy in 1990, and then newly independent Croatia in France eight years later. Full-back Jarni actually played for both Yugoslavia and Croatia in 1990, then only Yugoslavia in 1991, before switching back – and permanently – to Croat colours in 1992 after the country officially joined UEFA and FIFA. Prosinečki scored in Croatia's 2-1 victory over the Netherlands to finish third in 1998, and is the only man to score at different FIFA World Cups for two different teams – following his strike in a 4-1 Yugoslavia victory over the United Arab Emirates in the first round in 1990.

PROSINEČKI

PERIŠIĆ

CZECH REPUBLIC

The most successful of the former Eastern Bloc countries, as Czechoslovakia, they finished as runners-up in the 1934 and 1962 FIFA World Cups. As Czech Republic, they have failed to qualify for the last three FIFA World Cups.

Joined FIFA: 1994
Biggest win: 11-0 v. Senegal, 1966
Highest FIFA ranking: 2nd
Home stadium: (rotation)
Honours: 1 UEFA European Championship (1976)

ČECH

30 MINUTES
Belgium's 1920 victory at the Olympic Games was overshadowed when Czechoslovakia walked off the pitch after only 30 minutes in protest at what they saw as biased refereeing. Czechoslovakia are still the only team in the history of Olympic football to have been disqualified.

NATIONAL LEGEND
ČECH CAP
Goalkeeper **Petr Čech** always wore a protective cap after suffering a fractured skull during an English Premier League match in October 2006. The young Čech had served notice of his talent when he was beaten by only one penalty in a shoot-out against France in the 2002 UEFA U-21 European Championship final, helping the Czechs win the trophy. He later claimed winner's medals as Chelsea won the UEFA Champions League in 2012 (he was named man of the match) and the UEFA Europa League a year later. He retired after the UEFA Europa League final in 2019, but just a few months later he was back between the posts as an ice hockey goalie in England. He even saved a penalty shot on his debut.

STAR PLAYER
FRESHMAN ADAM
Striker Adam Hložek became the youngest Czech Republic international on his debut in September 2020 in a 3-1 away win against Slovakia in the UEFA Nations League. He was aged 18 years and 41 days, three days younger than Jan Polak had been against Poland in April 1999. Hložek opened his international goalscoring account 13 months later to help beat Belarus 2-0 in a FIFA World Cup qualifier. The country's oldest player remains Jan Koller, aged 36 years and 159 days for his 91st and final cap against Slovakia in September 2009.

NEDVĚD

NATIONAL LEGEND
THE CANNON COLLECTS
Pavel Nedvěd's election as European Footballer of the Year in 2003 ended a long wait for fans in the Czech Republic who had seen a string of outstanding players overlooked since Josef Masopust had been honoured back in 1962. Masopust, a midfield general, had scored the opening goal in the FIFA World Cup final that year before Brazil hit back to win 3-1 in the Chilean capital of Santiago. Years later, Masopust was remembered by Pelé and nominated as one of his 125 greatest living footballers. At club level, Masopust won eight Czechoslovak league titles with Dukla Prague, the army club.

MOST APPEARANCES:
1 **Petr Čech**, 124
2 **Karel Poborský**, 118
3 **Tomáš Rosický**, 105
4 **Jaroslav Plašil**, 103
5 **Milan Baroš**, 93

7

Striker Mojmír Chytil marked his Czech Republic debut with a hat-trick in the first 23 minutes of a 5–0 friendly victory against the Faroe Islands in November 2022, making him the nation's seventh man to hit an international treble.

TEAM TRIVIA
SEVEN UP

The Czech Republic's wait to reach a first FIFA World Cup since 2006 goes on after losing 1–0 to Sweden in their qualifying play-off semi-final in March 2022. In November 2021, the Czechs equalled their biggest ever win, seeing off Kuwait 7–0 in a friendly in Olomouc, including a brace by winger Jakub Pešek and a goal for captain **Tomáš Souček**. The Czech Republic previously beat San Marino 7–0 in October 2006 and September 2009, and they won 8–1 against Andorra in June 2005. The former Czechoslovakia defeated Yugoslavia 7–0 back in August 1920. Defensive midfielder Souček became only the sixth man to hit a hat-trick for the Czech Republic in a 6–2 FIFA World Cup qualifier triumph over Estonia in March 2021.

SOUČEK

NATIONAL LEGEND
TEN OUT OF TEN

Jan Koller is Czech football's all-time leading international marksman with 55 goals in 91 appearances. Koller scored on his debut against Belgium and struck ten goals in ten successive internationals. He scored six goals in each of the 2000, 2004 and 2008 UEFA European Championship qualifying campaigns. He began his career with Sparta Prague, who converted him from goalkeeper to goalscorer. Then, in Belgium, he was top scorer with Lokeren, before scoring 42 goals in two league title-winning campaigns with Anderlecht. Later, with Borussia Dortmund in Germany, he once went in goal after Jens Lehmann had been sent off and kept a clean sheet – having scored in the first half.

1934
The final of the 1934 FIFA World Cup was the first to go into extra time, with Czechoslovakia ultimately losing 2–1 to hosts Italy.

TOP SCORERS:

1 Jan Koller, 55

2 Milan Baroš, 41

3 Vladimir Šmicer, 27

4 Tomáš Rosický, 23

5 Pavel Kuka, 22 (plus 7 for Czechoslovakia)

KOLLER

1976
In 1976, Antonín Panenka invented the calmly-chipped penalty style – still performed to this day and now known as a "Panenka" – to win Czechoslovakia that year's UEFA European Championship in a penalty shoot-out final triumph over West Germany.

1

Debut-making substitute Zdeněk Ondrášek scored with his first shot in international football, a late winner to beat England 2–1 in Prague in a UEFA EURO 2020 qualifier in October 2019. This came seven months after the same opponents had inflicted the Czechs' heaviest post-independence defeat – 5–0 at Wembley.

NATIONAL LEGEND
SCHICK TO THE SYSTEM

Bayer Leverkusen striker **Patrik Schick**'s five goals at UEFA EURO 2020 put him level with Milan Baroš for Czech Republic goals at major tournaments – Baroš having won the Golden Boot when his five helped his country to the semi-finals at the 2004 European Championship. They could only make the quarter-finals this time, Schick's consolation strike not quite enough in a 2–1 defeat to Denmark. His second in the Czechs' 2–0 opening victory over Scotland, however, set a new record for the longest-distance goal recorded at a European Championship – struck from 49.7 metres after goalkeeper David Marshall had wandered towards the halfway line. Schick also scored in his country's surprise 2–0 second round victory over the Netherlands, set up by Tomáš Holeš, who had scored the first.

SCHICK

43

DENMARK

They have been playing football since 1908 but Denmark's crowning moment came in 1992 when they walked away with the UEFA European Championship crown in one of the biggest-ever international football shocks.

Joined FIFA: 1908

Biggest win: 17-1 v. France, 1908

Highest FIFA ranking: 3rd

Home stadium: Parken Stadium, Copenhagen

Honours: 1 UEFA European Championship (1992)

STAR PLAYER
CHRISTIAN AID

Denmark went into UEFA EURO 2020 looking for inspiration from star playmaker **Christian Eriksen**. A popular T-shirt ahead of the 2018 FIFA World Cup summed up their tactics as passing to Eriksen and waiting for him to score, after his hat-trick in a 5-1 play-off victory away to the Republic of Ireland clinched their place in Russia. Eriksen celebrated his 100th appearance for Denmark in October 2020 by scoring the only goal, a penalty, to defeat England at Wembley in the UEFA Nations League. But his sudden collapse, due to a cardiac arrest in the closing minutes of their UEFA Euro 2020 opener against Finland in Copenhagen, shocked the sporting world. It also also won praise for captain Simon Kjær and his team-mates as they formed a protective ring around Eriksen while paramedics battled to save his life. Inter Milan midfielder Eriksen, who previously played for Ajax and Tottenham Hotspur, thankfully regained consciousness. Eriksen was later fitted with a cardioverter-defibrillator and returned to top-flight football in January 2022 with English Premier League club Brentford before moving to Manchester United that summer. He scored with his first touch back in a Denmark shirt, two minutes in as a second-half substitute against the Netherlands in March 2022, and captained his country in their third and final Group D game at the 2022 FIFA World Cup, a 1–0 defeat to Australia.

ERIKSEN

16 SECONDS
Ebbe Sand scored the fastest-ever FIFA World Cup goal by a substitute when he netted a mere 16 seconds after coming onto the pitch in Denmark's clash with Nigeria at France 1998.

2

Midfielder Morten Wieghorst is the only player to be sent off twice while playing for Denmark – yet he also received a special award for fair play after deliberately missing a wrongly awarded penalty.

NATIONAL LEGENDS
BROTHERS IN ARMS

Denmark's two finest footballers came from the same family: **Michael** (104 games, 37 goals) and **Brian Laudrup** (82 games, 37 goals). The brothers spread their creative playmaking skills across Europe: Michael in Italy with Lazio and Juventus and in Spain with Barcelona and Real Madrid, Brian in Italy with Fiorentina and AC Milan, in Scotland with Rangers, and in England with Chelsea. Only Brian shared in Denmark's 1992 UEFA European Championship glory though – Michael had temporarily quit international football after falling out with then coach Richard Møller Nielsen.

MICHAEL **LAUDRUP**

BRIAN **LAUDRUP**

★ STAR PLAYER
IF THE SHIRT FITS

Denmark's emotional UEFA EURO 2020 saw them overcome the trauma of Christian Eriksen's collapse to reach the semi-finals, setting several new standards along the way. They became the first country in UEFA European Championship history to make the knock-out stages despite losing their first two games – 1-0 to Finland and 2-1 to Belgium. A 4-1 victory over Russia in their final Group B fixture was followed by a 4-0 defeat of Wales in the second round, making Denmark the first side at a UEFA European Championship to score four times in successive games. Their campaign ended in a 2-1 defeat to England, a semi-final match that began with England captain Harry Kane, a former Tottenham Hotspur team-mate of Eriksen's, presenting a signed England shirt saying "ERIKSEN 10" to Danish skipper Simon Kjær.

KASPER
SCHMEICHEL

🏆 TOURNAMENT TRIVIA
THE UNEXPECTED IN 1992

Few Danish football fans will ever forget June 1992, their national team's finest hour, when they won the UEFA European Championship, despite not actually qualifying for the finals in Sweden. Ten days before the tournament opened, UEFA invited the Danes – who had finished second to Yugoslavia in their qualifying group – to take the Yugoslavs' place following their exclusion. Expectations were minimal, but then the inconceivable happened. Relying heavily on goalkeeper Peter Schmeichel, his defence, and the creative Brian Laudrup, Denmark caused one of the biggest shocks in football history by winning the tournament, culminating in a 2-0 victory over world champions Germany.

20

Mikkel Damsgaard, aged 20 years and 353 days, became Denmark's youngest scorer at a major tournament with the opener in their 4-1 first round victory over Russia at UEFA EURO 2020. He then gave his team the lead with a free-kick in the semi-final defeat to England.

MOST APPEARANCES:

1. Peter Schmeichel, 129
2. Dennis Rommedahl, 126
3. Simon Kjær, 124
4. Christian Eriksen, 120
5. Jon Dahl Tomasson, 112

PETER
SCHMEICHEL

🌐 NATIONAL LEGEND
GOLDEN GLOVES

Peter Schmeichel, a European champion with Denmark in 1992, was rated by many as the world's best goalkeeper in the early 1990s. His son **Kasper Schmeichel** has since emulated his father by enjoying club success in England and becoming Denmark's first-choice keeper. Peter was a very animated fan in the stands at the 2018 FIFA World Cup as Kasper saved three spot kicks when Denmark lost their round-of-16 match against Croatia, 3-2 on penalties. Kasper had previously broken his father's Danish record of the longest stretch without conceding an international goal, reaching 533 minutes at the 2018 FIFA World Cup and going on unbeaten for a further 38 until Australia's Mile Jedinak scored from the penalty spot in a 1-1 draw.

🌐 NATIONAL LEGEND
TOMASSON'S JOINT TOP

Jon Dahl Tomasson, Denmark's joint-top goalscorer with 52, became his national side's assistant manager in 2016, working with Norwegian-born head coach Åge Hareide. His final goal for Denmark came in a 3-1 defeat to Japan in the first round of the 2010 FIFA World Cup - tucking away the rebound after his penalty was saved by Eiji Kawashima. Tomasson won 112 caps, while Poul "Tist" Nielsen's 52 strikes came in just 38 appearances between 1910 and 1925. Pauli Jørgensen was also prolific, scoring 44 goals in just 47 games between 1925 and 1939.

TOMASSON

5

After Denmark failed to make it past the first round of the 2022 FIFA World Cup, their next five goals were all scored by Rasmus Højlund – a hat-trick in a 3-1 UEFA European Championship qualifying win against Finland, then a brace in a surprise 3-2 defeat to Kazakhstan.

TOP SCORERS:

1. Poul Nielsen, 52
   = Jon Dahl Tomasson, 52
3. Pauli Jørgensen, 44
4. Ole Madsen, 42
5. Christian Eriksen, 39

GREECE

There is no argument about Greece's proudest footballing moment – their shock triumph at the 2004 UEFA European Championship, one of the game's greatest international upsets. It was only the Greeks' second appearance at a UEFA EURO finals.

Joined FIFA: 1929

Biggest win: 8-0 v. Syria, 1949

Highest FIFA ranking: 8th

Home stadium: Olympic Stadium, Athens

Honours: 1 UEFA European Championship (2004)

SAMARAS

44

Striker Dimitrios Salpingidis struck the only goal of Greece's 2010 FIFA World Cup qualifying play-off against Ukraine, sealing their place in South Africa. He then scored Greece's first goal at a FIFA World Cup, with a 44th-minute strike in a 2–1 victory over Nigeria.

TOURNAMENT TRIVIA

GORGEOUS GEORGE

Georgios Samaras won and converted the last-minute penalty that sent Greece through to the knock-out stages of a FIFA World Cup for the first time, clinching a dramatic 2-1 victory over Group C opponents Côte d'Ivoire at the 2014 tournament in Brazil. The goal, following a foul by Giovanni Sio, was former Celtic striker Samaras's ninth goal for his country – his first coming on his debut against Belarus in February 2006. Samaras could actually have played international football for Australia because his father, Ioannis, was born in Melbourne and moved to Greece aged 13. Ioannis won 16 caps for Greece between 1986 and 1990, but he is a long way behind his son, who made 81 appearances.

77

The 77 caps won by midfielder Tasos Mitropoulos – nicknamed "Rambo" – between 1978 and 1994 included captaining Greece at their first FIFA World Cup in his final international appearance, a 2–0 Group D defeat to Nigeria in 1994. Greece's first skipper at an international tournament had been midfielder Giorgos Koudas – nicknamed "Alexander the Great" – whose 43 internationals between 1967 and 1982 took in the 1980 UEFA European Championship, where Greece again departed in the first round.

17

Goalkeeper Stefanos Kapino became Greece's youngest international when he made his debut in November 2011 in a friendly against Romania at the age of 17 years and 241 days – 80 days younger than the previous record-holder, striker Thomas Mavros, had been when he faced the Netherlands in February 1972.

NATIONAL LEGEND
SIMPLY THEO BEST

Theodoros "Theo" **Zagorakis** – born near Kavala on 27 October 1971 – was captain of Greece when they won the UEFA European Championship in 2004, and the defensive midfielder picked up the prize for the tournament's best player. He is the second most-capped Greek footballer of all time, with 120 caps. But it was not until his 101st international appearance – ten years and five months after his debut – that he scored his first goal for his country, in a FIFA World Cup qualifier against Denmark in February 2005. He retired from international football after making a 15-minute cameo appearance against Spain in August 2007.

ZAGORAKIS

NATIONAL LEGEND
KING OTTO

German coach Otto Rehhagel became the first foreigner to be voted "Greek of the Year" in 2004 after leading the country to glory at that year's UEFA European Championship. He was also offered honorary Greek citizenship. His nine years in charge, after being appointed in 2001, made him Greece's longest-serving international manager. Rehhagel was 65 at EURO 2004, making him the oldest coach to win the UEFA European Championship – although that record was taken off him four years later when 69-year-old Luis Aragonés lifted the trophy with Spain. Rehhagel was also the first foreign coach to lead another country to glory at either the UEFA European Championship or the FIFA World Cup.

ANOSTOPOULOS

TEAM TRIVIA
GOOD NIK

Greece's all-time leading goalscorer was also the first to find the net for the country at a major tournament. Nikos Anostopoulos's equalising header against defending champions Czechoslovakia, in what proved to be a 3–1 defeat, was Greece's only strike of the 1980 UEFA European Championship in Italy. His 29 goals for his nation came in 74 appearances, beginning with a debut against Romania in September 1977 and ending against Denmark in May 1989.

KARAGOUNIS

MOST APPEARANCES:

1 Giorgos Karagounis, 139
2 Theodoros Zagorakis, 120
3 Kostas Katsouranis, 116
4 Vasileios Torisidis, 101
5 Angelos Basinas, 100

TOP SCORERS:

1 Nikos Anostopoulos, 29
2 Angelos Charisteas, 25
3 Theofanis Gekas, 24
4 Dimitris Saravakos, 22
5 Mimis Papaioannou, 21

CHARISTEAS

NEW COLOUR

Greece wore blue up to 2004, but switched to white after wearing their second kit when winning the 2004 UEFA European Championship.

NATIONAL LEGEND
RIGHT ANGELOS

Only Nikos Anostopoulos has scored more goals for Greece than **Angelos Charisteas**, but no one can have struck a more important one than Charisteas, whose second-half header defeated hosts Portugal in the 2004 UEFA European Championship final. He had already scored the equaliser against Spain in the first round as well as the match-winner against holders France in the quarter-finals. Striker Charisteas made his international debut in February 2001, scoring twice in a 3-3 draw against Russia. He also went on to score Greece's sole goal in their unsuccessful trophy defence and opening-round exit at UEFA EURO 2008.

1

Only one team – Greece – has beaten both the holders and the hosts on the way to winning either a UEFA European Championship or a FIFA World Cup. In fact, the Greeks beat hosts Portugal twice – in both the tournament's opening game and the final, with a quarter-final victory over defending champions France in between.

NATIONAL LEGEND
GRIEF AND GLORY
FOR GIORGOS

It was a bittersweet day for captain **Giorgos Karagounis** when he equalled the Greek record for international appearances, with his 120th cap against Russia in their final Group A game at UEFA EURO 2012. The midfielder scored the only goal of the game, giving Greece a place in the quarter-finals at Russia's expense, but a second yellow card of the tournament ruled him out of the match, which the Greeks lost to Germany. Karagounis was one of three survivors from Greece's UEFA EURO 2004 success, along with fellow midfielder Kostas Katsouranis and goalkeeper Kostas Chalkias, who a match earlier had become Greece's oldest international at the age of 38 years and 13 days against the Czech Republic.

HUNGARY

For a period in the early 1950s, Hungary possessed the most talented football team on the planet. They claimed Olympic gold at Helsinki in 1952 but finished as runners-up in the 1954 FIFA World Cup.

Joined FIFA: 1902
Biggest win: 13-1 v. France, 1927
Highest FIFA ranking: 18th
Home stadium:
Puskás Aréna, Budapest
Honours: -

NATIONAL LEGEND
DOM ON THE DOT

Hungary had to wait 30 years to play at a major tournament, between their first-round appearance at the 1986 FIFA World Cup and their progress to the second round of the 2016 UEFA European Championship in France. They followed up by reaching EURO 2020, thanks to a dramatic late comeback against Iceland in a qualifying play-off in Budapest's Puskás Arena in November 2020. The visitors were leading with just two minutes left, only for Hungary to score twice, first through right-back Loic Nego before a quickfire last-gasp winner by star playmaker **Dominik Szoboszlai,** who later became the first footballer to be named Hungarian Sportsman of the Year. Sadly a thigh muscle injury ruled him out of the UEFA European Championship in 2021. Without him Hungary finished bottom of so-called "Group Of Death" Group F, despite draws with France and Germany.

5.4
Hungary's average of 5.4 goals per game at the 1954 FIFA World Cup remains an all-time high for the tournament.

109

Balázs Dzsudzsák set a record for international appearances for Hungary with his 109th and final cap in a 2–1 victory over Greece on 20 November 2022 in the capital Budapest's Puskás Aréna. The win came courtesy of Zsolt Kalmár's free-kick strike three minutes into stoppage-time.

SCORING RECORD
YEARS OF PLENTY

Hungary's dazzling line-up of the early 1950s was known as the Aranycsapat – or Golden Team. They set a record for international matches unbeaten, going 31 consecutive games without defeat between May 1950 and their July 1954 FIFA World Cup final loss to West Germany – a run that included clinching Olympic gold at Helsinki 1952. That 31-match tally has since been overtaken only by Brazil and Spain.

73

Hungary in the 1950s also set a record for most consecutive games scoring at least one goal: 73 matches.

NATIONAL LEGEND
GOLDEN HEAD

Sándor Kocsis, top scorer at the 1954 FIFA World Cup with 11 goals, was so good in the air that he was known as the "Golden Head". In 68 internationals, he scored an incredible 75 goals, including a then-record seven hat-tricks. His tally included two decisive extra-time goals in the 1954 FIFA World Cup semi-final against Uruguay, when Hungary had appeared to be on the brink of defeat.

PUSKÁS

NATIONAL LEGEND
GALLOPING MAJOR

In Hungarian football history, no one can compare with **Ferenc Puskás**, who netted 84 goals in 85 international matches for Hungary as well as 514 goals in 529 matches in the Hungarian and Spanish leagues. Blessed with a lethal left foot, he was known as the "Galloping Major" – by virtue of his playing for the army team Honved before joining Real Madrid and going on to play for Spain. During the 1950s, he was the top scorer and captain of the legendary Mighty Magyars (another nickname given to the Hungarian national team) and Honved.

SALLAI

1

Only one Hungarian has won the Ballon d'Or for player of the year: Flórián Albert in 1967.

TEAM TRIVIA
SALLAI ARMY

Wait 60 years for a win against England, then two came along at once. Hungary's most momentous victories came in 1953 and 1954 – a majestic 6–3 triumph at Wembley followed by an even more emphatic 7–1 triumph in Budapest. But after defeating England 2–1 at the 1962 FIFA World Cup on the way to reaching the quarter-finals, Hungary went six decades and 15 matches without winning against the same opponents until Dominik Szoboszlai's penalty made the difference in their UEFA Nations League A clash in Budapest's Puskás Aréna in June 2022. Ten days later, Hungary twisted the knife by winning the return fixture at Molineux in Wolverhampton 4–0, including a brace by striker **Roland Sallai**, whose father Sándor won 55 caps for Hungary.

10-1

No team has scored more goals in one game at a FIFA World Cup than in Hungary's 10–1 victory over El Salvador at the 1982 finals in Spain, including a hat-trick by László Kiss, the first substitute to hit a treble at a FIFA World Cup.

NATIONAL LEGENDS
THE RIGHT TROUSERS

Goalkeeper **Gábor Király**'s international career got off to a dramatic start when he saved a penalty just four minutes into his Hungary debut away to neighbours Austria in March 1998, a game his side went on to win 3–2. Király was recognisable for the grey tracksuit trousers he wore when on the field – often compared with pyjama bottoms. He holds the record for the oldest man to play at a UEFA European Championship, aged 40 years and 86 days as Belgium won 4–0 in the second round at the 2016 tournament. He has played more times for Hungary than any man other than midfielder Balázs Dzsudzsák, who not only captained the nation at UEFA EURO 2016 but also scored the second and third goals for his side in a 3–3 draw with eventual champions Portugal, which clinched a place in the knock-out stages.

KIRÁLY

NORTHERN IRELAND

Northern Ireland have played as a separate country since 1921 – before that, there had been an all-Ireland side. They last appeared at a major tournament in 2016, at the UEFA European Championship.

Joined FIFA: 1921
Biggest win: 7-0 v. Wales, 1930
Highest FIFA ranking: 20th
Home stadium:
Windsor Park, Belfast
Honours: -

NATIONAL LEGEND
GEORGE IS BEST

One of the greatest players never to grace a FIFA World Cup, **George Best** (capped 37 times by Northern Ireland) nevertheless won domestic and European honours with Manchester United – including a European Champions Cup medal and the European Footballer of the Year award in 1968. He also played in the United States, Hong Kong and Australia before his "final" retirement in 1984.

BEST

17

Norman Whiteside became the then-youngest player at a FIFA World Cup finals (beating Pelé's record) when he represented Northern Ireland in Spain in 1982 at the age of 17 years and 41 days.

DAVIS

2 MINUTES
Peter Watson is thought to have had the shortest Northern Ireland international career, spending just two minutes on the pitch in a 5-0 UEFA European Championship qualifying win over Cyprus in April 1971.

STAR PLAYER
THE BOY DAVIS

Midfielder **Steven Davis** became Northern Ireland's youngest post-war captain when he led the side out against Uruguay in May 2006, aged just 21 years, five months and 20 days. Davis became Northern Ireland's most-capped player in October 2020 against Bosnia and Herzegovina, representing his country for the 120th time. His 126th appearance, against Bulgaria in March 2021, took him past former England goalkeeper Peter Shilton for the all-time British record.

2

Bailey Peacock-Farrell saved two penalties in a week in September 2021 for Northern Ireland in FIFA World Cup qualifiers, first in a 4–1 win in Lithuania and then in a goalless draw at home to Switzerland. His country would ultimately miss out on the finals, finishing third in UEFA's Group C, but another clean sheet, in a goalless final match, denied Italy top spot.

NATIONAL LEGEND
THE RIGHT BING

Billy Bingham played for Northern Ireland the first time the country reached the FIFA World Cup in 1958. They reached the quarter-finals, the smallest country to go so far, before being beaten 4–0 by France. Bingham cemented his place as a national hero by then managing Northern Ireland twice and twice returning them to the FIFA World Cup, in 1982 and 1986. Bingham's Northern Ireland were also the last team to win the old British Home Championship – annually contested with neighbours England, Scotland and Wales – in 1984, before it was wound up. He died aged 90 in June 2022. Billy Hamilton, who set up Gerry Armstrong's winner against hosts Spain in 1982, said: "Going to the World Cup was a dream for all of us and Bingy was the inspiration behind it all."

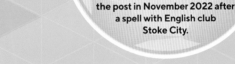

BINGHAM

118

Billy Bingham managed Northern Ireland a record 118 times across two stints, 20 games between 1967 and 1971 and then 98 from 1980 to 1993. Next on the list is former winger Michael O'Neill, who oversaw 72 matches from December 2011 to April 2020, including taking Northern Ireland to the 2016 UEFA European Championship. O'Neill returned to the post in November 2022 after a spell with English club Stoke City.

Veteran centre-back Gareth McAuley, aged 36, was the surprise first name on the goalsheet for Northern Ireland when they beat Ukraine 2–0 in the group stage of the 2016 UEFA Championship. Unfortunately he also found the net in the round of 16, scoring an own goal in a 1–0 defeat by neighbours Wales.

36

MOST APPEARANCES:
1 **Steven Davis**, 140
2 **Pat Jennings**, 119
3 **Aaron Hughes**, 112
4 **Jonny Evans**, 100
5 **David Healy**, 95

HEALY

NATIONAL LEGEND
HERO HEALY

Northern Ireland's leading goalscorer **David Healy** got off to the ideal start, scoring a brace on his international debut against Luxembourg in February 2000, but perhaps his two greatest days for his country came when he scored the only goal against Sven-Göran Eriksson's England in September 2005 – securing Northern Ireland's first victory over England since 1972 – and then, 12 months later, scoring a hat-trick to beat eventual champions Spain 3-2 in a 2008 UEFA European Championship qualifier.

TOURNAMENT TRIVIA
HOSTILE HOSTS

Northern Ireland topped their first-round group at the 1982 FIFA World Cup thanks to a 1-0 win over hosts Spain at a passionate Mestalla Stadium in Valencia. Watford striker Gerry Armstrong scored the goal, and the Northern Irish held on despite defender Mal Donaghy being sent off. A 4-1 second-round loss to France denied Northern Ireland a semi-finals place. Armstrong joined Spanish side RCD Mallorca the following year and, predictably, was regularly booed by rival fans.

TOP SCORERS:
1 **David Healy**, 36
2 **Kyle Lafferty**, 20
3 **Colin Clarke**, 13
= **Steven Davis**, 13
= **Billy Gillespie**, 13
5 **Gerry Armstrong**, 12
= **Joe Bambrick**, 12
= **Iain Dowie**, 12
= **Jimmy Quinn**, 12

NATIONAL LEGEND
GIANT JENNINGS

Pat Jennings' previous record 119 appearances for Northern Ireland also stood as an international record at one stage. The former Tottenham Hotspur and Arsenal goalkeeper made his international debut, aged just 18, against Wales on 15 April 1964, and played his final game in the 1986 FIFA World Cup, against Brazil, on his 41st birthday. On 26 February 1983, Jennings became the first player in English football to make 1,000 senior appearances, and he marked the occasion with clean sheet in a 0-0 draw for Arsenal at West Bromwich Albion.

NORWAY

Although they played their first international, against Sweden, in 1908 and qualified for the 1938 FIFA World Cup, it would take a further 56 years, and the introduction of a direct brand of football, before Norway reappeared at a major international tournament.

Joined FIFA: 1908
Biggest win: 12-0 v. Finland, 1946
Highest FIFA ranking: 2nd
Home stadium: Ullevaal Stadion, Oslo
Honours: -

MOST APPEARANCES:

1. **John Arne Riise,** 110
2. **Thorbjørn Svenssen,** 104
3. **Henning Berg,** 100
4. **Erik Thorstvedt,** 97
5. **John Carew,** 91
   = **Brede Hangeland,** 91

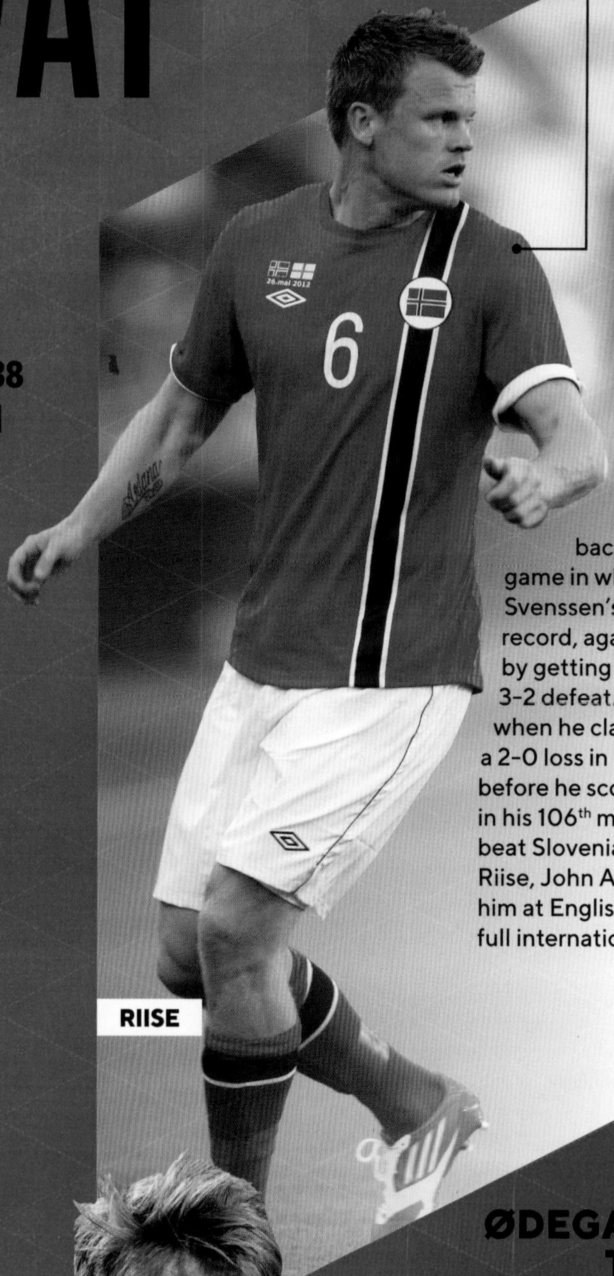

RIISE

NATIONAL LEGEND

LONG-DISTANCE RIISE

Fierce-shooting ex-Liverpool, AS Monaco and AS Roma left-back **John Arne Riise** marked the game in which he matched Thorbjørn Svenssen's Norwegian appearances record, against Greece in August 2012, by getting onto the scoresheet, albeit in a 3-2 defeat. He was also on the losing side when he claimed the record for himself, a 2-0 loss in Iceland the following month, before he scored his 16th international goal in his 106th match four days later as Norway beat Slovenia 2-1. Midfielder Bjorn Helge Riise, John Arne's younger brother, joined him at English club Fulham, and made 35 full international appearances.

15

Egil Olsen, one of Europe's most eccentric coaches, signed up for a surprise second spell as Norwegian national team coach in 2009, 15 years after he had led the unfancied Scandinavians to the 1994 FIFA World Cup finals.

STAR PLAYER

ØDEGAARD REPLACES THE OLD GUARD

Creative midfielder Martin Ødegaard became Norway's youngest international when making his debut as a substitute against the United Arab Emirates in August 2014 at the tender age of 15 years and 253 days. He beat the record previously held since September 1910 by Tormod Kjellsen, who was 15 years and 351 days old when first on the field for Norway in a 4-0 defeat to Sweden. Ødegaard, who joined Arsenal from Real Madrid in January 2021, initially on loan, was named Norway's new captain in March that year, aged just 20.

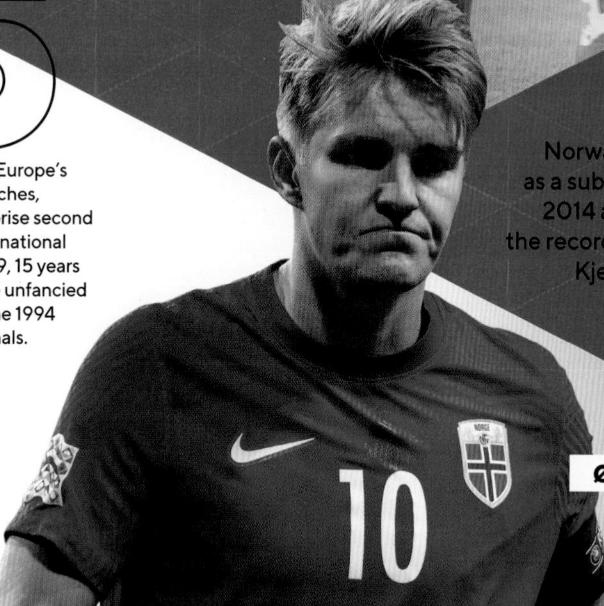

ØDEGAARD

0

Norway are the only country in the world to have played Brazil and never lost. Their record stands at won two, drawn two, lost zero.

ERIK THORSTVEDT

9

Striker Joshua King scored five times in nine games for Norway in 2019, but had to wait until March 2022 to next find the net for his country, albeit hitting a hat-trick in a 9-0 friendly victory over Armenia. Norway's record win remains their 12-0 trouncing of Finland in June 1946, while their biggest defeat was by the same scoreline, to Denmark in October 1917.

HÅLAND

NATIONAL LEGEND
ERIK THE VIKING (AND SON)

Erik Thorstvedt – fondly known to English fans as "Erik the Viking" during his time at Tottenham Hotspur, where he would throw his gloves into the crowd after every game – was a key figure helping Norway to the 1994 FIFA World Cup, their first appearance at the finals since 1938. He played a Norwegian goalkeeping record of 97 internationals between 1982 and 1996. His son, midfielder Kristian, made his Norway debut against Austria in November 2020, and opened his international scoring account in a 3-0 victory over Gibraltar four months later.

STAR PLAYER
STERLING ERLING

Norway's latest striking star **Erling Braut Håland** has proved himself a fast starter. Aged 16, he scored on his cup and league debuts for Molde FK in 2017. Subsequent scoring feats include four goals in the first 21 minutes away to SK Brann in July 2018, six goals in his first three UEFA Champions League appearances for Austria's Red Bull Salzburg in 2018-2019, and a hat-trick on his January 2020 debut for Germany's Borussia Dortmund in just 23 minutes, entering the fray as a substitute. Born in Leeds in July 2000, Håland was been eligible to play for England – his father Alf-Inge Håland, who won 34 Norway caps, was playing in England at the time – but he chose Norway. Håland won the Golden Boot at the FIFA U-20 World Cup 2019 in Poland. Håland signed for his father's old club Manchester City in June 2022 for £51.2million. That same month, he scored consecutive braces in UEFA Nations League B victories over neighbours Sweden and ended the calendar year on 23 goals from only 21 international appearances. He also passed a half-century of goals for Manchester City during his first season in England.

93

He may no longer hold Norway's record for most international appearances but Thorbjorn Svenssen – nicknamed "Klippen", or "The Rock" – captained the country more than any other player – 93 times.

NATIONAL LEGEND
JUVE DONE IT ALL

Jørgen Juve netted his national record 33 international goals in 45 appearances between 1928 and 1937. He did not score as Norway claimed bronze at the Berlin 1936 Olympics, but he played when Norway beat Germany 2-0 in the quarter-finals, prompting Adolf Hitler and other Nazi leaders to storm out of the stadium in fury. After retiring in 1938, he worked as a legal scholar and sports journalist and wrote books on the Olympics and football.

JUVE

TOP SCORERS:

1 Jørgen Juve, 33

2 Einar Gundersen, 26

3 Harald Hennum, 25

4 John Carew, 24

5 Tore André Flo, 23
= Ole Gunnar Solskjær, 23

TOURNAMENT TRIVIA
LONG-STAY TRAVELLERS

Norway's best finish at an international tournament was the bronze medal they clinched at the 1936 Summer Olympics in Berlin, losing to Italy in the semi-finals but beating Poland 3-2 in a medal play-off thanks to an Arne Brustad hat-trick. That year's side has gone down in Norwegian football history as the *Bronselaget*, or *Bronze Team*. However, they had entered the tournament with low expectations and were forced to alter their travel plans ahead of the semi-final against Italy on 10 August – Norwegian football authorities had originally booked their trip home for the previous day, not expecting their team to get so far.

POLAND

Poland first qualified for the FIFA World Cup in 1938 and finished in third place at both the 1974 and 1982 tournaments. They also notably co-hosted UEFA EURO 2012 with Ukraine, although they made a first-round exit.

Joined FIFA: 1921

Biggest win: 10-0 v. San Marino, 2009

Highest FIFA ranking: 5th

Home stadium: Stadion Narodowy, Warsaw

Honours: -

STAR PLAYER
LOVING LEWANDOWSKI

Poland's all-time leading goalscorer **Robert Lewandowski** was named The Best FIFA Men's Player in 2020 after spearheading Bayern Munich to UEFA Champions League glory earlier that year. But his international efforts were in vain as Poland finished bottom of their first-round groups at the 2018 FIFA World Cup and the delayed 2020 UEFA European Championship. Lewandowski was rejected by Legia Warsaw aged 16, but he is now the only Polish player to score at three UEFA European Championship finals – in 2012, 2016 and 2020 – and managed his first FIFA World Cup goal in a 2-0 Group C victory over Saudi Arabia at the 2022 finals in Qatar. His 78th international goal was a stoppage-time penalty in a 3-1 defeat to France in the second round.

NATIONAL LEGEND
POLE GOALIES

In 2022, **Wojciech Szczęsny** became only the third goalkeeper to save two in-game penalties at one FIFA World Cup, following on from compatriot Jan Tomaszewski in 1974 and the USA's Brad Friedel in 2002. Szczęsny's stops came from Saudi Arabia's Salem al-Dawsari in a 2-0 win for Poland and then Lionel Messi of eventual champions Argentina in a 2-0 defeat. It marked a turnaround in major tournament fortunes for Szczęsny. He was sent off against Greece in UEFA EURO 2012's curtain-raiser, and injured in the opening game four years later. He scored an own goal when Poland lost to Finland in their first game at UEFA EURO 2020. The Juventus player's 66th appearance, a 1-0 UEFA Nations League win in Wales in September 2022, made him Poland's most-capped goalkeeper.

SZCZĘSNY

100

Centre-back Kamil Glik became the fifth Polish man to reach a century of caps in his country's opening match at the 2022 FIFA World Cup, a 0-0 draw with Mexico in which captain Robert Lewandowski had a penalty saved by Mexico goalkeeper Guillermo Ochoa.

LEWANDOWSKI

TOP SCORERS:

1 **Robert Lewandowski**, 78
2 **Włodzimierz Lubański**, 48
3 **Grzegorz Lato**, 45
4 **Kazimierz Deyna**, 41
5 **Ernest Pohl**, 39

NATIONAL LEGEND
PEERLESS PRESIDENTS

Grzegorz Lato is Poland's fourth most-capped player and third-highest scorer, the only Polish winner of the Golden Boot with his seven goals at the 1974 FIFA World Cup, and a member of the gold medal-winning team at the 1972 Summer Olympics. He was also a leading figure in Poland's co-hosting with Ukraine of the 2012 UEFA European Championship, having become president of the country's FA in 2008. He vowed: "I am determined to change the image of Polish football, to make it transparent and pure." He was succeeded as president in 2012 by Zbigniew Boniek, arguably Poland's finest-ever player. Boniek's time as president ended in August 2021, succeeded by former Polish top-flight footballer Cezary Kulesza.

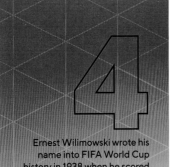

4

Ernest Wilimowski wrote his name into FIFA World Cup history in 1938 when he scored four goals but still finished on the losing side. Poland went down 6-5 after extra time to Brazil in a first-round tie in Strasbourg, France.

TEAM TRIVIA
BIG BUKSA

Robert Lewandowski has scored a national record six hat-tricks for Poland – including four goals against Gibraltar in September 2014 – but the country's most recent treble was hit by 6ft 4in striker **Adam Buksa** in only his second international, a 7-1 away win against San Marino in a FIFA World Cup qualifier in September 2021. Poland finished second behind England in Group I then clinched their place at the 2022 FIFA World Cup through the play-offs. Awarded a semi-final walkover victory over Russia following the invasion of Ukraine, they beat Sweden 2-0 in their March 2022 final thanks to a Lewandowski penalty and a second by midfielder Piotr Zieliński. The Sweden game was manager Czesław Michniewicz's second game in charge.

BUKSA

2000

Michał Żewłakow and brother Marcin became the first twins to line up together for Poland, against France in February 2000.

MOST APPEARANCES:
1 Robert Lewandowski, 140
2 Jakub Błaszczykowski, 108
3 Kamil Glik, 103
4 Michał Żewłakow, 102
5 Grzegorz Lato, 100

KOZŁOWSKI

STAR PLAYER
TRIUMPH AND TRAGEDY

Jakub Błaszczykowski was one of his country's few players to come out of EURO 2012 with credit, despite going into the tournament in testing circumstances. He joined the rest of the squad only after attending the funeral of his father. As a ten-year-old, Błaszczykowski had witnessed his mother being stabbed to death by his father, who served 15 years in prison. Błaszczykowski was encouraged to pursue football by his uncle Jerzy Brzęczek, a former Poland captain and 1992 Olympic Games silver medallist. Błaszczykowski became the third Pole to reach 100 caps, doing so against Senegal in Poland's 2018 FIFA World Cup opener.

BŁASZCZYKOWSKI

5

Poland had five different goalscorers when they beat Peru 5-1 at the 1982 FIFA World Cup: Włodzimierz Smolarek, Grzegorz Lato, Zbigniew Boniek, Andrzej Buncol and Włodzimierz Ciołek.

16

Aged just 16 years and 188 days, and on his debut, Włodzimierz Lubański scored Poland's third goal in a 9-0 victory over Norway in 1963 to become their youngest-ever scorer.

NATIONAL LEGEND
KOZ FOR CELEBRATION

England midfielder Jude Bellingham became the youngest ever player at a UEFA European Championship coming on as a substitute at EURO 2020, against Croatia, aged 17 years 349 days. But his record lasted just six days. Poland midfielder **Kacper Kozłowski** played the last 35 minutes of his country's 1-1 draw with Spain at the age of 17 years 246 days. He made his debut, aged 17 years 163 days in March 2021, as a substitute in a 3-0 FIFA World Cup qualifier win over Andorra. Only one man has played for Poland at a younger age: Włodzimierz Lubański, who was only 16 years 188 days old when he marked his debut with a goal in a 9-0 victory over Norway in September 1963.

PORTUGAL

Despite producing some of Europe's finest-ever players, Portugal's international history was one of near misses – until they triumphed in the 2016 UEFA European Championship and the UEFA Nations League in 2019.

Joined FIFA: 1921

Biggest win:
8-0 v. Lichtenstein, 1994 & 1999, v. Kuwait, 2003

Highest FIFA ranking: 3rd

Home stadium:
Estadio de Luz, Lisbon

Honours: 1
UEFA European Championship (2016),
1 UEFA Nations League (2019)

5

At Qatar 2022, Cristiano Ronaldo's penalty in a 3–2 Group H win over Ghana made him the first man to score at five different FIFA World Cups.

STAR PLAYER
PRESIDENTIAL POWER

Cristiano Ronaldo dos Santos Aveiro was given his second name because his father was an admirer of United States President Ronaldo Reagan. The five-time FIFA World Player of the Year lifted the 2016 UEFA European Championship trophy for his country. He scored five times in three games at UEFA Euro 2020, becoming the first man to play at five UEFA European Championships, and equalling Iranian Ali Daei's international record of 109 goals. Ronaldo claimed the record outright in September 2021 with two headed goals in a 2–1 FIFA World Cup qualifier win over the Republic of Ireland. The following month, he became the first man to score ten international hat-tricks with a treble against Luxembourg. In December 2022, he was dropped to the bench for Portugal's two knock-out round matches at the FIFA World Cup in Qatar. On 23 March 2023, he became the most-capped man of all-time, scoring a brace against Liechtenstein in his 197th international.

RONALDO

2
Portugal became the first team in FIFA World Cup or UEFA EURO history to score two own goals in one game in a 4-2 defeat to Germany at UEFA EURO 2020.

ÉDER

TOURNAMENT TRIVIA
HAPPY ÉDER AFTER

Substitute striker **Éder** was the unlikely hero when Portugal finally ended their long wait for an international trophy at UEFA EURO 2016. The forward – who spent the 2015-16 season on loan at French club Lille – scored the only goal of the final in Paris, in the 109th minute, to defeat host nation France. It was the latest opening goal scored in any UEFA European Championship final. Portugal, coached by Fernando Santos, drew their three first-round games to qualify as one of the best third-placed teams.

TOP SCORERS:

1 Cristiano Ronaldo, 122

2 Pauleta, 47

3 Eusébio, 41

4 Luís Figo, 32

5 Nuno Gomes, 29

MOST APPEARANCES:

1. Cristiano Ronaldo, 198
2. Joao Moutinho, 146
3. Pepe, 133
4. Luis Figo, 127
5. Nani, 112

PEPE

NATIONAL LEGEND
PEPE UP

Centre-back **Pepe** became Portugal's oldest international in March 2022, aged 39 years and 31 days, in a 2-0 victory over North Macedonia in a 2022 FIFA World Cup qualification play-off final in Porto, having missed the 3-1 semi-final win against Turkey five days earlier. At the finals in Qatar, he scored in Portugal's 6-1 second round victory over Switzerland, making him the oldest man to find the net in a FIFA World Cup knock-out game – aged 39 years and 283 days. Portugal's youngest international remains Paulo Futre, aged 17 years and 204 days for his debut against Finland in September 1983.

NATIONAL LEGEND
ENGINEERING SUCCESS

Fernando Santos managed Portugal to glory at not only the 2016 UEFA European Championship but also the inaugural UEFA Nations League in 2019, when substitute Gonçalo Guedes scored the only goal of the final against the Netherlands. After Portugal's quarter-final exit at the 2022 FIFA World Cup, Santos – who has a degree in electrical engineering – was sacked after 109 matches in charge since 2014: 67 wins, 23 draws and 19 defeats. Santos had earlier led Greece to the quarter-finals of the 2012 UEFA European Championship and to the knock-out stages of the FIFA World Cup for the first time in 2014. He was appointed Poland manager in January 2023.

1000

In a May 2018 FIFA World Cup warm-up against Tunisia, André Silva scored Portugal's 1,000th international goal in a 2-2 draw.

3

Benfica striker Gonçalo Ramos made his first FIFA World Cup start as a surprise replacement for Cristiano Ronaldo in Portugal's second round tie against Switzerland in 2022. He marked the call-up with a hat-trick in his side's 6-1 win, the first treble scored in the knock-out stages since Czechoslovakia's Tomáš Skuhravý against Costa Rica in 1990.

SANTOS

STAR PLAYER
NICE ONE, SAN

Renato Sanches is Portugal's youngest player at an international tournament – he was 18 years and 301 days old for their 2016 UEFA European Championship opener against Iceland. He was one of the stars of the tournament, and was voted the best young player. His superb long-range strike against Poland in the quarter-finals made him the youngest scorer in any UEFA European Championship knock-out round, at the age of 18 years and 316 days. Ten days later, he became the youngest man to play in a UEFA European Championship final.

NATIONAL LEGEND
THE BLACK PANTHER

Born in Mozambique, **Eusébio da Silva Ferreira** was named Portugal's "Golden Player" to mark UEFA's 50th anniversary in 2004. Signed by Benfica in 1960 at the age of 18, he scored a hat-trick in his second game – against Santos in a friendly tournament in Paris – even outshining their young star, Pelé. He helped Benfica win a second European Cup in 1962, was named European Footballer of the Year in 1965 and led Portugal to third place in the 1966 FIFA World Cup, finishing as top scorer with nine goals.

EUSÉBIO

REPUBLIC OF IRELAND

Ever since Jack Charlton took the team to UEFA EURO '88, Ireland have been regulars at major international tournaments.

Joined FIFA: 1924
Biggest win: 8-0 v. Malta, 1983
Highest FIFA ranking: 6th
Home stadium: Aviva Stadium, Dublin
Honours: -

NATIONAL LEGEND
BRIEF RETURN OF THE MICK

Mick McCarthy holds all of the following records: the first man to captain the Republic of Ireland at a FIFA World Cup – Italy 1990 – the last man to manage them at the finals – Japan/Korea Republic 2002 – and, in 2018, the first man to have two spells as permanent manager. The Yorkshireman, whose father was Irish, was first coach between 1996 and 2004, and he began his second spell with successive 1-0 victories over Gibraltar. After setting up a EURO 2020 qualifying play-off against Slovakia, McCarthy stepped down in April 2020 following the postponement of the finals, and was succeeded by his assistant **Stephen Kenny**. The new man in charge took up coaching in his 20s, managing clubs in Ireland and Scotland before guiding the Republic of Ireland's U-21s to the 2021 UEFA EURO U-21s. Kenny's Ireland lost that play-off semi-final to Slovakia 4-2 on penalties in October 2020, following a goalless draw after extra-time – with Alan Browne and Matt Doherty missing from the spot.

KENNY

MCCARTHY

4

Paddy Moore became the first player to score four goals in a FIFA World Cup qualifier when Ireland came from behind to draw 4-4 with Belgium on 25 February 1934. The feat was emulated by Don Givens, who scored all four goals of the game in a UEFA European Championship qualifier against Turkey in Dublin in October 1975.

STARPLAYER
BRADY BUNCH

Irish eyes were smiling again at Italy's expense in their final first-round group game at the 2016 UEFA European Championship, when **Robbie Brady** headed a late winning goal. It gave Martin O'Neill's team a place in the round of 16, where they took the lead against France through a Brady penalty, but eventually succumbed 2-1. Brady was the first Republic of Ireland player to score in consecutive UEFA European Championship games; Robbie Keane also achieved the feat at the 2002 FIFA World Cup.

BONNER

TOURNAMENT TRIVIA
WINNING JERSEY MISSING IN ACTION?

Irish fans' memories of their past FIFA World Cup adventures were reawakened in June 2017 when rapper M.I.A. appeared to be wearing one of goalkeeper **Packie Bonner**'s shirts in a photoshoot. Bonner starred at the 1988 European Championship and the 1990 and 1994 FIFA World Cups, and suggested that one of several red-and-yellow patterned jerseys he gave away for charity after USA '94 may have ended up with one of M.I.A.'s stylists. Bonner enhanced his national hero status by saving Daniel Timofte's penalty in the second-round shoot-out victory against Romania at Italy '90, before David O'Leary's winning spot kick clinched their place in the quarter-finals where they lost 1-0 to hosts Italy.

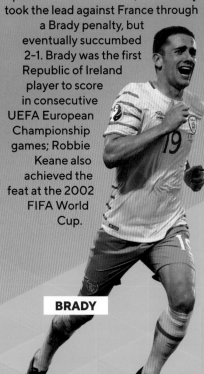

BRADY

CHARLTON

MOST APPEARANCES:

1 **Robbie Keane**, 146
2 **Shay Given**, 134
3 **John O'Shea**, 118
4 **Kevin Kilbane**, 110
5 **Steve Staunton**, 102

NATIONAL LEGEND
CHAMPION CHARLTON

Jack Charlton won the 1966 FIFA World Cup as a centre-back for England, but he was hailed by the Football Association of Ireland as a hero after he died aged 85 in July 2020. Charlton had become Republic of Ireland manager in 1986 and took them to their first major tournament, the 1988 UEFA European Championship – where they opened their campaign by beating England 1–0. He also took Ireland to two FIFA World Cups, including a quarter-final defeat to Italy in 1990 and a group-stage victory over the same opponents four years later. He resigned in 1996 after failing to qualify for that year's UEFA European Championship in England.

NATIONAL LEGEND
KEANE CARRY ON

Few star players have walked out on their country quite as dramatically as Republic of Ireland captain **Roy Keane** in 2002 at their FIFA World Cup training camp in Saipan, Japan. The midfielder quit before a competitive ball had been kicked, complaining about a perceived lack of professionalism in the Irish preparations – and his loss of faith in manager Mick McCarthy. The Irish reached the second round without him, losing on penalties to Spain, but his behaviour divided a nation. When McCarthy stepped down, Keane and the FAI brokered a truce, and he returned to international duty in April 2004 under new boss Brian Kerr. Dominant central midfielder Keane scored nine goals in 67 games for his country, all his strikes coming in competitive fixtures – six in FIFA World Cup qualifiers and the other three in UEFA European Championship qualification campaigns.

ROBBIE **KEANE**

NATIONAL LEGEND
ROBBIE KEEN

Much-travelled striker **Robbie Keane** broke the Republic of Ireland's scoring record in October 2004 and added to it right up to 31 August 2016, when he marked his 146th and final appearance with his 68th goal in a 4–0 friendly victory against Oman. His most famous goals were last-minute equalisers against Germany and Spain at the 2002 FIFA World Cup. He marked the final game at the old Lansdowne Road with a hat-trick against San Marino in November 2006 and, four years later, won his 100th cap in the inaugural game at its replacement, the Aviva Stadium. Keane celebrated his goals with a somersault and mock firing of invisible pistols.

118 SECONDS
The Republic of Ireland hold the record for scoring the quickest penalty at the UEFA European Championship – after just 118 seconds of their 2016 clash with France.

TOP SCORERS:

1 **Robbie Keane**, 68
2 **Niall Quinn**, 21
3 **Frank Stapleton**, 20
4 **John Aldridge**, 19
= **Tony Cascarino**, 19
= **Don Givens**, 19

33

Goalkeeper David Forde finally played his first competitive international for the Republic of Ireland against Sweden in a FIFA World Cup qualifier in March 2013, aged 33 – older than any other debutant in the country's history.

17

The Republic of Ireland's three youngest internationals have all played for England's Tottenham Hotspur. Left-back Jimmy Holmes is the youngest, at 17 years and 200 days old against Austria in May 1971. Robbie Keane made his debut aged 17 years and 259 days against the Czech Republic in March 1998. Fellow striker **Troy Parrott** is third, debuting in a 3–1 win against New Zealand in November 2019, at the age of 17 years and 282 days.

PARROTT

ROY **KEANE**

66

Only England's Billy Wright, with 70, played more consecutive internationals than **Kevin Kilbane**, whose 109th Republic of Ireland cap against Macedonia in March 2011 was also his 66th in a row, covering 11 years and five months.

ROMANIA

MUTU

Since 1938, Romania have qualified for the finals of the FIFA World Cup only four times in 16 attempts. The country's football highlight came in 1994 when, inspired by Gheorghe Hagi, they reached the quarter-finals.

Biggest win:
9-0 v. Finland, 1973

Highest FIFA ranking: 3rd

Home stadium: Arena Nationala, Bucharest

Honours: -

Romania conceded just two goals throughout the qualifying competition for the 2016 UEFA European Championship (the fewest of any team) – but then let in that same number in the tournament's opening match, a 2–1 defeat by hosts France.

NATIONAL LEGEND
MUCH ADO ABOUT MUTU

Romania lost only once when **Adrian Mutu** found the net – a feat made all the better since, with 35 goals, he is matched only by Gheorghe Hagi in the nation's all-time scoring ranks. His final international goal, an equaliser against Hungary in a March 2013 FIFA World Cup qualifier, was his first for 21 months.

NATIONAL LEGEND
CENTURY MAN

Gheorghe Hagi, Romania's "Player of the Century", scored three goals and was named in the Team of the Tournament at the 1994 FIFA World Cup in the United States, at which Romania lost out on penalties to Sweden after a 2–2 draw in the quarter-finals. Hagi made his international debut in 1983, aged just 18, scored his first goal aged 19 (in a 3–2 defeat to Northern Ireland) and remains Romania's joint-top goalscorer with 35 goals in 125 games. His son Ianis Hagi was born in 1998. Striker Ianis made his debut as a substitute in a 3–0 UEFA Nations League victory over Lithuania in November 2018.

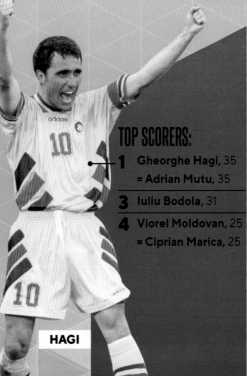

HAGI

TOP SCORERS:

1. Gheorghe Hagi, 35
= Adrian Mutu, 35
3. Iuliu Bodola, 31
4. Viorel Moldovan, 25
= Ciprian Marica, 25

TEAM TRIVIA
FATHER AND SON

Anghel Iordănescu served three spells in charge of Romania, having previously scored 21 goals in 57 appearances for his country. His most successful stint saw Romania reach the quarter-finals of the 1994 FIFA World Cup, with a team starring Florin Răducioiu (four goals that tournament), Ilie Dumitrescu (three) and Gheorghe Hagi (two). They were knocked out on penalties by Sweden. Anghel won 35 of his 73 matches as Romania boss in stints between 1993 and 1998, 2001 and 2004, and 2014 and 2016. In January 2022 ,the job was given to his son Edward Iordănescu. Edward never played for Romania but, like his father, began his playing and managerial careers with Steaua Bucharest.

3

Despite playing as a centre-back or defensive midfielder, Gheorghe Popescu is one of three men to score more than one hat-trick for Romania – both he and Florin Răducioiu have struck a pair apiece, all in the 1990s, while Iuliu Bodola managed three in the 1930s.

MOST APPEARANCES:

1 **Dorinel Munteanu**, 134
2 **Gheorghe Hagi**, 124
3 **Gheorghe Popescu**, 115
4 **Răzvan Raț**, 113
5 **Ladislau Bölöni**, 102

MUNTEANU

BÖLÖNI

NATIONAL LEGEND
ENDURING DORINEL

Nobody has played for Romania more than **Dorinel Munteanu**, although at one point his former team-mate Gheorghe Hagi's 124-cap record looked safe. Versatile defensive midfielder Munteanu was stuck on 119 appearances throughout an 18-month absence from the international scene before being surprisingly recalled at the age of 37 by manager Victor Piturca in February 2005. He ended his Romania career two years later, having scored 16 times in 134 games.

31

Iulia Bodola scored 31 goals for Romania in 48 internationals between 1931 and 1939, including appearances at the 1934 and 1938 FIFA World Cups. He then scored four in 13 for Hungary between 1940 and 1948. Bodola was one of 14 footballers who played for Romania in the 1930s and Hungary in the 1940s when Northern Transylvania was part of the Kingdom of Hungary.

102

Midfielder **Ladislau Bölöni** became the first Romanian to win 100 caps in a 2-0 away defeat to the Republic of Ireland in March 1988. His 23 goals for his country included the winner in a 1-0 victory over Italy in April 1983. The goal was crucial in helping Romania qualify for the UEFA European Championship for the first time.

TOURNAMENT TRIVIA
RUDOLF BY ROYAL APPOINTMENT

Romania played in the inaugural FIFA World Cup, in Uruguay in 1930, where they beat Peru 3-1 before being eliminated 4-0 by the hosts. Coach Constantin Rădulescu filled in as a linesman for some games, but not for those featuring his own side. It is claimed that the squad was picked by King Carol II. Their captain was Rudolf Wetzer, the only Romania player to score five goals in a game – in a pre-tournament 8-1 victory over Greece in May 1930.

15

Midfielder Enes Sali became Romania's youngest player when coming on as a late substitute against Liechtenstein in November 2021, in a FIFA World Cup qualifier his side won 2-0. He was aged just 15 years and 264 days.

TOURNAMENT TRIVIA
BLONDE AMBITION

Despite topping Group G ahead of England, Colombia and Tunisia at the 1998 FIFA World Cup, that particular Romanian vintage is perhaps best remembered for their collective decision to dye their hair blond ahead of their final first-round game. The newly bleached Romanians struggled to a 1-1 draw against Tunisia, before being knocked out by Croatia in the round of 16, 1-0.

RUSSIA

Before the break-up of the Soviet Union (USSR) in 1992, the team was a world football powerhouse. While playing as Russia since August 1992, the good times have eluded them – although they were quarter-finalists at Russia 2018.

Joined FIFA: 1992
Biggest win:
9-0 v. Faroe Islands, 2019
Highest FIFA ranking: 3rd
Home stadium: Luzhniki Stadium, Moscow
Honours: -

SCORING RECORD
ARTEM'S TIME

Captain Artem Dzyuba's penalty against Denmark in their final Group B fixture at UEFA Euro 2020 in June 2021 was not enough to prevent his side losing 4-1 and being eliminated, finishing bottom of their table. But it did pull him level with Aleksandr Kerzhakov at the top of Russia's scoring ranks, with 30 goals. Russia's biggest post-Soviet victory, 9-0 against the Faroe Islands in June 2019, included four goals by Dzyuba, who had also scored four times in a 7-0 defeat of Luxembourg in September 2004. Russia's sole win at Euro 2020 came in their second match, against Finland, with Aleksei Miranchuk scoring the game's only goal in first half stoppage-time.

NATIONAL LEGEND
GOLDEN BOY

Igor Netto captained the USSR national side to their greatest successes: gold at the 1956 Olympics in Melbourne and victory in the first-ever UEFA European Championship in France in 1960. Born in Moscow in 1930, Netto was awarded the Order of Lenin – the highest civilian honour in the Soviet Union – in 1957 and became an ice-hockey coach after retiring from football. He also scored 37 goals in 367 league games for Spartak Moscow, winning five Soviet championships.

NETTO

17
The youngest Soviet-era debutant was Eduard Streltsov, who hit a hat-trick on his debut against Sweden in June 1956, at the age of 17 years and 340 days, and then scored another treble in his second game, against India.

TOURNAMENT TRIVIA
HAPPY HOSTS

Expectations on the field for 2018 FIFA World Cup hosts Russia, at 70th the lowest team in the FIFA/Coca-Cola World Ranking, were not great, but in the opening game, they cruised past Saudi Arabia 5-0 and then downed Egypt 3-1 to guarantee a second-round place. Once there, Russia beat Spain on penalties before losing, again in a shoot-out, to Croatia in the last eight. Manager Stanislav Cherchesov, a former Russia goalkeeper, spoke of the pride felt nationwide by their unexpected progress.

109
Centre-back Viktor Onopko – now part of Valeri Karpin's Russia coaching staff – became the first man to reach a century of caps for Russia in a 1-0 win against Cyprus on 2 February 2003. He went on to reach 109, ending with a 4-3 victory against Lithuania on 18 August the following year. His brother Sergey played eight times for Ukraine's U-21s. They were both born in Luhansk in eastern Ukraine when it was part of the Soviet Union.

DZYUBA

MOST APPEARANCES:

1. **Sergei Ignashevich**, 127
2. **Igor Akinfeev**, 111
3. **Viktor Onopko**, 109
4. **Yuri Zhirkov**, 104
5. **Vasili Berezutskiy**, 101

127

Long-serving captain and centre-back Sergei Ignashevich, Russia's most-capped player with 127 caps, bowed out of international football for the second time after losing on penalties to Croatia in their 2018 FIFA World Cup quarter-final, the 38-year-old having done his bit by converting from the spot. He previously retired from internationals after the 2016 UEFA European Championship but was persuaded to return.

IGNASHEVICH

18

Igor Akinfeev became post-Soviet Russia's youngest international footballer when he made his debut in a friendly against Norway on 28 April 2004. The CSKA Moscow goalkeeper was just 18 years and 20 days old.

YASHIN

TEAM TRIVIA
INTERNATIONAL EXILE

Artem Dzuba and Aleksandr Yerokhin top-scored for Russia with three goals apiece in their UEFA qualification campaign for the 2022 FIFA World Cup. Coached by former international striker Valeri Karpin, the country finished second behind Croatia in Group H. Russia were then drawn against Poland in the play-offs, to play either Sweden or the Czech Republic in the final for a place at Qatar 2022, but their opponents were handed a walkover win when Russian sides were suspended from competing in UEFA and FIFA competitions following the military action against Ukraine in February 2022. UEFA announced in September 2022 that Russia would be barred from the 2024 UEFA European Championship.

TOP SCORERS:

1. **Artem Dzyuba**, 30
= **Aleksandr Kerzhakov**, 30
3. **Vladimir Beschastnykh**, 26
4. **Roman Pavlyuchenko**, 21
5. **Andrey Arshavin**, 17
= **Valeri Karpin**, 17

NATIONAL LEGEND
KERZH LIFTS THE CURSE

Only one man was in Russia's squads for the 2002 FIFA World Cup finals and the next time they qualified, in 2014: **Aleksandr Kerzhakov**. He made his international debut as a 19-year-old in March 2002, and he played just eight minutes of the finals three months later. With five goals, he was Russia's main man in qualifying for the 2014 finals. Kerzhakov joined Vladimir Beschastnykh as his country's top scorer, coming on as a substitute in Russia's 2014 FIFA World Cup opener against South Korea and equalising in a 1-1 draw. His 30th and final goal for Russia helped defeat Belarus in a June 2015 friendly.

KERZHAKOV

4

Winger Denis Cheryshev scored four goals at the 2018 FIFA World Cup. He replaced Alan Dzagoev against Saudi Arabia and scored, making him the first-ever substitute to score in a FIFA World Cup opening game.

NATIONAL LEGEND
SUPER STOPPER

Lev Yashin made it into the FIFA World Cup All-Time Team. In a career spanning 20 years, Yashin played 326 league games for Dynamo Moscow – the only club side he ever played for – and won 78 caps for the Soviet Union, conceding, on average, less than a goal a game (only 70 in total). With Dynamo, he won five Soviet championships and three Soviet cups, the last of which came in his final full season in 1970. He saved around 150 penalties in his career, and kept four clean sheets in his 12 FIFA World Cup matches.

SCOTLAND

A country with a vibrant domestic league and a rich football tradition – it played host to the first-ever international football match, against England, in November 1872 – Scotland have rarely put in the performances on the international stage to match their lofty ambitions.

Joined FIFA: 1910

Biggest win:
11-0 v. Ireland, 1901

Highest FIFA ranking: 13th

Home stadium:
Hampden Park, Glasgow

Honours: -

DALGLISH

TOP SCORERS:

1 **Kenny Dalglish**, 30
= **Denis Law**, 30
3 **Hughie Gallacher**, 23
4 **Lawrie Reilly**, 22
5 **Ally McCoist**, 19

NATIONAL LEGEND
KING KENNY

Kenny Dalglish is Scotland's joint-top international goalscorer (with Denis Law) and remains the only player to have won more than a century of caps for the national side, with 102 in total – 11 more than the next highest, goalkeeper Jim Leighton. Dalglish made his name spearheading Celtic's domestic dominance in the 1970s, winning four league titles, four Scottish Cups and one League Cup. He then went on to become a legend at Liverpool, winning a hat-trick of European Cups (1978, 1981 and 1984) before leading the side as player-manager to a league and cup double in 1986.

LAW

4

Denis Law twice scored four goals in a match for Scotland, the first against Northern Ireland on 7 November 1962 – helping the Scots to win the British Home Championship – and then against Norway in a friendly on 7 November 1963.

40

Rangers centre-back **David Weir**, Scotland's oldest-ever player, retired in October 2010 after winning 69 caps, his last coming at the ripe old age of 40 years and 150 days.

TOURNAMENT TRIVIA
UNOFFICIAL WORLD CHAMPIONS

One of the victories most cherished by Scotland fans is the 3-2 triumph over arch-rivals and reigning world champions England at Wembley in April 1967 – the first time Sir Alf Ramsey's team had lost since clinching the 1966 FIFA World Cup. Scotland's man of the match that day was ball-juggling left-half/midfielder Jim Baxter, while it was also the first game in charge for Scotland's first full-time manager, Bobby Brown. Less fondly recalled is Scotland's 9-3 trouncing by the same opposition at the same stadium in April 1961.

WEIR

71

Former footballer and primary school headteacher Craig Brown holds the record for most matches as Scotland manager – 71 between 1993 and 2001, including competing at the 1996 UEFA European Championship in England and the FIFA World Cup in France two years later.

TEAM TRIVIA
PLAY-OFF OFF-NIGHT

It was third time unlucky for Scotland when attempting to qualify for the 2022 FIFA World Cup, having last reached the finals in 1998. The country previously reached the tournament twice via the play-offs, seeing off Wales in 1977 and Australia eight years later. But after finishing second behind Denmark in UEFA's Group H, with striker Lyndon Dykes and midfielder John McGinn hitting four goals apiece, Steve Clarke's side were beaten 3-1 by Ukraine in Glasgow in a play-off semi-final. John McGinn and older brother Paul are among three sets of siblings to play for Scotland since the Second World War.

17

The youngest-ever Scotland captain is John Lambie, who led the team out at the age of 17 years and 92 days against Ireland in March 1886; the youngest since 1900 is Darren Fletcher, who was 20 years and 115 days old against Estonia in May 2004.

STAR PLAYER
GREAT SCOTT

Manchester United midfielder **Scott McTominay** had only scored once in 37 appearances for Scotland before 2023 – an injury-time winner against Israel in October 2021 in a 2022 FIFA World Cup qualifier. But he scored four times in four days in March 2023 in his country's first two 2024 UEFA European Championship qualifiers: twice in a 3-0 victory in Cyprus and then both goals at Glasgow's Hampden Park in a first win over Spain since 1984. McTominay was born in Lancaster in northern England but qualified for Scotland through his father Frank's Helensburgh ancestry. His four-goal salvo came a month after helping Manchester United win the 2023 League Cup at Wembley against Newcastle United.

McTOMINAY

MOST APPEARANCES:

1 **Kenny Dalglish**, 102
2 **Jim Leighton**, 91
3 **Darren Fletcher**, 80
4 **Alex McLeish**, 77
5 **Paul McStay**, 76

NATIONAL LEGEND
HOW GEMMILL DANCED TO THE MUSIC OF SCOTLAND'S WORLD CUP TIME

Archie Gemmill scored Scotland's greatest goal on the world stage in a surprise 3-2 victory over the Netherlands at the 1978 FIFA World Cup, jinking past three defenders before chipping the ball neatly over Dutch goalkeeper Jan Jongbloed. Amazingly, in 2008, this magical moment was turned into a dance in the English National Ballet's "The Beautiful Game", and was referenced in cult in 1990s film, *Trainspotting*, which is set in Edinburgh.

GEMMILL

STAR PLAYER
MARSHALL LAW

Goalkeeper **David Marshall** made his Scotland international debut back in 2004 and endured long spells without another call-up. Yet 16 years later he proved crucial in leading Scotland to a first major tournament, UEFA Euro 2020, for the first time since the 1998 FIFA World Cup. Marshall was the penalty-saving hero in shoot-out victories over Israel in an October 2020 play-off semi-final and then again against Serbia in the play-off final a month later. He was less fortunate in the finals. Scotland's opening match ended in 2-0 defeat to the Czech Republic, the second goal lobbed from the halfway line by Patrik Schick after Marshall had strayed beyond his own penalty area. A goalless draw against England at Wembley in London was followed by a 3-1 defeat to Croatia at Hampden Park.

MARSHALL

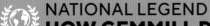

SERBIA

The former Yugoslavia was one of the strongest football nations in Eastern Europe. Serbia broke from Montenegro in 2006 and last featured at a major tournament in 2018 at the FIFA World Cup.

Joined FIFA: 2006

Biggest win: 6-1 v. Azerbaijan, 2007, v. Bulgaria, 2008, v. Wales, 2012

Highest FIFA ranking: 19th

Home stadium: Rajko Mitić Stadium, Belgrade

Honours: -

STAR PLAYER
HITMAN MIT

Serbia's all-time leading scorer Aleksandar Mitrović missed a shoot-out penalty to give Scotland victory in a November 2020 play-off to reach UEFA EURO 2020. But he enjoyed sweet redemption two Novembers later when heading a stoppage-time winner from Dušan Tadić's cross away to Portugal to clinch top spot ahead of them in UEFA's Group A and qualify for the 2022 FIFA World Cup. Serbia won just one point in Qatar, with Mitrović twice on the scoresheet in a 3–3 draw with Cameroon and a 3–2 loss to Switzerland, which both followed a 2–0 defeat by Brazil. Mitrović was the first man to score more than once for modern-day Serbia at a FIFA World Cup.

NATIONAL LEGEND
ENTER, THE DRAGAN

Yugoslavia's last appearance at a FIFA World Cup, before the country's dissolution, saw them reach the quarter-finals in Italy in 1990 – spearheaded by one of their most stylish footballers, playmaker **Dragan Stojković**. He scored both goals as Spain were beaten 2-1 in the second round, but was among those missing a penalty in a shoot-out in a defeat to defending champions and eventual runners-up Argentina. Stojkovic won the European Cup in 1993 with French club Marseille despite missing the final against AC Milan through injury, two years after losing the final to his former club Red Star Belgrade. Stojković became Serbia's tenth manager in ten years when he was appointed to the job in March 2021.

1930
The first man to captain and then coach his country at the FIFA World Cup was Milorad Arsenijević, who captained Yugoslavia to the semi-finals at the inaugural tournament in Uruguay in 1930 and then managed their squad in Brazil 20 years later.

TOP SCORERS:

1 **Aleksandar Mitrović**, 52

2 **Stjepan Bobek**, 38

3 **Milan Galić**, 37
= **Blagoje Marjanović**, 37
= **Savo Milošević**, 37

28

Siniša Mihajlović, who died aged 53 in December 2022 after suffering from leukaemia, scored 10 goals in 63 appearances for Yugoslavia between 1991 and 2003, including a run to the quarter-finals of the 2000 UEFA European Championship. Mihajlović also set the record for most direct free-kick goals in Italy's Serie A, 28. He was Serbia manager from May 2012 to October 2013.

TOURNAMENT TRIVIA
A TAD SPECIAL

Serbia's 5-0 victory over Russia in Belgrade in November 2020, in the UEFA Nations League, equalled their record winning margin, following a similar scoreline against Romania in October 2009 and 6-1 victories over Azerbaijan in October 2007, Bulgaria in November 2008 and Wales in September 2012. The Wales trouncing included a first international goal for playmaker **Dušan Tadić**. His four goals helped Serbia qualify for the 2018 FIFA World Cup, where an opening 1-0 win over Costa Rica was not enough to help the country through the first round. Tadić was made captain in 2021.

MITROVIĆ

TADIĆ

STAR PLAYER
BRAN POWER

Versatile defender **Branislav Ivanović**, who became Serbia's most-capped player with two appearances at the 2018 FIFA World Cup, has enjoyed scoring significant late goals against Portuguese opposition. His first goal for his country was an 88th-minute equaliser in a UEFA European Championship qualifier away to Portugal in September 2007. His stoppage-time header gave Chelsea victory over Benfica in the final of the UEFA Europa League in 2013, a year after suspension had ruled him out of the club's UEFA Champions League final triumph over Bayern Munich.

IVANOVIĆ

MOST APPEARANCES:

1 Branislav Ivanović, 105
2 Dejan Stanković, 103
3 Savo Milošević, 102
4 Dušan Tadić, 96
5 Aleksandar Kolarov, 94

87

Dragan Džajić, one of the former Yugoslavia's greatest talents, scored the goal that beat England and took his team to the final of the UEFA European Championship in 1968. Džajić scored again in a 1-1 draw with Italy in the final, but his side lost the replay 2-0.

3

Midfielder Dejan Stanković is the only man to have represented three different countries at separate FIFA World Cups, playing for Yugoslavia in 2002, Serbia and Montenegro in 2006, and Serbia in 2010.

NATIONAL LEGEND
ACCLAIM FOR ANTIĆ

In April 2019, tributes were paid to **Radomir Antić** after his death aged 71 in Madrid. Antić was the only man to manage Spanish giants Barcelona, Real Madrid and Atlético Madrid – leading the latter to a Spanish league and cup double in 1995-96. Fellow Serbian Milinko Pantić, who scored Atlético's Copa del Rey final winner against Barcelona, described him as a "father". Antić also led Serbia at the 2010 FIFA World Cup in South Africa, the first finals to feature Serbia solely after Montenegro's independence. They exited after the first round but marked their campaign with a 1-0 Group D victory over Germany thanks to winger Milan Jovanović's first-half strike.

ANTIĆ

NATIONAL LEGEND
STAN'S THE MAN

Dejan Stanković scored twice on his international debut for Yugoslavia in 1998. He also twice scored memorable volleyed goals from virtually on the halfway line – once for Internazionale against Genoa in 2009-10, with a first-time shot from the opposing goalkeeper's clearance, and an almost identical finish against German club Schalke 04 in the UEFA Champions League the following season. Stanković tied Savo Milošević's Serbian appearances record with his final competitive international in October 2011, but went one better in October 2013 when he played the first ten minutes of a 2-0 friendly defeat of Japan in Novi Sad.

STANKOVIĆ

100

Savo Milošević was the first Serbian player to reach a century of international appearances – and he can claim to have played for his country in four different guises, representing Yugoslavia before and after it broke up, Serbia & Montenegro, and finally Serbia alone.

MILOŠEVIĆ

SLOVAKIA

Slovakia have finally begun to claim some bragging rights over their neighbours, the Czech Republic. The Slovakians qualified for their first FIFA World Cup in 2010, at which they upset defending champions Italy 3-2 and reached the second round.

Joined FIFA: 1994

Biggest win:
7–0, v. Liechtenstein, 2004, v. San Marino, 2007, v. San Marino, 2009

Highest FIFA ranking: 14th

Home stadium:
Tehelné pole, Bratislava

Honours: -

MOST APPEARANCES:

1 **Marek Hamšík**, 136
2 **Peter Pekarik**, 117
3 **Miroslav Karhan**, 107
4 **Martin Škrtel**, 104
5 **Juraj Kucka**, 97

4

Four men have scored a hat-trick for Slovakia: Jan Arpas against Croatia in April 1944, Róbert Vittek against Liechtenstein in September 2004, Filip Sebo against Malta in August 2006 and Ondrej Duda against Malta in November 2021.

22
Striker Adolf Scherer holds the record for most goals scored by a Slovak-born footballer playing for the united Czechoslovakia. He scored 22 in 36 games between 1958 and 1964, including three at the 1962 FIFA World Cup, where the country finished runners-up to Brazil, among them a quarter-final winner against Hungary and the third as Yugoslavia were beaten 3-1 in the semi-final.

HAMŠÍK

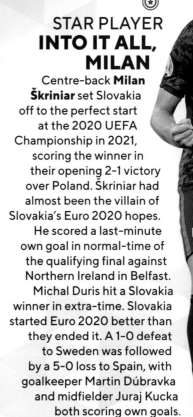

STAR PLAYER
INTO IT ALL, MILAN

Centre-back **Milan Škriniar** set Slovakia off to the perfect start at the 2020 UEFA Championship in 2021, scoring the winner in their opening 2-1 victory over Poland. Škriniar had almost been the villain of Slovakia's Euro 2020 hopes. He scored a last-minute own goal in normal-time of the qualifying final against Northern Ireland in Belfast. Michal Duris hit a Slovakia winner in extra-time. Slovakia started Euro 2020 better than they ended it. A 1-0 defeat to Sweden was followed by a 5-0 loss to Spain, with goalkeeper Martin Dúbravka and midfielder Juraj Kucka both scoring own goals.

ŠKRINIAR

TOURNAMENT TRIVIA
MAREK OFF THE MARK

Slovakia's biggest win is 7-0, a result they have achieved three times – with wing-back Marek Čech the only man to play in all three games: against Liechtenstein in September 2004 and twice versus San Marino, in October 2007 and June 2009. He scored twice in the most recent match and, in fact, four of his five international goals since his 2004 debut came against San Marino – he also scored a brace in a 5-0 victory in November 2007.

STAR PLAYER
CUTTING EDGE HAMŠÍK

Playmaker **Marek Hamšík** often stood out from the crowd with his Mohawk hairstyle. However, he fulfilled a promise to shave it off if his club Napoli won the 2012 Coppa Italia. Two years earlier, he had captained Slovakia when they knocked holders Italy out in the 2010 FIFA World Cup first round. Hamšík became Slovakia's most-capped player with his 108th appearance in October 2018, marking the occasion with a goal in a 2-1 defeat to the Czech Republic. He then equalled and swiftly overtook Róbert Vittek as the nation's leading scorer with a brace as Azerbaijan were beaten 4-1 the following June.

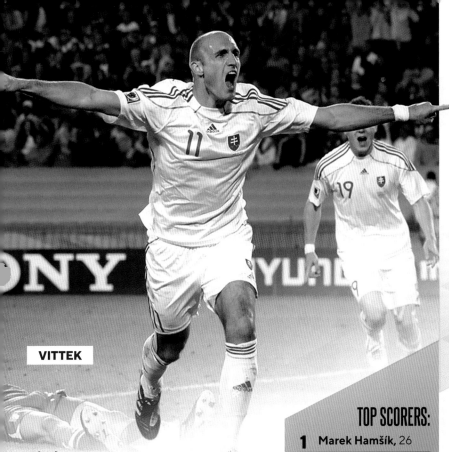

VITTEK

Ondrej Duda scored Slovakia's first goal at a UEFA European Championship, just 52 seconds after coming on as a substitute in their 2–1 defeat to Wales in the first round of the 2016 tournament. A 2–1 win over Russia and 0–0 draw with England helped Slovakia into the knock-out stages, ahead of a 3–0 defeat to reigning world champions Germany.

DUDA

TOP SCORERS:

1. **Marek Hamšík**, 26
2. **Róbert Vittek**, 23
3. **Szilárd Németh**, 22
4. **Róbert Mak**, 15
5. **Miroslav Karhan**, 14
= **Marek Mintál**, 14

NATIONAL LEGEND
RÓBERT THE HERO

At South Africa 2010, Slovakia's **Róbert Vittek** became only the fourth player from a FIFA World Cup debutant to score as many as four goals in one tournament. He hit one against New Zealand, two against defending champions Italy, and a late penalty in a second-round defeat to the Netherlands. The previous three players to have done so were Portugal's Eusébio in 1966, Denmark's Preben Elkjær in 1986, and Croatia's Davor Šuker in 1998.

TEAM TRIVIA
HIT FOR SIX

Slovakia missed out on a place at the 2022 FIFA World Cup despite losing just twice in their ten UEFA Group H qualification games. Managed by Štefan Tarkovič until June 2022, Slovakia signed off the campaign in style with a 6–0 victory in Malta in November 2021, the country's biggest-ever away win. Midfielder Ondrej Duda hit a hat-trick in a game that came three days after what was thought to be Slovak legend Marek Hamšík's last international, a 2–2 draw with Slovenia. But Hamšík returned for a 136th and final appearance in November 2022, a 2–2 friendly draw with Chile in Slovakia's capital Bratislava. Duda's international debut had been as a second-half substitute for Hamšík against Finland in November 2014.

107

Miroslav Karhan became the first Slovakia player to pass 100 caps and he retired in 2011 with 107 to his name.

NATIONAL LEGEND
VLAD ALL OVER

Three relatives named **Vladimir Weiss** – different generations of the same family – have represented their country in international football, with two of them featuring at the 2010 FIFA World Cup. The first Vladimir made three appearances for Czechoslovakia, including the 1964 Olympics final, in which he scored an own goal as Hungary triumphed 2–1. The second Vladimir won 19 caps for Czechoslovakia and 12 for Slovakia. The third reached 77 caps in June 2022, when he took his scoring tally to eight with the only goal against Azerbaijan in their UEFA Nations League C clash.

8

Eight of Czechoslovakia's triumphant 1976 UEFA European Championship side were born in modern-day Slovakia, including captain Anton Ondruš and both their scorers in the 2–2 draw: Ján Švehlík and Karol Dobiaš.

WEISS

SWEDEN

LARSSON

Twelve appearances at the FIFA World Cup finals (with a best result of second, as tournament hosts, in 1958) and three Olympic medals (including gold in London in 1948) bear testament to Sweden's rich history on the world football stage.

Joined FIFA: 1908

Biggest win: 12-0 v. Latvia, 1927, v. Korea Republic 1948

Highest FIFA ranking: 2nd

Home stadium: Friends Arena, Stockholm

Honours: -

6 Alvin Hallbäck scored a Swedish record six goals in one game in his side's 12–0 victory over Latvia on 29 May 1927. The most goals in one Sweden match came when they beat Norway 11–3 on 12 July 1908.

NATIONAL LEGEND
ONE MORE ENCORE AGAIN

One of the most famous and decorated Swedish footballers of modern times, **Henrik Larsson** (a star on the club scene with both Celtic and Barcelona), quit international football after the 2002 FIFA World Cup and again after the 2006 FIFA World Cup in Germany. He then made a further comeback in the 2010 FIFA World Cup qualifiers. With 37 goals in his 106 appearances, including five in his three FIFA World Cups, fans and officials clamoured for his return each time he tried to walk away. His son Jordan, also a striker, made his Sweden debut against Estonia in January 2018 and scored his first international goal to beat Moldova in a friendly two years later.

4 Emil Forsberg's four goals at UEFA EURO 2020 set a Swedish record for a UEFA European Championship, beating three apiece by Tomas Brolin in 1992 and Henrik Larsson in 2004. Forsberg's 19th for his country came in a 1–1 draw with Slovenia in September 2022, which sealed Sweden's relegation from UEFA Nations League B. They thus became the first country to be demoted twice in the UEFA Nations League.

SCORING RECORD
ANDERS KEEPERS

Midfielder **Anders Svensson** celebrated equalling Thomas Ravelli's Sweden appearances record by scoring in both his 142nd and 143rd games for his country: a long-range strike as Norway were beaten 4–2 and then the winning goal against the Republic of Ireland in a qualifier for the 2014 FIFA World Cup. He then became his country's most-capped player in a 1–0 victory over Kazakhstan, but he did not score. Svensson retired from international football in 2013, aged 37, after Sweden lost to Portugal in a 2014 FIFA World Cup qualifying play-off. He made 148 appearances, and scored 21 goals.

SVENSSON

MOST APPEARANCES:

1 Anders Svensson, 148

2 Thomas Ravelli, 143

3 Andreas Isaksson, 133
= Sebastian Larsson, 133

5 Kim Källström, 131

NATIONAL LEGEND
IBRA-CADABRA

Few modern footballers can claim such consistent success – or boast such an unrepentant ego – as Swedish forward **Zlatan Ibrahimović**. His proclamations have included "There's only one Zlatan", "I am like Muhammad Ali" and – in response to criticism from Norway's John Carew – "What Carew does with a football, I can do with an orange". He christened the newly built Friends Arena in Solna with all four goals as hosts Sweden beat England 4-2 in a November 2012 friendly – his final strike topping the lot, a 30-yard overhead kick which won the FIFA Puskás Award for goal of the year.

TOP SCORERS:

1. **Zlatan Ibrahimović**, 62
2. **Sven Rydell**, 49
3. **Gunnar Nordahl**, 43
4. **Henrik Larsson**, 37
5. **Gunnar Gren**, 32

40

Zlatan Ibrahimović ended five years of international retirement in 2021 to play again for Sweden. He holds the record as Sweden's oldest international – aged 40 years and 177 days – after coming on as a substitute in his country's 2-0 FIFA World Cup qualifying play-off final defeat to Poland in March 2022, alongside 19-year-old team-mate Anthony Elanga.

▼ STAR PLAYER
SEB STEPS UP

Midfielder Sebastian Larsson, renowned for his long-range strikes, spent much of his career in England after joining Arsenal as a 16-year-old. He helped Sweden reach the 2018 FIFA World Cup quarter-finals, where they were defeated by England. Larsson won his 100th cap in Sweden's last pre-2018 FIFA World Cup friendly against Peru, before scoring twice in a 4-0 victory over Malta in October 2019 to help his country qualify for UEFA EURO 2020. Larsson played in Sweden's 2-1 extra-time defeat to Ukraine in the second round of UEFA Euro 2020, becoming his country's oldest starter at a tournament, aged 36 years and 23 days, since Gunnar Gren turned out in the 1958 FIFA World Cup final aged 37 years and 241 days.

17

Alexander Isak became Sweden's youngest international scorer on 12 January 2017 when he netted the opener in a 6-0 friendly defeat of Slovakia in Abu Dhabi at the age of 17 years and 113 days.

IBRAHIMOVIĆ

2ND

Sweden's best result at a FIFA World Cup is runners-up. Englishman George Raynor, who led the Swedes to Olympic gold at London 1948, steered them to third place and the runners-up spot at the 1950 and 1958 FIFA World Cups, respectively.

RAVELLI

NATIONAL LEGEND
GRE-NO-LI OLYMPIC AND ITALIAN GLORY

Having conquered the world by leading Sweden to gold at the 1948 Olympics in London, **Gunnar Gren**, Gunnar Nordahl and Nils Liedholm were snapped up by AC Milan. Their three-pronged "Gre-No-Li" forward line led the Italian giants to their 1951 *Scudetto*. Nordahl, who topped the *Serie A* scoring charts five times between 1950 and 1955, remains Milan's all-time top scorer with 221 goals in 268 games. Gren and Liedholm went on to appear for the Swedish national team in the 1958 FIFA World Cup, where they finished runners-up.

GREN

NATIONAL LEGEND
CAMEO ROLES

Sweden's Magnus Erlingmark could claim to have the shortest-ever FIFA World Cup finals career, amounting to nothing more than his appearance as an 89th-minute substitute against Russia in the first round of the 1994 tournament. His only rival for the unenviable record is Bulgaria's Petar Mihtarski, another last-minute replacement that summer in his country's second round victory over Mexico on penalties. Sweden and Bulgaria went on to meet in the third-place play-off, which Sweden won 4-0. In goal for Sweden was the country's most-capped keeper **Thomas Ravelli**, who had saved two Romania penalties to help win a quarter-final shoot-out. Ravelli ended his international career having conceded 143 goals in 143 games.

SWITZERLAND

Switzerland may not be an international football powerhouse, but it is the home of both FIFA and UEFA. Switzerland co-hosted UEFA EURO 2008 with Austria, and reached the semi-finals of the inaugural UEFA Nations League in 2019.

TOURNAMENT TRIVIA
CLEAN SHEET WIPE-OUT

Switzerland remain the only team to exit the FIFA World Cup without conceding a goal in regulation time, which they did in 2006. However, in the shoot-out defeat to Ukraine in the second round, following a goalless 120 minutes, they failed to score a single penalty and lost 3-0. Despite being beaten three times in the shoot-out, goalkeeper **Pascal Zuberbühler's** performances in Germany earned him a Swiss record for consecutive clean sheets at an international tournament.

ZUBERBÜHLER

Joined FIFA: 1905
Biggest win:
9–0 v. Lithuania, 1924
Highest FIFA ranking: 3rd
Home Stadium:
Stade de Suisse Wankdorf, Bern
Honours: -

NATIONAL LEGEND
FREI-S AND LOWS

In April 2011, citing abuse from his own fans during recent matches, **Alexander Frei** announced his retirement from international football following a string of underwhelming results with the national side. He stepped down as Switzerland's all-time leading goalscorer with 42 in 84 games. Frei was joined in international retirement by strike partner Marco Streller, who had scored 12 goals in 37 games.

2004

After being compared to a llama by an angry Swiss sports press for spitting at Steven Gerrard at UEFA EURO 2004, Alexander Frei, Switzerland's all-time top scorer, adopted a llama at Basel Zoo as part of his apology to the nation.

3

Yann Sommer is only the third goalkeeper to score a FIFA World Cup own goal, after Spain's Andoni Zubizarreta in 1998 and Noel Valladeres of Honduras in 2014. Sommer saw a penalty from Costa Rica rebound off his head and into the net in 2018.

FREI

TOP SCORERS:

1 Alexander Frei, 42

2 Max Abegglen, 34
= Kubilay Türkyilmaz, 34

4 André Abegglen, 29
= Jacques Fatton, 29

MOST APPEARANCES:

1 **Heinz Hermann**, 118

2 **Granit Xhaka**, 113

3 **Alain Geiger**, 112
= **Xherdan Shaqiri**, 112

5 **Stephan Lichtsteiner**, 108

22

Legendary Swiss international player and manager **Jakob "Köbi" Kuhn** was only 22 years old when he was sent home from the 1966 FIFA World Cup for missing a curfew.

STAR PLAYER
SHAQIRI LOYALTY TEST

Kosovo-born Swiss playmaker **Xherdan Shaqiri** indicated that he would be prepared to switch allegiance to his native land in 2016, but FIFA ruled against it. Shaqiri's eight goals at major tournaments are a Swiss record. He opened the scoring in his side's 3–2 Group G victory over Serbia at the 2022 FIFA World Cup. This followed three strikes at UEFA EURO 2020 and a hat-trick against Honduras at the 2014 FIFA World Cup. Shaqiri scored with an overhead kick in a 1–1 second round draw against Poland at the 2016 UEFA European Championship, but the Poles won on penalties. At UEFA EURO 2020, he equalised for Switzerland in their quarter-final against Spain, only for his country to again lose in a shoot-out after a 1–1 draw.

SHAQIRI

STAR PLAYER
HARIS, FRANCE

Striker **Haris Seferovic** found the net three times at UEFA EURO 2020, making him only the third Swiss player – after Xherdan Shaqiri and Admir Mehmedi – to score at both a FIFA World Cup and a European Championship. His goals included a brace against reigning world champions France in the second round, when Switzerland came back from 3-1 down with just nine minutes of normal time remaining to draw 3-3. Seferovic bagged his second of the game in the 81st minute then Mario Gavranović equalised in stoppage-time. Goalkeeper Yann Sommer was the hero in the shoot-out, saving from Kylian Mbappe as the Swiss won 5-4 on penalties. Seferovic headed in after 55 seconds of Switzerland's 1-0 win over Portugal in June 2022 – the fastest goal in UEFA Nations League history.

TEAM TRIVIA
BREEL DEAL

In 2022, Breel Embolo became the first man to score at a FIFA World Cup for his adopted country against the land of his birth with the only goal of Switzerland's opening Group G game against Cameroon. The striker was born in Cameroon's capital Yaoundé but moved to Switzerland with his family as a young child. He opted not to celebrate the strike, out of respect. Embolo found the net again in his side's 3–2 victory over Serbia before Switzerland crashed out in the second round, losing 6–1 to Portugal. Switzerland had qualified for Qatar as winners of UEFA's Group C ahead of European champions Italy. Switzerland clinched top spot in September 2021 by beating Bulgaria 4–0 while Italy could only draw 0–0 with Northern Ireland.

EMBOLO

4

Switzerland have lost all four quarter-finals reached: at the FIFA World Cups of 1934, 1938 and 1954 and at UEFA EURO 2020.

NATIONAL LEGEND
NEARLY MAN HERMANN

Switzerland's most-capped player Heinz Hermann unfortunately found his playing career coinciding with his country's lengthy spell between major tournaments. Midfielder Hermann scored 15 goals in 118 appearances for his country between 1978 and 1991, and was named Swiss Footballer of the Year four times. His career fell in the void between Switzerland's first-round exit from the 1966 FIFA World Cup and their progress to the second round of the 1994 FIFA World Cup.

4

Karl Rappan, who pioneered pressurising defending and positional fluidity, managed Switzerland in four separate spells between 1937 and 1963.

SEFEROVIC

TURKEY

MOST APPEARANCES:

1 Rüştü Reçber, 120
2 Hakan Şükür, 112
3 Bülent Korkmaz, 102
4 Emre Belözoğlu, 101
5 Arda Turan, 100

Turkey qualified for the FIFA World Cup only twice in the 20th century. Since 2000, however, Turkish fans have had plenty to cheer about, including a third-place finish at the 2002 FIFA World Cup in Japan and Korea Republic.

Joined FIFA: 1923

Biggest win:
7–0 v. Syria, 1949, v. Korea Republic, 1954, v. San Marino, 1996

Highest FIFA ranking: 5th

Home stadium:
Atatürk Olympic Stadium, Istanbul

Honours: -

REÇBER

NATIONAL LEGEND
RÜŞTÜ TO THE RESCUE

With his distinctive ponytail and charcoal-black warpaint, Turkey's most-capped international, **Rüştü Reçber** always stood out, but perhaps never more so than as a star of Turkey's third-place performance at the 2002 FIFA World Cup, as he was named in the FIFA World Cup All Star Team. He was on the bench by UEFA EURO 2008 but played in the quarter-final after first-choice goalkeeper Volkan Demirel was sent off in the final group game and suspended – and Reçber was the hero again, saving from Croatia's Mladen Petrić in a penalty shoot-out to send Turkey into their first UEFA European Championship semi-final, a narrow defeat to Germany.

NATIONAL LEGEND
TAKE FAT

It was the end of an epic era when **Fatih Terim**'s third spell as national manager finished abruptly in July 2017, but Terim remains the dominant force in Turkish football history. After coaching Galatasaray to the UEFA Cup in 2000 – the nation's first European trophy – he led Turkey on their surprise run to the UEFA European Championship semi-finals in 2008. Turkey led in the semi-final only to concede a last-minute winner to Germany. Terim returned to Galatasaray in 2009 but became national manager for the third time in 2013.

TERIM

STAR PLAYER
LOTS TO TALK ABOUT

Turkey took part in their first FIFA World Cup in 1954 after winning the drawing of lots, following a 2–2 draw with Spain in a qualification play-off in Rome after each team had beaten the other in their home ties. Turkey's two matches at the tournament in Switzerland were a 4–1 defeat to eventual champions West Germany and a 7–0 victory over South Korea. Their goalkeeper that tournament was Turgay Şeren, whose 52 caps for his country between 1950 and 1966 included 35 as captain. Turkey had to wait until 2002 for their only other FIFA World Cup. They missed out on 2022 in Qatar after losing their UEFA qualification semi-final 3–1 to Portugal. It was the 77th and last international played by striker Burak Yılmaz, who scored Turkey's goal but missed a penalty that would have equalised for 2–2.

136

Fatih Terim managed Turkey for 136 matches, winning 70, drawing 34 and losing 32.

🏆 TOURNAMENT TRIVIA
THREE AND OUT

Turkey went into the 2020 UEFA European Championship in 2021 with what looked a promising blend of youth and experience. They were managed by 69-year-old Şenol Güneş, who had led them to third place at the 2002 FIFA World Cup and took charge again in 2019, some 15 years after first leaving his post. Their Euro 2020 squad was the youngest at the tournament, with an average age of 24 years and 353 days. But they lost 3–0 to Italy in Rome in the opening game, conceding as many goals in one match as they had in all ten Group H qualifiers – including a 2–0 victory and 1–1 away draw against world champions France. Turkey were beaten in all three Group A Euro 2020 clashes, losing 2–0 defeat to Wales and 3–1 to Switzerland. Star striker **Burak Yılmaz**, second only to Hakan Şükür in Turkey's all-time scoring ranks, scored his a hat-trick in a 4–2 victory over the Netherlands in March 2021 in a 2022 FIFA World Cup qualifier, but he failed to find the net at the Euros.

YILMAZ

17
Playmaker Nuri Şahin became both Turkey's youngest international and youngest goalscorer on the same day. Şahin was 17 years and 32 days old when he made his debut against Germany in Istanbul on 8 October 2005, and his goal, one minute from time, gave Turkey a 2–1 win.

👥 TEAM TRIVIA
SEVEN HEAVEN

Turkey have won 7–0 on three occasions, most notably against Korea Republic at the 1954 FIFA World Cup, including a hat-trick by Burhan Surgan, who hit seven goals in eight internationals. The other two occasions came at home, against Syria in November 1949 and San Marino in November 1996. They have won 6–0 twice away – against Kazakhstan in a June 2005 FIFA World Cup qualifier and in Lithuania in the UEFA Nations League in June 2022. The win over Lithuania included a brace by German-born striker **Serdar Dursun**. He racked up seven goals in his first seven games for Turkey having only made his international debut nine days before his 30th birthday.

DURSUN

15
Zeki Riza Sporel scored Turkey's first goal in international football, against Romania on 26 October 1923. He actually hit a brace that day in a 2–2 draw – the first of 16 games for Turkey in which he hit 15 goals.

94
The last-ever FIFA World Cup "golden goal" was scored by Turkey substitute İlhan Mansız, instantly ending and winning their 2002 quarter-final against Senegal four minutes into extra time. By the 2006 FIFA World Cup, the old system of two 15-minute periods and penalties – if necessary – had returned.

⚽ SCORING RECORD
SUPER ŞÜKÜR

Turkey beat Korea Republic 3–2 to claim third place at the 2002 FIFA World Cup, their finest-ever performance in the competition, helped in no small part by an 11-second strike from Hakan Şükür. Şükür's total of 51 goals (in 112 games) is more than double his nearest competitor in the national team ranking. His first goal came in only his second appearance, as Turkey beat Denmark 2–1 on 8 April 1992. He went on to score four goals in a single game twice – in the 6–4 win over Wales on 20 August 1997 and in the 5–0 crushing of Moldova on 11 October 2006.

ŞÜKÜR

TOP SCORERS:
1. **Hakan Şükür**, 51
2. **Burak Yılmaz**, 29
3. **Tuncay Şanlı**, 22
4. **Lefter Küçükandonyadis**, 21
5. **Nihat Kahveci**, 19
= **Metin Oktay**, 19
= **Cemil Turan**, 19

11
Hakan Şükür scored the fastest-ever FIFA World Cup finals goal – he needed only 11 seconds to score Turkey's opener in their third-place play-off against Korea Republic at the 2002 FIFA World Cup.

UKRAINE

YAREMCHUK

Since gaining independence in 1991, Ukraine has become a footballing force in its own right. They reached the quarter-finals at the 2006 FIFA World Cup in Germany and UEFA EURO 2000 and were co-hosts of UEFA EURO 2012.

Joined FIFA: 1992

Biggest win:
9-0 v. San Marino, 2013

Highest FIFA ranking: 11th

Home stadium: (rotation)

Honours: -

TOURNAMENT TRIVIA
WORLDWIDE SUPPORT

Ukraine were many neutrals' favourites to get through the UEFA European play-offs and reach the 2022 FIFA World Cup amid the suffering of the country after Russia's military invasion in February 2022. Many Ukrainian players were called up to fight in the army but the squad was given special dispensation to prepare for the play-offs at a training camp in Brdo in Slovenia. Their play-off semi-final against Scotland, scheduled for the March 2022, was delayed until June, when they won 3-1 at Hampden Park in Glasgow with goals by Andriy Yarmolenko, Roman Yaremchuk and Artem Dovbyk. But they fell short in the final four days later, losing 1-0 away to Wales. Yaremchuk previously scored three goals in Ukraine's Group D qualification campaign, in which they finished second behind world champions France, including a record five draws in a row. During the campaign, manager Andriy Shevchenko resigned in August 2021 to be succeeded by Oleksandr Petrakov. The defeat to Wales meant Ukraine have now failed in six tournament play-offs.

93

Andriy Pyatov became Ukraine's most-capped goalkeeper with his 93rd appearance in a 2-2 draw away to Serbia in November 2019, which clinched his country's place at UEFA EURO 2020. He previously set a national record by going 752 minutes without conceding a goal between March and November 2013.

YARMOLENKO

TOP SCORERS:

1 Andriy Shevchenko, 48

2 Andriy Yarmolenko, 45

3 Yevhen Konoplyanka, 21

4 Serhiy Rebrov, 15

5 Oleh Husyev, 13
= Roman Yaremchuk, 13

STAR PLAYER
IN YARM'S WAY

At UEFA EURO 2020, winger **Andriy Yarmolenko** and striker Roman Yaremchuk became the first pair of players to both score in each of their country's opening two games at a single UEFA European Championship – in a 3-2 defeat to the Netherlands and a 2-1 victory over North Macedonia. No man other than Andriy Shevchenko has scored more often for Ukraine than Yarmolenko, who also holds the country's record for fastest goal – just 14 seconds into a 3-2 friendly loss to Uruguay in September 2011.

NATIONAL LEGEND
REB ALERT

Serhiy Rebrov scored Ukraine's first-ever FIFA World Cup goal, giving them a 1–0 win over Northern Ireland in an August 1996 qualifier for the 1998 tournament. Rebrov was later part of the squad for Ukraine's first FIFA World Cup finals in 2006, scoring against Saudi Arabia to help his side progress to the quarter-finals where they lost 3–0 to eventual champions, Italy. Rebrov had become Ukraine's youngest international when making his debut against the USA in June 1992, aged 18 years and 24 days.

MOST APPEARANCES:

1. **Anatoliy Tymoshchuk**, 144
2. **Andriy Yarmolenko**, 112
3. **Andriy Shevchenko**, 111
4. **Andriy Pyatov**, 102
5. **Ruslan Rotan**, 100

TYMOSHCHUK

NATIONAL LEGEND
ROCKET MAN

Andriy Shevchenko was the first Ukrainian to reach a century of international appearances – but defensive midfielder **Anatoliy Tymoshchuk** overtook him and retired in 2016 as the country's most-capped player with 144 appearances. He also had the rare honour of seeing his name in space when Ukrainian cosmonaut Yuri Malenchenko was launched into orbit in 2007 while wearing a Zenit St Petersburg shirt with Tymoshchuk on the back.

NATIONAL LEGEND
LEADING FROM THE FRONT

Oleh Blokhin, Ukraine's coach on their first appearance at a major tournament finals, made his name as a striker with his hometown club Dynamo Kyiv. Born in 1952, when Ukraine was part of the Soviet Union, Blokhin scored a record 211 goals in another record 432 appearances in the USSR national league. He also holds the goals and caps records for the USSR, with 42 in 112 games. Always a high flyer, Blokhin led Ukraine to the finals of the 2006 FIFA World Cup in Germany, where they lost to eventual winners Italy 3–0 in the quarter-finals after knocking Switzerland out in the second round.

120:37

Artem Dovbyk's extra-time stoppage-time winner for Ukraine against Sweden in the second round of UEFA EURO 2020 was the latest match-winning goal in European Championship history. Timed at 120 minutes and 37 seconds, it overtook Michel Platini's strike after 118 minutes and 53 seconds that defeated Portugal at the 1984 tournament.

3

Marko Dević became the first man to score a hat-trick for Ukraine in an 8–0 victory away to San Marino in October 2013. The only player to do so since is Andriy Yarmolenko, with all three goals in an away win over Luxembourg in November the following year.

8

There were eight different scorers in Ukraine's 9–0 thrashing of San Marino in a FIFA World Cup qualifier in 2013 – still the country's biggest-ever win.

3

Three Ukrainians have won the Ballon d'Or as European Footballer of the Year: Oleh Blokhin in 1975 and Igor Belanov in 1986 when part of the Soviet Union and, post-independence, Andriy Shevchenko in 2004.

NATIONAL LEGEND
SUPER SHEVA

Andriy Shevchenko was a promising boxer as a youngster before deciding to focus on football full time. He lifted trophies at every club he played for and retired as Ukraine's second-most capped player and top goalscorer with 48 goals in 111 games, which included two at the 2006 FIFA World Cup, where he captained his country in their first-ever major finals appearance, and a double to secure a 2–1 comeback win over Sweden in Ukraine's first match co-hosting UEFA EURO 2012. Shevchenko was Ukraine's assistant coach to Mikhail Fomenko at UEFA EURO 2012 before taking the top job and, despite missing out on the 2018 FIFA World Cup, led them to the EURO 2020 quarter-finals before a 4–0 defeat to England in Rome.

SHEVCHENKO

WALES

In a land where rugby union has long been the main national obsession, recent progress – including a semi-final appearance at UEFA EURO 2016 – has inspired unprecedented excitement and optimism.

Joined FIFA: 1906

Biggest win:
11-0 v. Ireland, 1888

Highest FIFA ranking: 8th

Home stadium:
Cardiff City Stadium, Cardiff

Honours: -

100 MILLION
Gareth Bale cost Real Madrid a world record EUR 100 million (GBP 86 million) when he moved from Tottenham Hotspur in August 2013.

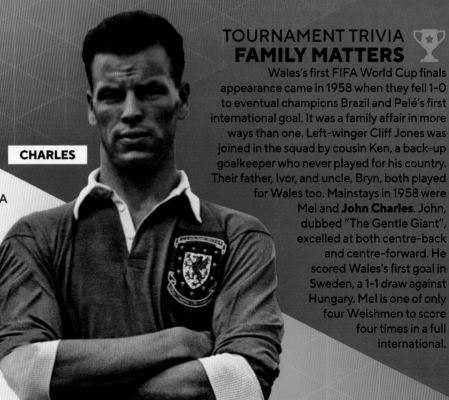

BALE

NATIONAL LEGEND
ALL HAIL BALE

Fittingly, Wales's first goalscorer at a FIFA World Cup since 1958 was Gareth Bale, whose late penalty gave his side a 1–1 draw against the USA in their Group B match at the 2022 finals in Qatar. This was followed by two defeats – 2–0 to Iran and 3–0 to England – which saw Wales eliminated in the first round. Bale announced his retirement shortly afterwards. He had also scored Wales's first post-1958 goal at a major tournament when finding the net with a free-kick to help beat Slovakia 2–1 at the 2016 UEFA European Championship. Bale, Wales's most-capped player and all-time leading scorer, was given an emotional farewell presentation at the Cardiff City Stadium on 28 March 2023 before Wales beat Latvia 1–0 in a 2024 UEFA European Championship qualifier.

Midfielder Aaron Ramsey became Wales's youngest captain, aged 20 years and 90 days, when he wore the armband against England in March 2011. The previous record was set in April 1964 by Mike England, who was 22 years and 135 days old when he skippered the side against Northern Ireland.

20

NATIONAL LEGEND
BILLY IDOL

Winger Harry Wilson became Wales' youngest full international when he replaced Hal Robson-Kanu in a 2014 FIFA World Cup qualifier in October 2013. At 16 years and 207 days, he was 108 days younger than previous record-holder Gareth Bale. Wales' oldest international is Billy Meredith, whose final international came at the age of 45 years and 229 days in March 1920. Wilson's UEFA EURO 2020 ended unhappily, sent off in Wales's second round 4-0 elimination by Denmark.

CHARLES

TOURNAMENT TRIVIA
FAMILY MATTERS

Wales's first FIFA World Cup finals appearance came in 1958 when they fell 1–0 to eventual champions Brazil and Pelé's first international goal. It was a family affair in more ways than one. Left-winger Cliff Jones was joined in the squad by cousin Ken, a back-up goalkeeper who never played for his country. Their father, Ivor, and uncle, Bryn, both played for Wales too. Mainstays in 1958 were Mel and **John Charles**. John, dubbed "The Gentle Giant", excelled at both centre-back and centre-forward. He scored Wales's first goal in Sweden, a 1–1 draw against Hungary. Mel is one of only four Welshmen to score four times in a full international.

TOP SCORERS:

1. **Gareth Bale**, 41
2. **Ian Rush**, 28
3. **Ivor Allchurch**, 23
   = **Trevor Ford**, 23
5. **Dean Saunders**, 22

Welsh striker Robert Earnshaw holds the remarkable record of scoring hat-tricks in all four divisions of English football, the FA Cup and the League Cup. He also grabbed a treble for Wales, against Scotland on 18 February 2004. In full internationals, Wales have registered 15 hat-tricks – each one by a different player.

15

PAGE

NATIONAL LEGEND
PAGE PUTS WALES BACK ON WORLD STAGE

No country had waited as long to return to a FIFA World Cup finals as Wales, who clinched their place at Qatar 2022 by beating Ukraine 1–0 in a European qualification play-off in Cardiff in June that year, the winning goal coming inevitably from Gareth Bale, albeit with a deflection off the visitors' Andriy Yarmolenko. Wales had last competed at the tournament in 1958. The longest waits had been for Egypt, from 1934 to 1990, and Norway, from 1938 to 1994. In charge for Wales was Rob Page, who had taken charge ahead of UEFA EURO 2020 and previously won 41 caps for the country as a defender. Goalkeeper Wayne Hennessey's clean sheet against Ukraine was the first against that side in nine FIFA World Cup qualifiers. The tournament itself turned sour for Hennessey, with a red card for a foul on Iran's Mehdi Teremi in a 2–0 defeat, making him the third goalkeeper to be sent off at a FIFA World Cup.

SPEED

NATIONAL LEGEND
SHOCK LOSS OF A MODEL PROFESSIONAL

The football world was united in shock and grief following the sudden death of Wales manager **Gary Speed** in November 2011. Former Leeds United, Everton, Newcastle United and Bolton Wanderers midfielder Speed, once the country's most-capped outfield player, was found at his home in Cheshire, England. The 42-year-old had been manager for 11 months, overseeing a series of encouraging performances that saw a rise in the world ranking from 116th to 48th and a prize for FIFA's Best Movers of 2011. An official memorial game was played in Cardiff in February 2012 between Wales and Costa Rica, the country against whom he had made his international debut in May 1990.

1906
Pioneer movie-makers Sagar Mitchell and James Kenyon filmed Wales v. Ireland in March 1906, making it the first international football match to be captured on film.

Wales and Chelsea defender Ethan Ampadu became the youngest player to be shown a straight red card at a UEFA European Championship, when sent off aged 20 years and 279 days for a foul on Italy's Federico Bernadeschi as his side lost 1–0 in their final Group A game at UEFA EURO 2020.

20

NATIONAL LEGEND
OH, BROTHER

Chris Gunter was 29 when he made his 93rd Wales appearance against Albania in November 2018, passing former binman-turned-Everton-goalkeeper Neville Southall as his country's most-capped player. Versatile full-back Gunter's parents had a dilemma after a 3–1 victory over Belgium in their 2016 UEFA European Championship quarter-final, thanks to goals by captain Ashley Williams, Hal Robson-Kanu and Sam Vokes – his brother Marc's wedding in Mexico coincided with the semi-final against Portugal. They opted to watch Chris in Lille, where Wales lost 2–0, bringing their memorable run to an end. Gunter became the first Wales international to reach a century of caps when Mexico were beaten 1–0 in a friendly in March 2021.

GUNTER

MOST APPEARANCES:

1. **Gareth Bale**, 111
2. **Chris Gunter**, 109
3. **Wayne Hennessey**, 108
4. **Neville Southall**, 92
5. **Ashley Williams**, 86

EUROPE : OTHER TEAMS

For some of the smaller countries in Europe, the thrill of representing their nation is more important than harbouring dreams of world domination.

Country: Iceland
Joined FIFA: 1947
Most appearances: Birkir Bjarnason, 113
Top scorer: Eiður Guðjohnsen/Kolbeinn Sigþórsson, 26

Country: San Marino
Joined FIFA: 1988
Most appearances: Matteo Vitaioli, 77
Top scorer: Andy Selva, 8

Country: Finland
Joined FIFA: 1908
Most appearances: Jari Litmanen, 137
Top scorer: Teemu Pukki, 37

Country: Luxembourg
Joined FIFA: 1910
Most appearances: Mario Mutsch, 102
Top scorer: Léon Mart, 16

Country: Gibraltar
Joined FIFA: 2016
Most appearances: Liam Walker, 69
Top scorer: Roy Chipolina, 5 = Liam Walker, 5

Country: Austria
Joined FIFA: 1905
Most appearances: Marko Arnautović, 106
Top scorer: Toni Polster, 44

Country: Georgia
Joined FIFA: 1992
Most appearances: Guram Kashia, 102
Top scorer: Shota Arveladze, 26

Country: North Macedonia
Joined FIFA: 1994
Most appearances: Goran Pandev, 122
Top scorer: Goran Pandev, 38

Country: Azerbaijan
Joined FIFA: 1992
Most appearances: Rashad Sadygov, 111
Top scorer: Gurban Gurbanov, 14

Country: Bosnia and Herzegovina
Joined FIFA: 1996
Most appearances: Edin Džeko, 127
Top scorer: Edin Džeko, 64

Country: Slovenia
Joined FIFA: 1992
Most appearances: Boštjan Cesar, 101
Top scorer: Zlatko Zahovič, 35

Country: Armenia
Joined FIFA: 1992
Most appearances: Sargis Hovsepyan, 132
Top scorer: Henrikh Mkhitaryan, 32

Country: Albania
Joined FIFA: 1932
Most appearances: Lorik Cana, 93
Top scorer: Erjon Bogdani, 18

Country: Belarus
Joined FIFA: 1992
Most appearances: Alyaksandr Kulchy, 102
Top scorer: Maksim Romaschenko, 20

Country: Andorra
Joined FIFA: 1996
Most appearances: Ildefons Lima, 134
Top scorer: Ildefons Lima, 11

Country: Montenegro
Joined FIFA: 2007
Most appearances: Fatos Bećiraj, 86
Top scorer: Stevan Jovetić, 31

Country: Kosovo
Joined FIFA: 2015
Most appearances: Amir Rrahmani, 51
Top scorer: Vedat Muriqi, 23

TOURNAMENT TRIVIA
UNDERDOGS HAVE THEIR DAY

Iceland's first goal at a tournament was scored by midfielder Birkir Bjarnason, now the nation's most-capped player, in their opening game at the 2016 UEFA European Championship – the equaliser in a 1–1 draw with eventual champions Portugal. Iceland reached the quarter-finals that summer, beating England 2–1 in the second round before they were knocked out by hosts France. Iceland then became the smallest nation to reach a FIFA World Cup, though did not make it beyond the group stages in Russia in 2018. Their first FIFA World Cup goal was hit by Alfreð Finnbogason in a 1–1 draw against Argentina.

BJARNASON

TOURNAMENT TRIVIA
FINALLY, FINLAND

Ten-goal **Teemu Pukki** starred as Finland qualified for a major international tournament for the first time, at the 33rd attempt, clinching a place at UEFA EURO 2020 as Group B runners-up behind Italy. Only Luxembourg had taken part in more qualifying contests – 35 – without reaching a finals. Pukki scored ten times in his first 59 matches, but had added another 20 goals in the next 31 going into the UEFA European Championship in summer 2021. His brace against Kazakhstan in October 2021, both goals of the game in a FIFA World Cup qualifier, took him past 32-goal Jari Litmanen as Finland's all-time leading scorer. But his side missed out on reaching the 2022 finals, finishing third in UEFA Group D behind France and Ukraine.

PUKKI

102

Centre-back Guram Kashia moved past midfielder Jaba Kankava and wide man Levan Kobiashvili as Georgia's most-capped player by making his 101st appearance in a 3-0 friendly defeat to Morocco in November 2022. He moved to 102 in Georgia's first 2024 UEFA European Championship qualifier, a 1-1 home draw with Norway.

SELVA

SCORING RECORD
SELVA SERVICE

San Marino, with a population of under 30,000, remain near the bottom of FIFA's world ranking, but they finally had something to celebrate in November 2014 thanks to a goalless draw with Estonia – their first-ever point in a UEFA European Championship qualifier – which ended a run of 61 successive defeats. Their only win was a 1-0 friendly triumph over Liechtenstein in April 2004, thanks to a fifth-minute strike by overall top scorer **Andy Selva**. The country's most-capped player is fellow striker Matteo Vitaioli, whose first and so far only goal for San Marino came in a 2-1 defeat to Lithuania in September 2015. It was the nation's first away goal for 14 years.

7-0
Iceland's captain at the 2016 UEFA European Championship and 2018 FIFA World Cup was midfielder Aron Gunnarson. He marked his 101st international with a hat-trick in Iceland's record 7-0 victory in a 2024 UEFA European Championship qualifier away to Liechtenstein in March 2023.

SCORING RECORD
REBORN BOURG

A long and painful wait finally ended for traditional whipping boys Luxembourg when they beat Northern Ireland 3-2 in September 2013. It was the *Red Lions*' first home win in a FIFA World Cup qualifier for 41 years, since overcoming Turkey 2-0 in October 1972. It was also five years to the day since their last FIFA World Cup qualifying victory, a 2-1 triumph in Switzerland in 2008. Luxembourg continued their eye-catching form with a surprise 1-0 away win to the Republic of Ireland in March 2021, in a 2022 FIFA World Cup qualifier, thanks to a late strike by midfielder Gerson Rodrigues. Three days later Rodrigues opened the scoring against reigning champions Portugal, though the game ended in a 3-1 defeat.

PANDEV

NATIONAL LEGEND
SUPER PAN

North Macedonia's first qualification for a major tournament came courtesy of their all-time top scorer, almost two decades after his international debut. **Goran Pandev** scored the only goal in their play-off win against Georgia in November 2020, clinching his nation a place at the following summer's UEFA European Championship. He had reached a century of caps in an earlier EURO 2020 qualifier, a 3-1 victory over Latvia in 2019. Pandev first topped his nation's goalscoring rankings – passing Georgi Hristov - with a first-half double in a 3-2 defeat by reigning European champions Spain in August 2009.

15

The break-up of the Soviet Union in 1990 led to 15 new footballing nations, although Russia initially played on at the 1992 UEFA European Championship as CIS, or the Commonwealth of Independent States – albeit without the involvement of Estonia, Latvia and Lithuania.

LIMA

HAPPY DAYS FOR ILDEFONS

Andorra's long-serving captain **Ildefons Lima** had double cause for celebration on 9 June 2017. Not only did he equal Óscar Sonejee's record of 106 international appearances, but Andorra also beat Hungary 1-0 in a 2018 FIFA World Cup qualifier – only their second-ever competitive victory and first in 66 matches. The winning goal came from Lima's central defensive partner Marc Rebés, his first for Andorra in his ninth game. The Andorrans ended a run of 56 consecutive defeats in UEFA European Championship qualifiers in October 2019 with a 1-0 victory over Moldova, thanks to a goal by another centre-back, Marc Vales.

 STAR PLAYER
ED BOY

Edin Džeko became Bosnia and Herzegovina's all-time leading scorer with a second-half hat-trick in an 8-1 2014 FIFA World Cup qualifier victory over Liechtenstein in September 2012. The goals not only took him past previous record-holder Elvir Bolić, but also ahead of Džeko's international team-mate

DŽEKO

Zvjezdan Misimović, whose brace earlier in the game had briefly put him in the lead. The pair jostled for position at the top of the charts for a while before Džeko took over for good. Džeko then became his country's most-capped international when he played against Austria in the UEFA Nations League in September 2018, scoring the only goal of the game for good measure.

54

Kazakhstan full-back Aybol Abiken scored from 54 metres in his country's 3-1 defeat to Albania in November 2020, the longest-distance goal scored in UEFA's Nations League. He lofted the ball into the net from the halfway line.

4

The Faroe Islands, UEFA's fourth-smallest nation by population, went on an unprecedented four-match unbeaten run in 2022. They beat Lithuania 2-1 at home, then drew 2-2 in Luxembourg and 1-1 in Lithuania before a surprise 2-1 home victory over Turkey, all in UEFA Nations League C. Left-back Viljormur Davidsen scored the Faroes' first in both victories.

POLSTER

MURIQI

TOURNAMENT TRIVIA
KOS FOR CELEBRATION

Kosovo made their debut in international competition in the 2018 FIFA World Cup qualifiers. Two years later, they marked their first UEFA European Championship qualifiers by finishing third behind England and the Czech Republic in Group A, clinching a play-off against North Macedonia. Top scorer for coach Bernard Challandes' side was striker **Vedat Muriqi**. He scored in a crucial 2-0 victory over Montenegro, as did centre-back Amir Rrahmani, who in 2022 pulled clear of team-mate right-back Mërgim Vojvoda as the fledgling nation's most-capped international. Vojvoda scored in Kosovo's joint-record win, 5-0 against Burkina Faso in March 2022, matching the margin of victory against Malta in 2018.

NATIONAL LEGEND
100 CLUB

Centre-back Aleksandar Dragović became only the second Austrian to win 100 caps for Austria – after midfielder Andreas Herzog – in a 2-2 draw against Scotland in March 2022. He was followed to a century of international appearances three months later by striker Marko Arnautović, in a 2-1 UEFA Nations League A defeat to Denmark. Three days earlier, Arnautović had scored his 33rd Austria goal in a 3-0 win away to Croatia, putting him one behind Johann Krankl and 11 behind **Anton Polster** in the country's all-time scoring ranks.

29

Māris Verpakovskis, Latvia's all-time leading scorer with 29 goals in 104 games, is also the only man to find the net for the nation at a major international tournament – in a 2–1 defeat to Czech Republic at the 2004 UEFA European Championship. He previously hit six in 10 qualifiers to help Latvia to the finals in Portugal.

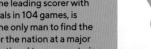

STAR PLAYER
BY JOVE

Stevan Jovetić struck seven goals in seven games for Montenegro between September 2016 and June 2017, taking him past strike partner and captain **Mirko Vučinić** as the country's leading scorer with 23. His 2018 FIFA World Cup qualifying hat-trick helped to down Armenia 4–1 in June 2017. Vučinić's 17 goals included a winner against Switzerland in a EURO 2012 qualifier, which he celebrated by removing his shorts and wearing them on his head – antics that earned him a yellow card.

VUCINIC

STAR PLAYER
XHAKA CLAN

Granit and Taulant Xhaka, both born in Swiss city Basel to Kosovo Albanian parents, became the first brothers to face each other on opposing sides at a UEFA European Championship on 11 June 2016 – midfielder Granit, 23, for Switzerland, 25-year-old defender Taulant for Albania. Granit and Switzerland won 1–0, though Albania did achieve their first victory at their first major tournament by beating Romania 1–0 eight days later.

STAR PLAYER
A SEQUEL TO HAMLET

Striker Hamlet Mkhitaryan played twice for post-Soviet state Armenia in 1994 before tragically dying two years later from a brain tumour at the age of just 33. His son, **Henrikh Mkhitaryan**, just seven when his father died, has gone on to become the country's all-time leading scorer – and one who often dedicates his achievements to his late father. The younger Mkhitaryan became Armenia's joint-top scorer, alongside Artur Petrosyan, with a goal against Denmark in June 2013. While Petrosyan's goals came in 69 games, Mkhitaryan's 11 were scored in 39 – and he pulled away on his own, with a 12th international strike, in a 2–2 draw with Italy in October 2013.

MKHITARYAN

TOURNAMENT TRIVIA
KAZAK JOY, SCOTTISH MISERY

Some 27,000 Kazakhstan fans celebrating a national new year had even more reason for joy in March 2019 with perhaps the country's finest footballing result, a surprise 3–0 trouncing of Scotland in their opening UEFA EURO 2020 qualifier in Astana – despite being ranked 117th in the world. Yuriy Pertsukh, Yan Vorogovskiy and Baktiyar Zaynutdinov were the goalscoring heroes in the first game in charge for new Kazakhstan coach, former Czech Republic midfielder and manager Michael Bílek. Kazakhstan had failed to register a win in their ten qualifiers for the 2018 FIFA World Cup.

100

Slovenia's Boštjan Cesar made his 100th appearance against Scotland in October 2017, but it was marred by a late red card and he retired after one more game.

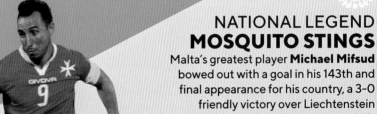

MIFSUD

NATIONAL LEGEND
MOSQUITO STINGS

Malta's greatest player **Michael Mifsud** bowed out with a goal in his 143th and final appearance for his country, a 3–0 friendly victory over Liechtenstein in November 2020, at the age of 39. Mifsud – just 1.65m tall and nicked "The Mosquito" – scored 42 times for his country, including five in a 7–1 win against Liechtenstein in March 2008, three of them in the first 21 minutes. His only goal of the game also ended Malta's 20-year wait for an away win in a competitive international at Armenia in June 2013 in a 2014 FIFA World Cup qualifier.

SOUTH AMERICA

South America has embraced association football with such passion that it boasts 10 triumphs in the FIFA World Cup and the world's oldest national team tournament in the *Copa América*, founded in 1916. The continent has also hosted the World Cup finals five times and is bidding to do so again in 2030.

Confederation founded: 1916

Number of associations: 10

Headquarters: Luque, Paraguay

Most continental championship wins:
Uruguay, 15
Argentina, 15

10

National teams from all 10 members of CONMEBOL, the South American football confederation, compete in the *Copa América*. At least two guest nations were invited between 1993 and 2019.

The first FIFA World Cup was held in South America: Uruguay hosted and won the tournament in 1930.

21

Brazil have competed at all 21 FIFA World Cups – more than any other nation – and have won five, also a record.

RIVALDO

RONALDO

The first football club established in South America was the Lima Cricket and Football Club, in Peru in 1859.

10

With only ten member associations, CONMEBOL has the fewest of any FIFA confederation.

ARGENTINA

MESSI

Argentina have been *Copa América* champions on 15 occasions, FIFA Confederations Cup winners in 1992, Olympic gold medallists in 2004 and FIFA World Cup winners in 1978, 1986 and 2022. Few countries can boast as much high-profile international success.

Joined FIFA: 1912

Biggest win:
12-0 v. Ecuador, 1942

Highest FIFA ranking: 1st

Home stadium:
Estadio Antonio Vespucio Liberti (El Monumental), Buenos Aires

Honours: 3 FIFA World Cup (1978, 1986, 2022), 15 *Copa Américas* (1921, 1925, 1927, 1929, 1937, 1941, 1945, 1946, 1947, 1955, 1957, 1959, 1991, 1993, 2021)

STAR PLAYER
LEO BRAVO

Lionel Messi's status as one of the finest footballers ever was not in doubt, but at the 2022 FIFA World Cup in Qatar he emulated compatriot Diego Maradona by lifting the most-prized trophy, too. Messi scored twice in the final against holders France as the game finished 3–3 after extra-time. He then put away the first spot-kick in the decisive shoot-out. Messi was also handed the Golden Ball as the FIFA World Cup's best player, making him the first man to win this twice. His international career made an awful start when he was sent off two minutes into his debut against Hungary in August 2005, but he has since become his country's record goalscorer, youngest FIFA World Cup scorer (in 2006, aged 19) and youngest captain (23, during the 2010 FIFA World Cup). He has more FIFA World Cup finals appearances – 26 – than any other man.

26

Lionel Messi's seven goals at the 2022 FIFA World Cup meant he has now scored 26 times combined across that competition and the *Copa América* (13 in each) – the most for any South American, surpassing the 25 struck by Brazil's Ronaldo (15 FIFA World Cup, 10 *Copa América*).

MASCHERANO

3

Argentina are one of only three teams, alongside France and Brazil, to have won the FIFA World Cup, FIFA Confederations Cup and Olympic Games gold medals.

STAR PLAYER
MASCHERANO'S GOLDEN GLOW

Before the introduction of the FIFA World Cup in 1930, eight Uruguayans had won football gold at both the 1924 and 1928 Summer Olympics. Only one man, Hungary's Dezso Novak in 1964 and 1968, had achieved a similar double before Argentina's defensive midfielder **Javier Mascherano** at Athens 2004 and Beijing 2008. Carlos Tevez got the only goal against Paraguay in 2004, while Ángel Di Mária struck the winner against Nigeria four years later in a game played in such heat that officials allowed water breaks. Mascherano – nicknamed "The Little Chief" – became Argentina's most-capped player at the 2018 FIFA World Cup, before retiring from international football following their 4-3 second round exit to eventual champions France. Lionel Messi surpassed Mascherano as Argentina's most-capped player during the 2021 *Copa América*.

DI MARÍA

TOP SCORERS:

1 Lionel Messi, 98
2 Gabriel Batistuta, 54
3 Sergio Agüero, 41
4 Hernán Crespo, 35
5 Diego Maradona, 34

14

Argentina have finished *Copa América* runners-up more times than any other country, 14, three more than Brazil, most recently in 2015 and 2016.

TOURNAMENT TRIVIA
RIGHT ÁNGEL

Ángel Di María has twice scored the winning goal in finals for Argentina – 13 years apart. After hitting the only goal of the 2008 Beijing Summer Olympics men's football final against Nigeria, he did similarly against hosts Brazil in 2021 to clinch the *Copa América* for Argentina – the country's first major international title since winning the same competition in 1993. It followed penalty shoot-out misery in both the 2015 *Copa América* final and the following year's *Copa América Centenario* final, both times against Chile after a goalless draw. Di María missed the 2014 FIFA World Cup final after suffering an ankle injury in the quarter-final, in which he set up Gonzalo Higuaín's winner against Belgium, but scored Argentina's second in their triumphant 2022 final versus France.

STAR PLAYER
SUPER MART

Emiliano Martínez was the goalkeeping hero for Argentina as they won the FIFA World Cup in 2022 in the final penalty shoot-out, saving from Kingsley Coman before seeing Aurélien Tchouaméni send France's third spot-kick wide. Minutes earlier, Martínez had made a point-blank save from France's Randal Kolo Muani in the closing stages of extra-time. Martínez was awarded the Golden Glove prize for the tournament's best goalkeeper. Sergio Romero remains the nation's most-capped goalkeeper, with 96 international appearances, but Martinez's 26th game for his country meant he joined Ubaldo Fillol (58 caps) and Nery Pumpido (36) in winning the FIFA World Cup with Argentina.

7.1

The number 10 shirt Diego Maradona wore when scoring two goals in the 1986 FIFA World Cup victory against England – one with his hand, the other later voted "Goal Of The Century" – sold at auction by Sotheby's in London in May 2022 for £7.1 milion.

NATIONAL LEGEND
BEGINNER'S LUCK

Aged just 27 years and 267 days old, Juan José Tramutola became the FIFA World Cup's youngest-ever coach when Argentina opened their 1930 campaign by beating France 1-0. Argentina went on to reach the final, only to lose 4-2 to Uruguay. Top scorer at the 1930 FIFA World Cup was Argentina's Guillermo Stábile, with eight goals in four games – the only internationals he played. He later won six *Copa América* titles as his country's longest-serving coach between 1939 and 1960.

NATIONAL LEGEND
DIVINE DIEGO

To many, **Diego Maradona** was the greatest footballer ever, and his death aged 60 on 25 November 2020 prompted loving worldwide tributes. Pelé said: "I have lost a great friend and the world has lost a legend." Maradona's dazzling skills, goals and achievements speak for themselves. After finding fame as a ball-juggling child at Argentinos Juniors, he was left out of his country's 1978 FIFA World Cup squad, then sent off at the 1982 tournament. But as Argentina captain in Mexico in 1986, Maradona scored a spectacular individual strike in the quarter-final win over England. He also set up Jorge Burruchaga's winner in the final against West Germany. Later he coached Argentina to the quarter-finals of the 2010 FIFA World Cup.

MARADONA

2
Midfielder Marcelo Trobbiani played just two minutes of FIFA World Cup football – the last two minutes of the 1986 final, after replacing winning goalscorer Jorge Burruchaga.

STAR PLAYER
KUN'S TON

Only Lionel Messi and Gabriel Batistuta have scored more goals for Argentina than Sergio Agüero. He became the country's seventh man to reach a century of caps in a 4-1 win over Bolivia in the last group game of the 2021 *Copa América* – a tournament his team went on to win. Nicknamed "Kun" after a cartoon character he is meant to have resembled, Agüero was top scorer in 2007 when Argentina won the FIFA World U-20 Championship for a record sixth time in Canada. He was forced to retire from football aged 33 in December 2021 after suffering from cardiac arrhythmia during a match.

AGÜERO

12

Argentina were responsible for the biggest win in *Copa América* history, when five goals by José Manuel Moreno helped them thrash Ecuador 12-0 in 1942.

NATIONAL LEGEND
THE ANGEL GABRIEL

Gabriel Batistuta, nicknamed "Batigol", is the only man to have scored hat-tricks in two separate FIFA World Cups. Argentina's former all-time leading goalscorer grabbed the first treble against Greece in 1994 and the second against Jamaica four years later. Hungary's Sándor Kocsis, France's Just Fontaine and Germany's Gerd Müller each scored two hat-tricks in the same FIFA World Cup. Batistuta, born in Avellaneda on 1 February 1969, also set an Italian league record by scoring in 11 consecutive *Serie A* matches for his club Fiorentina at the start of the 1994–95 season.

BATISTUTA

TOURNAMENT TRIVIA
YELLOW GOODBYE

Some 20 years before France were forced to wear local Argentine team Club Atlético Kimberley's kit at the 1978 FIFA World Cup, Argentina faced similar embarrassment before their first-round match against West Germany at the 1958 tournament in Sweden. They had neglected to bring along a second kit, and a colour clash with their opponents meant borrowing the yellow shirts of Swedish side IFK Malmö. Despite taking a third-minute lead, Argentina lost 3-1 and departed the tournament bottom of Group A.

TOURNAMENT TRIVIA
SUPER MARIO

Two Argentina players have finished a FIFA World Cup as the tournament's top scorer. Guillermo Stabile's eight strikes at the inaugural finals in Uruguay in 1930 helped his country to the final, where they lost 4-2 to the hosts. His eight goals in four games were also his only appearances as a player for Argentina – although he did coach them to six *Copa América* triumphs in the 1940s and 1950s. **Mario Kempes** went one better on the pitch, when his brace in the 1978 final in the Argentininan capital Buenos Aires not only took him to six goals for the tournament, but also clinched the trophy with a 3-1 victory over the Netherlands.

5

Argentina have won more FIFA World Cup penalty shoot-outs than any other country. Their 2022 victories over the Netherlands in the quarter-finals and France in the final took them to five triumphs from six – their only spot-kicks defeat coming against hosts Germany in 2006.

KEMPES

NATIONAL LEGEND
THE OTHER MAIN LIONEL

Lionel Scaloni, a former right-back, played seven times for his country and was a relative novice in coaching when appointed Argentina's caretaker manager in 2018 alongside 52-cap Pablo Aimar. He was given the top job on a permanent basis the following year and, in 2022, led the nation to their third FIFA World Cup triumph. He also became, at 44, the youngest manager to lift the trophy since compatriot César Luis Menotti, who was 39 when Argentina won as hosts in 1978. Scaloni and Argentina began the 2022 tournament badly, going down to a shock 2–1 defeat by Saudi Arabia, but went on to become the second country – after Spain in 2010 – to end as champions despite losing their first game. He is the third manager to win both the *Copa América* (in 2021) and the FIFA World Cup, following Brazil's Mário Zagalo and Carlos Alberto Parreira. Argentina's decisive penalty in the 2022 final shoot-out was scored by defender Gonzalo Montiel, who had earlier come on in extra-time and given away the spot-kick for handball that enabled France to equalise at 3–3 through Kylian Mbappé.

NATIONAL LEGEND
SECOND TIME LUCKY

Luisito Monti is the only man to play in a FIFA World Cup final for two different countries. The centre-half, born in Buenos Aires on 15 May 1901 but with Italian family origins, was highly influential in Argentina's run to the 1930 final. They lost the game 4–2 to Uruguay – after Monti allegedly received mysterious pre-match death threats. Following a transfer to Juventus the following year, he was allowed to play for Italy and was on the winning side when the *Azzurri* beat Czechoslovakia in the 1934 final. Another member of the 1934 team was Raimundo Orsi, who had also played for Argentina before switching countries in 1929.

NATIONAL LEGEND
FRINGE PLAYERS

Daniel Passarella was a demanding captain when he led his country to glory at the 1978 FIFA World Cup. He was the same as coach. After taking over the national side in 1994, he refused to pick anyone unless they had their hair cut short – and ordered striker Claudio Caniggia to get rid of his "girl's hair".

SCALONI

PASSARELLA

MOST APPEARANCES:

1. **Lionel Messi**, 172
2. **Javier Mascherano**, 147
3. **Javier Zanetti**, 143
4. **Ángel Di María**, 129
5. **Roberto Ayala**, 114

TOURNAMENT TRIVIA
NUMBERS GAME

Argentina's FIFA World Cup squads of 1978 and 1982 were given numbers based on alphabetical order rather than positions, which meant the no. 1 shirt was worn by midfielders Norberto Alonso in 1978 and Osvaldo Ardiles in 1982. The only member of the 1982 squad whose shirt number broke the alphabetical order was no. 10, Diego Maradona. Italian club Napoli retired the number 10 in tribute to Maradona, who starred for the team at his peak.

36

Martín Palermo is Argentina's oldest international goalscorer. He was aged 36 years and 27 days when making the score 2–0 against France in the final minutes of a Group B match at the 2010 FIFA World Cup. Less impressively, he missed a hat-trick of penalties in a 3–0 defeat to Colombia at the 1999 *Copa América*.

BRAZIL

No country has captured the soul of the game to the same extent as Brazil. The only nation to appear in every FIFA World Cup finals, Brazil have won the competition a record five times.

Joined FIFA: 1923

Biggest win:
10–1 v. Bolivia, 1949

Highest FIFA ranking: 1st

Home stadium:
Maracanã, Rio de Janeiro

Honours: 5 FIFA World Cups (1958, 1962, 1970, 1994, 2002), 9 *Copa Américas* (1919, 1922, 1949, 1989, 1997, 1999, 2004, 2007, 2019), 4 FIFA Confederations Cups (1997, 2005, 2009, 2013)

26

1970 FIFA World Cup star Tostão retired at the age of 26 in 1973, after an eye injury.

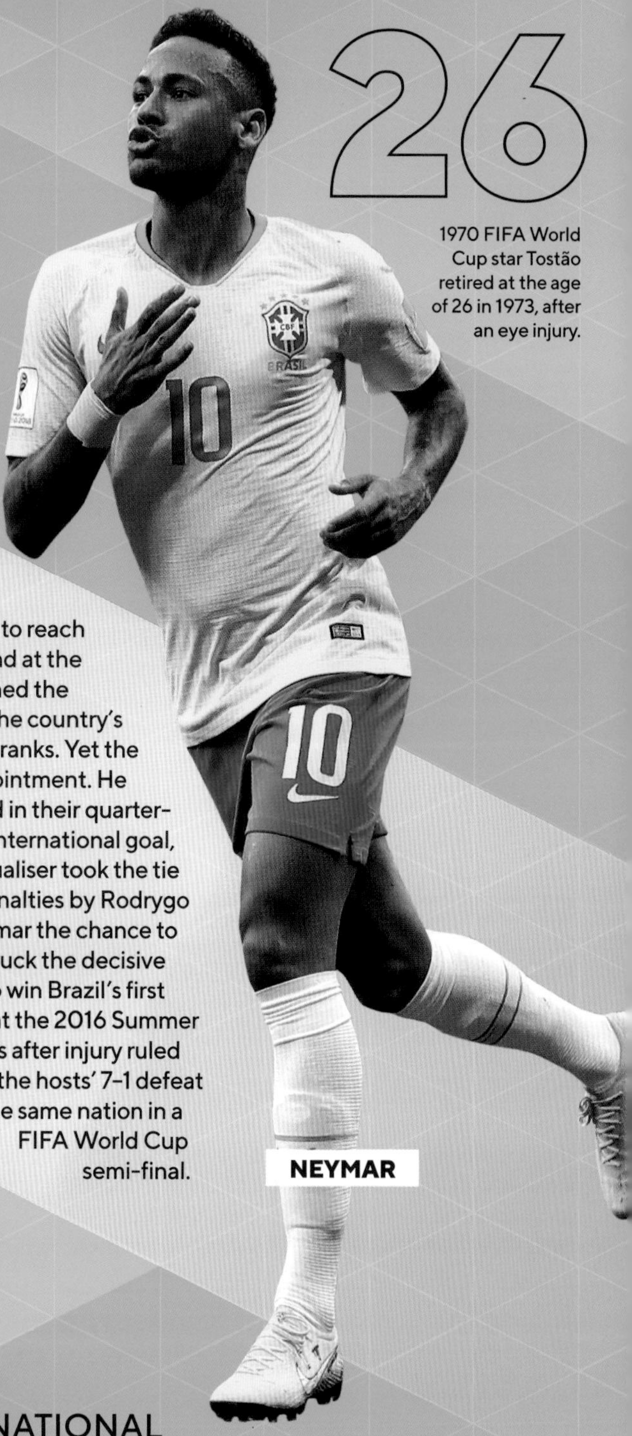

STAR PLAYER
STAR NEYM

Neymar is the youngest man to reach a century of caps for Brazil, and at the 2022 FIFA World Cup he joined the legendary Pelé at the top of the country's all-time international scoring ranks. Yet the tournament ended in disappointment. He gave Brazil an extra-time lead in their quarter-final against Croatia, his 77th international goal, but a late Bruno Petković equaliser took the tie to a shoot-out and missed penalties by Rodrygo and Marquinhos denied Neymar the chance to even take his. Neymar had struck the decisive spot-kick against Germany to win Brazil's first Olympic football gold at the 2016 Summer Games, two years after injury ruled him out of the hosts' 7–1 defeat to the same nation in a FIFA World Cup semi-final.

NEYMAR

3

Neymar became only the third Brazilian, after Pelé and Ronaldo, to score at three different FIFA World Cups when hitting his country's third in a 4–1 victory over Korea Republic in the Round of 16 at the 2022 tournament.

NATIONAL LEGEND
BRAZIL HAVE HAD THEIR BIG PHIL

The return of "Big Phil" **Luiz Felipe Scolari** as Brazil coach in November 2012 was meant to culminate, in 2014, with a repeat of his success spearheading the country to triumph at the 2002 FIFA World Cup. Although his second reign did bring glory at the 2013 FIFA Confederations Cup, the following year's FIFA World Cup on home turf will be remembered for the many unwanted records his team set and the embarrassment with which their efforts ended – most notably, the 7–1 defeat by Germany in their Belo Horizonte semi-final. Scolari was relieved of his role just days after a 3–0 defeat to the Netherlands in the third place play-off.

SCOLARI

TOP SCORERS:

1	Pelé,	77
=	Neymar,	77
3	Ronaldo,	62
4	Romário,	55
5	Zico,	48

NATIONAL LEGEND
THE KING

PELÉ

The world mourned when **Pelé** – considered by many as the greatest player of all time – died aged 82 on 29 December 2022. He was revered globally and not only for his exploits on the pitch. After scoring his 1,000th goal, Pelé dedicated it to the poor children of Brazil. More than 230,000 people attended the public wake in Santos, where "O Rei" ("The King") played his entire career other than two years at the New York Cosmos. Pelé began playing for Santos aged 15 and won his first FIFA World Cup two years later in 1958, scoring twice in the final. He gained further winners' medals in 1962 and again in 1970, when he headed the first goal as Brazil beat Italy 4–1 in the final. No other man is a triple FIFA World Cup champion as a player.

7

Pelé leads the way with seven hat-tricks for Brazil, followed by Zico and Romário on four – but only one-time Flamengo and Barcelona centre-forward Evaristo de Macedo has scored five goals in one game for Brazil, against Colombia in March 1957.

VINÍCIUS JÚNIOR

STAR PLAYER
THE JUNIOR EXPERIENCE

Tricky winger **Vinícius Júnior** became the world's most expensive footballer aged under 19 when Spain's Real Madrid agreed a €45m deal to sign him from Flamengo in May 2017, when he was still two months short of his 17th birthday. He went on to score the winning goal in Madrid's 2022 UEFA Champions League final against Liverpool, helping his club lift the trophy for a record 14th time. His first Brazil goal came in a March 2022 FIFA World Cup qualifier against Chile, a 4–0 home win, and he opened his FIFA World Cup account with the first in a 4–1 victory over Korea Republic at the 2022 finals in Qatar.

1954
The world-renowned yellow and blue kit now worn by Brazil was not adopted until 1954, as a replacement for their former all-white strip.

TOURNAMENT TRIVIA
LAND OF FOOTBALL

No country is more deeply identified with football success than Brazil, who have won the FIFA World Cup a record five times – in 1958, 1962, 1970, 1994 and 2002. They are also the only team never to have missed a FIFA World Cup finals and are favourites virtually every time the competition is staged. After winning the trophy for a third time in Mexico in 1970, Brazil kept the Jules Rimet Trophy permanently. Sadly, it was stolen from the association's headquarters in 1983 and was never recovered.

NATIONAL LEGEND
JOY OF THE PEOPLE

Garrincha, one of Brazil's greatest legends, was really Manuel Francisco dos Santos at birth but his nickname meant "Little Bird" – inspired by his slender, bent legs. Despite the legacy of childhood illness, he was a star right-winger at Botafogo from 1953 to 1965. He and Pelé were explosively decisive newcomers for Brazil at the 1958 FIFA World Cup finals. In 1962 Garrincha was voted player of the tournament. He died in January 1983 at just 49. His epitaph was the title often bestowed on him in life: "The Joy of the People".

GARRINCHA

TOURNAMENT TRIVIA
EVER-PRESENT

Only Brazil have taken part in every FIFA World Cup, and they comfortably reached the 2022 tournament for their 22nd appearance, topping South America's 10-team qualification table, only to lose on penalties to Croatia in the quarter-finals in Qatar. There was some consolation, however, for three-goal striker **Richarlison**. His brace in Brazil's opening game, a 2–0 victory over Switzerland, included a spectacular bicycle kick strike that was later voted the tournament's best goal. The Tottenham Hotspur forward also scored in the Round of 16 against Korea Republic, not only celebrating with his trademark "pigeon dance" but also seeing coach Tite join in with his team-mates in doing so. It proved their last dance together.

13

In their 2022 quarter-final against Croatia, Brazil became the 13th team in FIFA World Cup history to take a 1–0 lead in extra-time, and the first of those to then be knocked out. They were also the first country to field 26 players across the tournament, including all three goalkeepers, at a FIFA World Cup.

STAR PLAYER
ALISSON WONDERLAND

Liverpool and Brazil goalkeeper Alisson went 14 hours and 59 minutes without conceding a goal for club or country before being finally beaten by a Paolo Guerrero penalty in the 2019 *Copa América* final – but Peru's goal in a 3-1 Brazil victory was the only one he let in all tournament. It was glorious 2019 for Alisson – winner of The Best FIFA Men's Goalkeeper award – as he also won the *Copa América*, UEFA Champions League and FIFA Club World Cup. He was joined as a triple medal-winner by team-mate Roberto Firmino.

3

Right-back **Djalma Santos** is one of only two players to be voted into the official all-star team of a FIFA World Cup on three different occasions.

RICHARLISON

SANTOS

TOURNAMENT TRIVIA
PLAYING *COPA* CATCH-UP

Brazil won just three of the first 33 *Copa América* tournaments yet have now won five of the last ten editions, after triumphing on home soil in 2019. It was also their first South American crown in 12 years. Brazil beat Peru 3-1 in the final in Rio's Maracanã stadium, despite the absence of injured superstar Neymar and Gabriel Jesus being sent off. The centre-forward set up Everton's opening goal and then scored Brazil's second before being dismissed for collecting two yellow cards. Brazil, even with ten men, extended their lead through a penalty from substitute Richarlison, allowing veteran captain **Dani Alves** to lift the trophy.

NATIONAL LEGENDS
THIAGO GOES ON

Thiago Silva succeeded fellow centre-back **Lúcio** as Brazil captain after the 2010 FIFA World Cup. In March 2022, aged 37, Silva equalled his former team-mate's tally of 105 caps, as he again wore the armband in a 4–0 FIFA World Cup qualifying win at home to Chile. Silva managed seven goals to Lúcio's four in those appearances, including the opener in 2-1 quarter-final victory over Colombia at Brazil's home FIFA World Cup in 2014. A second yellow card of the tournament ruled him out of the semi-final, a 7-1 humiliation by Germany. By contrast, Lúcio had set a FIFA World Cup record during the 2006 finals by playing for 386 minutes without conceding a foul – only ended by Brazil's 1–0 quarter-final defeat to France.

LÚCIO

SILVA

RONALDO

NATIONAL LEGEND
WHITHER RONALDO?

Only one person knows exactly what happened to **Ronaldo** in the hours before the 1998 FIFA World Cup final – the man himself. He sparked one of the biggest mysteries in FIFA World Cup history when his name was left off the teamsheet before the game, only for it to reappear just in time for kick-off. It was initially reported that Ronaldo had an ankle injury, and then a upset stomach. Finally, team doctor Lídio Toledo revealed the striker had been rushed to hospital after suffering a convulsion in his sleep, but that he had been cleared to play after neurological and cardiac tests. He did score both goals in the final four years later as Brazil beat Germany 2-0, giving him the Golden Boot with eight overall. Only Germany's Miroslav Klose has scored more FIFA World Cup goals than his 15.

RONALDINHO

MARCELO

STAR PLAYER
INAUSPICIOUS START

Left-back/left-winger **Marcelo** achieved the dubious "honour" of being the first player to score the opening goal of a FIFA World Cup finals in his own net. He inadvertently gave Croatia the lead in the 2014 tournament's curtain-raiser in São Paulo, but Brazil did come back to win 3-1, thanks to a pair of goals from Neymar and one from Oscar. Marcelo, who a couple of weeks earlier had scored for his club, Real Madrid, as they won the UEFA Champions League final, also became the first Brazil player ever to score past his own goalkeeper in the FIFA World Cup finals.

BEBETO

ROMÁRIO

MOST APPEARANCES:

1. **Cafu**, 142
2. **Roberto Carlos**, 125
3. **Dani Alves**, 122
4. **Neymar**, 124
5. **Thiago Silva**, 113

NATIONAL LEGEND
ROM NUMBERS

Brazilian goal poacher supreme **Romário** is one of the few footballers to claim more than 1,000 career goals. He is also the last man to win both the FIFA World Cup and the Golden Ball award as the best player at the same tournament, something he achieved in 1994. The former Barcelona and Fluminense forward moved into politics after retiring from playing to become elected as an MP, as did his 1994 FIFA World Cup strike partner **Bebeto**. Brazil were undefeated in the 23 international matches Romário and Bebeto played together: 17 wins and six draws, including 33 goals scored between them, eight at the 1994 FIFA World Cup.

TOURNAMENT TRIVIA
SUPER POWERS' POWER CUT

There was a new addition to the international calendar in 2011: the Superclásico de las Américas, a two-legged event between fierce rivals Brazil and Argentina. Brazil were the first winners and retained the crown a year later, edging a first leg at home 2–1 before the return game in Chaco was postponed after a power cut. The rearranged game ended 2–1 to Argentina, but Brazil won 4–3 on penalties. The two nations only played once in qualification for the 2022 FIFA World Cup, a goalless draw in San Juan. Two months earlier, their meeting in São Paulo had been abandoned after four Argentina players had allegedly breached Covid-19 rules. The match was cancelled after both countries reached the finals. That left Brazil on 43 wins to Argentina's 40, with 26 draws.

CHILE

1 Alexis Sánchez, 50
2 Eduardo Vargas, 40
3 Marcelo Salas, 37
4 Iván Zamorano, 34
5 Arturo Vidal, 33

Chile were one of four founding members of CONMEBOL, South America's football confederation, in 1916. Their greatest glories were hosting and finishing third at the 1962 FIFA World Cup and winning their first two *Copa América* titles in 2015 and 2016.

Joined FIFA: 1912
Biggest win:
7-0 v. Venezuela, 1979, v. Armenia, 1997, v. Mexico, 2016
Highest FIFA ranking: 3rd
Home stadium:
Estadio Nacional Julio Martínez Prádanos, Santiago
Honours: 2
Copa Américas (2015, 2016)

SÁNCHEZ

⭐ STAR PLAYER
SÁNCHEZ SETS MORE CHILE RECORDS

The winning spot kick against Argentina to secure Chile's first *Copa América* in 2015 was struck by the well-travelled **Alexis Sánchez**, then of Arsenal in England, following spells in Italy with Udinese and in Spain with Barcelona. Sánchez holds the record as Chile's youngest international, having made his debut against New Zealand in April 2006 at the age of 17 years and four months. At the 2017 FIFA Confederations Cup, Sánchez passed Marcelo Salas to become Chile's all-time record goalscorer. Then, in 2018, and while with Manchester United, he took over at the top of the appearances list too.

SCORING RECORD
LUCKY LEO

For many years, Leonel Sánchez held the Chilean record for international appearances, scoring 23 goals in 84 games. But he was lucky to remain on the pitch for one of them. Sánchez escaped an early bath despite punching Italy's Humberto Maschio in the face during their so-called "Battle of Santiago" clash at the 1962 FIFA World Cup, when English referee Ken Aston could have sent off more than just the two players he did dismiss. Sánchez, a left-winger who was born in Santiago on 25 April 1936, finished the 1962 FIFA World Cup as one of six four-goal leading scorers – along with Garrincha, Vavá, Valentin Ivanov, Drazan Jerković and Flórián Albert.

Iván Zamorano holds the national record for most goals in one international, scoring five in a 6-0 victory over Venezuela in a FIFA World Cup qualifier in April 1997.

5

SALAS

🌐 NATIONAL LEGEND
SALAS DAYS

Chile's third leading scorer **Marcelo Salas** formed a much-feared striking partnership with **Iván Zamorano** during the late 1990s and early 21st century. Salas scored four goals as Chile reached the round of 16 at the 1998 FIFA World Cup in France despite not winning a game. The striker spent two years in international retirement, from 2005 to 2007, but returned for the first four games of qualification for the 2010 FIFA World Cup. He scored twice in Chile's 2-2 draw with Uruguay on 18 November 2007, but his international career ended for good three days later, following a 3-0 defeat to Paraguay.

ZAMORANO

STAR PLAYER
MOTHER COUNTRY

One of Chile's latest striking stars was born in Stoke-on-Trent in England in April 1999 and known as Ben Brereton when helping his birth country win the 2017 UEFA European U-17 Championship, managing three goals to finish as the tournament's joint-top scorer. But he has a Chilean mother Andrea as well as an English father Martin and when fans of the computer game Football Manager noticed he was half-Chilean, they campaigned online for him to be called up by his mother's nation. After switching international allegiance, he adopted the name **Ben Brereton Díaz** and made his Chile debut at the 2021 *Copa América* in a 1–1 group-stage draw with Argentina. The 22-year-old scored in both of his first two games, and added three more in the 2022 FIFA World Cup qualifiers, but Chile missed out on the finals for the second time running.

BRERETON DÍAZ

48

Chile went precisely 48 years between victories at a FIFA World Cup, from a 1–0 third-place play-off success against Yugoslavia on 16 June 1962 to a first-round victory by the same scoreline over Honduras on 16 June 2010.

BEAUSEJOUR

1930
Chile forward Carlos Vidal – nicknamed "Little Fox" – was the first man to miss a penalty at a FIFA World Cup, seeing his spot kick saved by France goalkeeper Alex Thépot in 1930.

150

Both forward Alexis Sánchez and defender/midfielder Gary Medel made their 150th appearances for Chile in a November 2022 friendly against Qatar in Austrian capital Vienna, a 2–2 draw. Sánchez opened the scoring, reaching 50 international goals.

MOST APPEARANCES:

1	Gary Medel,	152
=	Alexis Sánchez,	152
3	Claudio Bravo,	144
4	Arturo Vidal,	137
5	Mauricio Isla,	136

STAR PLAYER
DEJU VU, BRAVO

You wait 90 years to win the *Copa América* for the first time – and then a second triumph comes around 12 months later. Just as in 2015, Chile beat Argentina in the final of the 2016 *Copa América* – this time in the USA, in the *Copa América Centenario* to mark the 100th anniversary of the tournament. Both finals ended goalless and went to a shoot-out, with Chile winning 4–1 on penalties in 2015 and 4–2 the following year. Goalkeeper and captain **Claudio Bravo** was named the tournament's best goalkeeper on both occasions – as he was again when Chile competed in their first FIFA Confederations Cup in Russia in 2017, yet this time they finished runners-up following a 1–0 defeat to Germany in the final. Bravo had been a shoot-out hero again in the semi-final, after another 0–0 draw, saving three Portugal spot kicks.

BRAVO

SCORING RECORD
BRAVO, BEAUSEJOUR

Chile's first goal at the 2010 FIFA World Cup in South Africa came from **Jean Beausejour** in a 1–0 win over Honduras. He then scored Chile's third in an opening-game 3–1 triumph over Australia in Brazil four years later, becoming the first Chilean player ever to score at more than one FIFA World Cup. In goal and captain at both tournaments was Claudio Bravo, Chile's most-capped goalkeeper of all time.

4

Eduardo Vargas scored four times as Chile matched their record win – and their biggest in a competitive match – by beating Mexico 7–0 in their June 2016 quarter-final at that summer's *Copa América Centenario*.

VARGAS

URUGUAY

Uruguay were the first country to win a FIFA World Cup, in 1930, and with a population of under four million, they remain the smallest to do so. They claimed the game's greatest prize for a second time in 1950.

Joined FIFA: 1916

Biggest win:
9–0 v. Peru, 1927

Highest FIFA ranking: 2nd

Home stadium: Estadio Centenario, Montevideo

Honours: 2 FIFA World Cups (1930, 1950), 15 *Copa Américas* (1916, 1917, 1920, 1923, 1924, 1926, 1935, 1942, 1956, 1959, 1967, 1983, 1987, 1995, 2011)

FORLÁN

32

Uruguay were the last of the 32 teams at the 2022 FIFA World Cup to find the net. Giorgian de Arrascaeta's brace beat Ghana 2–0 in their final Group H game, but Uruguay were knocked out after finishing third behind Korea Republic, who had the same points and goal difference but scored more goals.

YOUNGEST

Centre-back José Giménez became Uruguay's youngest player at a FIFA World Cup when he came on as a substitute against England aged 19 years and 149 days at the 2014 tournament in Brazil.

NATIONAL LEGEND
FORLÁN HERO

Uruguay achieved their best FIFA World Cup since 1970 when again finishing fourth in South Africa in 2010. Forward **Diego Forlán** took home the Golden Ball for best player and finished joint top scorer with five goals. He did better than his father Pablo, a member of the Uruguay squad knocked out in the first round in 1974. The following year Forlán not only became Uruguay's most-capped player, he also matched Héctor Scarone's 31 goals for the country – a record since 1930 – with two goals to help beat Paraguay 3–0 in the *Copa América* final. His grandfather, Juan Carlos Corazzo, had been head coach when Uruguay won the tournament in 1959.

NATIONAL LEGEND
CLASS APART

Óscar Tabárez, a former schoolteacher known as "The Maestro", led Uruguay to the second round of the 1990 FIFA World Cup and returned for a second spell in 2006, taking them back to the tournament in 2010 – and a fourth-place finish. When he took charge of his 168th Uruguay game in 2016, he passed West Germany's Sepp Herberger for the most matches coached for one team. Tabárez became the first international manager to oversee 200 matches when winger Brian Rodríguez gave Uruguay a 1–0 friendly win over Peru in Montevideo's Estadio Centenario in October 2019. He was dismissed in November 2001, having managed Uruguay for a total of 228 full internationals – 111 wins, 57 draws and 60 defeats.

TABÁREZ

228

When Oscar Tabárez was dismissed as Uruguay manager in November 2021 after poor results in 2022 FIFA World Cup qualifiers, his record across two spells in charge was 228 games, 111 wins, 57 draws and 60 defeats. Those comprised 34 matches between 1988 and 1990 and 194 from 2006 to 2021.

TOURNAMENT TRIVIA
DIFFERENT BALL GAME

Uruguay were the inaugural hosts – and the first winners – of the FIFA World Cup in 1930, having won football gold at the Olympics of 1924 in Paris and 1928 in Amsterdam. Uruguay beat arch-rivals Argentina 4-2 in the 1930 final, a game in which two different footballs were used – Argentina's choice in the first half, in which they led 2-1, before Uruguay's was used for their second-half comeback. Uruguay declined the chance to defend their title in 1934, refusing to travel to host country Italy in pique at only four European nations visiting in 1930.

17

No man has played more times for Uruguay at the FIFA World Cup than goalkeeper **Fernando Muslera**, with 17 appearances at the 2010, 2014, 2018 and 2022 tournaments. His tally was matched by striker Edinson Cavani at the 2022 finals, where Muslera remained on the bench. Muslera's two shoot-out saves had helped defeat Ghana in the 2010 quarter-finals.

MUSLERA

STAR PLAYER
BITE CLUB

Notoriety has cast many shadows over the career of **Luis Suárez**. He earned infamy with a deliberate goal-line handball in the last minute of extra time when Uruguay and Ghana were level in their 2010 FIFA World Cup quarter-final, celebrating wildly when Asamoah Gyan missed the penalty. Worse followed at the 2014 FIFA World Cup, when he bit into the shoulder of Italian defender Giorgio Chiellini, earning a four-month suspension from all football. His scoring instincts are much more admirable – his international goals total includes four during Uruguay's triumphant 2011 *Copa América*. Suárez scored the first goal of South America's 2022 FIFA World Cup qualifying campaign with a penalty in a 2-1 win over Chile in Montevideo in October 2020, having previously done similarly at the beginning of the 2010 and 2014 campaigns. Team-mate Martín Cáceres got the opening goal ahead of the 2018 finals.

STAR PLAYER
GET IN, GODÍN

Centre-back **Diego Godín** was the third man to reach win 100 caps for Uruguay, and he became their most-capped player in the final of the 2019 China Cup, as Uruguay beat Thailand 4-0. Godín has a knack for scoring crucial goals, especially three in May and June 2014. The first secured a first Spanish league title in 18 years for his club Atlético Madrid; he then gave them the lead in the UEFA Champions League final (although they lost 4-1 to Real Madrid); and he headed the late goal that beat Italy and secured Uruguay's place in the FIFA World Cup round of 16.

GODÍN

1901
Uruguay's 3-2 home defeat to neighbours Argentina, in Montevideo on 16 May 1901, was the first official international match outside the UK.

TOURNAMENT TRIVIA
HAPPY ANNIVERSARY

A so-called *Mundialito* or "Little World Cup", was staged in December 1980 and January 1981 to mark the 50th anniversary of the FIFA World Cup – and, as in 1930, Uruguay emerged triumphant. The tournament was meant to involve all six countries who had previously won the tournament, though 1966 champions England turned down the invitation and were replaced by 1978 runners-up the Netherlands. Uruguay beat Brazil 2-1 in the final, a repeat of the scoreline from the final match of the 1950 FIFA World Cup. The *Mundialito*-winning Uruguay side was captained by goalkeeper Rodolfo Rodríguez and coached by Roque Máspoli, who had played in goal in that 1950 final.

SUÁREZ

TOP SCORERS:

1	Luis Suárez,	68
2	Edinson Cavani,	58
3	Diego Forlán,	36
4	Héctor Scarone,	31
5	Ángel Romano,	28

SOUTH AMERICA: OTHER TEAMS

With only ten nations in South America, CONMEBOL is competitive. Though there are minnows who don't have the history or prowess of Brazil or Argentina, the rest of South America has still produced wonderful stories football over the years.

Country: Colombia
Joined FIFA: 1938
Most appearances: David Ospina, 127
Top scorer: Radamel Falcao, 36
Honours: 1 *Copa América* (2001)

Country: Peru
Joined FIFA: 1925
Most appearances: Roberto Palacios, 128
Top scorer: Paulo Guerrero, 38
Honours: 2 *Copa Américas* (1939, 1975)

Country: Bolivia
Joined FIFA: 1926
Most appearances: Ronald Raldes, 102
Top scorer: Marcelo Moreno / Marcelo Martins, 30
Honours: 1 *Copa América* (1963)

Country: Paraguay
Joined FIFA: 1925
Most appearances: Paulo da Silva, 148
Top scorer: Roque Santa Cruz, 32
Honours: 2 *Copa Américas* (1953, 1979)

Country: Ecuador
Joined FIFA: 1930
Most appearances: Iván Hurtado, 168
Top scorer: Enner Valencia, 38
Honours: -

Country: Venezuela
Joined FIFA: 1952
Most appearances: Juan Arango, 129
Top scorer: Salomón Rondon, 38
Honours: -

STAR PLAYER
HERO GUERRERO

Veteran playmaker **Paolo Guerrero** had to wait a very long time before he could lead Peru at the 2018 FIFA World Cup, their first appearance in the finals for 36 years. He scored in a 2-0 win over Australia, but Peru went out at the group stage. That goal was his record-extending 35th for Peru and it came 14 years after his debut. He achieved even more at the 2019 *Copa América*, when his three goals made him joint top scorer. Guerrero led Peru to the final, and scored, but his side ultimately lost 3-1 to Brazil.

35,742
The smallest national stadium in South America is the Estadio Olímpico Atahualpa, Quito, Ecuador, which holds 35,742.

DÍAZ

STAR PLAYER
HAPPY DÍAZ

Although Lionel Messi was awarded the Golden Boot at the 2019 *Copa América* due to providing more assists, Colombia's **Luis Díaz** also scored three goals as his side reached the semi-finals. Colombia lost to eventual champions Argentina 3-2 on penalties following a 1-1 draw, before securing third place with a 3-2 victory over Peru in the play-off. Díaz scored the last two goals against Peru, having earlier in the tournament hit a spectacular acrobatic volley opener against Brazil. Díaz began his career with Barranquilla and then Atlético Junior in his homeland, before securing moves to Portugal's Porto in July 2019 and then Liverpool in England during the January 2022 transfer window.

MARTINS

4

Bolivia's only win at *Copa América* came as hosts in 1963. They led Brazil 2-0 and 4-2 in their final match, only for Máximo Alcócer to clinch a 5-4 victory with just four minutes left.

CASTING CASTILLO ASPERSIONS

Ecuador qualified for the FIFA World Cup in 2022 for the first time in eight years by finishing fourth in CONMEBOL's ten-team qualifying system. They had been left sweating on their participation in Qatar when eliminated Peru and Chile launched legal appeals. Ecuador were accused of ineligibly fielding right-back Byron Castillo, with allegations the right-back was born in the Colombian city of Tumaco rather than Playas in Ecuador as claimed. FIFA and the Court of Arbitration for Sport ruled he could be deemed an Ecuadorian national, but they did dock Ecuador three points from their qualification campaign for the 2026 FIFA World Cup for false use of a document.

TEAM TRIVIA
MARCELO'S SOLACE

Bolivia finished ninth out of ten in South America's qualification process for the 2022 FIFA World Cup, with only Venezuela below them. Yet the overall leading scorer, with ten, was Bolivia's all-time top marksman, known as **Marcelo Martins** in Bolivia and Marcelo Moreno elsewhere. His ten goals were two more than his nearest challengers, Neymar of Brazil and Uruguay's Luis Suárez. He finished the qualifiers with 30 for his country in 96 internationals. He had actually played for Brazil's Under-18s, due to his Brazilian ex-footballer father Mauro Martins, but switched allegiance to the country of his birth. His early goals for Bolivia included the opener in a 6-1 thrashing of Argentina, in April 2009, in which strike partner Joaquín Botero scored a hat-trick.

44

Peru were coached at the 1982 FIFA World Cup by Tim, who had been waiting an unprecedented 44 years to return to the FIFA World Cup finals – after playing once as striker for his native Brazil in the 1938 tournament.

39
Seven-goal striker Juan Enrique García remains Venezuela's oldest international, aged 39 years and 51 days for his 49th and final appearance, a 1–0 FIFA World Cup qualifier victory away to Bolivia in June 2009.

TEAM TRIVIA
HIGH LIFE

Bolivia and Ecuador play their home internationals at higher altitudes than any other teams on earth. Bolivia's showpiece Estadio Hernando Siles stadium, in the capital La Paz, is 3,637 metres (11,932 feet) above sea level, while Ecuador's main Estadio Olímpico Atahualpa, in Quito, sits 2,800 metres (9,185 feet) above sea level. Opposing teams have complained that the rarefied nature of the air makes it difficult to breathe, let alone play, but a FIFA ban on playing competitive internationals at least 2,500 metres (8,200 feet) above sea level, first introduced in May 2007, was suspended entirely in May 2008.

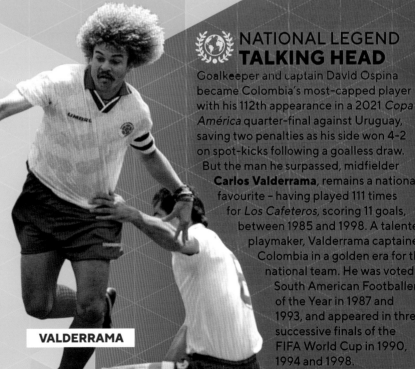

VALDERRAMA

NATIONAL LEGEND
TALKING HEAD

Goalkeeper and captain David Ospina became Colombia's most-capped player with his 112th appearance in a 2021 *Copa América* quarter-final against Uruguay, saving two penalties as his side won 4-2 on spot-kicks following a goalless draw. But the man he surpassed, midfielder **Carlos Valderrama**, remains a national favourite – having played 111 times for *Los Cafeteros*, scoring 11 goals, between 1985 and 1998. A talented playmaker, Valderrama captained Colombia in a golden era for the national team. He was voted South American Footballer of the Year in 1987 and 1993, and appeared in three successive finals of the FIFA World Cup in 1990, 1994 and 1998.

HURTADO

NATIONAL LEGEND
ABOVE-PAR PARAGUAY

Paraguay's two most-capped players, centre-back Paulo da Silva (148 appearances, first against Bolivia on 27 July 2000) and goalkeeper Justo Villar (120 caps, debut v. Guatemala, 3 March 1999) were mainstays in their country's most successful FIFA World Cup performance: topping their group in 2010 and reaching the quarter-finals, only losing to eventual champions Spain. Both were still in the side in October 2016, helping Paraguay win a FIFA World Cup qualifier in Argentina for the first time – thanks to a Derlis González strike.

SCORING RECORD
NOT SO FAB

Colombia full-back Frank Fabra endured a bittersweet *Copa América* first at the 2016 *Centenario* tournament when he scored for both teams in one match – no other player had done this in the competition's 100-year history. He found the net at both ends as his side lost 3-2 to Costa Rica in the first round, although Colombia did recover to qualify for the next stage and ultimately reached the semi-finals.

168

With 168 caps, **Iván Hurtado** of Ecuador is the most capped South American footballer of all time.

NATIONAL LEGEND
WINNING RON

Bolivia's most-capped player, centre-back Ronald Raldes, scored just his second-ever international goal against Ecuador at the 2015 Copa América, helping secure Bolivia's first victory in the tournament since 1997. Their failure to qualify for the 2022 FIFA World Cup means that 1930, 1950 and 1994 remain their only finals. The 2018 campaign did include back-to-back wins for the first time since 1998, including a surprise 2–0 victory over Argentina thanks in part to a goal from Marcelo Martins, who had gone ten internationals without scoring beforehand.

RONDÓN

BABY GOAL
Striker **Roque Santa Cruz** was known as "Baby Goal" on his international debut aged 17 in 1998. He has scored more for Paraguay than anyone else.

SANTA CRUZ

TEAM TRIVIA
GOING CARACAS FOR FOOTBALL

Venezuela is the only CONMEBOL nation not to qualify for a FIFA World Cup, yet it achieved a record high 25th position in the FIFA/Coca-Cola World Ranking in November 2019. After lavish investment in new stadiums, Venezuela staged its first *Copa América* in 2007 as captain and record cap-holder Juan Arango helped them through to the knockout stages for the first time. Much-travelled striker **Salomón Rondón** became Venezuela's first man to reach 30 goals for his country with a 26-minute hat-trick to win the 2019 Kirin Cup, beating Japan 4-1 in November 2019. Another treble, when beating Bolivia by the same scoreline in January 2022, was a rare highlight of Venezuela's failed 2022 FIFA World Cup qualification campaign.

SCORING RECORD
FALCAO FIGHTS BACK

Colombia captain and leading goalscorer **Radamel Falcao** made a remarkable recovery to play at the 2018 FIFA World Cup finals in Russia. Four years earlier, it had been feared a knee injury might bring his goal-hungry career to a premature end. In 2009, FC Porto bought Falcao for GBP 2m, and it proved a bargain as he led them to a 2011 treble of league, cup and UEFA Europa League. Following a move to Spain's Atlético Madrid, he repeated the Europa League triumph 12 months later. He then moved to AS Monaco, where he was top scorer in their 2016-17 Ligue 1 title win.

Colombia lost only two of the 32 matches in which star striker Radamel Falcao scored his 36 international goals by the end of 2022 – 2-1 to Venezuela in an August 2009 friendly and 2-1 to Paraguay in October 2017 in a FIFA World Cup qualifier.

FALCAO

Colourful Paraguayan goalkeeper José Luis Chilavert also liked to take free-kicks and scored 67 times in his career, including eight strikes for his country – an international record. Seven came in FIFA World Cup qualifiers between 1989 and 2001, with the other the opener in a 1-1 draw with Argentina at the 1997 *Copa América*.

TOURNAMENT TRIVIA
RUID AWAKENING

Peru ended a 31-year wait to beat Brazil with a 1-0 win in the first round of the 2016 *Copa América Centenario*. It put Ricardo Gareca's side in the quarter-finals and eliminated Dunga's Brazilians. The goal was contentious, however, as Raúl Ruidíaz seemed to knock the ball into the goal with his hand from Andy Polo's cross. Ruidíaz insisted he had used his thigh and denied comparisons to Diego Maradona's "Hand of God" goal at the 1986 FIFA World Cup, claiming his strike was "thanks to God". Peru's captain that day was the country's all-time leading scorer Paolo Guerrero, though at the time he was still a goal behind Jefferson Farfán's then-national record of 27.

VALENCIA

NATIONAL LEGEND
HIGHS AND LOWS FOR LOLO

Teodoro "Lolo" Fernández scored six goals in two games for Peru at the 1936 Summer Olympics, including five in a 7-3 defeat of Finland and another in a 4-2 victory over Austria, though the that match was ruled void. Peru withdrew from the tournament in protest, while Austria went on to claim silver. But Fernández and his team-mates had a happier ending at the *Copa América* three years later, with Peru crowned champions and Fernández finishing as top scorer with seven goals. Fernández hit 24 goals in 32 internationals, a Peru record that stood until being overtaken by Teófilo Cubillas's 26 from 81 between 1968 and 1982. The top ranking later passing to Jefferson Farfán, then Paolo Guerrero.

SCORING RECORD
ENNER VALUE

Ecuador's all-time leading goalscorer **Enner Valencia** has scored six of his country's last six seven goals at FIFA World Cups – three in 2014 and another three at the 2022 tournament in Qatar. These included two to beat the hosts in the tournament's opening game then the equaliser in a 1-1 draw against Netherlands. Portugal's Eusébio in 1966, Italy's Paolo Rossi in 1982 and Russia's Oleg Salenko in 1994 previously scored six FIFA World Cup goals in a row for their countries. Moises Caicedo pulled Ecuador level in their last Group A game against Senegal, but a 2-1 defeat saw them eliminated. Valencia's opener against Qatar was the first time the FIFA World Cup's first goal had come from a penalty.

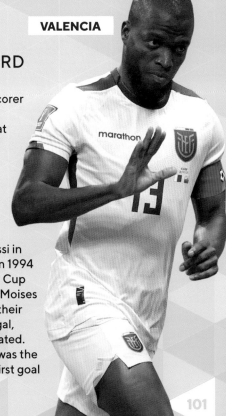

AFRICA

The African Football Confederation is one of the largest in the world game, with 54 FIFA member associations. It was created in the mid-1950s and launched the CAF Cup of Nations in 1957 as more and more nations demanded recognition on the international stage. South Africa was the continent's first World Cup host in 2010.

Founded: 1957

Number of associations: 54 (+1 non-FIFA member)

Headquarters: Cairo, Egypt

Most continental championship wins: Egypt, 7 (1957, 1959, 1986, 1998, 2006, 2008, 2010)

5

Africa is split into five regional confederations. Patrice Motsepe of South Africa is the first CAF president to come from within COSAFA.

UNAF (Southern Africa)

WAFU-UFOA (West Africa)

CECAFA (East Africa)

UNIFFAC (Central Africa)

COSAFA (Southern Africa)

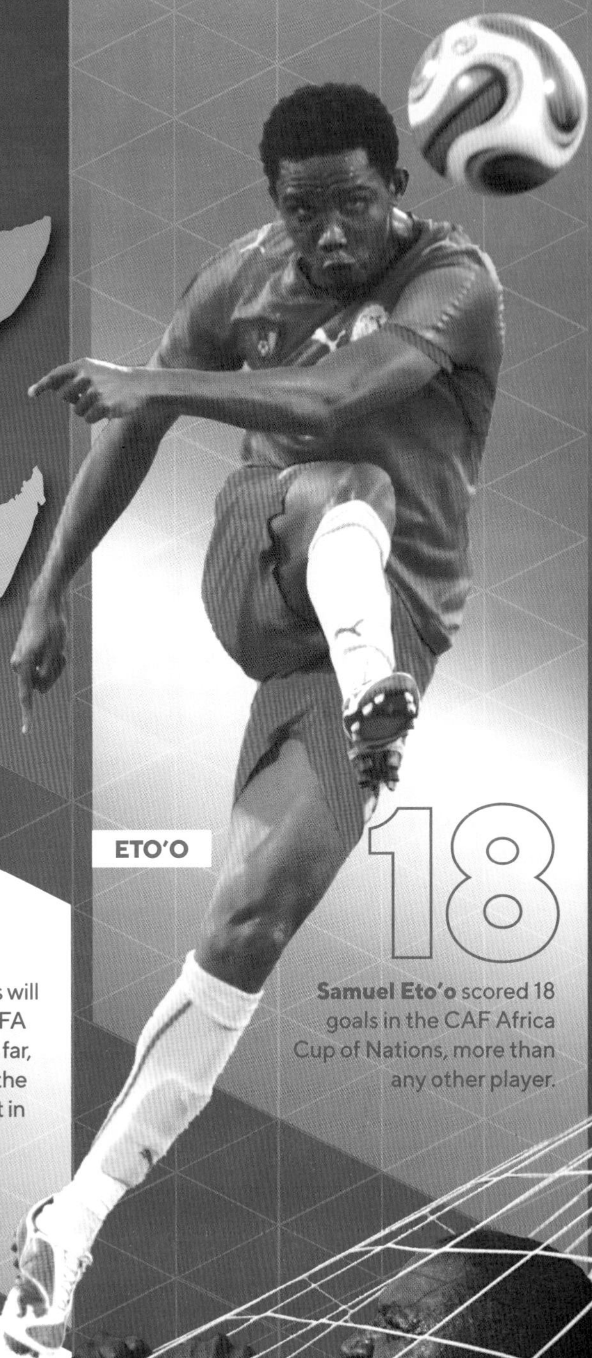

ETO'O

18

Samuel Eto'o scored 18 goals in the CAF Africa Cup of Nations, more than any other player.

9

A record nine African nations will compete at the expanded FIFA World Cup finals in 2026. So far, a best-ever six competed at the finals in their home continent in South Africa in 2010.

In Italy in 1990, Cameroon became the first African nation to reach the quarter-finals of the FIFA World Cup. They lost 3–2 in extra time to England in Naples.

2

Nigeria became the first African side to reach consecutive FIFA World Cup knockout stages – in 1994 and 1998.

NORTH AFRICA

The most successful regional zone within Africa, the north of the continent has produced the most successful CAF Africa Nations Cup side of all time, Egypt, along with the first African team to win a FIFA World Cup match, Tunisia.

Country: Algeria
Joined FIFA: 1964
Most appearances:
Lakhdar Belloumi, 100
Top scorer:
Islam Slimani, 41
Honours: 2 Africa Cup of Nations (1990, 2019)

Country: Egypt
Joined FIFA: 1923
Most appearances:
Ahmed Hassan, 184
Top scorer:
Hossam Hassan, 68
Honours: 7 Africa Cup of Nations (1957, 1959, 1986, 1998, 2006, 2008, 2010)

Country: Libya
Joined FIFA: 1964
Most appearances:
Muhammad Nashnoush, 72
= Ahmed Saad Osman, 72
Top scorer: Ali Al-Biski, 35
Honours: -

Country: Morocco
Joined FIFA: 1960
Most appearances:
Noureddine Naybet, 115
Top scorer:
Ahmed Faras, 36
Honours: 1 Africa Cup of Nations (1976)

Country: Sudan
Joined FIFA: 1948
Most appearances:
Haitham Mustafa, 111
Top scorer:
Nasr Eddin Abbas, 27
Honours: 1 Africa Cup of Nations (1970)

Country: Tunisia
Joined FIFA: 1960
Most appearances:
Radhi Jaïdi, 105
Top scorer:
Issam Jemâa, 36
Honours: 1 Africa Cup of Nations (2004)

TOURNAMENT TRIVIA
MOKHTAR RUNS AMOK

Egypt had to play only two matches to qualify for the 1934 FIFA World Cup, becoming the first African representatives at the tournament. Both qualifiers were against a Palestine side under the British mandate – and the Egyptians won both games handsomely, 7-1 in Cairo and 4-1 in Palestine. Captain and striker Mahmoud Mokhtar scored a hat-trick in the first leg, a brace in the second. Turkey were also meant to contest qualifiers against the two sides, but withdrew, leaving the path to the finals free for Egypt.

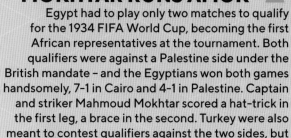

4

Four nations founded CAF, but South Africa were expelled before they could join on account of the apartheid regime, the other three competing in the first Africa Cup of Nations: Egypt, Ethiopia and Sudan.

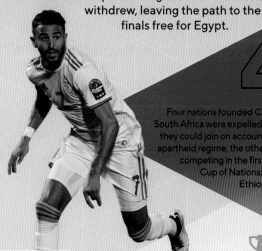

MAHREZ

TOURNAMENT TRIVIA
ALGERIA HYSTERIA

Playmaker **Riyad Mahrez** had been billed as the star of the show at the 2019 CAF Africa Cup of Nations, and was one of four Algerian players named in the team of the tournament. But striker Baghdad Bounedjah was the ultimate hero as his deflected long-range strike won the final against Senegal in Egypt. Manager and former Algeria international midfielder Djamel Belmadi had only taken charge the previous August. This was Algeria's second African championship, having previously won it in 1990, spearheaded by star striker Rabah Madjer. In 2016, Mahrez had become the first African footballer to be voted England's Footballer of the Year by his fellow professionals after helping underdogs Leicester City win the Premier League . He was named CAF Footballer of the Year that same year. But individual 2019 CAF Africa Cup of Nations prizes went to his international team-mates Ismaël Bennacer as best player and Raïs M'Bolhi as best goalkeeper.

STAR PLAYER
SALAH THE FOOTBALLING PHAROAH

Egypt winger **Mohamed Salah** has established himself as one of the world's outstanding players in recent years. Salah scored a hat-trick against Zimbabwe in the 2014 World Cup qualifiers before his goals for both Egypt and Swiss club Basel earned an GBP 11m transfer to Chelsea. Salah ended up at Liverpool in 2017 and was voted footballer of the year in 2018 by both the Football Writers' Association and Professional Footballers' Association; he suffered a shoulder injury early in Liverpool's defeat against Real Madrid in the UEFA Champions League final in 2018 but was on the scoresheet a year later when the Reds claimed the title against Tottenham Hotspur.

SALAH

TOURNAMENT TRIVIA
FIFTEEN LOVE

The 2021 Africa Cup of the Nations was Tunisia's 15th in a row, breaking Egypt's previous record of 14. A key player was forward Wahib Khazri, whose two goals in a 4–0 victory over Mauritania helped the Eagles Of Carthage through to the knock-out stages before they were lost 1–0 to Burkina Faso in the quarter-finals. Khazri's brace against Mauritania took him to 24 goals for his country. He had previously scored the winner against Panama at the 2018 FIFA World Cup, but both teams were eliminated at the group stage. Two months after losing to Burkina Faso, Tunisia clinched a place in their sixth FIFA World Cup by beating Mali 1–0 on aggregate in their play-off.

15
Sudan's 3–1 away win in Chad in September 2019 was their first in 15 FIFA World Cup qualifiers – following three draws and 11 defeats. Striker Ramad Agab hit their first-ever FIFA World Cup hat-trick.

5
Mohamed Salah's five goals in 2018 FIFA World Cup qualifiers helped take Egypt to the finals for the first time in 38 years. Sala scored both goals, including a crucial last-minute penalty, in a 2–1 win over Congo that took the Pharaohs through.

TOURNAMENT TRIVIA
MOROCCAN ROLL

At Mexico 1986, Morocco became the first African team to top a FIFA World Cup group, finishing above England, Poland and Portugal. At the 2022 tournament in Qatar, they became first African country to reach the semi-finals – knocking out Spain in the second round and Portugal in the quarter-finals along the way. Goalkeeper **Yassine Bounou** was the star against Spain, saving twice in the shoot-out following a goalless draw. This also made him the first African goalkeeper to keep three clean sheets in a single FIFA World Cup. He added another when Portugal were beaten 1–0 thanks to a header by Youssef En-Nesyri. France won their semi-final 2–0 and Croatia the third-place play-off 2–1, but Morocco returned home as heroes. They donated their tournament earnings to child poverty charities.

SCORING RECORD
NOT SO SLIM PICKINGS

Algeria striker **Islam Slimani** topped the individual goal charts in Africa's qualifying campaign for the 2022 FIFA World Cup, with eight. He also became his nation's all-time leading scorer, reaching 40 strikes in 80 appearances, surpassing previous record-holder Abdelhafid Tasfaout's 36. Slimani hit four in an 8–0 drubbing of Djibouti in September 2021, a brace when Niger were beaten 6–1 the following month, and the only goal away to Cameroon in the first leg of their final play-off. A 2–1 defeat at home in the second leg meant Algeria were denied a place in the Qatar tournament. Centre-back Rafik Alliche has played most games for Algeria at FIFA World Cups, with seven appearances.

SLIMANI

BOUNOU

JAÏDI

TOURNAMENT TRIVIA
IN TUNE FOR TUNISIA

Tunisia became the first African team to win a match at a FIFA World Cup finals when they beat Mexico 3-1 in Rosario, Argentina, in 1978, thanks to goals from Ali Kaabi, Néjib Ghommidh and Mokhtar Dhouib. They later reached three successive FIFA World Cups, in 1998, 2002 and 2006, while also winning their first – and so far only – CAF Africa Cup of Nations as hosts in 2004, thanks to a 2-1 final victory over Morocco. Among those featuring in all four of those tournaments was the country's most-capped player, 105-appearance centre-back **Radhi Jaïdi**, whose club career took him from Esperance in Tunisia to Bolton Wanderers, Birmingham City and Southampton in England.

4-2

Ethiopia's only Africa Cup of Nations triumph came as hosts in the third tournament in 1962, when only four teams competed. They only played two matches, winning both 4-2 – the semi-final against Tunisia and a final that went to extra-time against Egypt.

TOURNAMENT TRIVIA
LUCKY ESCAPE

Libya would probably still hold the record for the highest score by an African nation if not for the fact that their Arab Nations Cup match against Oman in April 1966 was abandoned after 80 minutes. They were leading 21-0 at the time. The biggest recorded victory for an African team was Sudan's 15-0 win over Muscat and Oman in 1965.

TOURNAMENT TRIVIA
SUDAN IMPACT

The first Africa Cup of Nations kicked off in Khartoum, Sudan, on 10 February 1957. Just three teams competed: Sudan, Ethiopia and Egypt. In 1970, Sudan became the last of the tournament's founders to win the trophy, thanks to Hasubu El-Sagheir's only goal of the final against Ghana. Sudan returned to the Africa Cup of Nations after nine years away for the 2021 tournament, held in early 2022 due to the pandemic, but were eliminated in the first round.

39

The first man to win the CAF Africa Cup of Nations both as a player and a manager was Egypt's Mahmoud Al-Gohary. He was top scorer in 1959's three-team tournament, thanks to a hat-trick when beating Ethiopia 4-0, and in charge 39 years later when his side beat South Africa 2-0 in the 2008 final in Burkina Faso.

STAR PLAYER
TOP CLASS HASSANS

Ahmed and Hossam Hassan share a surname as well as top billing when it comes to success and endurance for Egypt, though they are not related. **Ahmed Hassan** has been capped more than any other man in the world, retiring from international football in 2012 with 33 goals in 184 appearances. He bowed out in a March 12 friendly against Kenya, 17 years after his debut. Hossam Hassan previously held the Egyptian caps record with 170, and his 68 goals for his country remain unsurpassed. He was joined in the side by a Hassan who was related: Hossam's brother Ibrahim, a right-back, played 131 times for Egypt, including appearances at the 1990 FIFA World Cup.

AHMED HASSAN

TOURNAMENT TRIVIA
OFFICIAL INFLUENCE

The first African to referee a FIFA World Cup final was Morocco's Said Belqola, who controlled the 1998 climax in which hosts France beat Brazil 3-0. Perhaps his most notable moment was sending off France's Marcel Desailly in the 68th minute – brandishing only the third red card to be shown in a FIFA World Cup final. Belqola was 41 at the time. He sadly died from cancer just under four years later.

115

Morocco's most-capped player, centre-back and former captain Nourredine Naybet became the country's first man to reach a century of international appearances in a 1-1 draw with South Africa at the 2004 Africa Cup of Nations. He was booked in the final as his side lost 2-1 to Tunisia. His 115th and last cap came in a goalless draw against Libya at the following tournament in 2006. No other Moroccan has yet made it to 100 appearances.

1934
Abdelrahman Fawzi became the first African footballer to score at a FIFA World Cup when he pulled a goal back for Egypt against Hungary in the first round of the 1934 tournament.

EL HADARY

45

Egypt goalkeeper **Essam El-Hadary**, at 45 years and 161 days, became the oldest player in World Cup history when he played in a 2-1 defeat by Saudi Arabia in 2018.

TOURNAMENT TRIVIA
ABOUD AWAKENING

After the political upheaval in Libya in 2011, little was expected of the country's footballers at the 2012 Africa Cup of Nations. Yet they brought some joy to supporters with a surprise 2-1 victory over Senegal in their final first-round match – the first time Libya had ever won an Africa Cup of Nations match outside their own country. Their kit bore the new flag of the country's National Transitional Council. Among the star performers were Ihaab al Boussefi – scorer of both goals against Senegal – and goalkeeper and captain **Samir Aboud**, at 39 the oldest player in the tournament.

ABOUD

KHAZRI

NATIONAL LEGEND
SO FARAS, SO GOOD

Ahmed Faras not only heads Morocco's all-time scoring charts with 36 goals between 1965 and 1979, he was also the captain who lifted the country's only Africa Cup of Nations trophy in 1976. He was also named the tournament's best player after scoring three goals in six games. He had previously come on twice as a sub when Morocco made their FIFA World Cup finals debut in 1970, the first African representatives since 1934.

NATIONAL LEGEND
KHAZRI IF YOU CAN

Wahbi Khazri was born in Ajaccio in France, and played once for the France U-21s in 2012 before switching allegiance to Tunisia. Despite being knocked out in the first round, he ended his country's 2022 FIFA World Cup campaign in style by scoring a surprise late winner to beat the country of his birth. It was his third FIFA World Cup goal – he had also hit the winner for Tunisia in their final game at Russia 2018, a 2-1 victory over Panama. Khazri announced his international retirement after Tunisia's 2022 exit, ending his career on 25 goals from 74 caps. Only Issam Jemâa, with 36 strikes in 84 games between 2005 and 2014, has been more prolific for Tunisia.

SUB-SAHARAN AFRICA

From the *Super Eagles* to the Black Stars, and from *Bafana Bafana* to *Les Éléphants*, Sub-Saharan football has delivered some of the biggest African stars of all time, and also hosted the first African FIFA World Cup in South Africa in 2010.

Country: South Africa
Rejoined FIFA: 1992
Most appearances: Aaron Mokoena, 107
Top scorer: Benni McCarthy, 31
Honours: 1 Africa Cup of Nations (1996)

Country: Ghana
Joined FIFA: 1958
Most appearances: André Ayew, 113
Top scorer: Asamoah Gyan, 51
Honours: 4 CAF Africa Cup of Nations (1963, 1965, 1978, 1982)

Country: Cameroon
Joined FIFA: 1962
Most appearances: Rigobert Song, 137
Top scorer: Samuel Eto'o, 56
Honours: 5 Africa Cup of Nations (1984, 1988, 2000, 2002, 2017)

Country: Nigeria
Joined FIFA: 1960
Most appearances: Ahmed Musa, 107
Top scorer: Rashidi Yakini, 37
Honours: 3 CAF Africa Cup of Nations (1980, 1994, 2013)
1 Olympic Games (1996)

Country: Gabon
Joined FIFA: 1966
Most appearances: Didier Ovono, 112
Top scorer: Pierre-Emerick Aubameyang, 30
Honours: -

Country: Mali
Joined FIFA: 1964
Most appearances: Seydou Keita, 102
Top scorer: Seydou Keita, 25
Honours: -

Country: Senegal
Joined FIFA: 1964
Most appearances: Henri Camara/Idrissa Gueye, 99
Top scorer: Sadio Mané, 34
Honours: - 1 Africa Cup of Nations (2021)

Country: Liberia
Joined FIFA: 1964
Most appearances: Joe Nagbe, 77
Top scorer: George Weah, 18
Honours: -

Country: Zimbabwe
Joined FIFA: 1965
Most appearances: Peter Ndlovu, 81
Top scorer: Peter Ndlovu, 37
Honours: -

Country: Côte d'Ivoire
Joined FIFA: 1964
Most appearances: Didier Zokora, 123
Top scorer: Didier Drogba, 65

Honours: 2 CAF Africa Cup of Nations (1992, 2015)

Country: Zambia
Joined FIFA: 1964
Most appearances: Kennedy Mweene, 122
Top scorer: Godfrey Chitalu, 79
Honours: 1 CAF Africa Cup of Nations (2012)

Country: Togo
Joined FIFA: 1964
Most appearances: Emmanuel Adebayor, 85
Top scorer: Emmanuel Adebayor, 32
Honours: -

Country: Botswana
Joined FIFA: 1978
Most appearances: Joel Mogorosi, 92
Top scorer: Jerome Ramatlhakwane, 24
Honours: -

STAR PLAYER
FOUR-MIDABLE MUSA

Winger Ahmed Musa is Nigeria's leading scorer at FIFA World Cups. He scored twice when his side were beaten 3–2 by eventual runners-up Argentina in Brazil in 2014 before going out in the second round 2–0 to France, following previous departures at that stage in 1994 and 1998. He hit another brace to beat Iceland 2–0 at the 2018 tournament in Russia, but it was not enough to take his country into the knock-outs. Musa became Nigeria's most-capped player, overtaking goalkeeper Vincent Enyeama and defender Joseph Yobo, by making his 102nd appearance as a late substitute for Kelechi Iheanacho against Liberia in November 2021.

1985
The first African country to win an official FIFA tournament was Nigeria, when their Golden Eaglets beat West Germany in the final of the 1985 FIFA World U-16 Championship.

MANÉ

ASAMOAH THE MOST

Ghana's **Asamoah Gyan** has scored more FIFA World Cup goals than any other player representing an African nation. He took his tally to six with two strikes at the 2014 FIFA World Cup in Brazil, putting him one ahead of Cameroon's Roger Milla. He also became the first African to score at three separate FIFA World Cups. Gyan had the chance to make Ghana Africa's first FIFA World Cup semi-finalists, but hit the bar with a penalty in the last minute of extra-time in their 2010 quarter-final. Minutes later, he scored from the spot in a shoot-out but in vain, as Uruguay went on to win.

2010

The Boateng brothers made FIFA World Cup history by playing against each other at the 2010 finals in South Africa, Jerome as left-back for Germany in their 1-0 victory over the Ghana side of his elder half-brother Kevin-Prince.

GYAN

STAR PLAYER
MANÉ THE MAIN MAN

Lions of Teranga star man **Sadio Mané** missed a seventh-minute penalty in Senegal's 2021 CAF Africa Cup of Nations final against Egypt in February 2022, but struck the decisive fifth spot-kick in the shoot-out, following a goalless draw, to clinch the title for the first time for his country. The two teams went head-to-head again the following month in a final qualifier for the 2022 FIFA World Cup. Again it went to penalties, after a 1-1 draw on aggregate, and again Mané hit the winning spot-kick. There was disappointment for Mané on the eve of the tournament when he was forced to miss the finals with a leg injury picked up playing for Bayern Munich. Senegal reached the knock-out stages for the second time in three FIFA World Cup appearances. The "Lions of Teranga" then lost 3-0 to England.

NATIONAL LEGEND
GOING FOR A SONG

Cameroon legend Rigobert Song, his country's most-capped player with 137 appearances, has experienced mixed fortunes at FIFA World Cups. In 1994, he became the youngest man to be sent off at a FIFA World Cup (aged 17 years and 358 days against Brazil). Four years later, he became the first player to receive two FIFA World Cup red cards, an unwanted feat later matched by France's Zinedine Zidane. Song came up against Brazil again at the 2022 finals, and this time enjoyed a happier occasion despite having been knocked out already. Now Cameroon manager, he saw his side beat the favourites 1-0 in their final Group G game with a stoppage-time winner by captain Vincent Aboubakar. Song had taken the job in March 2022 when he oversaw a victory over Algeria in their two-leg play-off.

NATIONAL LEGEND
JOLLY ROGER

Cameroon striker **Roger Milla**, famous for dancing around corner flags after his goals, became the FIFA World Cup's oldest scorer against Russia in 1994 – aged 42 years and 39 days. Milla, born in Yaoundé on 20 May 1952, had retired from professional football for a year before Cameroon President Paul Biya persuaded him to join the 1990 FIFA World Cup squad. He finally ended his international career after the 1994 FIFA World Cup in the United States, finishing with 77 caps and 43 goals to his name.

MILLA

116

Zambians believe the world record for goals in a calendar year should belong to their own Godfrey Chitalu and not to Lionel Messi. In 2012, Messi scored 91 goals for Argentina and Barcelona, but the Zambian FA insists that Chitalu had scored 116 goals, apparently unnoticed abroad, in 1972.

15

Fifteen-year-old Samuel Kuffour became the youngest footballer to win an Olympic medal when Ghana took bronze at the 1992 Olympics in Barcelona – 27 days before his 16th birthday.

SHOCK NEWCOMERS COMOROS

Comoros not only qualified for their first CAF Africa Cup of Nations by making the 2021 tournament, delayed until January and February 2022, but caused a sensation when there before unfortunately bowing out. They knocked out heavyweights Ghana in the group-stages with a 3–2 win. The opening goal came from the country's all-time top scorer Ben Nabouhane before a brace by **Ahmed Mogni**, his first strikes for Comoros in his 18th international. Nabouhane had also scored the only goal to secure Comoros' first victory in a competitive international, against Botswana in 2016. Their 2021 ACN run ended in the round of 16, losing to hosts Cameroon 2–1. In that match, left-back Chaker Alhadhur had to play in goal due to Covid-19 regulations ruling out goalkeeper Ali Ahamada. Their most-capped player **Youssof M'Changama** had provided late hope with a free-kick goal from 30 yards.

MOGNI

M'CHANGAMA

NATIONAL LEGEND
THE FOURMOST

The only two African footballers to play at four FIFA World Cups – and the only three to be named in the squads for four – are all from Cameroon. Striker Samuel Eto'o became the latest in 2014, after also playing in 1998, 2002 and 2010. He emulated defender Rigobert Song, who was in the Cameroon squad in 1994, 1998, 2002 and 2010. Goalkeeper Jacques Songo'o was named in the country's squads for the four FIFA World Cups between 1990 and 2002, but he only actually played in the 1994 and 1998 versions.

1996

Apartheid-era South Africa spent 32 years suspended by world governing body FIFA. South Africa returned in 1992 with a 1–0 victory over Cameroon. Four years later, they lifted the CAF Africa Cup of Nations as hosts, beating Tunisia 2–0 in the final.

1992
Zimbabwe's leading scorer Peter Ndlovu was the first African footballer to appear in the English Premier League when he appeared for Coventry City in August 1992.

NATIONAL LEGEND
SUPER FRED

In 2007, Frédéric Kanouté became the first non-African-born player to be named African Footballer of the Year. The striker was born in Lyon, France, and played for France U-21s. But the son of a French mother and Malian father opted to play for Mali in 2004, scoring 23 goals in 37 appearances before retiring from international football after the 2010 CAF Africa Cup of Nations. As well as going down in history as one of Mali's greatest ever players, he is also a hero to fans of Spanish side Sevilla FC, for whom he scored 143 goals, winning two UEFA Cups along the way. Only three men have scored more goals for the club.

NATIONAL LEGEND
PRESIDENT GEORGE

George Weah made history in December 2017 when he became the first former African footballer to become president of his country. In Liberia's first democratic handover in decades, Weah succeeded Ellen Johnson Sirleaf, Africa's first elected female president. Weah, raised in a slum in the capital Monrovia, is the only former FIFA World Player of the Year whose country has never qualified for the World Cup finals. He starred in attack for Monaco, Paris Saint-Germain and AC Milan, played for Chelsea and Manchester City, and dipped into his own earnings to help pay for his national team's travel costs and kit.

WEAH

NATIONAL LEGEND
FIRST ADE

Togo's all-time leading goalscorer – and 2008 African Footballer of the Year – **Emmanuel Adebayor** was captain during the country's only FIFA World Cup finals appearance, in Germany in 2006. They failed to win a game, but Adebayor's European club career was more successful, with stints in France with FC Metz and AS Monaco, in Spain with Real Madrid, in England with Arsenal, Manchester City, Tottenham Hotspur and Crystal Palace, and in Turkey with İstanbul Başakşehir and Kayserispor.

22

In 2022, Ghana attacker Mohammed Kudus became the second-youngest African man to hit a brace in a FIFA World Cup match, aged 22 years, 118 days. His goals helped beat Korea Republic 3-2. The only younger double hero was Ahmed Musa, aged 21 years, 254 days, when scoring for Nigeria against Argentina eight years earlier.

8

Vincent Aboubakar's eight goals for hosts Cameroon at the 2021 CAF Africa Cup Nations was the highest individual tally since Zaire/DR Congo's Ndaye Mulamba hit nine in 1974. Côte d'Ivoire's Laurent Pokou is the only other man to score eight at a single tournament, in 1970.

DISCIPLINARY-RELATED
HISTORY LESSON

Senegal made FIFA World Cup history in 2018 as the first country to be eliminated on yellow cards. *The Lions of Teranga* and Japan finished their group on four points apiece, but the tiebreaker came down to a new fair play regulation. They drew their match 2-2 and finished with the same points, the same goal difference and the same number goals scored, but Senegal "lost" 6-5 on bookings so Japan went into the second round, and Senegal went home.

NATIONAL LEGEND
LUCKY BENNI

South Africa's all-time leading scorer **Benni McCarthy** was also the first man to find the net for them in the FIFA World Cup finals. This was an equaliser in a 1-1 draw with Denmark in their second match of the 1998 tournament in France, following a 3-0 defeat to the hosts. McCarthy scored 31 goals in 79 internationals after making his debut against the Netherlands in 1997, two more than Shaun Bartlett. Unfortunately fitness concerns cost him the opportunity to play for the hosts at the 2010 FIFA World Cup finals.

MCCARTHY

NATIONAL LEGENDS
AYEW AND AYEW AND AYEW

The three Ayew brothers who have played for Ghana in recent years have impressive footballing pedigree. Their father, Abedi Pele, ranks as one of his country's greats. He appeared at more CAF Africa Cup of Nations than any other player (nine) and lifted the trophy in 1982. **André Ayew**, now Ghana's most-capped player, missed their 2022 FIFA World Cup away-goals victory over Nigeria in March 2022, which secured their place at the tournament, through suspension. But he captained Ghana in Qatar and scored their first goal in a 3-2 defeat to Portugal. Younger brother Jordan Ayew played at the 2014 and 2022 FIFA World Cups, while older brother Ibrahim was part of the squad alongside André in 2010.

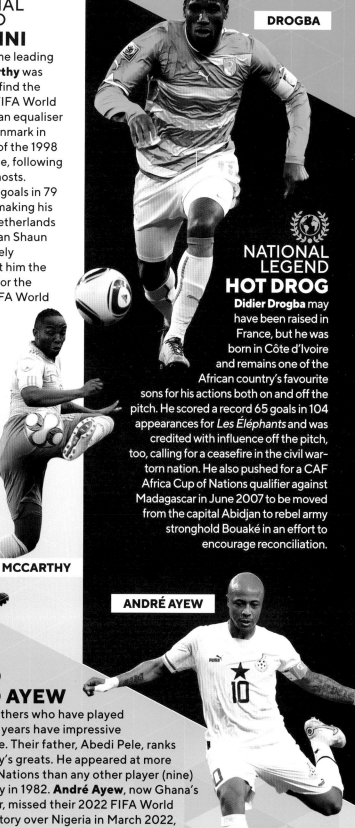

DROGBA

NATIONAL LEGEND
HOT DROG

Didier Drogba may have been raised in France, but he was born in Côte d'Ivoire and remains one of the African country's favourite sons for his actions both on and off the pitch. He scored a record 65 goals in 104 appearances for *Les Éléphants* and was credited with influence off the pitch, too, calling for a ceasefire in the civil war-torn nation. He also pushed for a CAF Africa Cup of Nations qualifier against Madagascar in June 2007 to be moved from the capital Abidjan to rebel army stronghold Bouaké in an effort to encourage reconciliation.

ANDRÉ AYEW

111

ASIA & OCEANIA

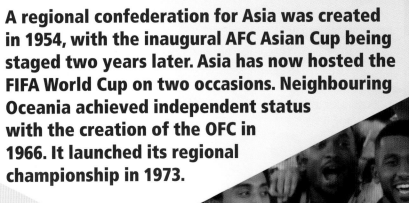

A regional confederation for Asia was created in 1954, with the inaugural AFC Asian Cup being staged two years later. Asia has now hosted the FIFA World Cup on two occasions. Neighbouring Oceania achieved independent status with the creation of the OFC in 1966. It launched its regional championship in 1973.

AFC

Confederation founded: 1954

Number of associations:
46 (+1 non-FIFA member)

Headquarters: Bukit Jalil, Kuala Lumpur, Malaysia

Most continental championship wins: Japan, 4

OFC

Confederation founded: 1966

Number of associations:
11 (+9 non-FIFA members)

Headquarters: Auckland, New Zealand

Most continental championship wins:
New Zealand, 5

88

Indian fans displayed their ever-growing enthusiasm for football with their huge support for the country's staging of the FIFA U-17 World Cup in 2017.

The FIFA World Cup 2022 in **Qatar** will be the first World Cup since Italy 1934, 88 years ago, in which the host nation will make their tournament debut.

DAEI

10

To mark the 60th anniversary of its foundation in 2014, the AFC created a Hall of Fame for Asian players, inducting ten players to begin with, including **Ali Daei** (IR Iran), **Harry Kewell** (Australia) and Yasuhiko Okudera (Japan).

KEWELL

1964

Israel won the Asian Cup in 1964, but they were expelled from the AFC ten years later before becoming a full member of UEFA in 1984.

12

The Asian Football Confederation was founded by 12 members in 1954 but has since grown to 47, although the Northern Mariana Islands are not a FIFA member.

AUSTRALIA

KUOL

Driven by new generations of players, many starring for top European clubs, Australia have become regular FIFA World Cup qualifiers. In 2015, they hosted and lifted the AFC Asian Cup for the first time.

Joined FIFA: 1922

Biggest win:
31–0 v. American Samoa, 2001

Highest FIFA ranking: 14th

Home stadium:
Stadium Australia, Sydney

Major honours:
4 OFC Nations Cups (1980, 1996, 2000, 2004), 1 AFC Asian Cup (2015)

🏆 TOURNAMENT TRIVIA
BACK-TO-BACK

In Qatar in 2022, Australia won their first FIFA World Cup match since 2010 then added another victory to secure a place in the knock-out stages for only the second time. Craig Goodwin gave them an early lead against holders France in a 4–1 defeat but they bounced back with 1–0 victories over Tunisia and Denmark, thanks to Mitchell Duke and then Mathew Leckie. **Garang Kuol** became Australia's youngest player at a FIFA World Cup as a sub against France, aged 18 years 68 days. He almost scored a late equaliser in their Round of 16 2–1 defeat to eventual champions Argentina. He is the second youngest player to feature in the World Cup knock-out stages after Brazil's Pelé in Sweden in 1958.

STAR PLAYER
A MILE AHEAD

Australia captain **Mile Jedinak** has scored his country's last three FIFA World Cup goals – all from the penalty spot. He found the net in their 3–2 defeat to the Netherlands in 2014, then four years later scored in a 2–1 defeat to France and a 1–1 draw with Denmark as Australia bowed out in the first round. Midfielder Jedinak had also scored a hat-trick to secure Australia's place in Russia – including two penalties – as the *Socceroos* saw off Honduras 3–1 on aggregate in their November 2017 play-off following a goalless first leg.

WILLIAMS

🌐 NATIONAL LEGEND
HERO HARRY

Harry Williams holds a proud place in Australian football history as the first Aboriginal player to represent the country in internationals. He made his debut in 1970 and was part of the first Australian squad to compete at a FIFA World Cup finals, in West Germany in 1974. Despite holding Chile to draw, the Australians finished bottom of their group, losing to both East Germany and eventual champions West Germany.

3

Ahead of the 2022 finals, former Australia captain Mile Jedinak had scored his country's past three FIFA World Cup goals – against the Netherlands in 2014 and against France and Denmark in 2018, all from the penalty spot.

CAHILL

NATIONAL LEGEND
CAHILL MAKES HISTORY

Tim Cahill scored Australia's first two FIFA World Cup goals, netting in the 84th and 89th minutes of a comeback 3-1 win over Japan in 2006, but he saved the most spectacular for last, a first-time volley in a 3-2 defeat to the Netherlands in 2014. Cahill also received his second yellow card of the competition later in that game and so missed Australia's final match. He scored twice in 2006, once in 2010 – when he was also red-carded – and twice in 2014. He retired from international football in November 2018, having won 108 caps and scored 50 goals – more than half of them (26) with his head.

29

Damian Mori's then-Australian record tally of 29 goals, in just 45 internationals, included no fewer than five hat-tricks: trebles against Fiji and Tahiti, four-goal hauls against the Cook Islands and Tonga, and five in Australia's 13-0 rout of the Solomon Islands in a 1998 FIFA World Cup qualifier.

SCORING RECORD
AUSSIES ON THE SPOT

Australia became the first team to reach a FIFA World Cup on penalties – and, 16-and-a-half years later, the second. The country's most-capped player, goalkeeper Mark Schwarzer made to crucial saves as Uruguay were beaten 4-2 in a Sydney shoot-out after a two-legged play-off against Uruguay ended 1-1 on aggregate. In June 2022, a one-off play-off against Peru in Qatar remained goalless after extra-time. The hero proved not to be first-choice goalkeeper Maty Ryan but instead penalty-saving Andrew Redmayne, who was substituted on in the closing moments for only his third international appearance. He danced along the line as each Peru player stepped up and his efforts paid off. Redmayne palmed away a crucial kick from Alex Valera to give Australia a 5-4 win and a place at the finals for the fifth time running.

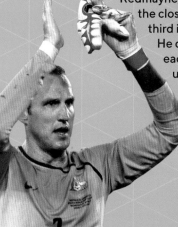

3.69

Damian Mori never played at a FIFA World Cup but he did claim a world record for scoring the fastest recorded goal ever – after just 3.69 seconds for his club side Adelaide City against Sydney United in 1996.

61

Peter Wilson and Lucas Neill jointly hold the record for most appearances as Australia captain – 61. Tough-tackling defender Neill had to wait until his 91st cap for his first international goal, completing a 4-0 win against Jordan in June 2013.

1000

In March 2015, Mile Jedinak scored Australia's 1,000th international goal, a stunning free kick in a 2-2 friendly draw against world champions Germany.

SCHWARZER

3

Josip Simunić, in 2006, was not the first player at a FIFA World Cup to receive three yellow cards in one game. The same had happened in an earlier game involving Australia, when their English-born midfielder Ray Richards was belatedly sent off against Chile at the 1974 FIFA World Cup.

SCORING RECORD
ARCHIE COSMIC

On 9 April 2001, Australia set an international record by beating Tonga 22-0 in a 2002 FIFA World Cup qualifier, but they went even better two days later by trouncing American Samoa 31-0. This included an unprecedented 13 goals from striker **Archie Thompson**, while team-mate David Zdrilic found the net "only" eight times. Both outscored the previous international record-holder, Iran's seven-goal Karim Bagheri. Thompson's debut goal against Tonga and his 13 in his next appearance meant he scored as many goals in his first two appearances (14) as he managed in his subsequent 51 games for his country.

THOMPSON

JAPAN

Japan co-hosted the FIFA World Cup in 2002 when the team reached the second round for the first time. AFC Asian Cup wins in 1992, 2000, 2004 and 2011 were all celebrated keenly as proof of surging standards.

Joined FIFA: 1950
Biggest win:
15–0 v. Phillippines, 1967
Highest FIFA ranking: 9th
Home stadium:
rotation
Major honours:
4 AFC Asian Cups (1992, 2000, 2004, 2011)

50
Shinji Okazaki's 50 goals for his country include hat-tricks in consecutive matches, against Hong Kong and Togo in October 2009.

NATIONAL LEGEND
HONDA INSPIRES

Skilful midfielder **Keisuke Honda** is Japan's top scorer at the FIFA World Cup – with four goals – and the only Japanese player to have found the net at three final competitions. It all started at South Africa in 2010 when he scored in Japan's victories over Cameroon and Denmark, and continued with a goal in the defeat against Costa Rica in Brazil four years later. Honda won two man-of-the-match awards at the 2010 FIFA World Cup and was named player of the tournament when Japan won the 2011 AFC Asian Cup. After Japan had exited the 2018 tournament – after he had scored against Senegal – Honda retired from international football.

HONDA

STAR PLAYER
TO DARE IS TO DŌ

Déjà vu reigned for Japan's super-sub winger **Ritsu Dōan** at the 2022 FIFA World Cup. The PSV Eindhoven player came off the bench when 1–0 down in their opening Group E game against Germany and hit a swift equaliser. Later, Takuma Asano hit a shock winner for Japan. After a 1–0 defeat to Costa Rica, Dōan emerged as a sub again to level against Spain ahead of Ao Tanaka's VAR-given strike to secure their side's place in the next round. Japan were only the third team in FIFA World Cup history to win twice at one tournament when losing at half-time. The victory over Germany was all the sweeter since eight players in the squad were signed to German clubs, against just seven with Japanese sides. Their adventure ended with a 3-1 defeat on penalties following a 1–1 draw with Croatia.

DŌAN

MOST APPEARANCES:

1 **Yasuhito Endō**, 152
2 **Yuto Nagatomo**, 142
3 **Maya Yoshida**, 126
4 **Masami Ihara**, 122
5 **Shinji Okazaki**, 119

After making his international debut in the 2011 AFC Asian Cup group-stage match against Jordan, striker Tadanari Lee could not have picked a better time to score his first goal for his country, finding the back of the net with just 11 minutes of extra time left in the final against Australia.

TOURNAMENT TRIVIA
POLITICAL FOOTBALL

Japan were surprise bronze medallists at the 1968 Olympic Football Tournament in Mexico City, with Star striker Kunishige Kamamoto finishing as top scorer with seven goals. He remains Japan's all-time top marksman with 75 goals in 76 games (Japan consider Olympic Games matches to be full internationals). Since retirement, he has combined coaching with being elected to Japan's parliament and serving as vice-president of the country's football association.

39

First-choice in goal at the 2010, 2014 and 2018 FIFA World Cups, Eiji Kawashima became Japan's oldest international in a 2022 FIFA World Cup qualifier against Vietnam in March 2022, a 1–1 draw. His 94th cap came nine days after his 39th birthday.

TOP SCORERS:

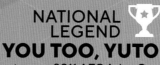

1 **Kunishige Kamamoto**, 75
2 **Kazuyoshi Miura**, 55
3 **Shinji Okazaki**, 50
4 **Hiromi Hara**, 37
= **Keisuke Honda**, 37

NATIONAL LEGEND
YOU TOO, YUTO

Full-back Yuto Nagatomo, a 2011 AFC Asian Cup winner and later captain of Italian giants Internazionale, skippered Japan when he became the seventh man to win 100 Samurai Blue caps in a 3–1 friendly defeat to Brazil in November 2017. Two years later, he equalled the 122 appearances of Masami Ihara – Japan's captain for their first AFC Asian Cup triumph in 1992 – when Japan beat Kyrgyzstan 2–0. A month earlier, Nagatomo had scored his fifth international goal, but his first for ten years, in a 6–0 victory over Mongolia. In 2022, Nagatomo became the first Japanese man to play at four different FIFA World Cups, taking his total appearances there to 15 – ahead of Makoto Hasebe and Eiji Kawashima (both 11).

KAMAMOTO

8

No man has scored more hat-tricks for Japan than **Kunishige Kamamoto** with eight, including six goals in his country's biggest win – 15–0 against the Philippines in Tokyo in September 1967. Kazuyoshi Miura has since matched his six in a game, in a 10–0 victory over Macau in June 1997.

ENDŌ

NATIONAL LEGEND
THE ENDŌ

Midfielder **Yasuhito Endō** scored the opening goal of Japan's defence of their AFC Asian Cup crown in 2015 as they began their campaign with a 4–0 win over debutants Palestine. However, after winning their three group matches without conceding a goal, Japan promptly lost in the quarter-finals to the United Arab Emirates, bowing out on penalties after a 1–1 draw. It was their worst showing at the AFC Asian Cup for 19 years. Endo had the consolation of becoming the first Japanese player to win 150 caps, but he left the international stage after the finals, having scored 15 times in 152 games.

21

No team has ever scored more goals in one AFC Asian Cup tournament than Japan's 21 in six matches in Lebanon in 2000. Nine different players scored, with Akinori Nishizawa and Naohiro Takahara bagging five apiece, including hat-tricks in an 8–1 first-round win over Uzbekistan. A single goal by Shigeyoshi Mochizuki was enough to settle the final against Saudi Arabia.

2018

Japan's fans and players impressed many at the 2018 FIFA World Cup with their displays – and their manners. Japanese fans were filmed meticulously tidying up after themselves in the stands at full time of their games, and the support staff took a similar approach to their dressing rooms, even after seeing a 2–0 lead slip away in their 3–2 defeat by Belgium in the round of 16.

NATIONAL LEGEND
KEN CAN DO

Japan's longest-serving manager had previously served his country as a player and later as president of the Japanese Football Association. Ken Naganuma won four caps as a forward between 1954 and 1961. He took charge in two spells between 1962 and 1969, then 1972 and 1976, including leading his nation to bronze at the 1968 Summer Olympics. He was JFA president from 1995 to 1998. He took charge a total of 73 games, ahead of Brazilian legend Zico's 71 from 2002 to 2006 – though Zico recorded three more victories in his time.

KOREA REPUBLIC

"Be the Reds!" was the rallying cry of Korea Republic's fervent fans during their country's co-hosting of the 2002 FIFA World Cup – and they saw their energetic team become the first Asian side to reach the semi-finals, ultimately finishing fourth.

Joined FIFA: 1948

Biggest win:
v. Nepal, 16-0, 2003

Highest FIFA ranking: 17th

Home stadium: Seoul World Cup Stadium

Major honours: 2 AFC Asian Cups (1956, 1960)

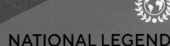

NATIONAL LEGEND
HONG SETS FIFA WORLD CUP RECORD

Defender **Hong Myung-bo** captained Korea Republic to fourth place in the 2002 FIFA World Cup on home soil and was voted third-best player of the tournament to boot. Ten years later, as coach of the U-23 squad, Hong led his side to Olympic bronze at the 2012 Summer Games after a 2-0 victory over Japan in the bronze medal match. Hong became Korea Republic's national team coach in June 2013, and he was still in charge at the 2014 FIFA World Cup, where one group game pitted him against Belgium and their coach Marc Wilmots – the pair having played against each other at the 1998 finals.

HONG

29
Korea Republic's goalless draw in Pyongyang in October 2019, in a 2022 FIFA World Cup qualifier, was their first international in neighbouring North Korea for 29 years.

56
Since the FIFA/Coca-Cola World Ranking was introduced in 1992, no top-ranked team had ever lost to a country as many as 56 places below them until defending champions Germany were beaten 2-0 by Korea Republic at the 2018 FIFA World Cup.

4
Korea Republic defender Hong Myung-bo was the first Asian footballer to appear in four consecutive FIFA World Cup finals tournaments, from 1990 to 2002.

NATIONAL LEGEND
"RUINED" BY AHN

Ahn Jung-hwan went from villain to hero at the 2002 FIFA World Cup during co-host Korea Republic's second-round victory over Italy. The striker missed a penalty then scored a golden-goal header to eliminate the Italians. As a result, Serie A club Perugia's owner Luciano Gaucci informed him that his loan contract would be torn up for having "ruined Italian football". Ahn shares the Korea Republic record for FIFA World Cup goals – three – with Son Heung-min and Park Ji-sung. Park became the first Asian player to claim a UEFA Champions League winner's medal when Manchester United beat Chelsea in 2008.

AHN

TOP SCORERS:

1 Cha Bum-kun, 58
2 Hwang Sun-hong, 50
3 Park Lee-chun, 36
4 Son Heung-min, 35
5 Kim Jae-han, 33
= Lee Dong-gook, 33

STAR PLAYER
HERE COMES THE SON

At the 2018 FIFA World Cup, Korea Republic's latest hero **Son Heung-min** scored his side's consolation goal in a 2-1 defeat by Mexico, and he later sealed their 2-0 win over Germany, just three minutes after Kim Young-gwon's injury-time opener, Son tapping the ball into an empty net after German goalkeeper Manuel Neuer was left stranded at the other end of the pitch. That lifted Son to 23 goals in 70 internationals and put him level with Park Ji-sung and Ahn Jung-hwan on three FIFA World Cup goals for his country. National icon Son captained his country at the 2022 FIFA World Cup wearing a face mask after fracturing his eye socket shortly before the tournament while playing for English club Tottenham Hotspur in the UEFA Champions League.

SON

7

Korea Republic captain Son Heung-min won FIFA's Puskás Award for "most beautiful" goal of the year in 2020, for a solo run from his own penalty area past seven opponents before finishing at the other end for Tottenham Hotspur at home to English Premier League rivals Burnley in December 2019.

NATIONAL LEGEND
CHA BOOM AND BUST

Even before Korea Republic made their FIFA World Cup breakthrough under Guus Hiddink in 2002, the country had a homegrown hero of world renown – thunderous striker **Cha Bum-kun**, known for his fierce shots and suitable nickname "Cha Boom". He helped pave the way for more Asian players to make their name in Europe by signing for German club Eintracht Frankfurt in 1979 and later played for *Bundesliga* rivals Bayer Leverkusen. His achievements in Germany included two UEFA Cup triumphs – with Frankfurt in 1980 and with Leverkusen eight years later – while his performances helped make him a childhood idol for future German internationals such as Jürgen Klinsmann and Michael Ballack.

NATIONAL LEGEND
SPIDER CATCHER

Goalkeeper Lee Woon-jae – nicknamed "Spider Hands" – made himself a national hero by making the crucial penalty save that took co-hosts Korea Republic into the semi-finals of the 2002 FIFA World Cup. He blocked Spain's fourth spot kick, taken by winger Joaquin, in a quarter-final shoot-out. Lee, who also played in the 1994, 2006 and 2010 FIFA World Cups, pulled off more penalty saves at the 2007 AFC Asian Cup – stopping three spot kicks in shoot-outs on his side's march to third place. Lee's form restricted his frequent back-up, Kim Byung-ji, to just 62 international appearances.

TOURNAMENT TRIVIA
COUNT ON KOREA

No Asian country has qualified for the FIFA World Cup as often as Korea Republic. Their first appearance at the finals in 1954 ended swiftly and brutally with a 9-0 defeat to eventual runners-up Hungary and a 7-0 loss to Turkey. After returning in 1986, they have taken part in every tournament since. Qatar 2022 was their tenth appearance in a row, and they reached the knock-out stages for the third time, after 2002 and 2010. **Cho Gue-Sung** became the first Korea Republic player to score more than once in a FIFA World Cup game, with both his country's goals in a 2-1 Group H victory over Ghana, also making him the first Asian player to score twice with his head in a FIFA World Cup match. A stoppage-time strike by Hwang Hee-chan then beat group leaders Portugal 2-1 to clinch a place in the next round, where they lost 4-1 to Brazil.

CHO

MOST APPEARANCES:

1	Hong Myung-bo,	136
	= Cha Bum-kun,	136
3	Lee Woon-jae,	133
4	Lee Young-pyo,	127
5	Kim Ho-kon,	124
	= Yoo Sang-chul,	124

CHA

5

Right-back Park Jin-sub was not a regular goalscorer, netting just five times in 35 appearances for his country. Amazingly, however, all of them came in the same game, Korea Republic's record 16-0 victory over Nepal in an AFC Asian Cup qualifier in September 2003.

ASIA : SELECTED : TEAMS

IR Iran won all 13 matches across their hat-trick of AFC Asian Cup triumphs in 1968, 1972 and 1976.

13

Though many of Asia's other nations have had limited footballing success on the world stage, their achievements in and passion and for the game are no less vibrant or impressive.

Country: Iraq
Joined FIFA: 1950
Most appearances: Younis Mahmoud, 148
Top scorer: Hussein Saeed, 78
Major honours: 1 AFC Asian Cup (2007)

Country: China PR
Joined FIFA: 1931
Most appearances: Li Weifeng, 112
Top scorer: Hao Haidong, 41
Major honours: -

Country: Qatar
Joined FIFA: 1970
Most appearances: Hassan Al-Haydos, 172
Top scorer: Mansoor Muftah/ Almeoz Ali, 42
Major honours: 1 AFC Asian Cup (2019)

Country: Saudi Arabia
Joined FIFA: 1956
Most appearances: Mohamed Al-Deayea, 178
Top scorer: Majed Abdullah, 72
Major honours: 3 AFC Asian Cups (1984, 1988, 1996)

Country: IR Iran
Joined FIFA: 1948
Most appearances: Javad Nekounam, 151
Top scorer: Ali Daei, 109
Major honours: 3 AFC Asian Cups (1968, 1972, 1976)

Country: Uzbekistan
Joined FIFA: 1994
Most appearances: Server Djeparov, 128
Top scorer: Maksim Shatskikh, 34
Major honours: -

Country: Syria
Joined FIFA: 1937
Most appearances: Maher Al-Sayed, 109
Top scorer: Firas Al Khatib, 36
Major honours: -

TOURNAMENT TRIVIA
IRAQ AND ROLL

One of the greatest – and most heart-warming – surprises in international football in recent years was Iraq's unexpected triumph at the AFC Asian Cup in 2007, barely a year after the end of the war that had ravaged the country and forced them to play "home" games elsewhere. Despite disrupted preparations, they eliminated Vietnam and Korea Republic en route to the 2007 final in which captain Younis Mahmoud's goal proved decisive against Saudi Arabia. They were unable to retain their title four years later, losing to Australia in the quarter-finals.

AL-HAYDOS

TOURNAMENT TRIVIA
QATAR STARS

Qatar, the 2022 FIFA World Cup hosts, were crowned continental champions for the first time in 2019, lifting the AFC Asian Cup after beating Japan 3–1 in the final in Abu Dhabi. One of their scorers that day was Almoez Ali, with a spectacular bicycle kick. Ali finished with a tournament record of nine goals – including four in 51 minutes in a first-round 6–0 defeat of Korea DPR. Japan's strike in the final was the only goal conceded all tournament by 19-goal Qatar, who were coached by Spaniard Félix Sánchez. They were captained by striker **Hassan Al-Haydos**, who has played for the country more often than any other player.

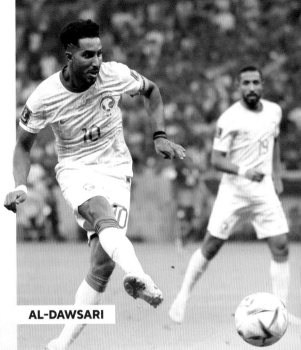

AL-DAWSARI

TOURNAMENT TRIVIA
CHINA STILL WAITING

Only the United Arab Emirates' Ali Mabkhout, with 14, scored more goals in Asia's qualification campaign for the 2022 FIFA World Cup than China forward **Wu Lei** with 12. But China still wait to reach only their second FIFA World Cup since their sole appearance in 2002, when they lost all three matches and failed to score. This is despite employing such high-profile national coaches as Italy's 2006 FIFA World Cup-winning manager Marcello Lippi and later his captain that summer Fabio Cannavaro. Lu Wei's 2022 qualifier efforts put him on 27 goals, behind only Haidong and his own modern-day team-mate Yang Xu, whose four strikes in a 7–0 victory over Guam in October 2019 made him the first man in 18 years, since Australia's Archie Thompson and David Zdrilic, to score four goals in the first half of a FIFA World Cup qualifier.

CUP RECORDS
AFC FIGUREHEADS

IR Iran dominate AFC Asian Cup records. They have played the most games (68), celebrated the most wins (41), had the most draws (19) and scored the most goals (131). South Yemen and Yemen both failed to score in their only appearance, and China PR have conceded the most goals (65) – and have suffered the most defeats (20) – while Myanmar and Singapore have conceded the fewest goals (four), but in only one appearance. Japan have won a record four championships; IR Iran and Saudi Arabia have three apiece.

130,000
The highest attendance for an Asian team in a home FIFA World Cup qualifier was the 130,000 who watched IR Iran draw 1-1 with Australia at the Azadi Stadium, Tehran, on 22 November 1997.

26

The 2015 AFC Asian Cup set a remarkable international tournament record for consecutive matches without a draw. All 24 matches in the group stage and then the first two quarter-finals turned up positive results after 90 minutes.

NATIONAL LEGEND
SAUDIS' SUPER SALEM

Saudi Arabia achieved not only the country's greatest victory but also one of the FIFA World Cup's greatest surprises by coming back from a goal behind – to a penalty by Lionel Messi – to beat eventual champions Argentina in their opening Group C match at the 2022 FIFA World Cup. Striker Saleh Al-Shehri hit the equaliser shortly after half-time before the decisive strike just five minutes later by winger **Salem Al-Dawsari**, who had previously scored the stoppage-time 2–1 winner in their dead-rubber game against Egypt at the 2018 FIFA World Cup. The Saudis did not make it out of the first round in Qatar, but Al-Dawsari did find the net again in their 2–1 defeat to Mexico, putting him level with the country's all-time second-top scorer Sami Al-Jaber on three FIFA World Cup goals.

KHARBIN

NATIONAL LEGEND
PRIDE OF SYRIA

In 2017, **Omar Kharbin** became the first Syrian to be named AFC Player of the Year. The free-scoring winger helped his Saudi Arabian club Al-Hilal to their first domestic league title in six years, and they also finished as AFC Champions League runners-up behind Japan's Urawa Red Diamonds. Kharbin, who made his debut as a 15-year-old for Al-Wahda in his home city of Damascus, also equalised for Syria in a 2019 AFC Asian Cup first-round defeat by defending champions Australia. Players from 2019 AFC Asian Cup winners Qatar claimed the AFC Player of the Year awards in 2018 and 2019, with winger Akram Afif succeeding defender Abdelkarim Hassan. The prize was cancelled in 2020 due to the COVID-19 pandemic.

NATIONAL LEGEND
HAPPY DAEI

IR Iran striker **Ali Daei** ended his career having scored 109 times for IR Iran in 149 internationals between 1993 and 2006 – although none of his goals came during FIFA World Cup finals appearances in 1998 and 2006. He is, however, the all-time leading scorer in the AFC Asian Cup, with 14 goals, despite never winning the tournament. His time as national team coach was less auspicious – he lasted only a year from March 2008 to March 2009 before being fired as the Iranians struggled in qualifiers for the 2010 FIFA World Cup.

Almoez Ali became the first player from outside Central America to win the Golden Boot for top scorer at a CONCACAF Gold Cup, when his four strikes took the prize and helped guest invitees Qatar claim bronze at the 2021 tournament in the USA. They included a brace in a 3–2 victory over El Salvador in the semi-finals.

1938
The first Asian country to play in a FIFA World Cup finals was Indonesia, who played in France in 1938 as the Dutch East Indies. The tournament was a straight knockout and Hungary beat them 6-0 in Reims on 5 June.

DAEI

TOURNAMENT TRIVIA
BHUTAN DO THE BEATING

Bhutan enjoyed an unprecedented winning streak in March 2015. The world's then-lowest-ranked nation had won only two official internationals in 34 years before they beat Sri Lanka twice in a two-legged 2018 FIFA World Cup qualifier. Tshering Dorji scored the only goal of the first leg, and the nation's only professional footballer – Chencho Gyeltshen – struck both goals in a 2-1 victory a week later. The Himalayan nation reached the second round of AFC qualification for the first time, but lost all eight matches with a goal difference of -52.

4-0
On the same day that Brazil and Germany contested the FIFA World Cup final on 30 June 2002, the two lowest-ranked FIFA countries were also taking each other on. Asian side Bhutan ran out 4-0 winners over Concacaf's Montserrat.

NATIONAL LEGEND
ONE OF BARCA'S BEST

The first Asian footballer to play for a European club was also, for almost a century, the all-time leading scorer for Spanish giants FC Barcelona, before being finally overtaken by Lionel Messi in March 2014. Paulino Alcántara, from the Philippines, scored 369 goals in 357 matches for the Catalan club between 1912 and 1927. He made his debut aged just 15, and remains Barcelona's youngest-ever first-team player. Alcántara was born in the Philippines, but had a Spanish father, and appeared in internationals for Catalonia, Spain and the Philippines, for whom he featured in a record 15-2 trouncing of Japan in 1917.

TOURNAMENT TRIVIA
FIRST-ROUND FIRST

In January 2019, India finally ended a 55-year wait for victory in the AFC Asian Cup finals when they defeated Thailand 4-1. Two goals from **Sunil Chhetri** took his overall record for his country to a national record 67, and he has since moved on to 84, while also playing a record 131 times for India. Those proved to be India's only points of the tournament, however. Thailand responded by firing their Serbian coach Milovan Rajevac and replacing him with Sirisak Yodyardthai. They recovered to reach the knockout stage for the first time in 47 years, before falling 2-1 to China PR in the round of 16.

CHHETRI

90+13

Iran's Mehdi Taremi scored the latest ever goal in regular time at a FIFA World Cup, 13 minutes into stoppage-time, for his second in his side's 6-2 defeat by England at the 2022 tournament. In their next Group B match, Iran beat Wales with goals eight and 11 minutes into added time.

NATIONAL LEGEND
FAB MABKHOUT

The United Arab Emirates' **Ali Mabkhout** did not just top the scoring charts in Asia's qualification process for the 2022 FIFA World Cup – his 14 goals were the most worldwide. Seeing off everyone else with his goal feats was nothing new – his 19 strikes in 13 appearances meant a calendar-year record in 2019. His most recent feats have only extended his lead as his country's all-time leading scorer. Mabkhout also scored the fastest goal in AFC Asian Nations Cup history, 14 seconds into his team's 2-1 first-round victory in 2015 on his way to winning the Golden Boot, with the UAE finishing third. His 2022 FIFA World Cup efforts helped his country reach a play-off against Australia. The play-off was held on 7 June 2022 in Qatar, where a 2-1 defeat ended the UAE's campaign.

SHATSKIKH

NATIONAL LEGEND
MAXIMUM MAKSIM

Uzbekistan's record marksman **Maksim Shatskikh** retired from international football after winning his 61st cap in a friendly against Oman in 2014. He had equalled previous top scorer Mirjalol Qosimov's 31-goal tally in a 7-3 defeat of Singapore in June 2008. Shatskikh also holds the Uzbek single-game record with five goals against Taiwan in 2007. While playing for Dynamo Kiev in Ukraine, Shatskikh joined ex-Alania Vladikavkaz striker Qosimov as the only Uzbeks to score in a UEFA club competition. Qosimov has been national coach twice, leading them to the AFC Asian Cup quarter-finals in 2015. The nation's most-capped player, however, is still forward Server Djeparov, who retired in 2017 on 128 caps.

1934

Palestine, then under British rule, were the first Asian team to enter the FIFA World Cup qualifiers. They lost 7-1 away to Egypt on 16 March 1934.

TEAM TRIVIA
THAT'S THE WAY TO DOO-IK

North Korea caused a sensation at the 1966 FIFA World Cup by beating Italy 1-0 at Middlesbrough in England and eliminating the then-two-time world champions from the tournament. Pak Doo-ik scored the winner in the 42nd minute, making his side the first Asian team to reach the quarter-finals, where they raced into a 3-0 lead against Eusébio's Portugal only to lose 5-3. North Korea have only made the finals once since, in 2010, with their now-most-capped player, keeper **Ri Myong-guk** managing to keep Brazil down to only a 2-1 victory in their opening game, though his side did lose all three matches. North Korea withdrew from 2022 FIFA World Cup qualifiers during the second round of Asia's process, citing Covid-19 pandemic concerns.

MABKHOUT

STAR PLAYER
HOME COMFORTS

Qatar enjoyed staging the 2022 FIFA World Cup – the first Middle East nation to do so – but their national side set some unwanted records on the pitch. They lost all three matches in the first round, the first host country to fail to win at least a point in three games: 2-0 to Ecuador in the tournament opener, 3-1 to Senegal and 2-0 to the Netherlands. A place in national history went to their first-ever FIFA World Cup goalscorer, Ghanaian-born striker Mohammed Muntari. His previous feats for Qatar included a hat-trick against Bhutan in a 15-0 FIFA World Cup qualifier win in September 2015.

RI MYONG-GUK

OCEANIA

Football in Oceania can claim some of the most eye-catching football statistics – although not necessarily in a way that many there would welcome, especially the long-suffering goalkeepers from minnow islands on the end of cricket-style scorelines.

Country: New Zealand
Joined FIFA: 1948
Most appearances: Ivan Vicelich, 88
Top scorer: Chris Wood, 33
Major honours: 5 OFC Nations Cups (1973, 1998, 2002, 2008, 2016)

Country: Fiji
Joined FIFA: 1964
Most appearances: Roy Krishna, 48
Top scorers: Roy Krishna, 32
Major honours: -

Country: Tahiti
Joined FIFA: 1989
Most appearances: Angelo Tchen, 34
Top scorer: Teaonui Tehau, 24
Major honours: 1 OFC Nations Cup (2012)

STAR PLAYER
THE WOOD LIFE

Not only was the 2020 OFC Nations Cup cancelled due to the Covid-19 pandemic, but the continent's qualification campaign for a possible place at the 2022 FIFA World Cup was reduced to a standalone tournament in Qatar in March 2022. New Zealand's **Chris Wood** finished as top scorer with five, as his country beat the Solomon Islands in the final to book a play-off against Costa Rica. His brace against Fiji in the group-stage took him past Vaughan Coveny to become the nation's all-time top scorer. His first international goal came back in October 2010 against Honduras. He was booked for celebrating by revealing underpants bearing his nickname "Woodzee". Wood had a potential equaliser disallowed for a foul when New Zealand missed out on a place at the 2022 FIFA World Cup, losing their qualification play-off 1-0 to Costa Rica in Qatar in June.

WOOD

3

Ricki Herbert is one of only three New Zealand-born men to be national coach, along with Barrie Truman who was in charge between 1970 and 1976, and Danny Hay, who took over in 2019.

NATIONAL LEGEND
RETURNING RICKI

Ricki Herbert is the only New Zealander to have featured in two FIFA World Cups. A left back at the 1982 tournament in Spain, he then coached the country in their second World Cup appearance, in 2010. Their second qualification came after a play-off defeat of AFC representatives Bahrain. Herbert resigned in November 2013, and then briefly took charge of the Maldives. In August 2019, former Leeds United defender Danny Hay – a winner of 31 caps between 1996 and 2007 – became All Whites coach. Hay and Herbert are the only men to have both captained and managed the side. Yet Hay stepped away from the job in autumn 2022 after New Zealand football's governing body asked him to reapply to be manager – an offer he declined.

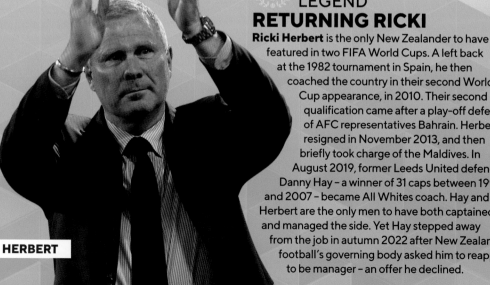

HERBERT

TOURNAMENT TRIVIA
BAD LUCK OF THE DRAW

Despite featuring at only their second-ever FIFA World Cup – and their first since 1982 – New Zealand did not lose a game in South Africa in 2010. They drew all three first-round matches, against Slovakia, Italy and Paraguay. The three points were not enough to secure a top-two spot in Group F, but their third-placed finish did see the Kiwis finish above defending world champions Italy. The only other three teams to have gone out despite going unbeaten in their three first-round group games were Scotland (1974), Cameroon (1982) and Belgium (1998).

STAR PLAYER
FOUR STAR

The Solomon Islands were beaten in the final of the OFC's qualifiers for the 2022 FIFA World Cup in March, but they unearthed one of the stars at the campaign: 18-year-old striker **Raphael Lea'i** emerged from it with four goals in his first four international appearances. He hit a hat-trick to beat Tahiti 3–1 in the first round and another goal as Papua New Guinea were downed 3–2 in the semi-finals. He had previously marked his 15th birthday by scoring four times to help beat Papua New Guinea on the opening day of the 2018 OFC U-16 Championship.

LEA'I

34

Commins Menapi is the Solomon Islands' all-time top scorer, with 34 goals in 37 games between 2000 and 2009.

24

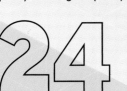

Tahiti conceded a whopping 24 goals in their three games at the FIFA Confederations Cup in 2013. Ten came against Spain in one match.

31–0
American Samoa set an unwanted international record by losing 31–0 to Australia in April 2001 – two days after the Australians had crushed Tonga 22–0.

KRISHNA

TOURNAMENT TRIVIA
TEHAU ABOUT THAT

Pacific Island underdogs Tahiti finally broke the stranglehold that Australia and New Zealand had over the OFC Nations Cup by winning the tournament when it was held for the ninth time in 2012. Tahiti scored 20 goals in their five games at the event in the Solomon Islands, 15 of which came from the Tehau family: brothers Lorenzo (five), Alvin and Jonathan (four each) and their cousin Teaonui (two). Steevy Chong Hue scored the only goal of the final, against New Caledonia, to give the team the trophy and a place at the FIFA Confederations Cup in 2013. Teaonui Tehau is Tahiti's all-time leading scorer, with 24 goals in 33 appearances.

STAR PLAYER
FIJI FIREPOWER

Roy Krishna has been capped more times (48) than any other Fijian. He pulled ahead as his country's all-time leading scorer with his 32nd goal in a 2–2 draw with the Solomon Islands in September 2022. He previously equalled Esala Masi's 31-goal tally with both goals to beat Vanuatu 2–1 in Qatar in a March 2022 friendly, just after Fiji had been eliminated and Vanuatu withdrew due to Covid-19 cases from the OFC's 2022 FIFA World Cup qualifiers being held there. Fiji's best international performance came at the 1998 OFC Nations Cup, at which Masi bagged a brace to help beat Tahiti 4–2 in the third-place play-off.

65

Centre-back Ivan Vicelich passed Vaughan Coveny's New Zealand record of 64 caps in the second leg of their 2010 FIFA World Cup qualifying play-off against Bahrain, helping his country to reach the tournament in South Africa.

125

CONCACAF

Canada, Mexico and USA will make football history when they co-host the FIFA World Cup in 2024 on behalf of Concacaf. This will be the first time three nations have shared the finals, which will feature a field of 48 teams for the first time. The Confederation of North, Central America and Caribbean Association Football was created in 1961.

Founded: 1961

Number of associations: 35 (+6 non-FIFA members)

Headquarters: Miami, USA

Most continental championship wins: Mexico, 11

2026 FIFA WORLD CUP™

The Member Associations of

CANADA, MEXICO, USA

have been selected by the FIFA Congress to host the 2026 FIFA World Cup™

3

Come 2026, Mexico will have hosted or co-hosted the FIFA World Cup three times, more than any other nation.

4

There are four Concacaf zones: North America, Central America, the Caribbean, and South America.

The best performance from a Concacaf team in the FIFA World Cup was in 1930, when the USA finished third.

2000

Mexico and United States have won all but one of the 16 Gold Cups since the CONCACAF Championship was relaunched in 1991. Canada broke their grip in 2000.

The Mexican national team is the only Concacaf team to have won a senior FIFA men's tournament, the FIFA Confederations Cup in 1999.

MEXICO

Mexico may well be the powerhouse of the Concacaf region – they have missed out on the FIFA World Cup final tournament only five times (in 1934, 1938, 1974, 1982 and 1990) – but they have struggled to impose themselves on the international stage.

Joined FIFA: 1927

Biggest win:
13–0 v. Bahamas, 1987

Highest FIFA Ranking: 4

Home stadium: Estadio Azteca, Mexico City

Honours: 11 Concacaf championships (1965, 1971, 1977, 1993, 1996, 1998, 2003, 2009, 2011, 2015, 2019), 1 FIFA Confederations Cup (1999)

MOST APPEARANCES:

1 Andrés Guardado, 179

2 Claudio Suárez, 177

3 Rafael Márquez, 147

4 Pável Pardo, 146

5 Gerardo Torrado, 144

3

Hugo Sánchez played for Mexico at three FIFA World Cups – 1978, 1986 and 1994 – and would surely have featured had they qualified in 1982 and 1990.

SÁNCHEZ

NATIONAL LEGEND
VICTOR HUGO

Javier Hernández may have overtaken Jared Borghetti as Mexico's all-time leading goalscorer, but perhaps the country's most inspirational striker remains **Hugo Sánchez**, famed for his acrobatic bicycle-kick finishes and somersault celebrations. During spells in Spain with Atlético Madrid and Real Madrid, he finished as *La Liga*'s top scorer five years out of six between 1985 and 1990. He was less successful as Mexico coach from 2006 to 2008, his best result being third in the 2007 *Copa América*.

39

Hugo Sánchez, who scored 29 goals in 58 matches for Mexico, was aged 39 years and 251 days for his farewell game, against Paraguay in March 1998 – though this was four years after his previous international and he played only the first minute before being replaced by Luis García.

MÁRQUEZ

NATIONAL LEGEND
MAKING HIS MÁRQUEZ

Centre-back **Rafael Márquez** holds many of Mexico's records in the FIFA World Cup. His 19 matches in the finals are seven more than Javier Hernández. He – along with Cuauhtémoc Blanco and Hernández – are the only Mexican players to have scored in three World Cup final tournaments. Also, at the age of 39 years and 139 days, Márquez is – by six days – the second-oldest outfielder to start a FIFA World Cup knock-out match; the only person who was older was England winger Stanley Matthews when he played against Uruguay in 1954.

NATIONAL LEGEND
INSPIRATIONAL IGNACIO

Mexican football mourned the country's longest-serving national coach Ignacio Trelles when he died at the age of 103 following a heart attack in April 2020. Trelles holds the record for most matches as Mexico coach – overseeing 50 victories in 106 games during three spells between 1958 and 1976. These included Mexico's first victory at a FIFA World Cup, beating Czechoslovakia 3-1 in 1962, although they departed Chile at the end of the first round as well as England at the same stage four years later. Trelles – known as "Don Nacho" – also oversaw a record 1,083 games as top-flight coach in Mexico, while only he and Victor Manuel Vucetich (Mexico manager for just 35 days in 2013) have won the country's league at the helm of four different clubs. Bora Milutinović was coach for 104 games over two stints (1983-86 and 1995-97), including Mexico's run to the quarter-finals as hosts in 1986.

42

Mexico's Manuel Rosas scored the first penalty ever awarded in the FIFA World Cup finals when he converted a 42nd-minute spot-kick in his country's match against Argentina in 1930.

NATIONAL LEGEND
NOTEWORTHY "MEMO"

No man has kept goal for Mexico more often than **Guillermo Ochoa**, who kept a clean sheet in a 2–0 Mexico win over Hungary on his international debut in December 2005. He was also on the winning side for his record 134th cap, a 2–1 victory against Saudi Arabia at the 2022 FIFA World Cup. However, Mexico failed to make the knock-out stages for the first time since 1978, not counting the FIFA World Cups they missed in 1982 and 1990. They finished third in Group C behind Poland on goal difference. Ochoa – nicknamed "Memo" – saved a penalty from Polish star striker Robert Lewandowski in the two sides' opening 0–0 draw.

22

Mexico's shock 7-0 trouncing by Chile in the quarter-finals of the 2016 *Copa América Centenario* was their heaviest defeat in an official competition – and it brought to an end a 22-match unbeaten run, a Mexican international record.

TOP SCORERS:

1 Javier Hernández, 52
2 Jared Borghetti, 46
3 Cuauhtémoc Blanco, 39
4 Carlos Hermosillo, 35
= Luis Hernández, 35

HERNANDEZ

STAR PLAYER
LITTLE PEA FROM A POD

Javier Hernández's goal against Costa Rica on 24 March 2017 saw him join Jared Borghetti as Mexico's leading scorer – both men with 46 goals from 89 games. Further goals have followed – as has Hernández's 100-cap milestone – and he reached 50 goals with a strike against Korea Republic at the 2018 FIFA World Cup. In June 2010, playing against South Africa in the opening match, he became the third generation of his family to play at a FIFA World Cup.

OCHA

11

The record for goals at one Concacaf Gold Cup is the 11 struck by Mexico forward Luís Roberto Alves, also known as Zague or Zaguinho, at the 1993 tournament his country won while co-hosting with the USA. Seven came in one game, a 9–0 victory over Martinique in Mexico's opener. He also scored his nation's third in the final, a 4–0 win against the USA in Mexico City's Azteca stadium.

GUARDADO

TOURNAMENT TRIVIA
TAKING GUARD

Mexico captain **Andrés Guardado** became the sixth man to play at five different FIFA World Cups at the tournament in 2022, and the third Mexican following goalkeeper Antonio Carbajal (1950, 1954, 1958, 1962 and 1966) and defender Rafael Márquez (2002, 2006, 2010, 2014 and 2018). Guardado previously captained Mexico to glory at the 2019 Concacaf Gold Cup, preventing a USA equaliser to Jonathan Dos Santos's goal when the ball rebounded off his face on the goal-line with two minutes left. Guardado's one appearance at the 2022 FIFA World Cup, in a 2–0 defeat to Argentina, was his 179th international appearance. He had broken Claudio Suárez's Mexico record of 177 in a 2–1 friendly defeat to Sweden ten days earlier.

USA

Over the years, football has steadily grown in both popularity and quality in the USA, which remains one of only 17 nations to have hosted the FIFA World Cup.

Joined FIFA: 1913

Biggest win: 8-0 v. Barbados, 2008

Highest FIFA ranking: 4th

Home stadium: (rotation)

Honours: 7 Concacaf Championships (1991, 2002, 2005, 2007, 2013, 2017, 2021)

DONOVAN

NATIONAL LEGEND
LANDON HOPE AND GLORY

The USA's joint all-time leading scorer **Landon Donovan** was the star of their 2010 FIFA World Cup campaign, scoring three goals in four matches, including a stoppage-time winner against Algeria to help his team top Group C. . His four games at the tournament meant he featured in 13 FIFA World Cup matches for the USA, two ahead of Earnie Stewart, Cobi Jones and DaMarcus Beasley. Donovan's goal in the second-round loss to Ghana also made him the USA's all-time top scorer in the finals, with five – one more than 1930 hat-trick hero Bert Patenaude and Clint Dempsey, who scored twice in 2014.

30

Clint Dempsey, nicknamed "Deuce", scored just 30 seconds into his country's first game at the 2014 FIFA World Cup against Ghana – the fifth-fastest goal in the tournament's history.

TOP SCORERS:

1. Landon Donovan, 57
   = Clint Dempsey, 57
3. Jozy Altidore, 42
4. Eric Wynalda, 34
5. Brian McBride, 30

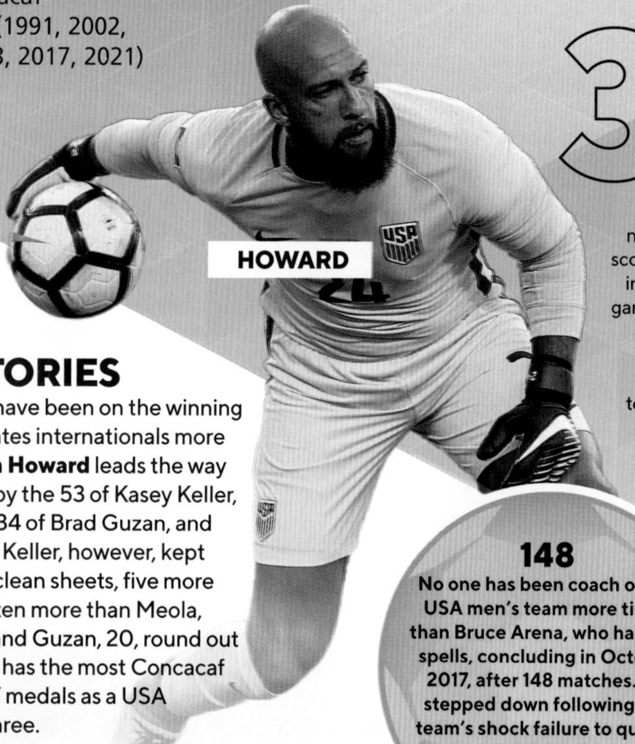

HOWARD

NATIONAL LEGENDS
GLOVE STORIES

Five goalkeepers have been on the winning team in United States internationals more than 25 times. **Tim Howard** leads the way with 62, followed by the 53 of Kasey Keller, 37 of Tony Meola, 34 of Brad Guzan, and 27 of Brad Friedel. Keller, however, kept a team-record 47 clean sheets, five more than Howard and ten more than Meola, while Friedel, 24, and Guzan, 20, round out the top five. Keller has the most Concacaf Gold Cup winners' medals as a USA goalkeeper with three.

148

No one has been coach of the USA men's team more times than Bruce Arena, who had two spells, concluding in October 2017, after 148 matches. He stepped down following the team's shock failure to qualify for the 2018 FIFA World Cup.

19

Jozy Altidore became the USA's youngest scorer of an international hat-trick in a 3-0 victory over Trinidad and Tobago on 1 April 2009, aged 19 years and 146 days.

STAR PLAYER
MAGIC CHRISTIAN

Philadelphia native **Christian Pulisic** moved to Germany as a 16-year-old in 2015 to sign for Borussia Dortmund, and less than four years later had become the most expensive US footballer of all-time when joining English club Chelsea for £58m. In March 2017, he scored the USA's fastest second-half goal, taking 12 seconds after the restart to find the net in a 6–0 victory over Honduras. In November the following year against Italy, he became the nation's youngest captain, aged 20 years and 63 days. Pulisic scored the only goal of the USA's final Group B match at the 2022 FIFA World Cup to edge past opponents Iran into the knock-out stages. He then set up Haji Wright's consolation goal in their 3–1 second round elimination by the Netherlands.

PULISIC

MOST APPEARANCES:

1. Cobi Jones, 164
2. Landon Donovan, 157
3. Michael Bradley, 151
4. Clint Dempsey, 141
5. Jeff Agoos, 134

DEMPSEY

3-2

The USA became inaugural winners of a new tournament, the Concacaf Nations League, involving all the region's countries in games aside from friendlies and FIFA World Cup qualifiers, by beating Mexico 3–2 after extra-time in the June 2021 final in Denver. Captain Christian Pulisic settled the match with a late penalty.

TOURNAMENT TRIVIA
ENGLAND STUNNED BY GAETJENS

USA's 1–0 win over England on 29 June 1950 ranks among the biggest surprises in FIFA World Cup history. England, along with hosts Brazil, were joint favourites to win the trophy. The USA had lost their last seven matches, scoring just two goals. Joe Gaetjens scored the only goal, in the 37th minute, diving to head Walter Bahr's cross past goalkeeper Bert Williams. England dominated the game, but USA keeper Frank Borghi made save after save. Defeats by Chile and Spain eliminated the USA at the end of the group stage, but their victory over England remains the greatest result in the country's football history.

TOURNAMENT TRIVIA
MILES AHEAD

Only two men played every minute for the USA at the 2021 Concacaf Gold Cup, at which they won their seventh title, defeating Mexico in the final. Fittingly, both players were rewarded beyond the trophy itself. Goalkeeper Matt Turner only conceded once in the whole tournament, a penalty, and was presented the Golden Glove prize, while centre-back Miles Robinson scored the only goal of the final, just three minutes before the end of extra-time. Some 61,114 fans crammed into Nevada's Allegiant Stadium in August 2021 after the lifting of Covid-19 pandemic-related restrictions.

WEAH

36

Striker **Tim Weah** – son of Liberia footballing legend and later state President George Weah – was born in Brooklyn, New York, and opted to play for the USA. He opened their account at the 2022 FIFA World Cup 36 minutes into their first match, a 1–1 draw with Wales.

STAR PLAYER
A FAMILY AFFAIR

The Reyna family became the first in the USA's history to have three members play international football for the country, when Borussia Dortmund midfielder **Giovanni Reyna** made his debut the day before his 18th birthday in a goalless draw friendly against Wales in November 2020. His father won 112 caps between 1994 and 2006, including captaining the USA at the 2006 FIFA World Cup in Germany, while his mother Danielle played six times for the women's team in 1993. In his second international four days later, Giovanni became the nation's third-youngest goalscorer with a brace in a 6–2 victory over Panama. In May 2018, Josh Sargent became the USA's fourth-youngest scorer, in the 52nd minute against Bolivia – only to be outdone seven minutes later by teammate Tim Weah, who is two days younger.

REYNA

CONCACAF: OTHER TEAMS

Mexico and the USA have dominated the Concacaf region down the years, but with recent standout performances from Costa Rica in FIFA World Cup competition, and Panama making the 2018 tournament, the region is starting to boast more and more talent.

Country: Costa Rica
Joined FIFA: 1927
Most appearances: Celso Borges, 158
Top scorer: Rolando Fonseca, 47
Honours: 3 Concacaf championships (1963, 1969, 1989)

Country: Honduras
Joined FIFA: 1946
Most appearances: Maynor Figueroa, 181
Top scorer: Carlos Pavón, 57
Honours: 1 Concacaf championships (1981)

Country: Canada
Joined FIFA: 1912
Most appearances: Atiba Hutchinson, 101
Top scorer: Cyle Larin, 25
Honours: 2 Concacaf Gold Cups (1985, 2000)

Country: El Salvador
Joined FIFA: 1938
Most appearances: Darwin Cerén, 89
Top scorer: Raúl Díaz Arce, 39
Honours: -

Country: Trinidad & Tobago
Joined FIFA: 1964
Most appearances: Angus Eve, 117
Top scorer: Stern John, 70
Honours: -

Country: Panama
Joined FIFA: 1938
Most appearances: Gabriel Gómez, 149
Top scorer: Luis Tejada, 43
Honours: -

NATIONAL LEGEND
PAN-TASTIC TORRES

Panama made their FIFA World Cup finals debut in Russia in 2018, captained by mighty centre-back **Róman Torres**, whose goal three minutes from time sealed a 2-1 win over Costa Rica and secured their place at the expense of the USA, who lost by the same scoreline to Trinidad & Tobago that night. Panama President Juan Carlos Valera declared a national holiday to celebrate. Panama lost all three games in Russia – 3-0 to Tunisia, 6-1 to England and 2-1 to Tunisia – but their fans celebrated exuberantly in Nizhny Novgorod when substitute Felipe Baloy scored their first-ever FIFA World Cup goal, against England.

TORRES

40
Canada's most-capped player Atiba Hutchinson became the country's first man to reach a century of caps in their 4-1 defeat to Croatia at the 2022 FIFA World Cup, where the 40-year-old midfielder was also the oldest player at the tournament.

TOURNAMENT TRIVIA
ALL FOR EL SALVADOR

El Salvador can claim to be the first Central American country to have qualified for the FIFA World Cup twice, doing so in 1970 and 1982. Recent years have brought more struggles, however, although left-back Alfredo Pacheco became his country's most-capped player with 86 appearances between 2002 and 2013.

JOHN

70
Only 17 men have netted more than the 70 international goals – in 115 matches – scored by Trinidad & Tobago's **Stern John** between his debut in 1995 and his final game in 2011.

STAR PLAYER
KEYLOR IS THE KEY

Costa Rica made their FIFA World Cup finals debut in 1990, and goalkeeper Luis Gabelo Conejo shared the best goalkeeper award with Argentina's Sergio Goycochea as his displays helped his team reach the knockout stages. *Los Ticos* did even better in 2014 and while goalscorers Joel Campbell and Bryan Ruiz impressed, again a goalkeeper was crucial: **Keylor Navas** was named Man of the Match four times in five games. At the other end of the pitch, the first man to score twice for Costa Rica at the FIFA World Cup was charismatic striker Paulo Wanchope, who found the net both times for his country when they lost the 2006 tournament's opening match 4-2 to hosts Germany. His record tally of 45 for Costa Rica was later passed by 47-goal striker Rolando Fonseca.

NAVAS

TEAM TRIVIA
O CANADA

Canada's youngest international **Alphonso Davies** became the country's first-ever scorer at a FIFA World Cup when he provided a second-minute lead in their second match at the 2022 finals. It was a brief moment to enjoy since the match ended 4-1 to Croatia. Managed by Englishman John Herdman, Canada then lost 1-0 to Belgium and finished with a 2-1 defeat to Morocco. That meant the country had lost all six World Cup fixtures, having been beaten three times at their only previous finals in 1986. Davies, who joined Bayern Munich in 2018, was born in a Ghana refugee camp to Liberian parents fleeing civil war. The family moved to Canada when Alphonso was five. He received Canadian citizenship a week before his international debut against Curaçao on 13 June 2017, and was aged just 16 days and 225 days when he took the field.

DAVIES

TOURNAMENT TRIVIA
FAMILY BUSINESS

El Salvador's most-capped player Darwin Cerén comes from a footballing family. His younger brother Óscar Cerén played 38 times for the country, while their sisters Brenda and Paola are internationals for the women's team. Darwin and Óscar were both members of El Salvador's squads at the 2017 and 2019 Concacaf Gold Cups, including a run to the quarter-finals in 2017. The country's all-time top scorer is Raúl Díaz Arce, who hit 39 goals in 72 appearances between 1991 and 2000, putting him ahead of Jorge González's 26 in 62. The latter, nicknamed "El Mágico", helped El Salvador reach the FIFA World Cup finals in 1982.

3 Canada, Haiti, Jamaica, Panama and Trinidad & Tobago all played three matches in their only World Cup finals appearances. Jamaica won once and Trinidad & Tobago drew once; all their other games were lost.

5 In 1938, Cuba scored five goals on their way to becoming the first island state of the CONCACAF region to reach the FIFA World Cup quarter-finals.

3 Joel Campbell scored the earliest goal in a FIFA World Cup intercontinental qualification play-off to secure Costa Rica's place at the 2022 tournament – finding the net just after three minutes against New Zealand in June that year, the only goal of the game in his 117th international.

NATIONAL LEGEND
REGGAE BOYZ

In 1998, Jamaica became the first team from the English-speaking Caribbean to reach a FIFA World Cup. Nicknamed the "Reggae Boyz", they included several players based in England, such as Chelsea's Frank Sinclair and Wimbledon's Robbie Earle. They were eliminated in the group stage, though did beat Japan 2-1 in their last game thanks to two goals by **Theodore Whitmore**, the country's third most-capped player behind Ian Goodison (128) and Linval Dixon (127), and manager since 2016.

WHITMORE

FIFA WORLD CUP

The FIFA World Cup finals in Qatar in November and December 2022 were the first to be staged in the northern hemisphere winter. They were also the first to be held in the Arab world. Argentina triumphed for the third time by defeating 2018 champions France.

First held:
1930

Current champions:
Argentina

Most wins:
Brazil, 5

Next edition:
Canada, Mexico, USA, 2026

211

All 211 FIFA members entered qualifying, including finals hosts Qatar, who were seeded directly to the finals. The tournament also doubled up with the Asian Cup preliminaries.

The 2022 FIFA World Cup saw stadia reach 94 per cent capacity. The matches were broadcast around the planet through 236 different media contracts and set numerous local TV ratings records. The final was watched in France by 24.1m, almost 5m more than the 2018 final between France and Croatia.

FIFA WORLD CUP
Qatar2022

MESSI

26

Leo Messi dominated the 2022 FIFA World Cup, inspiring Argentina to glory after the shock of defeat in their opening group game by Saudi Arabia. The climactic victory over France saw Argentina's captain take his total of finals appearances to a record 26, ahead of Germany's Lothar Matthäus (25) and Miroslav Klose (24).

172

The FIFA World Cup in Qatar saw 172 goals at an average of 2.68 per game.

The **Azteca Stadium** in Mexico is the only stadium to have hosted the FIFA World Cup final twice. Brazil's Maracanã has hosted the deciding game twice, but in 1950, the tournament was held in a round-robin format with no set final.

WORLD CUP 2022 REPORT

32 Nations

The FIFA World Cup Qatar 2022 made history several times over with the choice of the Gulf state as the smallest nation ever to play host. Qatar's population of 2.9m and area of 11,571 sq.km were below comparative figures for inaugural 1930 host Uruguay. The finals saw a historic breakthrough for international football with Morocco becoming both the first African nation and the first Arab nation to reach the FIFA World Cup semi-finals.

🏆 TOURNAMENT TRIVIA
KEEPING TIME

FIFA surprised fans, coaches and players in Qatar with a new, stricter policing of stoppage times to allow for minutes taken up with injuries, celebrations, video assistant referee (VAR) reviews and substitutions. During the group stages, referees added a total of 563 minutes of play – more than nine hours. England's 6–2 defeat of Iran ran to a record 117 minutes. Overall, the finals took up 29 days between November 20 and December 18. This made it the shortest tournament since 1978. The format remained unchanged, with eight first-round groups followed by four elimination rounds with extra-time and penalties when necessary.

22

Qatar 2022 was the 22nd finals tournament. The Gulf state followed in the proud footsteps of previous hosts Uruguay, Italy (twice), France (twice), Brazil (twice), Switzerland, Sweden, Chile, England, Mexico (twice), Germany (twice), Argentina, Spain, United States, Japan and Korea Republic jointly, South Africa and Russia.

🏆 TOURNAMENT TRIVIA
BACK TO THE START

Qatar were the first national team, after inaugural World Cup hosts Uruguay in 1930, to welcome the world without ever having previously appeared in the finals. The finals were awarded to Qatar in December 2010 by world football federation FIFA, which later decided to abandon the traditional June/July dates to protect players, officials and fans from the high summer temperatures. This was the last time the finals were contested by 32 teams. The finals will expand to 48 teams in Canada, Mexico and the United States in 2026.

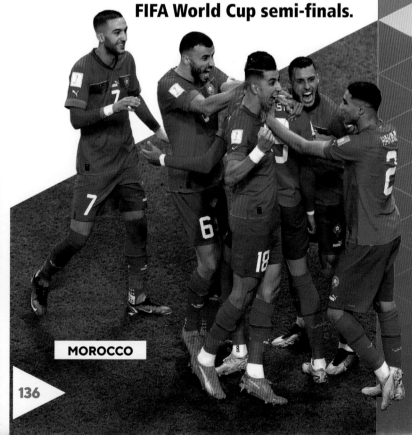

MOROCCO

2

Fans were enabled to attend at least two matches every day in Qatar because of the compact nature of the country. This was in sharp contrast to the finals in 2014 in Brazil and 2018 in Russia when hours of flying time separated many venues. Teams were also able to stay in one training centre for the entire tournament.

THE HUB

The central home of the 2022 finals was the city of Doha, which is home to a majority of the population of Qatar. The city was founded in the 1820s and officially declared the country's capital on independence from the former British protectorate in 1971.

TOURNAMENT TRIVIA
HISTORIC HOSTS

Qatar has been hosting international football championships since 1985, when it stepped in at short notice to stage a FIFA Youth Cup. Since then, it has welcomed the FIFA Club World Cup™ in 2019 and 2020 and the FIFA Arab Cup™ in December 2021. One of the most notable venues was Stadium 974, constructed out of shipping containers and taking its name from Qatar's international dialling code.

TOURNAMENT TRIVIA
ALL-NEW START TO FINISH

Seven of the eight venues for the finals were newly-built, the exception being the redeveloped Khalifa International Stadium. The Opening Match featuring hosts Qatar in Group A was staged in the 68,895-capacity Al Bayt Stadium in Al Khor. Originally the first match was scheduled to be a tie between Senegal and Netherlands, but the programme was rearranged with Qatar's match being moved forward 24 hours. The climax of the 2022 finals, with Argentina's shootout victory over France, was staged in the Lusail Iconic Stadium on December 18, which was also a public holiday as Qatar National Day. Lusail, like all the other stadiums except 974, was cooled using solar power. It was intended to be reduced to a 40,000 capacity in post-World Cup redevelopment.

THE VENUES:

LUSAIL ICONIC STADIUM
World Cup Capacity: 88,996
Ten matches including a semi-final and the final.

AL BAYT STADIUM
World Cup Capacity: 68,895
Nine matches including a semi-final and the ceremonial Opening Match.

STADIUM 974
World Cup Capacity: 44,089
Seven matches including one round of 16 tie.

AL THUMAMA STADIUM
World Cup Capacity: 44,400
Eight matches including a quarter-final.

EDUCATION CITY STADIUM
World Cup Capacity: 44,667
Eight matches including a quarter-final.

AHMAD BIN ALI STADIUM
World Cup Capacity: 45,032
Seven matches including one round of 16 tie.

KHALIFA INTERNATIONAL STADIUM
World Cup Capacity: 45,857
Eight matches including the third place play-off.

STADIUM AL JANOUB
World Cup Capacity: 44,325
Seven matches including one round of 16 tie.

FIFA WORLD CUP TEAM RECORDS

From the most decorated nations in world football to those that have only played a single game, and every team in-between.

TOURNAMENT TRIVIA
AFRICAN HEROES

Morocco thrilled their own and their adopted local Arab/Asian fans at the 2022 FIFA World Cup on becoming the first African team ever to reach the semi-finals. They had been the first African team to top their first-round group this century and upset European football aristocracy twice over in the knockout rounds. First goalkeeper **Yassine Bounou** achieved hero status by saving two penalties in a 3–0 shootout win over Spain, then a goal from Youssef En-Nesyri earned a 1–0 win over Portugal. The third-place playoff proved one step too far as the Atlas Lions lost 2–1 to the World Cup experience of Croatia. Morocco had history. In 1986, they were the first African team to progress beyond the group stage.

BOUNOU

7

Brazil's record of seven wins in the 2002 FIFA World Cup – a 100 per cent record – is the most by any country at any tournament ever.

TOURNAMENT TRIVIA
ENGLAND STALEMATE

England's goalless draw against United States in the group stage of the 2022 FIFA World Cup was their record 22nd draw at the finals. Italy are second with 21. England returned to winning ways next time out with a 3–0 win over Wales. Marcus Rashford's second goal was England's 100th in the World Cup finals. England had opened their World Cup account in Brazil in 1950 through Stan Mortensen. The Blackpool forward scored after 39 minutes in a 2–0 win over Chile. Wilf Mannion scored the second goal six minutes into the second half. It was England's last goal in the tournament. They were eliminated after 1–0 defeats by United States and Spain.

NATIONAL LEGEND
BRAZIL OFF COLOUR

Brazil's yellow shirts are famous around the world, but the team wore white shirts at the first four FIFA World Cup finals. Their 2–1 loss to Uruguay in the 1950 tournament's final match – when a draw would have given them the cup – was such a shock that they switched to yellow. The Brazilian FA insisted no further colour change would follow the shock of the 7–1 semi-final defeat by Germany and 3–0 third-place play-off loss to the Netherlands in 2014.

SOUTH AFRICA
South Africa is the only host country to fail to progress from the first round of a FIFA World Cup.

MOST APPEARANCES IN A FIFA WORLD CUP FINAL:

1 Germany/West Germany – 8

2 Brazil – 7

3 Argentina 6
= Italy 6

4 France 4

5 Netherlands 3

138

MOST APPEARANCES IN FINALS TOURNAMENTS:

1 Brazil – 22

2 Germany/West Germany – 20

3 Italy – 18
= Argentina – 18

5 Mexico – 17

FRANCE
France hold the record for the worst performance by defending champions: they scored no goals and managed a single draw in 2002.

KIT TRIVIA
EVER RED

England's victory in 1966 remains the only time the FIFA World Cup final has been won by a team wearing red. Spain, who usually wear red, changed into blue for their 2010 victory over the Netherlands to avoid a colour-clash. **Luka Modrić** and his Croatia teammates did wear their unique red-and-white checks in the 2018 final but lost to France. Wearing red also proved unlucky for losing finalists Czechoslovakia in 1934 and then Hungary in both 1938 and 1954.

MODRIĆ

TOURNAMENT TRIVIA
LIONS ROAR INTO HISTORY

Cameroon became the first African team to beat Brazil at a World Cup in the concluding Group G match at the 2022 FIFA World Cup. The record five-times champions were already sure of a place in the knockout stage before conceding a late winning goal to Vincent Aboubakar two minutes into second-half stoppage time. The Indomitable Lions' captain ripped off his shirt in delight and, as well as being mobbed by team-mates, collected a red card after an earlier booking. Aboubakar was the first player to both score and be sent off since France's Zinedine Zidane in the 2006 final against Italy.

NATIONAL RECORD
GAVI ON TARGET FOR SPAIN'S NEW GENERATION

Spain set a national record with the single-match margin of their 7–0 victory over Costa Rica in the group stage at the 2022 FIFA World Cup. Their fifth goal fell to the Barcelona midfielder **Gavi**, who was the youngest scorer at the finals in Qatar, at 18 years 110 days. Spain's coach was former international midfielder Luis Enrique, who played for Spain in three FIFA World Cups in 1994, 1998 and 2002. One of his national team predecessors, Vicente Del Bosque, is one of only two men to lead teams to success in both the FIFA World Cup and the UEFA Champions League, which he won with Real Madrid. The other double winner was Marcello Lippi, with Italy in 2006 and Juventus in 1996.

GAVI

Switzerland hold the record for the least number of goals conceded in one tournament (2006), despite losing in the round of 16 on penalties to Ukraine.

Tunisia's pride in 2022 was seeing Wahbi Khazri become the first African player to score in three consecutive World Cup starts.

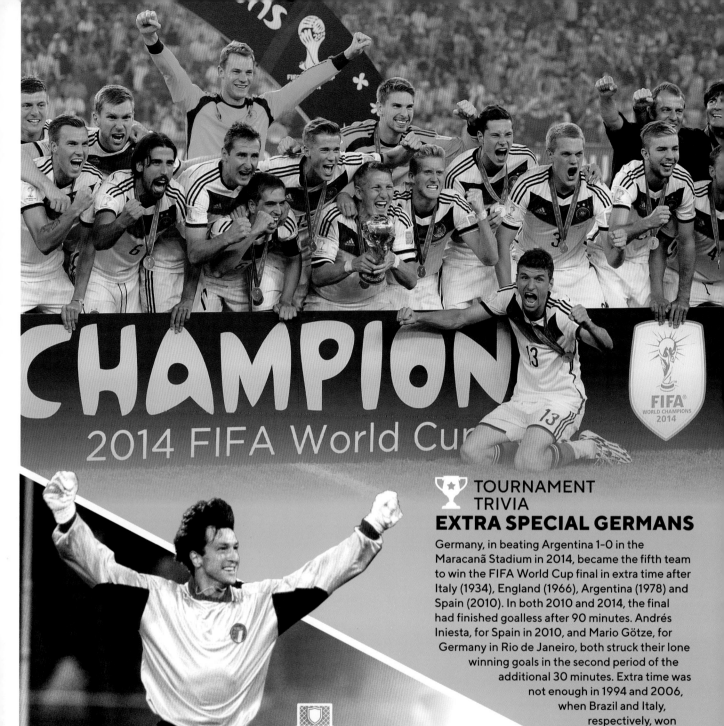

CHAMPIONS

2014 FIFA World Cup

🏆 **TOURNAMENT TRIVIA**

EXTRA SPECIAL GERMANS

Germany, in beating Argentina 1-0 in the Maracanã Stadium in 2014, became the fifth team to win the FIFA World Cup final in extra time after Italy (1934), England (1966), Argentina (1978) and Spain (2010). In both 2010 and 2014, the final had finished goalless after 90 minutes. Andrés Iniesta, for Spain in 2010, and Mario Götze, for Germany in Rio de Janeiro, both struck their lone winning goals in the second period of the additional 30 minutes. Extra time was not enough in 1994 and 2006, when Brazil and Italy, respectively, won on penalties.

DEFENSIVE RECORD

ITALY KEEP IT TIGHT

Italy set the record for the longest run without conceding a goal at the FIFA World Cup finals. They went five games without conceding at the 1990 finals, starting with their 1-0 group win over Austria. Goalkeeper **Walter Zenga** was unbeaten until Claudio Caniggia scored Argentina's equaliser in the semi-final. However, a watertight defence did not bring Italy the glory it craved: Argentina reached the final by winning the penalty shoot-out 4-3.

ZENGA

1

Hosts Qatar were the only FIFA World Cup finals debutants in 2022 after two newcomers in 2018: Iceland and Panama.

🏆 TOURNAMENT TRIVIA
SAUDI SHOCKERS

The extent of the shock of Saudi Arabia's victory over Argentina in their opening match of the 2022 FIFA World Cup was illustrated by the comparative status of the two teams. Saudi Arabia, at 53, were the second-lowest ranked nation at the finals, while fourth-rated Argentina had been on a 36-match unbeaten run. Not only that but Argentina had taken the lead after only 10 minutes when Leo Messi converted a penalty. The Albiceleste had more "goals" ruled out for offside but were shocked when the Saudis took the lead early in the second half through Saleh Al-Shehri and Salem Al-Dawsari. To the delight of their fans, veteran coach **Hervé Renard**'s side held out for more than 40 minutes to record one of the finals' greatest upsets.

RENARD

DEFENSIVE RECORD
THE FEWEST GOALS CONCEDED

FIFA World Cup winners France (1998), Italy (2006) and Spain (2010) hold the record for the fewest goals conceded on their way to victory. All three conceded just two. Spain also hold the record for fewest goals scored by FIFA World Cup winners. They netted just eight in 2010, below the 11 scored by Italy in 1938, England in 1966 or Brazil in 1994.

73

Brazil have won more matches, 73, at the FIFA World Cup finals than any other nation. They are also the only ever-presents.

🏆 TOURNAMENT TRIVIA
STUBBORN SCOTS

England and Scotland may be where international football began but none of the home nations, including Wales and Northern Ireland, entered the FIFA World Cup until 1950, as they were not members of FIFA in the 1930s. England and Scotland both qualified for the 1950 finals but the Scots refused to go to Brazil out of principle, because they "only" finished second in the British qualifying group.

ÁLVAREZ

SCORING RECORD
KEEPING IT TIGHT

Argentina's 15 goals on their way to success in the 2022 World Cup finals in Qatar were shared among only six players: Leo Messi (seven), **Julián Álvarez** (four), Enzo Fernández, Alex Mac Allister, Nahuel Molina and Ángel di María. This had also been the winning number for France in 2018, when their 12 goals were split among Antoine Griezmann and Kylian Mbappé (four each), Benjamin Pavard, Paul Pogba, Samuel Umtiti and Raphaël Varane. Italy's winning side in 2006 had 12 goals distributed among a record 10 players: Marco Materazzi and Luca Toni (two each), Alessandro del Piero, Alberto Gilardino, Fabio Grosso, Vincenzo Iaquinta, Filippo Inzaghi, Andrea Pirlo, Francesco Totti and Gianluca Zambrotta.

TOURNAMENT TRIVIA
HOME DISCOMFORT

South Africa became the first host nation to fail to reach the second round of a FIFA World Cup, when staging the 2010 tournament – though their first-round record of one win, one draw and one defeat was only inferior on goal difference to the opening three games played by hosts Spain, in 1982, and the USA, in 1994, both of whom reached the second round. Uruguay's 3–0 victory over South Africa in Pretoria on 16 June 2010 equalled the highest losing margin suffered by a FIFA World Cup host, following Brazil's 5–2 win over Sweden in the 1958 final and Italy's 4–1 trouncing of Mexico in their 1970 quarter-final.

DEFENSIVE RECORD
BRAZIL'S GOAL GLOOM

The 14 goals conceded by Brazil in the 2014 FIFA World Cup finals are the most ever conceded by the host nation. The overall record was 16 goals shipped by Korea Republic in Switzerland in 1954. In those finals, West Germany let in 14 but still won the tournament for the first time. That included conceding eight in a group match against beaten finalists Hungary.

TOURNAMENT TRIVIA
BRAZIL PROFIT FROM RIMET'S VISION

Jules Rimet, President of FIFA from 1921 to 54, was the driving force behind the first FIFA World Cup, in 1930. The tournament, in Uruguay, was not high-profile, with only 13 nations taking part. The long sea journey kept most European teams away, and only Belgium, France, Romania and Yugoslavia made the trip. Rimet's dream of a truly global competition has long since been realised and the FIFA World Cup has grown enormously in popularity. Brazil have been the competition's most successful team, winning five times. The only ever-presents at FIFA World Cup finals, they have more wins (76) than any other country and now lead Germany 114 to 112 in their tally of matches. Germany and Italy are the most successful European nations, with four World Cup wins apiece. Argentina rank next overall after their third success in Qatar, followed by Uruguay, the inaugural hosts, and France as two-times champions. England have won once as hosts in 1966 while Spain failed as hosts in 1982 then made amends in 2010 in South Africa.

RIMET

TOURNAMENT TRIVIA
CRASHING THE INTERNET

Argentina broke Instagram records with Leo Messi's first post celebrating their third FIFA World Cup triumph in Qatar. Within 24 hours, the post had almost 70 million likes, making it the most-liked post in the site's history. Football's social media revolution had already been in evidence earlier in the game when France's dramatic equalising goal in normal time generated 24,400 tweets per second, the highest ever for a World Cup. Surveys of the main social media sites reported that Argentina received almost double the mentions of France and 57 per cent of all mentions of the 32 World Cup teams. Lionel Messi was the most mentioned player during the finals, followed by **Kylian Mbappé**.

MOST GOALS IN FIFA WORLD CUP FINALS:

1	**Brazil,**	237
2	**Germany/West Germany,**	232
3	**Argentina,**	152
4	**France,**	136
5	**Italy,**	128

KIT TRIVIA
KIT CONFUSION

France had to wear the green-and-white striped shirts of local club Kimberley in a 1978 FIFA World Cup group tie in Argentina. Confusion over colours meant they forgot to take an agreed change strip to Mar del Plata to play Hungary. France won the tie 3–1 but both teams were eliminated. Italy won the group ahead of hosts Argentina.

MBAPPÉ

TOURNAMENT TRIVIA
DISPOSSESSORS

Japan made modern FIFA World Cup finals history in Qatar in beating Spain 2–1 in their first-round tie in Group E. Spain dominated the game to such an extent that Japan managed only 17.7 per cent possession – the lowest rating for any winning team. The Blue Samurai, ever-present at the finals since 1998, were 1–0 down at halftime then hit back to win with two high-speed goals from Ritsu Dōan and **Ao Tanaka**. Victory meant they finished top of the group while Spain sneaked through as runners-up, ahead of eliminated Germany on goal difference.

TANAKA

13

Only 13 nations participated in the first FIFA World Cup. Pioneered by Jules Rimet, it was held in Uruguay in 1930.

143

FIFA WORLD CUP GOALSCORING

11

Hakan Şükür of Turkey holds the record for the fastest-ever FIFA World Cup goal, scored after 11 seconds against Korea Republic in 2002.

7-5

The highest-scoring game in the FIFA World Cup finals was the quarter-final between Austria and Switzerland on 26 June 1954, which ended 7-5 to Austria.

9

Brazil have scored more goals than any other nation in opening matches of the FIFA World Cup: 9.

2,500

Tunisia's Fakhreddine Ben Youssef scored the 2,500th FIFA World Cup finals goal, against Panama in 2018.

TOURNAMENT TRIVIA
PENALTY PROGRESS

The 2018 FIFA World Cup finals in Russia equalled the number of shoot-outs in the knockout stage, with four matches decided from the penalty spot, matching the number in 1990, 2006 and 2014. Croatia became only the second team, after Argentina in 1990, to win consecutive shoot-outs, against Denmark and Russia. They were also the first team to be taken to extra time in all three knockout ties on their way to the final, meaning that they played 90 minutes more than final opponents France.

The goals are what everyone remembers from the FIFA World Cup. Over the years, some of the world's greatest strikers have showcased their talents on the world stage.

TOURNAMENT TRIVIA
RONALDO'S RECORD

With his penalty in Portugal's opening victory over Ghana, **Cristiano Ronaldo** became the only player to have scored at least one goal in five finals tournaments, having hit the net in 2006, 2010, 2014 and 2018. He also became, at 37 years 292 days, the oldest player to score for Portugal at the World Cup, having been the youngest, at 21 years 132 days, in 2006. Three players have scored goals in four tournaments: Pelé in 1958, 1962, 1966, 1970, West Germany's Uwe Seeler in 1958, 1962, 1966 and 1970, and Leo Messi in 2006, 2014, 2018 and 2022.

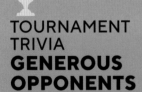

TOURNAMENT TRIVIA
GENEROUS OPPONENTS

Chile were the first team to benefit from an opponent's own goal at the FIFA World Cup. Mexico's Manuel Rosas put the ball into his own net during the Chileans' 3-0 win at the inaugural 1930 finals in Uruguay. France, courtesy of two in both 2014 and 2018, are out on their own as recipients of the most own goals with six; Germany and Italy have four apiece. In 2018, **Mario Mandžukić** of Croatia scored the first own goal in a FIFA World Cup final, while the other own goal to benefit France came from Australia's Aziz Behich in the group stage.

MANDŽUKIĆ

RONALDO

PELÉ

LEADING ALL-TIME FIFA WORLD CUP GOALSCORERS:

1 Miroslav Klose, Germany – 16 (2002, 2006, 2010, 2014)

2 Ronaldo, Brazil – 15 (1998, 2002, 2006)

3 Gerd Müller, West Germany – 14 (1970, 1974)

4 Just Fontaine, France – 13 (1958)

5 Lionel Messi, Argentina - 13 (2006, 2014, 2018, 2022)

GONÇALO GLORY

Gonçalo Ramos, replacing Cristiano Ronaldo, hit the first hat-trick of the 2022 finals in Portugal's 6–1 win over Switzerland.

KLOSE

NATIONAL LEGEND
PELÉ SO UNLUCKY

Pelé would surely have been the all-time FIFA World Cup top scorer but for injuries. He was sidelined early in the 1962 finals, and again four years later. He scored six goals in Brazil's 1958 triumph, including two in the 5-2 final victory over Sweden. He also netted Brazil's 100th FIFA World Cup goal as they beat Italy 4-1 in the 1970 final. Despite his bad luck with injuries, Pelé, who died at 82 just 11 days after the 2022 final, is the only man to have been a member of three World Cup-winning squads.

NATIONAL LEGEND
KLOSE ENCOUNTERS

Germany's 2014 World Cup-winning striker Miroslav Klose is the World Cup's all-time leading marksman with 16 goals (in 2002, 2006, 2010 and 2014). Behind him come Brazil's Ronaldo Luís Nazário de Lima (15, in 1994, 1998, 2002 and 2006), West Germany's Gerd Müller (14, in 1970 and 1974) then France's Just Fontaine and Argentina's Lionel Messi both on 13. Fontaine, who died in March 2023, holds the single-event record after scoring all his goals as France finished third in Sweden in 1958. The magnitude of Fontaine's achievement is underlined by the fact that Messi needed five tournaments to match him.

MOST GOALS IN ONE FIFA WORLD CUP:

1 Hungary – 27 (1954)

2 West Germany – 25 (1954)

3 France – 23 (1958)

4 Brazil – 22 (1950)

5 Brazil – 19 (1970)

SCORING RECORD
MBAPPÉ PROVES A FINAL MATCH FOR HURST

Kylian Mbappé emulated the achievement of England's Geoff Hurst in 1966 when he scored a hat-trick for France against Argentina in the FIFA World Cup final in Qatar. Both Hurst and Mbappé needed extra-time to complete their trebles. Mbappé exploded into devastating action in the 80th, 81st and 118th minutes of the final. He was rewarded with the tournament's Golden Boot as eight-goal leading marksman, but ended up a loser after France's defeat in a penalty shootout. He is the fifth man to score in more than one FIFA World Cup Final, along with Brazil's Vavá and Pelé, West Germany's Paul Breitner and France's Zinedine Zidane.

FIFA WORLD CUP APPEARANCES

Since the dawn of the FIFA World Cup, many players have left their mark on the competition. But some have left bigger legacies than others...

MARADONA

TOURNAMENT TRIVIA
THE "DOUBLE" CHAMPIONS

Didier Deschamps joined Franz Beckenbauer and Mário Zagallo in the history books at the 2018 FIFA World Cup finals. Until France's victory in Russia under Deschamps, their 1998 winning captain, Zagallo and Beckenbauer had been the only men to win the World Cup as both player and manager. Zagallo won the World Cup in 1958 and 1962 on the wing; he took over at short notice from João Saldanha as Brazil manager and secured his third triumph at the 1970 final. Beckenbauer played in 1970 too for West Germany, whom he captained to victory on home soil in 1974. Beckenbauer was appointed national coach in 1984, and won the FIFA World Cup in 1990.

DESCHAMPS

NATIONAL LEGEND
LEADING CAPTAINS

Five players have been team captain in the FIFA World Cup final on two occasions. **Diego Maradona** lifted the trophy for Argentina in 1986 but was on the losing side in 1990. Reverse the order for fellow Argentinian Leo Messi, who was a runner-up in 2014 then a winner in 2022. Dunga of Brazil was a trophy-lifting captain in 1994 but a loser in 1998. France's Hugo Lloris led his team to glory in 2018 but was on the losing side in Qatar. West Germany's Karl-Heinz Rummenigge was the losing captain in both 1982 and 1986.

NATIONAL LEGEND
PROSINEČKI'S SCORING RECORD

Robert Prosinečki is the only player to have scored for different countries in FIFA World Cup finals tournaments. He netted for Yugoslavia in their 4-1 win over the United Arab Emirates in the 1990 tournament. Eight years later, following the break-up of the old Yugoslavia, he scored for Croatia in their 3-0 group-game win over Jamaica, and then netted the first goal in his side's 2-1 third-place play-off victory over the Netherlands.

PROSINEČKI

MOST APPEARANCES IN FIFA WORLD CUP FINALS:

1. Lionel Messi (Argentina) – 26
2. Lothar Matthäus (Germany) – 25
3. Miroslav Klose (Germany) – 24
4. Paolo Maldini (Italy) – 23

NICO WILLIAMS

IÑAKI WILLIAMS

4

The three fastest substitutions in the history of the FIFA World Cup have been made in the fourth minute: Steve Hodge (England, 1986), Giuseppe Bergomi (Italy, 1998) and Peter Crouch (England, 2006).

17

Northern Ireland's Norman Whiteside is the youngest player in FIFA World Cup finals history, being just 17 years and 41 days old when he started against Yugoslavia in 1982.

TOURNAMENT TRIVIA
BROTHERLY STARDOM

Iñaki Williams of Ghana and **Nico Williams** of Spain made FIFA World Cup history on becoming the first full siblings to play for different countries at the same finals. At least they did not play against each other. In 2010 and 2014, half-brothers Jerome and Kevin-Prince Boateng were twice on opposite sides. In South Africa, Jerome was on the winning side for Germany against Kevin-Prince's Ghana. Their World Cup paths crossed again in Brazil in a 2–2 group stage draw.

16

Manchester City sent 16 players to the finals in both 2018 and 2022. That made them the best-represented club in Russia, but they lost that status in Qatar to Bayern Munich, who sent 17 players to the tournament.

4

The most players sent off in one FIFA World Cup finals game is four during a match between Portugal and the Netherlands, refereed by Russian official Valentin Ivanov in 2006.

SHARING THE GLORY

Portugal's Cristiano Ronaldo and Argentina's Lionel Messi have been old rivals out on the pitch, but they share a record in the history books. The 2022 finals saw them join Germany's Lothar Matthäus plus Mexico's Antonio Carbajal, Rafael Márquez and Andrés Guardado in playing at five different World Cups.

FEDERATION HISTORY
GERMANY UNITED

Germany and West Germany are counted together in FIFA World Cup records because the Deutscher Fussball-Bund, founded in 1900, Germany's governing body, was in charge of the national game before World War II, during the East-West split and post-reunification. German sides have won the World Cup four times and appeared in the final a record eight times. In 2014, match-deciding substitutes André Schürrle and Mario Götze were the first players born in Germany since reunification to win the World Cup, while team-mate Toni Kroos was the only 2014 squad member to have been born in what was East Germany. Kroos was also the first player from the former East Germany to win the World Cup.

PEPE

NATIONAL LEGEND
PEPE'S PRIDE

Pepe, Portugal's 39-year-old centre back or defensive midfielder, became the second-oldest outfield player to appear in the World Cup finals in the 2–0 group stage victory over Uruguay. He also became the second-oldest player to score at a World Cup in the 6–1 win over Switzerland. Cameroon's Roger Milla remains the oldest World Cup outfield player as a 42-year-old in the United States in 1994. Overall record veteran is Egyptian goalkeeper Essam El-Hadary, who was 45 at the 2018 finals.

FASTEST SENDINGS-OFF IN THE FIFA WORLD CUP FINALS:

1. José Batista (Uruguay) v. Scotland, 1986 – 1 min
2. Carlos Sánchez (Colombia) v. Japan, 2018 – 4 min
3. Giorgio Ferrini (Italy) v. Chile, 1962 – 8 min
4. Zezé Procópio (Brazil) v. Czechoslovakia, 1938 – 14 min
5. Mohammed Al Khlaiwi (Saudi Arabia) v. France 1998 – 19 min
= Miguel Bossio (Uruguay) v. Denmark, 1986 – 19 min

FIFA WORLD CUP GOALKEEPING

The FIFA World Cup has produced a fair few legends between the sticks. From the old dependables to the crazy keepers, many have written their names in the history books.

RIGHT WAY FOR RICARDO

Spain's Ricardo Zamora became the first man to save a penalty in a FIFA World Cup finals match, stopping Waldemar de Brito's spot-kick for Brazil in 1934. Spain went on to win 3–1.

BEIRANVAND

MARTÍNEZ

RECENT HISTORY
CONCUSSION PROTOCOL

Iran goalkeeper Hossein Hosseini became the first player declared a 'concussion substitute' when he took over from **Alireza Beiranvand** in their opening defeat by England in the FIFA World Cup in Qatar. In the first half, Beiranvand collided with defender Majid Hosseini. Beiranvand played on after several minutes' treatment on the pitch, but sank to the ground moments later and had to be replaced. Under the new concussion protocol, a ruling of suspected concussion meant Iran could still use their standard five substitutes. Beiranvand had been Iran's first-choice keeper at the 2018 finals, where he saved a penalty from Cristiano Ronaldo. In Qatar, he missed Iran's second game against Wales and returned for the 1–0 defeat to United States.

NATIONAL LEGEND
EMI BETTER LATE THAN NEVER

Emiliano Martínez climaxed a remarkable two years when he was awarded the Golden Glove as top goalkeeper at the 2022 FIFA World Cup after Argentina defeated holders France in a penalty shootout. The Aston Villa goalkeeper was the first South American to win the prize after keeping three clean sheets and conceding only seven goals. Yet he had only become a guaranteed starter in the English Premier League after leaving Arsenal for Aston Villa in 2020. A year later, Martínez made his full debut for Argentina. This was 10 years after he had first been called up as an unused substitute.

NATIONAL LEGEND
NETTING FRENCH RECORDS

Goalkeepers **Hugo Lloris** and Steve Mandanda both made French football history at the 2022 FIFA World Cup finals in Qatar. Tottenham goalkeeper Lloris won a national record 143rd cap, overtaking Lilian Thuram, in the quarter-final victory over England. Loris extended his total to 144 in the semi-final defeat of Morocco and to 145 in the final against Argentina. Earlier, reserve goalkeeper Mandanda, at 37 years 247 days, had become the oldest French player to appear at the finals in their 1–0 group stage defeat by Tunisia.

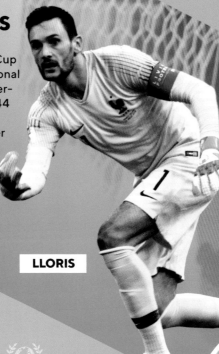

LLORIS

NEUER

3 Three goalkeepers managed clean sheets at the World Cup finals in Qatar: Argentina's Emi Martínez, England's Jordan Pickford and Morocco's Yassine Bounou.

4 Dominik Livaković of Croatia made a record-equalling four saves in penalty shootouts at the 2022 FIFA World Cup in Qatar.

16 Tim Howard famously made an incredible 16 saves in the USA's round-of-16 clash with Belgium in 2014.

OLIVER'S ARMS

Germany's Oliver Kahn is the only goalkeeper to have received the adidas Golden Ball as the tournament's best player, winning the award at the 2002 FIFA World Cup – despite taking a share of the blame for Brazil's winning goals in the final.

NATIONAL LEGEND
BATTERING RAMÓN

Argentina's 6–0 win over Peru at the 1978 FIFA World Cup aroused suspicion because the hosts needed to win by four goals to reach the final at the expense of arch-rivals Brazil – and Peruvian goalkeeper Ramón Quiroga had been born in Argentina. He insisted, though, that his saves prevented the defeat from being even more embarrassingly emphatic. Earlier in the same tournament, Quiroga had been booked for a foul on Grzegorz Lato after running into the Polish half of the field.

TOURNAMENT TRIVIA
DOWNHILL SLALOM

Goalkeeper **Manuel Neuer** came down to earth in more ways than one during the 2022 FIFA World Cup. Neuer had won the World Cup with Germany in Brazil in 2014, but he was unable to prevent the four-time champions crashing out in the group stage in both 2018 and then 2022. Neuer flew home from Qatar with 117 international appearances to his credit, sixth in Germany's all-time rankings. However, a freak accident on a skiing holiday left Neuer with a broken right leg and damaged left hand, ruling him out for the rest of the season.

NATIONAL LEGEND
ITALY'S ELDER STATESMEN

Dino Zoff became both the oldest player and oldest captain to win the FIFA World Cup when Italy lifted the trophy in Spain in 1982. He was 40 years and 133 days old. A predecessor as goalkeeper and captain of both Italy and Juventus, Gianpiero Combi, had led Italy to World Cup glory in 1934. Zoff also holds the record (1,142 minutes) for the longest stretch without conceding in international football, set between 1972 and 1974.

ZOFF

FIFA WORLD CUP MANAGERS

Behind every great team is a tactical mastermind, and the FIFA World Cup has introduced the world to some of the greatest minds football has ever seen.

27

Juan José Tramutola was the youngest-ever FIFA World Cup finals coach, leading Argentina to the 1930 final at the age of 27 years and 267 days.

HERDMAN

SCALONI

NATIONAL LEGEND
HERDMAN'S DUAL TRACK STRATEGY

John Herdman was unique at the 2022 FIFA World Cup in Qatar as the only team manager who had also managed at the Women's World Cup. Born and brought up in north-east England, Herdman emigrated to New Zealand, where the local FA appointed him as director of development. He led the New Zealand women's senior squad to the World Cup in 2007 and 2011, after which he took over Canada's women's team. Canada won bronze medals at the 2012 and 2016 Olympic Games, and reached the quarter-finals, as hosts, of the Women's World Cup in 2015. In 2018, Herdman switched roles to become head coach of the Canada men's team, and in Qatar he led them to their first men's World Cup finals in 36 years.

NATIONAL LEGEND
SCALONI'S TRIUMPHANT REUNION

Lionel Scaloni had no idea what a glorious World Cup destiny was in store when he and Leo Messi left the pitch together after victory over Mexico in the round of 16 at the 2006 finals. Scaloni was a fullback at the peak of his career while Messi was just starting out. Both played for clubs in Spain – Scaloni with Deportivo de La Coruña and Messi with Barcelona. That 2006 World Cup brought a parting of the ways that lasted for 12 years. Then in 2018, Scaloni was promoted from under-20s boss to take over Argentina's seniors and link up once more with Messi. It was to prove a winning partnership – first with the *Copa América* in 2021 then with the greatest prize of all in Qatar.

TOURNAMENT TRIVIA
VITTORIO'S VICTORIES

Italy's Vittorio Pozzo continues to hold a record, established in 1938, as the only manager to have led his nation to two successive FIFA World Cup triumphs. A Manchester United admirer during a study spell in England in the 1920s, Pozzo returned home to become a major figure in the Italian federation. He was appointed national team coach in 1929 and built a team who won the World Cup in both 1934 and 1938 as well as the Olympic football gold medal in between at the 1936 Berlin Games. Pozzo stepped down after a 4–0 defeat in Turin to England in 1948. The hopes harboured by Didier Deschamps of matching Pozzo's double achievement at the 2022 World Cup ended in a penalty shootout in the final.

NATIONAL LEGEND
CRASHING BORA

Only one tournament behind record-holder Carlos Alberto Parreira, **Bora Milutinović** has coached at five different FIFA World Cups – with a different country each time, two of them being the hosts. As well as Mexico in 1986 and the USA in 1994, he led Costa Rica in 1990, Nigeria in 1998 and China PR in 2002. He reached the knockout stages with every country except China PR – who failed to score a single goal.

MILUTINOVIC

TITE

71

The oldest manager in the finals was German Otto Rehhagel, aged 71 years and 307 days, when he led Greece in South Africa in 2010.

25

West Germany's Helmut Schön was coach for more FIFA World Cup matches than any other man – 25, across the 1966, 1970, 1974 and 1978 tournaments.

6

Carlos Alberto Parreira holds the record for most FIFA World Cups attended as a coach. Parreira won with Brazil in 1994 and fell at the quarter-finals with them in 2006, but also led Kuwait (1982), the United Arab Emirates (1990), Saudi Arabia (1998) and hosts South Africa (2010).

7

Seven managers were sacked or quit immediately after their team's exit from the 2022 FIFA World Cup finals.

TOURNAMENT TRIVIA
PUFF DADDIES

The coaches of the two sides appearing at the 1978 FIFA World Cup final were such prolific smokers that an oversized ashtray was produced for Argentina's César Luis Menotti and the Netherlands's Ernst Happel so they could share it on the touchline. Menotti, the triumphant coach that day, also managed Barcelona and Atlético Madrid in an illustrious managerial career.

NATIONAL LEGEND
LAST WALTZ FOR TITE

Brazil coach **Tite** threw himself enthusiastically into the dance routine of his goalscoring stars during the five-time champions' 4–1 victory over Korea Republic in the round of 16 at the 2022 FIFA World Cup. The 61-year-old imitated Richarlison's "pigeon dance" from the touchline after the Tottenham forward's goal. He explained: "It shows the connection I have with a younger generation. I am 61 years old and I work with players who are 21 and 22. They could be my grandchildren. If I have to dance to connect with them, I will continue dancing." Unfortunately for Tite, Brazil's next match, against Croatia, saw the dance cut short by a quarter-final defeat on penalties.

LAST TEN COACHES TO WIN FIFA WORLD CUP:

2022: Lionel Scaloni, Argentina

2018: Didier Deschamps, France

2014: Joachim Löw, Germany

2010: Vicente del Bosque, Spain

2006: Marcello Lippi, Italy

2002: Luiz Felipe Scolari, Brazil

1998: Aimé Jacquet, France

1994: Carlos Alberto Parreira, Brazil

1990: Franz Beckenbauer, Germany

1986: Carlos Bilardo, Argentina

FIFA WORLD CUP ATTENDANCES

From the modest hundreds of 1930 to the hundreds of thousands who watch these days, FIFA World Cups are all about the fans. Every four years, millions pack into the stadiums to watch the greatest show on Earth.

FUTURE TOURNAMENTS
THREE-WAY WINNERS

The FIFA World Cup finals in 2026 will make history twice over. Firstly, they will feature 48 teams – playing 80 matches – after world football's governing body decided to open up the finals to more national teams than the current 32 that competed in Qatar in 2022. Secondly, staging the finals will be shared between three countries after the USA, Canada and Mexico were awarded hosting rights by the FIFA Congress in Moscow in June 2018. Canada and Mexico will host ten matches each with the USA the other 60, including all ties from the quarter-finals onwards.

1.8 MILLION
More than 1.8m fans visited the FIFA Fan Festival at the Al Bidda Park in Doha during the 2022 finals. Every match was shown live with entertainment from the likes of Diplo, Maluma, Kizz Daniel, Nora Fatehi, Trinidad Cardona and Calvin Harris.

ATTENDANCE RECORD
MORBID MARACANÃ

The largest attendance for a FIFA World Cup match was at Rio de Janeiro's Maracanã for the last clash of the 1950 tournament – though no one is quite sure how many were there. The final tally was officially given as 173,850, though some estimates suggest as many as 210,000 witnessed the host country's traumatic defeat. Tensions were so high at the final whistle; FIFA president Jules Rimet described the crowd's overwhelming silence as "morbid, almost too difficult to bear". Uruguay's triumphant players barricaded themselves inside their dressing room for several hours before they judged it safe enough to emerge.

NATIONAL STADIUM
LOST IN THE DESERT

Qatar, Arab host of the FIFA World Cup in 2022, were also the first host nation to lose both the Opening Match and all their other group games. That meant a first round exit after three matches in which they conceded seven goals and scored just one. Previously, South Africa in 2010 had been the only host to fail to progress beyond the initial stage. Qatar opened up with a 2-0 defeat to Ecuador before further losses to Senegal and Netherlands sealed their fate. These were all the more surprising since Qatar were the reigning Asian champions. The one player who could rate the finals a success was Mohammed Muntari, who made history by scoring Qatar's first-ever World Cup goal to temporarily reduce the deficit in the 3-1 defeat to Senegal, four minutes after coming on as a substitute.

3
Mexico will stage the World Cup for a record third time in 2026 as cohost with Canada and United States, having been sole host in 1970 and 1986.

17
Some 17 countries have staged the World Cup finals: Argentina, Brazil, Chile, England, France (twice), Germany (twice), Italy (twice), Japan, Korea Republic, Mexico (twice), Qatar, Russia, South Africa, Spain, Sweden, Switzerland and Uruguay.

ATTENDANCE RECORD
QUEUEING IN QATAR

The 2022 FIFA World Cup was the third-highest attended in history. The 64 matches were watched by a total attendance of 3,404,252 fans. That averaged out at 52,191 per match. More than one million tickets were sold to Qatari fans, followed by purchasing orders from United States, neighbouring Saudi Arabia, England, Mexico, the United Arab Emirates, Argentina, France, Brazil and Germany. These statistics disproved pre-tournament concerns that foreign fans would stay away because of the November/December staging and other issues. The United States holds the record aggregate for the 1994 tournament, which saw a total attendance figure of 3,587,538.

300

The 300 people who were recorded as watching Romania beat Peru 3-1 in 1930 formed the FIFA World Cup finals' smallest attendance, at the Estadio Pocitos in Montevideo. A day earlier, ten times as many people are thought to have been there for France's 4-1 win over Mexico.

ATTENDANCE RECORD
ABSENT FRIENDS

Only 2,823 spectators turned up at the Råsunda Stadium in Stockholm to see Wales play Hungary in a first-round play-off match during the 1958 FIFA World Cup. More than 15,000 had attended the first game between the two sides, but boycotted the replay in tribute to executed Hungarian uprising leader Imre Nagy. It's not the lowest-ever attendance at a FIFA World Cup match, though: that honour goes to Romania v. Peru at Estadio Pocitos in Montevideo, Uruguay, in 1930. Just 300 fans showed their faces.

TOP TEN
FIFA WORLD CUP ATTENDANCES:

1 **173,850 – Maracanã Stadium,** Rio De Janeiro, Brazil, 1950

2 **114,600 – Azteca Stadium,** Mexico City, Mexico, 1986

3 **107,412 – Azteca Stadium,** Mexico City, Mexico, 1970

4 **98,000 – Wembley Stadium,** London, England, 1966

5 **94,194 – Rose Bowl,** Pasadena, USA, 1994

6 **93,000 – Estadio Centenario,** Montevideo, Uruguay, 1930

7 **90,000 – Estadio Santiago Bernabéu,** Madrid, Spain, 1982

8 **88,966 Lusail Iconic Stadium,** Lusail, Qatar, 2022

9 **88,668 Lusail Iconic Stadium,** Lusail, Qatar, 2022

10 **88,235 Lusail Iconic Stadium,** Lusail, Qatar, 2022

172

Qatar's air-conditioned staging brought a finals record of 172 goals, one more than the 171 achieved in France in 1998 and Brazil in 2014. Runners-up France outscored eventual champions Argentina by 16 goals to 15.

 ## TOURNAMENT TRIVIA
GENDER EQUALITY

Only two stadiums have hosted the finals of the FIFA World Cup for both men and women. The Rose Bowl, in Pasadena, California, was the venue for the men's final in 1994 – when Brazil beat Italy – and the women's showdown between the victorious USA and China PR five years later, which was watched by 90,185 people. But Sweden's Råsunda Stadium, near Stockholm, just about got there first – though it endured a long wait between the men's final in 1958 and the women's in 1995.

FIFA WORLD CUP PENALTIES

A quick-draw battle of nerves from 12 yards, the penalty shoot-out is either one of the most anticipated moments of a FIFA World Cup, or one of the most dreaded: it often depends on your history…

35

The tightly-matched drama of the FIFA World Cup finals has been illustrated by the need for 35 penalty shootouts since the first in 1982. A record five shootouts featured at the finals in Qatar.

TOURNAMENT TRIVIA
WOE FOR ASAMOAH

Ghana striker Asamoah Gyan is the only player to have missed two penalties during match time at FIFA World Cups. He hit the post from a spot kick against the Czech Republic during a group game at the 2006 tournament, then struck a shot against the bar with the final kick of extra time in Ghana's 2010 quarter-final versus Uruguay. Had he scored then, Gyan would have given Ghana a 2-1 win – following Luis Suárez's goal-stopping handball on the goal line – and a first African place in a FIFA World Cup semi-final. Despite such a traumatic miss, Gyan scored Ghana's first penalty in the shoot-out. His team still lost 4-2, though.

LAST FIVE FIFA WORLD CUP PENALTY SHOOT-OUTS:

1 **Argentina 4-2 France, final, 2022** (3-3 AET)

2 **Argentina 4-3 Netherlands, semi-final, 2022** (2-2 AET)

3 **Croatia 4-2 Brazil, quarter-final, 2022** (0-0 AET)

4 **Morocco 3-0 Spain, round of 16, 2022** (0-0 AET)

5 **Croatia 3-1 Japan, round of 16, 2022** (1-1 AET)

SCORING RECORD
GERMAN EFFICIENCY

Germany have won all four of their penalty shootouts in the FIFA World Cup. Their first was also the first in the finals after none had been needed in 1978, when the facility was introduced. In the semi-finals in Seville, Spain, in 1982, West Germany and France ended extra-time all-square at 3-3. The Germans won 5-4 on penalties. France's Michel Platini ended on the losing side despite twice being successful from the spot – once in normal time and once in the shootout. Settling the tie needed 12 penalty kicks, the joint-longest shootout together with Sweden's 5-4 win over Romania in the quarter-finals in 1994. The shortest seven-kick shootouts saw West Germany beat Mexico in 1986 and Morocco beat Spain in 2022.

16

The round of 16 proved devastating for Spain in both 2018 and 2022. Each time they were eliminated in a penalty shootout. In 2018, Spain lost 4-3 after a 1-1 draw with hosts Russia and four years later they succumbed 3-0 after a 0-0 draw with Morocco.

KANE

TOURNAMENT TRIVIA
CRUEL FOR KANE

England's **Harry Kane** has established a reputation over the years as one of the most reliable takers of penalties in the domestic and international game. Yet no-one is infallible when it comes to the one-on-one duel against an opposing goalkeeper with victory and defeat, progress and elimination at stake. England were reminded of this against holders France in the quarter-finals of the 2022 FIFA World Cup in Qatar. France went ahead only for England to level through a Kane penalty. That strike brought him level with Wayne Rooney as England's 53-goal all-time top scorer. But later Kane, again facing his Tottenham club-mate Hugo Lloris, put a second spot-kick into the crowd. France went on to win 2-1 and England went home. Still Kane's record remained an impressive 17 conversions out of 21.

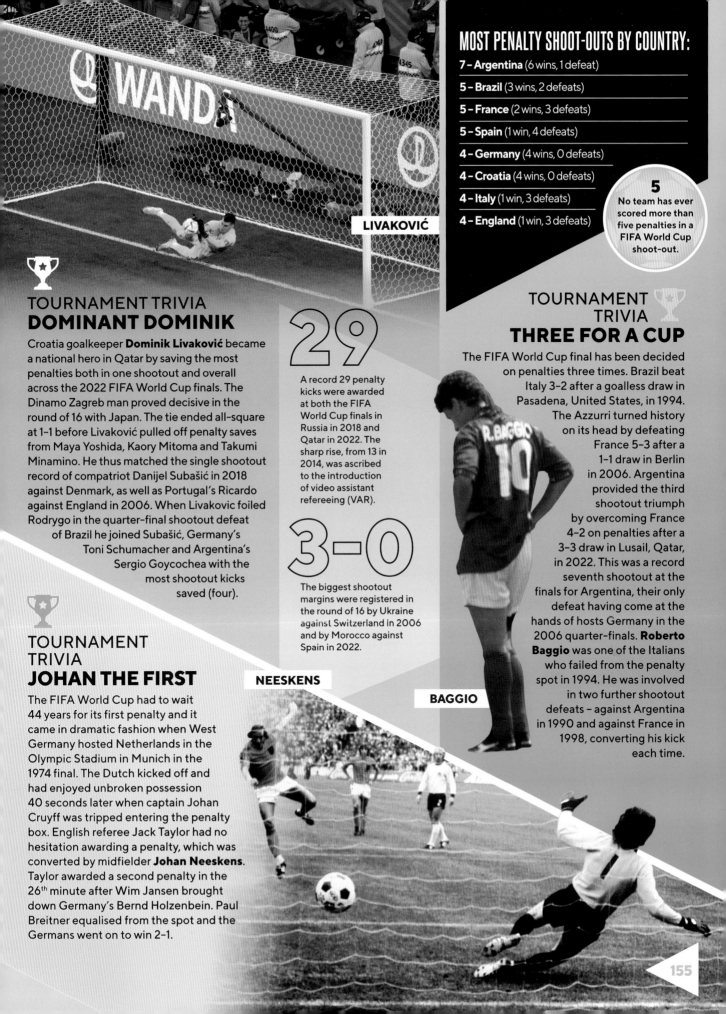

MOST PENALTY SHOOT-OUTS BY COUNTRY:

7 – Argentina (6 wins, 1 defeat)

5 – Brazil (3 wins, 2 defeats)

5 – France (2 wins, 3 defeats)

5 – Spain (1 win, 4 defeats)

4 – Germany (4 wins, 0 defeats)

4 – Croatia (4 wins, 0 defeats)

4 – Italy (1 win, 3 defeats)

4 – England (1 win, 3 defeats)

LIVAKOVIĆ

5
No team has ever scored more than five penalties in a FIFA World Cup shoot-out.

TOURNAMENT TRIVIA
DOMINANT DOMINIK

Croatia goalkeeper **Dominik Livaković** became a national hero in Qatar by saving the most penalties both in one shootout and overall across the 2022 FIFA World Cup finals. The Dinamo Zagreb man proved decisive in the round of 16 with Japan. The tie ended all-square at 1–1 before Livaković pulled off penalty saves from Maya Yoshida, Kaory Mitoma and Takumi Minamino. He thus matched the single shootout record of compatriot Danijel Subašić in 2018 against Denmark, as well as Portugal's Ricardo against England in 2006. When Livakovic foiled Rodrygo in the quarter-final shootout defeat of Brazil he joined Subašić, Germany's Toni Schumacher and Argentina's Sergio Goycochea with the most shootout kicks saved (four).

29

A record 29 penalty kicks were awarded at both the FIFA World Cup finals in Russia in 2018 and Qatar in 2022. The sharp rise, from 13 in 2014, was ascribed to the introduction of video assistant refereeing (VAR).

3–0

The biggest shootout margins were registered in the round of 16 by Ukraine against Switzerland in 2006 and by Morocco against Spain in 2022.

TOURNAMENT TRIVIA
THREE FOR A CUP

The FIFA World Cup final has been decided on penalties three times. Brazil beat Italy 3–2 after a goalless draw in Pasadena, United States, in 1994. The Azzurri turned history on its head by defeating France 5–3 after a 1–1 draw in Berlin in 2006. Argentina provided the third shootout triumph by overcoming France 4–2 on penalties after a 3–3 draw in Lusail, Qatar, in 2022. This was a record seventh shootout at the finals for Argentina, their only defeat having come at the hands of hosts Germany in the 2006 quarter-finals. **Roberto Baggio** was one of the Italians who failed from the penalty spot in 1994. He was involved in two further shootout defeats – against Argentina in 1990 and against France in 1998, converting his kick each time.

BAGGIO

NEESKENS

TOURNAMENT TRIVIA
JOHAN THE FIRST

The FIFA World Cup had to wait 44 years for its first penalty and it came in dramatic fashion when West Germany hosted Netherlands in the Olympic Stadium in Munich in the 1974 final. The Dutch kicked off and had enjoyed unbroken possession 40 seconds later when captain Johan Cruyff was tripped entering the penalty box. English referee Jack Taylor had no hesitation awarding a penalty, which was converted by midfielder **Johan Neeskens**. Taylor awarded a second penalty in the 26th minute after Wim Jansen brought down Germany's Bernd Holzenbein. Paul Breitner equalised from the spot and the Germans went on to win 2–1.

FIFA WORLD CUP QUALIFIERS

To get to the greatest show on Earth, first countries must fight it out in regional confederations.

BIGGEST-EVER QUALIFYING WINS:

1. **Australia 31-0 American Samoa**
   11 April 2001
2. **Australia 22-0 Tonga**
   9 April 2001
3. **Iran 19, Guam 0**
   24 November, 2000
4. **Maldives 0-17 IR Iran**
   2 June 1997
5. **Tajikistan 16, Guam 0**
   11 June 1997
   = **Fiji 16, Tuvalu 0**
   27 August, 2007
7. **Vanuatu 15, American Samoa 0**
   30 August, 2007
   = **Qatar 15, Bhutan 0**
   3 September, 2015
9. **Iran 14, Cambodia 0**
   10 October, 2019
   = **Mongolia 0, Japan 14**
   30 March, 2021

NATIONAL QUALIFICATION RECORD
MESSI SHOWS THE WAY

Lionel Messi played an inspirational captain's role in leading Argentina to the finals in 2022. Captain Messi was not distracted from the World Cup task by his headline-grabbing transfer from Barcelona to Paris Saint-Germain in the summer of 2021. He scored all three goals in Argentina's 3-0 win over Bolivia and ended the campaign with seven goals, level with team-mate Lautaro Martínez. Bolivia's Marcelo Moreno was the South American group's 10 goals leading marksman followed, on eight goals each, by Messi's former Barcelona club-mates Neymar (Brazil) and Luis Suárez (Uruguay).

KANE

117 SECONDS
Abdel Hamid Bassiouny of Egypt scored the fastest-ever qualification hat-trick in their 8-2 win over Namibia on 13 July 2001.

SCORING RECORD
HAPPY HARRY

Harry Kane, six-goal top scorer at the 2018 finals, picked up in the 2022 qualifiers where he left off in Russia. England's captain scored a hat-trick in a 5-0 home win over Albania then four goals in the 10-0 away victory over San Marino with which England topped their group. Kane's late surge meant he finished as 12-goal joint top scorer in the European section along with Netherlands' Memphis Depay. Next came Poland's captain Robert Lewandowski with nine goals, eight in group play and one in the playoffs.

32

Just 32 countries entered qualification for the 1934 FIFA World Cup. Sweden and Estonia played the first match on 11 June 1933.

1

Hosts of the 2022 FIFA World Cup Qatar are the only one of the 32 finalists never to have reached this stage previously.

41

At 41, Zambia's Kalusha Bwalya is the oldest player to have scored a match-winning goal in a FIFA World Cup qualifying match.

OFF THE MARK

Norjmoogiin Tsedenbal of Mongolia scored the first goal of the 2022 FIFA World Cup qualification campaign in a 2-0 defeat of Brunei Darussalam on 6 June 2019.

NATIONAL QUALIFICATION RECORD
SWITCH IN TIME FOR MUSIALA

MUSIALA

Germany were the first European team to secure a place in the finals in Qatar. The four-times champions earned a 20th successive appearance after a 4-0 victory in North Macedonia in Group J. Former England youth international **Jamal Musiala** opened the scoring as Germany reached the finals with two games to spare. The next day, Denmark followed suit by defeating Austria 1-0 in Copenhagen in Group F. Denmark owed victory to a second-half goal from Joakim Maehle.

NATIONAL QUALIFICATION RECORD
ABSENT HEROES

The 2022 finals went ahead without the regional champions of Europe and Oceania. European champions Italy failed to qualify for only the third time in their history. They finished runners-up in their World Cup group to Switzerland before falling to North Macedonia in the playoff semi-finals. Oceania champions New Zealand reached the intercontinental playoffs but lost the decider 1-0 in Qatar to Costa Rica. Regional champions who have made the finals are Argentina (South America), United States (Central and North America), Senegal (Africa) and hosts Qatar (Asian champions).

ALL-TIME QUALIFICATIONS BY REGIONAL CONFEDERATION:

1 Europe – 259
2 South America – 89
3 Africa – 49
4 North/Central America & Caribbean – 46
5 Asia – 43
6 Oceania – 4

NATIONAL QUALIFICATION RECORD
THE "FOOTBALL WAR"

War broke out between El Salvador and Honduras after El Salvador beat Honduras 3-2 in a play-off on 26 June 1969 to qualify for the 1970 finals. Tensions had been running high between the neighbours over a border dispute and there had been rioting at the match. El Salvador lost all three matches at the 1970 FIFA World Cup, and left without scoring a single goal.

NATIONAL QUALIFICATION RECORD
RETURN OF THE DRAGONS

Ukraine came within 90 minutes of defying the qualifying odds. The military invasion by Russia in February brought football in the country to a halt and forced the national team to prepare for their delayed World Cup qualifying playoffs at a training camp in Slovenia. Goals from Andriy Yarmolenko, Roman Yaremchuk and Artem Dobvyk brought a 3-1 semi-final win over Scotland in Glasgow. Yarmolenko then headed into his own net against Wales in Cardiff. Inspired by their talismanic winger Gareth Bale, Wales won 1-0 to reach the finals for the first time since 1958.

CWPAN Y BYD FIFA 2022
DIOLCH I'R WAL GOCH
#TOGETHERSTRONGER

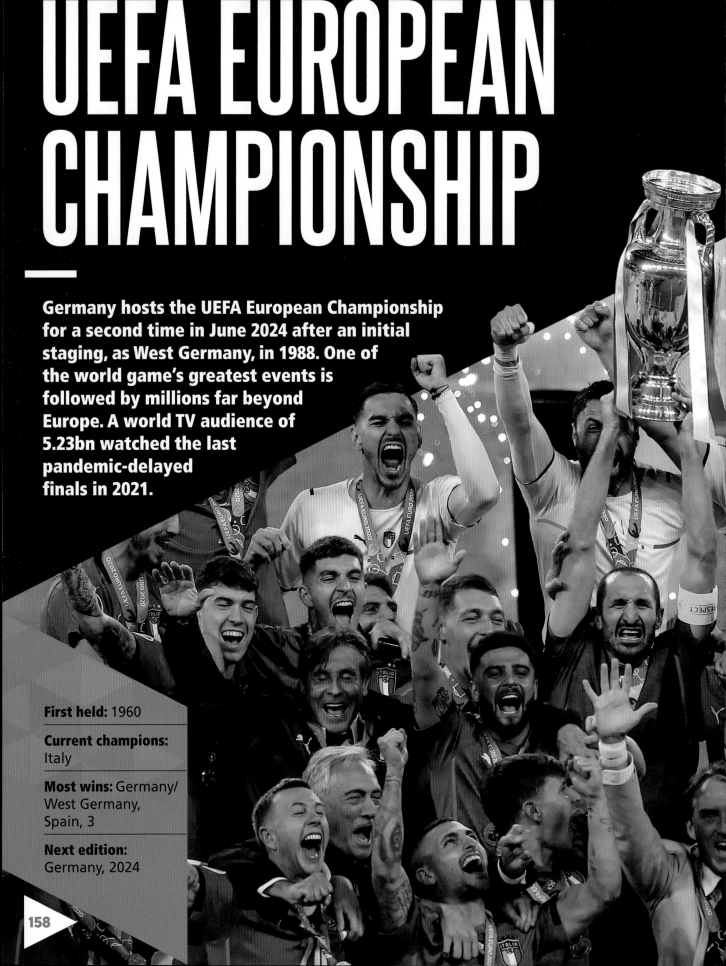

UEFA EUROPEAN CHAMPIONSHIP

Germany hosts the UEFA European Championship for a second time in June 2024 after an initial staging, as West Germany, in 1988. One of the world game's greatest events is followed by millions far beyond Europe. A world TV audience of 5.23bn watched the last pandemic-delayed finals in 2021.

First held: 1960

Current champions: Italy

Most wins: Germany/ West Germany, Spain, 3

Next edition: Germany, 2024

1968

The 1968 finals in Italy were used as a backdrop to a famous English-language film – **The Italian Job**, starring Michael Caine – about a British gang who use the cover of the finals to stage a daring gold robbery in Turin.

142

The 24-team UEFA European Championship in 2021 boasted more goals than any previous UEFA EURO – 142 in all. The rate of goals per game was also an all-time high, coming in at 2.78 per match.

9

In 1984, **Michel Platini** scored more goals than any player in a single UEFA European Championship finals.

PLATINI

3

France have **hosted the tournament three times**, more than any other nation.

BIERHOFF

Germany's **Oliver Bierhoff** scored the first golden goal in the history of the tournament when he hit the winner against the Czech Republic in the UEFA Euro '96 final at Wembley on 30 June.

UEFA EURO 2024 PREVIEW

The UEFA European Championship finals in Germany will mark the 70th anniversary of the creation of the continental governing body in 1954. Initial interest in host rights was expressed by a four-nation Nordic group, an Estonia/Russia partnership and sole bids from Germany, Netherlands and Turkey. By the confirmation deadline, only the bids from Germany and Turkey were left standing. The UEFA executive committee voted for Germany by 12 votes to four.

1000

Hosts Germany, seeded directly to the finals, played preparatory matches instead during the qualifying competition. One was the 1,000th official international played by *Die Mannschaft*, a 3-3 draw against Ukraine.

2

Europe's most coveted crown has been won twice on a penalty shootout - by Czechoslovakia in 1976 and by Italy in the 2020 tournament.

TOURNAMENT TRIVIA

BACK TO BERLIN

Berlin's Olympic Stadium will be staging its third major international football final on July 14. The venue, built for the 1936 Olympic Games, hosted the FIFA World Cup Final in 2006 and the UEFA Champions League Final in 2015. It stages the German Cup Final every year and is home to the Bundesliga club BSC Hertha. The Opening Match will be held in Munich on June 14. Munich also hosted matches at the 1988 finals, but in the Olympic Stadium. This was replaced as the city's main football venue by the newly-constructed Allianz Arena in 2005. UEFA and FIFA regulations on stadium naming rights see it labelled for international competitions as the Munich Football Arena. It hosted the Opening Match in the 2006 FIFA World Cup finals. Gelsenkirchen is another city providing a different venue compared with 1988. EURO matches then were staged at the Parkstadion, which has been succeeded by the Arena AufSchalke.

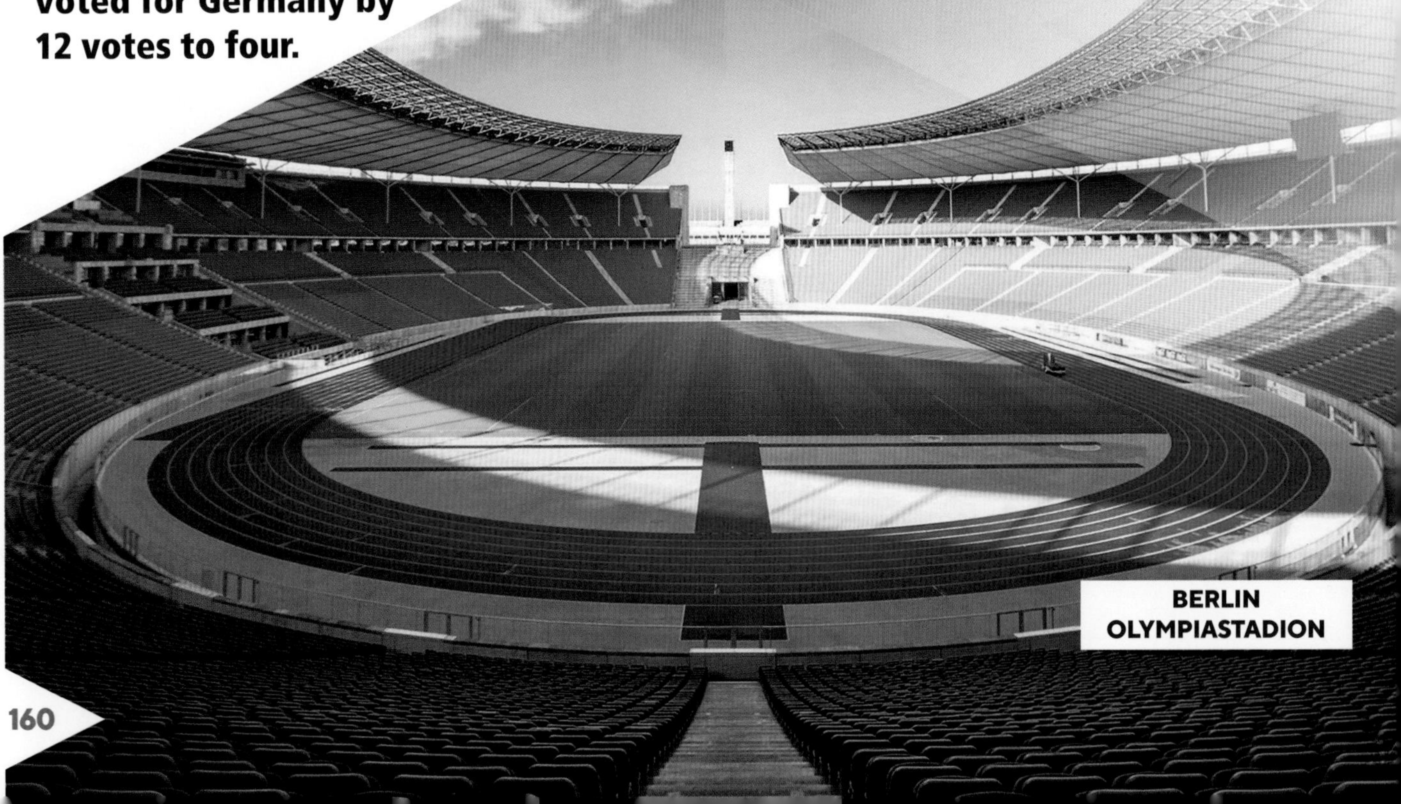

BERLIN OLYMPIASTADION

3

Germany and Spain have both won the European title three times, followed by Italy and France with two victories each.

LAHM

FILIP FOR PHILIPP

Tournament director **Philipp Lahm** knows all about football's big occasions from both sides of the touchline. Lahm won 21 trophies with Bayern Munich and played 113 times in defence for Germany, whom he captained to victory in the 2014 FIFA World Cup in Brazil. In 2017, he was named honorary ambassador for Germany's EURO bid and subsequently was appointed tournament director. Lahm says: "In Germany, we always look back on 2006 and how hosting the FIFA World Cup brought us closer together while also providing the opportunity to welcome others to our country. We plan to replicate that, updated for modern times – 2006 was very special and EURO 2024 offers the chance to do it again."

TOURNAMENT TRIVIA
BEAR ESSENTIAL

A mascot has led the marketing and promotional effort for each edition of the UEFA European Championship finals ever since 1980. In 1988, a rabbit named Berni was the commercial face of the finals in West Germany. Evolution means 2024 will be fronted this time by a bear – a homage to the iconic children's teddy bear, claimed to have originated simultaneously in Germany and the United States more than a century ago.

Fans were asked to choose its name from among four options: Albärt, Bärnardo, Bärnheart or Herzi von Bär.

THE FINAL STORY SO FAR

1960, FRANCE
Soviet Union 2, Yugoslavia 1 (AET)

1964, SPAIN
Spain 2, Soviet Union 1

1968, ITALY
Italy 1, Yugoslavia 1 (AET)
Replay: Italy 2, Yugoslavia 0

1972, BELGIUM
West Germany 3, Soviet Union 0

1976, YUGOSLAVIA
Czechoslovakia 2, West Germany 2
Czechoslovakia 5-3 on penalties, AET

1980, ITALY
West Germany 2, Belgium 1

1984, FRANCE
France 2, Spain 0

1988, WEST GERMANY
Netherlands 2, Soviet Union 0

1992, SWEDEN
Denmark 2, Germany 0

1996, ENGLAND
Germany 2, Czech Republic 1
(Golden goal in extra time)

2000, BELGIUM/NETHERLANDS
France 2, Italy 1
(Golden goal in extra time)

2004, PORTUGAL
Greece 1, Portugal 0

2008, AUSTRIA/SWITZERLAND
Spain 1, Germany 0

2012, POLAND/UKRAINE
Spain 4, Italy 0

2016, FRANCE
Portugal 1, France 0 (AET)

2020*
Italy 1, England 1
Italy 3-2 on penalties, AET

*The 2020 finals were postponed until 2021 by the COVID-19 pandemic. Matches were played in 11 cities in 11 countries across Europe

THE VENUES:

BERLIN OLYMPIASTADION
Capacity: 70,000
Group stage: three matches
KO stage: round of 16, quarter-final, final

COLOGNE STADIUM
Capacity: 47,000
Group stage: four matches
KO stage: round of 16

BVB STADION DORTMUND
Capacity: 66,000
Group stage: four matches
KO stage: round of 16, semi-final

DÜSSELDORF ARENA
Capacity: 47,000
Group stage: three matches
KO stage: round of 16, quarter-final

FRANKFURT ARENA
Capacity: 46,000
Group stage: four matches
KO stage: round of 16

GELSENKIRCHEN ARENA AUFSCHALKE
Capacity: 50,000
Group stage: three matches
KO stage: round of 16

HAMBURG VOLKSPARKSTADION
Capacity: 50,000
Group stage: four matches
KO stage: quarter-final

LEIPZIG STADIUM
Capacity: 42,000
Group stage: three matches
KO stage: round of 16

MUNICH FOOTBALL ARENA
Capacity: 67,000
Group stage: four matches
KO stage: round of 16, semi-final

STUTTGART ARENA
Capacity: 54,000
Group stage: four matches
KO stage: quarter-final

9 GOALS

Michel Platini holds the record for goals at one tournament. Platini scored nine times in just five games as he led France to glory on home soil in 1984. He is three ahead of compatriot Antione Griezmann, who struck six times in 2016 when France hosted the tournament for a record third time.

UEFA EUROPEAN CHAMPIONSHIP TEAM RECORDS

Over the past six decades, the UEFA European Championship has grown to become arguably the most important international football tournament after the FIFA World Cup.

France, on home soil in 1984, were the first team to win all their matches since the finals expanded beyond four teams. They won them without any shoot-outs too (unlike Spain in 2000), beating Denmark 1-0, Belgium 5-0 and Yugoslavia 3-2 in their group, Portugal 3-2 after extra time in the semi-finals and Spain 2-0 in the final. Michel Platini was the star of the tournament for the French, netting nine goals; Platini went on to pick up his second Ballon d'Or that year.

4-5

France and Yugoslavia set a nine-goal match aggregate scoreline that has never been beaten when the Slavs defeated their hosts in the semi-finals in 1960.

17

Only 17 nations entered the initial tournament in 1958-60, which featured a four-team finals and victory for the Soviet Union. By comparison a full UEFA complement of 55 took part in qualifying for EURO 2020 – the second expanded finals with 24 teams.

TOSS FAVOURS THE HOSTS

Italy reached the 1968 final on home soil thanks to the toss of a coin: the only game in finals history decided in such fashion. Italy drew 0-0 against the Soviet Union after extra time in Naples on 5 June 1968.

TOURNAMENT TRIVIA
SAME OLD SPAIN

Spain not only cruised to the largest winning margin of any UEFA European Championship final by trouncing Italy 4-0 in the climax to 2012, they also became the first country to successfully defend the title. Spain also equalled the record match-winning margin when they defeated Slovakia 5-0 in a group stage tie in Seville in the 2020 finals. Four others had achieved that precise scoreline: France (1984 v Belgium, Denmark (1984 v Yugoslavia), Sweden (2004 v Bulgaria). Netherlands are the only team have scored six in one game, defeating Yugoslavia 6-1 in 2000, with a hat-trick from **Patrick Kluivert**.

KLUIVERT

TOURNAMENT TRIVIA
FANCY SEEING YOU AGAIN

When Spain beat Italy 4-0 in the 2012 final, it was the fourth time that UEFA European Championship opponents had faced each other twice in the same tournament. Each time, it followed a first-round encounter. The Netherlands lost to the Soviet Union, then beat them in the 1988 final; Germany beat the Czech Republic twice at UEFA EURO '96, including the final; and Greece did the same to Portugal in 2004. Spain and Italy drew in UEFA EURO 2012's Group C, with Cesc Fàbregas cancelling out Antonio Di Natale's opener for Italy. Their second showdown was rather less even.

VOGTS

TOURNAMENT TRIVIA
GERMANY IN THE ASCENDANCY

Germany, also as West Germany, and Spain have each won the European crown a record three times. The Germans have played most matches (53) and won the most (27), they have also scored more goals (78) than anyone else as well as conceding the most (55). They have contested the most finals tournaments (13). Former defender **Berti Vogts** remains the only man to have won the tournament as both player (1972) and coach (1996). England's shootout defeat in the 2020 final means they are the team who have played the most matches (38) without carrying off the Henri Delaunay trophy.

DELLAS

SCORING RECORD
DELLAS TIMES IT RIGHT FOR GREECE

Greece secured the only "silver goal" victory in EURO history in their 2004 semi-final. (The silver goal rule meant that a team leading after the first period of extra time won the match.) **Traianos Dellas** headed Greece's winner seconds before the end of the first period of extra time against the Czech Republic in Porto on 1 July. Both golden goals and silver goals were abandoned for UEFA EURO 2008, and drawn knockout ties reverted to being decided over the full 30 minutes of extra time, and penalties if necessary.

UEFA EUROPEAN CHAMPIONSHIP WINNERS:

1 3 – West Germany/ Germany
= 3 – Spain

3 2 – France
= 2 – Italy

4 1 – Soviet Union
= 1 – Czechoslovakia
= 1 – Netherlands
= 1 – Denmark
= 1 – Greece
= 1 – Portugal

3

Czechoslovakia's 3-1 semi-final win over the Netherlands in Zagreb, on 16 June 1976, featured a record three red cards.

TOURNAMENT TRIVIA
DENMARK'S UNEXPECTED TRIUMPH

Denmark were unlikely winners of UEFA EURO '92. They had not even expected to take part after finishing behind Yugoslavia in their qualifying group, but they were invited to complete the final eight when Yugoslavia were excluded. Goalkeeper **Peter Schmeichel** was their hero – in the semi-final shoot-out win over the Netherlands and again in the final against Germany, when goals by John Jensen and Kim Vilfort earned the Danes a 2-0 win.

SCHMEICHEL

142

A record 142 goals were scored in the 2020 finals, surpassing 108 at the first expanded 24-team competition in 2016.

UEFA EUROPEAN CHAMPIONSHIP PLAYER RECORDS

The UEFA European Championship has featured some of football's most memorable moments delivered by some of the continent's all-time finest players.

SCORING RECORD
KOZŁOWSKI ENDS UP WITH AGE ADVANTAGE

KOZŁOWSKI

Poland midfielder **Kacper Kozłowski** became the youngest player to appear in the EURO finals, at 17 years 246 days, when he substituted Mateusz Klich in a 2020 group stage game against Spain a. The record had been set only six days earlier when England's Jude Bellingham (17 years 349 days) replaced Kalvin Phillips in a 4-0 win over Ukraine in the quarter-finals in Rome. Youngest player records had been set earlier in the same finals by Spain's Pedri (18 years 215 days) against Croatia in the round of 16 and then, a day later, by Germany's Jamal Musiala (18 years 117 days) as a substitute against England. Musiala had played for England under-21s before deciding to opt for Germany at competitive senior level.

37

North Macedonia's Goran Pandev, at 37 years 321 days, became the second-oldest marksman in EURO finals history against Austria in2020. Austria's Ivica Vastić remains the oldest, at 38 years 257 days, with a goal against Poland in 2008.

TOURNAMENT RECORD
GOLDEN ONE-TOUCH

Spain striker Fernando Torres claimed the UEFA EURO 2012 Golden Boot, despite scoring the same number of goals – three – as Italy's Mario Balotelli, Russia's Alan Dzagoev, Germany's Mario Gómez, Croatia's Mario Mandžukić and Portugal's Cristiano Ronaldo. The decision came down to number of assists – with Torres and Gómez level on one apiece – and then the amount of time played. The 92 fewer minutes spent on the pitch by Torres, compared to Gómez, meant his contributions were deemed better value for the prize.

7

Karim Benzema marked his EURO debut with four goals for France at the 2020 finals. This placed him fifth in the all-time French charts behind Michel Platini (nine), Antoine Griezmann (seven), Thierry Henry (six) and Zinedine Zidane (five).

SHEARER

NATIONAL LEGEND
SHEARER TALLY BOOSTS ENGLAND

Alan Shearer is the only Englishman to have topped the finals scoring chart, leading the way with five goals as England lost on penalties to Germany in the UEFA EURO '96 semi-final at Wembley. He netted against Switzerland, Scotland and the Netherlands (two) in the group and gave England a third-minute lead against the Germans. He added two more goals at UEFA EURO 2000 and is behind only Michel Platini and Cristiano Ronaldo in the all-time list.

10

The most red cards were shown at EURO 2000, when the ten dismissals included Romania's Gheorghe Hagi, Portugal's Nuno Gomes, Italy's Gianluca Zambrotta and the Czech Republic's Radoslav Látal who, having been sent off at EURO 96, is the only man to be dismissed in two tournaments.

SCORING RECORD
VONLANTHEN BEATS ROONEY RECORD

The youngest scorer in finals history is Switzerland midfielder **Johan Vonlanthen**. He was 18 years and 141 days old when he netted in the Swiss' 3-1 defeat by France on 21 June 2004, beating the record set by England forward Wayne Rooney four days earlier. Rooney was 18 years and 229 days old when he scored the first goal in England's 3-0 win over the Swiss. Vonlanthen retired at the age of 26 in May 2012 due to a knee injury.

VONLANTHEN

SCORING RECORD
PONEDELNIK'S MONDAY MORNING FEELING

Striker Viktor Ponedelnik headed the Soviet Union's extra-time winner to beat Yugoslavia 2-1 in the first final on 10 July 1960 – and sparked some famous headlines in the Soviet media. The game in Paris kicked off at 10pm Moscow time on Sunday, so it was Monday morning when Ponedelnik – whose name means "Monday" in Russian – scored. He said: "When I scored, all the journalists wrote the headline '*Ponedelnik zabivayet v Ponedelnik*' – 'Monday scores on Monday'." This goal, in the 113th minute, remains the latest ever in a European Championship/Nations Cup final.

ILYIN MAKES HISTORY
Anatoli Ilyin of the Soviet Union scored the first-ever goal in the UEFA European Championship when he netted after four minutes in a first-round tie against Hungary on 29 September 1958.

1

Only one man has been sent off in a UEFA European Championship final: France defender Yvon Le Roux, who received a second yellow card with five minutes remaining of his team's 2-0 triumph over Spain in 1984.

NATIONAL LEGEND
BIERHOFF NETS FIRST GOLDEN GOAL

Germany's **Oliver Bierhoff** scored the first golden goal in the history of the tournament when he hit the winner against the Czech Republic in the UEFA EURO '96 final at Wembley on 30 June. (The golden goal rule meant the first team to score in extra time won the match.) Bierhoff netted in the fifth minute of extra time, his shot from 20 yards deflecting off defender Michal Horňák and slipping through goalkeeper Petr Kouba's fingers.

BIERHOFF

TOP SCORERS IN UEFA EURO FINALS HISTORY:

1 **Cristiano Ronaldo,** Portugal, 14

2 **Michel Platini,** France, 9

3 **Antoine Griezmann,** France, 7

= **Alan Shearer,** England, 7

5 **Nuno Gomes,** Portugal, 6

= **Thierry Henry,** France, 6

= **Zlatan Ibrahimović,** Sweden, 6

= **Patrick Kluivert,** Netherlands, 6

= **Romelu Lukaku,** Belgium, 6

= **Alvaro Morata,** Spain, 6

= **Wayne Rooney,** England, 6

= **Ruud van Nistelrooy,** Netherlands, 6

UEFA EUROPEAN CHAMPIONSHIP OTHER RECORDS

KJÆR

The UEFA European Championship has provided tons of trivia over the years, from the goal droughts to the host countries and everything in between.

🕐 RECENT HISTORY
GOALS AREN'T EVERYTHING

UEFA EURO 2020 set a record for its goals-per-game ratio since the group stage was introduced for the 1980 finals in Italy. The record high of 142 goals produced a mark of 2.78 goals per match. This surpassed the previous best of 2.74 in Belgium and Netherlands in 2000. However, it was far short of the 4.75 goals-per-match ratio set in 1976 – but those finals featured only four teams and 19 goals in a four-match knockout event. The 2020 finals set a record with 11 own goals, overtaking the total of nine recorded at all the previous tournaments. First unlucky player was Turkey's Merih Demiral in the Opening Match against Italy and the last Denmark's captain **Simon Kjær** in their semi-finals defeat by England.

6

Six red cards were shown at EURO 2020, with Wales collecting two for Harry Wilson and Ethan Ampadu. Referees issued 151 yellow cards. England's Alan Mullery was the first player ever sent off in the finals, against Yugoslavia in Florence in 1968.

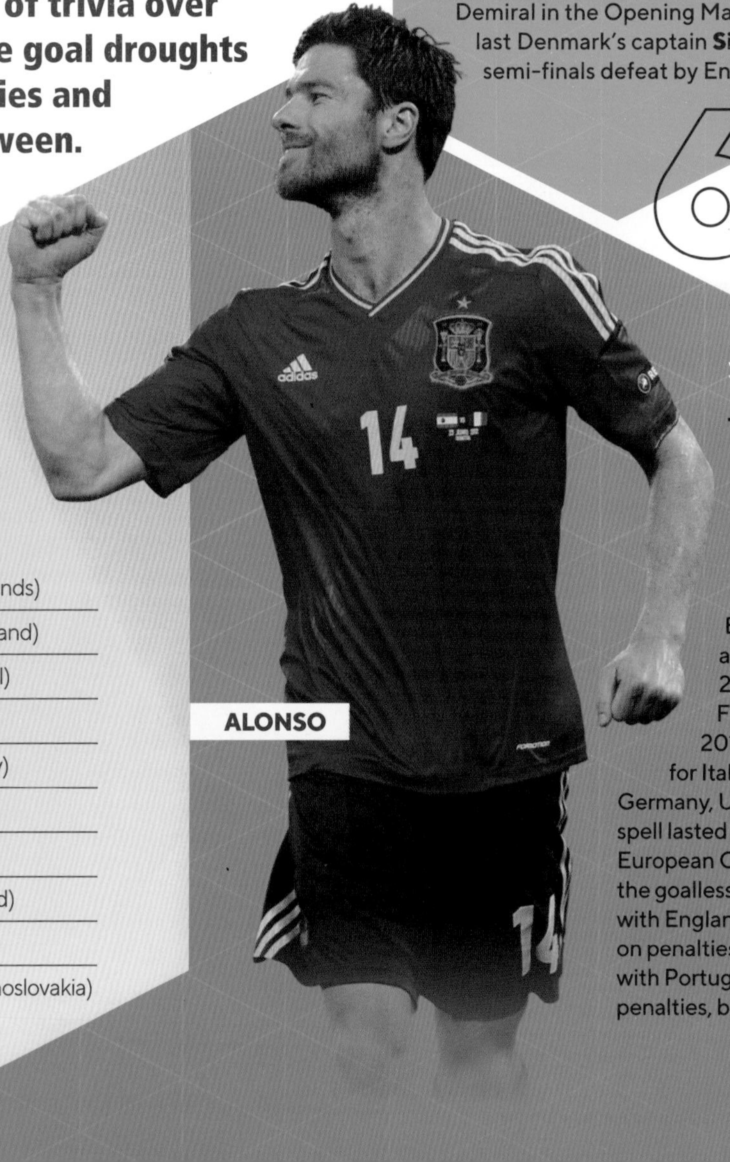

ALONSO

LAST TEN UEFA EUROPEAN CHAMPIONSHIP FINAL REFEREES:

2020 – Bjorn Kuipers (Netherlands)

2016 – Mark Clattenburg (England)

2012 – Pedro Proença (Portugal)

2008 – Roberto Rosetti (Italy)

2004 – Markus Merk (Germany)

2000 – Anders Frisk (Sweden)

1996 – Pierluigi Palretto (Italy)

1992 – Bruno Galler (Switzerland)

1988 – Michel Vautrot (France)

1984 – Vojtech Christob (Czechoslovakia)

🏆 TOURNAMENT RECORD
RECORD UEFA EURO GOAL DROUGHT

Between **Xabi Alonso**'s added-time penalty in Spain's 2-0 quarter-final defeat of France, and Mario Balotelli's 20th-minute semi-final strike for Italy in their 2-1 victory against Germany, UEFA EURO 2012's goalless spell lasted 260 minutes – a UEFA European Championship record. In the goalless interim, Italy drew 0-0 with England before beating them on penalties, and Spain drew 0-0 with Portugal before beating them on penalties, both after extra time.

3-0

Greece withdrew from their qualifier against Albania in the 1964 tournament because the countries were still technically at war. Albania were thus handed a 3-0 walkover. Greece formally declared an end to war only in 1987.

REFEREE TRIVIA
TAKE CLATT

In 2012, Pedro Proença from Portugal achieved the double feat of refereeing the UEFA Champions League final between Chelsea and Bayern Munich and that summer's UEFA European Championship final between Spain and Italy. English referee **Mark Clattenburg** went one better in 2016: he took charge of his homeland's FA Cup final between Manchester United and Crystal Palace, the UEFA Champions League final between Real Madrid and Atlético Madrid in May, and the UEFA European Championship final between France and Portugal in July.

CLATTENBURG

79,115

The highest attendance at a EURO final was 79,115 in the Estadio Santiago Bernabeu in Madrid in 1964, who saw hosts Spain beat the Soviet Union 2-1.

NATIONAL LEGEND
LÖW AT LAST SIGHT

Joachim Löw, who retired as Germany coach after EURO 2020, holds the record for the most UEFA European Championship matches and victories in charge. His side's defeat by England in the round of 16 placed him on 21 matches across the four tournaments in 2008, 2012, 2016 and 2020, with 13 victories. Germany's best finish during his 15 years in charge was runners-up to Spain in 2008. However, he did lead Germany to success in the 2014 FIFA World Cup in Brazil and the FIFA Confederations Cup in Russia in 2017. Between July 2010 and June 2012, Germany won a record 15 consecutive international competitive matches.

LÖW

2020

The 2020 European Championship final between Italy and hosts England was the seventh to go to extra-time and the first decided on penalties. Italy won the shootout 3-2 after a 1-1 draw.

HOST HISTORY
SHARE AND SHARE ALIKE

Ten venues across France were used for the 2016 UEFA European Championship. This equalled the record set by Portugal in 2004, and was two more than the eight stadiums that were used in the three shared tournaments (four in each country): Belgium and the Netherlands in 2000; Austria and Switzerland in 2008; and Poland and Ukraine in 2012. It will be all change for the finals in 2021, however, as, for the first time, the first-round group stage and first two knock-out rounds will be played across 12 cities in 12 different countries. England will have the honour of hosting both semi-finals and the final, with all three to be played at London's Wembley Stadium.

HOST HISTORY
BACK TO SQUARE ONE IN 2024

Germany will play host in 2024, bringing the EURO finals back to the original concept of a single-country host. This contrasts with the staging of the 2020 tournament in 11 venues across the length and breadth of Europe. European federation UEFA had decided in 2012 to celebrate 60 years of the EUROS by staging matches from Azerbaijan in the east to Spain in the west, from St Petersburg in the north to Italy in the south. This set a venues record that surpassed the 10 used in Portugal alone in 2004. England's Wembley was the busiest stadium, with three group matches and six in the knockout stage including both semi-finals and the final.

1992

Players wore their names as well as their numbers on the back of their shirts for the first time at UEFA EURO '92. They had previously been identified only by numbers.

UEFA NATIONS LEAGUE

European federation UEFA set out on a pioneering mission when it created the Nations League. Initially club managers, players and media were sceptical, but their doubts soon faded as the league ended the litany of unpopular friendly matches and offered an extra qualifying route into major tournament finals.

RODRI

CASHING IN

UEFA was so happy with the initial reaction of broadcasters and sponsors that it rapidly increased the Nations League prize money. In 2019, the overall winners received €7.5m. By 2023, this had risen to €10.5m, with €9m for the runners-up.

TOURNAMENT HISTORY
HOW AND WHY AND WHEN

The Nations League was devised by European federation UEFA to insert a revenue-raising competition into dates set aside in the international calendar for increasingly unpopular friendly matches. First mooted in 2011, it was finally unveiled in 2017. Europe's 55 national teams were ranked according to a computation of notional points per game, known as a coefficient. League A contained the 12 highest-ranked teams, League B the next 12 teams, League C the 15 following and League D the last 16. Those leagues were sub-divided into four groups of three or four teams. Promotion and relegation decide the groups' make-up for the subsequent event. The Nations League also fed into the qualifying competition for the finals of both Euro 2020 and Euro 2024.

6

Norway's Erling Haaland was joint six-goal overall leading scorer in the 2023 Nations League qualifying groups along with Serbia's Aleksandar Mitrović. They were followed, on five goals apiece, by Georgia's Khvicha Kvaratskhelia, Kosovo's Vedat Muriqi and Latvia's Vladislavs Gutkovskis.

TOURNAMENT TRIVIA
SPAIN REIGN IN ROTTERDAM

Spain's success in the 2023 UEFA Nations League saw them join France as the second nation to have carried off Europe's newest trophy, the FIFA World Cup and the UEFA European Championship. Real Madrid rightback Dani Carvajal converted the decisive kick that delivered a 5–4 shootout defeat of Croatia in the final in Rotterdam after a goalless extra-time draw. Victory eased painful memories of Spain's shootout defeat by Morocco at the FIFA World Cup in Qatar. Coach Luis de la Fuente, 61, thus needed only six matches to emulate José Villalonga (Euro 1964), Luis Aragonés (Euro 2008) and Vicente del Bosque (2010 FIFA World Cup and Euro 2012).

GUEDES

NATIONAL LEGEND
HOME AT LAST

Hosts Portugal won the inaugural UEFA Nations League in June 2019 to make eventual amends for defeat in front of their own fans in the European Championship final in 2004. Back then a teenaged Cristiano Ronaldo had been among the tearful runners-up. Some 15 years later, he was captain and three-goal leading scorer as his Portuguese team defeated Netherlands 1-0 in the final in Porto. **Gonçalo Guedes** scored the goal that secured a second prize in three years for Portugal after their UEFA Euro 2016 triumph in France.

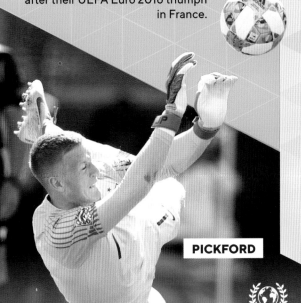

PICKFORD

NATIONAL LEGEND
PICKFORD SPOT ON

Jordan Pickford was twice the shoot-out hero when England edged Switzerland to finish third in the inaugural finals in 2019. The playoff went to penalties after finishing goalless at the end of extra time in Guimarães. The Everton goalkeeper not only saved from Josip Drmić in the shootout but also converted his own spot-kick as the Three Lions won 6-5 on penalties. England thus finished third in a senior tournament for the first time since Euro 1968. They had reached the finals by winning their group thanks to a concluding 2-1 win over Croatia.

2023 FINALS (IN NETHERLANDS)

Semi-finals: Netherlands 2, Croatia 4 (AET)
Spain 2, Italy 1
Third place playoff: Netherlands 2, Italy 3
Final: Croatia 0, Spain 0 (Spain 5-4 on penalties, AET)

LEAGUE A

Group A1							
Croatia	6	4	1	1	8	6	13
Denmark	6	4	0	2	9	5	12
France	6	1	2	3	5	7	5
Austria	6	1	1	4	6	10	4

Group A3							
Italy	6	3	2	1	8	7	11
Hungary	6	3	1	2	8	5	10
Germany	6	1	4	1	11	9	7
England	6	0	3	3	4	10	3

Group A2							
Spain	6	3	2	1	8	5	11
Portugal	6	3	1	2	11	3	10
Switzerland	6	3	0	3	6	9	9
Czech Rep.	6	1	1	4	5	13	4

Group A4							
Netherlands	6	5	1	0	14	6	16
Belgium	6	3	1	2	11	8	10
Poland	6	2	1	3	6	12	7
Wales	6	0	1	5	6	11	1

LEAGUE B

Group B1							
Scotland	6	4	1	1	11	5	13
Ukraine	6	3	2	1	10	4	11
Rep. Ireland	6	2	1	3	8	7	7
Armenia	6	1	0	5	4	17	3

Group B3							
Bosnia & H.	6	3	2	1	8	8	11
Finland	6	2	2	2	8	6	8
Montenegro	6	2	1	3	6	6	7
Romania	6	2	1	3	6	8	7

Group B2							
Israel	4	2	2	0	8	6	8
Iceland	4	0	4	0	6	6	4
Albania	4	0	2	2	4	6	2
Russia	0	0	0	0	0	0	0*
*disqu.							

Group B4							
Serbia	6	4	1	1	13	5	13
Norway	6	3	1	2	7	7	10
Slovenia	6	1	3	2	6	10	6
Sweden	6	1	1	4	7	11	4

LEAGUE C

Group C1							
Turkey	6	4	1	1	18	5	13
Luxembourg	6	3	2	1	9	7	11
Faroe Islands	6	2	2	2	7	10	8
Lithuania	6	0	1	5	2	14	1

Group C3							
Kazakhstan	6	4	1	1	8	6	13
Azerbaijan	6	3	1	2	7	4	10
Slovakia	6	2	1	3	5	6	7
Belarus	6	0	3	3	3	7	3

Group C2							
Greece	6	5	0	1	10	2	15
Kosovo	6	3	0	3	11	8	9
N Ireland	6	1	2	3	7	10	5
Cyprus	6	1	2	3	4	12	5

Group C4							
Georgia	6	5	1	0	16	3	16
Bulgaria	6	2	3	1	10	8	9
N Macedonia	6	2	1	3	7	7	7
Gibraltar	6	0	1	5	3	18	1

LEAGUE D

Group D1							
Latvia	6	4	1	1	12	5	13
Moldova	6	4	1	1	10	6	13
Andorra	6	2	2	2	6	7	8
Liechtenstein	6	0	0	6	1	11	0

Group D2							
Estonia	4	4	0	0	10	2	12
Malta	4	2	0	2	5	4	6
San Marino	4	0	0	4	0	9	0

**12 teams access the UEFA Euro 2024 qualifying play-offs

$80

President of world governing body FIFA Gianni Infantino was so impressed by the Nations League that he came up with a proposal for a Global Nations League. Encouraged by promises of financial support from an international consortium, Infantino envisaged a worldwide nations league every two years with up to $80m for the winners. Initially this proved too ambitious, but other confederations have adopted the concept for themselves in their own regions.

COPA AMÉRICA

June and July of 2024 will see the 108ᵗʰ anniversary of the *Copa América*. CONMEBOL organised the first event in 1916. Four countries took part: Argentina, Brazil, Chile and winners Uruguay. The 2024 finals will be hosted in the United States and feature all 10 CONMEBOL nations plus six from CONCACAF.

Founded: 1916

Current champions:
Argentina

Most wins:
Argentina, Uruguay,
15 titles

Next edition:
United States, 2024

2 Brazil became only the second nation to host consecutive *Copa Américas* in 2019 and 2021. The only previous example had been Uruguay, in 1923 and 1924.

In 1984, CONMEBOL adopted the policy of rotating the right to host the *Copa América* among the ten member associations.

3 The *Copa América* has been hosted across the whole continent three times (1975, 1979, 1983).

In 1916, the current *Copa América* trophy was purchased from Casa Escasany, a jewellery shop in Buenos Aires, at the cost of 3,000 Swiss francs.

Across more than 100 years of the *Copa América*, there have been only three editions in which neither Argentina nor Brazil finished in the top four (1939, 2001, 2011).

COPA AMÉRICA TEAM RECORDS

South America was the first region to organise its own confederation, which led to the creation, in 1916, of the South American Championship. Four countries contested that opening tournament – hosts Argentina as well as Brazil, Chile and Uruguay, who were the inaugural winners.

150

The longest match in the history of the *Copa América* was the 1919 final between Brazil and Uruguay. It lasted 150 minutes, 90 minutes of regular time plus two extra-time periods of 30 minutes each.

TOURNAMENT TRIVIA
RECORD-BREAKERS

On winning the 2021 *Copa América* in Brazil, Argentina extended their proud record of the most victories in the history of the tournament: 127. The Argentinians have also scored the most goals, with 474, the last of which was claimed by Ángel Di María in the 1-0 defeat of hosts Brazil in the final in Maracanã. Neighbours Uruguay hold the unwanted record of six defeats in penalty shootouts. The Celeste suffered their latest upset by 4-2 against Colombia after a 0-0 draw in the 2021 quarter-finals in Brasília. Goalkeeper **David Ospina** was Colombia's hero after saving Matías Viña's last kick.

OSPINA

COPA AMÉRICA TITLES:

1 **Uruguay, 15** (1916, 1917, 1920, 1923, 1924, 1926, 1935, 1942, 1956, 1959, 1967, 1983, 1987, 1995, 2011)
= **Argentina, 15** (1921, 1925, 1927, 1929, 1937, 1941, 1945, 1946, 1947, 1955, 1957, 1959, 1991, 1993, 2021)

3 **Brazil, 9** (1919, 1922, 1949, 1989, 1997, 1999, 2004, 2007, 2019)

4 **Peru, 2** (1939, 1975)
= **Paraguay, 2** (1939, 1979)
= **Chile, 2** (2015, 2016)

7 **Bolivia, 1** (1963)
= **Colombia, 1** (2001)

TOURNAMENT TRIVIA
SUB-STANDARD

During the 1953 *Copa América*, Peru were awarded a walkover win when Paraguay tried to make one more substitution than they were allowed. Would-be substitute Milner Ayala was so incensed that he kicked English referee Richard Maddison and was banned from football for three years. Yet Paraguay remained in the tournament and went on to beat Brazil in the final – minus, of course, the disgraced Ayala. The entire tournament was staged at the Estadio Nacional de Perú.

TOURNAMENT TRIVIA
HISTORY MEN

Four nations entered the inaugural *Copa América* when it launched in 1916: Argentina, Brazil, Chile and Uruguay. Bolivia, Colombia, Ecuador, Paraguay, Peru and Venezuela had all joined by 1967. In 1910, an unofficial South American championship was won by Argentina, who beat Uruguay 4-1 in the decider – although the final match had been delayed a day after rioting fans burnt down a stand at the Gimnasia stadium in Buenos Aires.

TOURNAMENT TRIVIA
WELCOME VISITORS

Nine guest nations have appeared in the *Copa América*. **Mexico**, from Central America, have not only been the most frequent guests with ten appearances but they nearly achieved what would have been embarrassing victories in 1993 and 2001, when they reached the final before losing 2-1 to Argentina and 1-0 to Colombia respectively. Four guests have appeared only once: Honduras (2001), Haiti and Panama (both in 2016), and Australia (2020).

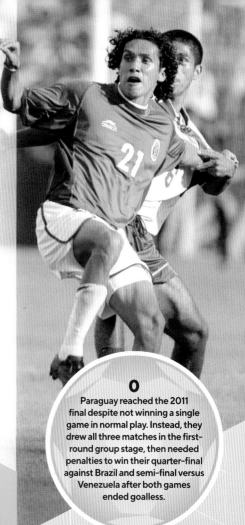

0
Paraguay reached the 2011 final despite not winning a single game in normal play. Instead, they drew all three matches in the first-round group stage, then needed penalties to win their quarter-final against Brazil and semi-final versus Venezuela after both games ended goalless.

HOSTING RIGHTS BY COUNTRY:

1 **Argentina, 9** (1916, 1921, 1925, 1929, 1937, 1946, 1959, 1987, 2011)

2 **Chile, 7** (1920, 1926, 1941, 1945, 1955, 1991, 2015)
= **Uruguay, 7** (1917, 1923, 1924, 1942, 1956, 1967, 1995)

3 **Peru, 6** (1927, 1935, 1939, 1953, 1957, 2004)
= **Brazil, 6** (1919, 1922, 1949, 1989, 2019, 2021)

31

In 1942, Ecuador and their goalkeeper Napoléon Medina conceded more goals in one tournament than any other team, when they let in 31 goals across six games – and six defeats.

ARISTIZÁBAL

11

In 2001, Colombia, who went on to win the trophy for the first and only time in their history, became the only country to go through an entire *Copa América* campaign without conceding a single goal. They scored 11 themselves, more than half of them from six-goal tournament top scorer **Victor Aristizábal**.

TOURNAMENT TRIVIA
MORE FROM MORENO

Argentina were not only responsible for the *Copa América*'s biggest win, but also the tournament's highest-scoring game, when they put 12 past Ecuador in 1942 – to no reply. José Manuel Moreno's five strikes in that game included the 500th goal in the competition's history. Moreno, born in Buenos Aires on 3 August 1916, ended that tournament as joint top scorer with team-mate Herminio Masantonio – hitting seven goals. Both men ended their international careers with 19 goals for their country, although Moreno did so in 34 appearances – compared to Masantonio's 21. Masantonio scored four in the defeat of Ecuador.

COPA AMÉRICA PLAYER RECORDS

For more than a century, the *Copa América* has showcased the very best of South America's football talent on the pitch. Unsurprisingly, its goalscoring and appearance records read as a who's who of the continent's most enduring footballing superstars.

FORLÁN

NATIONAL LEGEND
LIKE GRANDFATHER, LIKE FATHER, LIKE SON

Diego Forlán's two goals in the 2011 *Copa América* final helped Uruguay to a 3–0 victory over Paraguay and a record 15th South American championship. They also ensured that he followed in family footsteps in lifting the trophy – his father **Pablo** was part of the Uruguay side who won in 1967, when his grandfather Juan Carlos Corazzo was the triumphant coach. Corazzo had previously managed Uruguay's winning team in 1959. The youngest Forlán's brace against Paraguay put him level with Héctor Scarone as Uruguay's all-time leading scorer, with 31 goals. Yet it was Forlán's strike partner Luis Suárez who was voted the player of the 2011 tournament.

NATIONAL LEGEND
FROG PRINCE

Chilean goalkeeper Sergio Livingstone holds the record for the most *Copa América* appearances, with 34 games from 1941 to 1953. Livingstone, nicknamed "The Frog", was voted the player of the tournament in 1941 – becoming the first goalkeeper to win the award – and he might have played even more *Copa América* matches had he not missed out on the 1946 competition. Livingstone, born in Santiago on 26 March 1920, spent almost his entire career in his home country – save for a season with Argentina's Racing Club in 1943–44. Overall, he made 52 appearances for Chile between 1941 and 1954 before retiring and becoming a popular TV journalist and commentator.

NATIONAL LEGEND
MAGIC ÁLEX

Ecuador's Álex Aguinaga, a midfielder born in Ibarra on 9 July 1969, played a total of 109 times for his country – 25 of them in the *Copa América*, a competition that yielded four of his 23 international goals. His *Copa América* career certainly began well: Ecuador went undefeated for his first four appearances, at the 1987 and 1989 events, but his luck had ran out by the time his Ecuador career was coming to an end: he lost his final seven *Copa América* matches.

MÉNDEZ

OVERALL TOP SCORERS:

1 **Norberto Méndez** (Argentina), 17
= **Zizinho** (Brazil), 17

3 **Teodoro Fernández** (Peru), 15
= **Severino Varela** (Uruguay), 15

5 **Paolo Guerrero** (Peru), 14
= **Eduardo Vargas** (Chile), 14

1917
The first *Copa América* own goal was scored by Chile's Luis García, giving Argentina a 1–0 win in 1917, the second edition of the tournament.

8

When Álex Aguinaga lined up for Ecuador against Uruguay in his country's opening game at the 2004 event, he became only the second man to take part in eight different *Copa Américas* – joining legendary Uruguayan goalscorer Ángel Romano.

MOST GAMES PLAYED:

1 **Sergio Livingstone** (Chile), 34

= **Lionel Messi** (Argentina), 34

3 **Zizinho** (Brazil), 33

4 **Víctor Ugarte** (Bolivia), 30

5 **Máximo Mosquera** (Peru) 28

NATIONAL LEGEND
START TO FINISH

Colombia playmaker Carlos Valderrama and defensive midfielder **Leonel Álvarez** played in all 27 of their country's *Copa América* matches between 1987 and 1995, winning ten, drawing ten and losing seven – including third-place finishes in 1987, 1993 and 1995. Valderrama's two *Copa América* goals came in his first and final appearances in the competition – in a 2-0 victory over Bolivia in 1987 and a 4-1 defeat of the USA eight years later.

17

Paraguayan midfielder Julio César Enciso was the youngest player to appear at the 2021 *Copa América*. He was 17 years 111 days when he appeared as a late substitute in a 3-1 win over Bolivia. Two years earlier, at 15, Enciso had been the youngest player to make a league debut for his club Libertad of Asunción.

4-0
The first-ever *Copa América* goal, in 1916, was scored by José Piendibene – setting Uruguay on the way to a 4-0 triumph over Chile.

ÁLVAREZ

NATIONAL LEGEND
REPEATING THE FEAT

Gabriel Batistuta is the only Argentinian to have twice won the award for leading marksman at the *Copa América*. He made his *Albiceleste* debut only days before the 1991 event in which his six goals – including a crucial strike in the concluding match (it was a mini group as opposed to a final) victory over Colombia – earned a transfer from Boca Juniors to Fiorentina. Nicknamed "Batigol" in Italy, he was joint top scorer in 1995, with four goals, along with Mexico's Luis García.

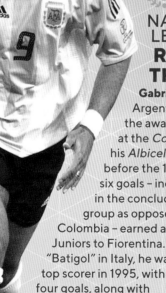

BATISTUTA

NATIONAL LEGEND
PELÉ'S INSPIRATION

Brazilian forward **Zizinho** shares the all-time goalscoring record in the *Copa América*, along with Argentina's Norberto Méndez. Méndez was top scorer once and runner-up twice and won championship medals on all three occasions, while Zizinho's 17 goals helped Brazil take the title once, in 1949. Zizinho, Pelé's footballing idol, would emerge from the 1950 FIFA World Cup as Brazil's top scorer and he was also voted the tournament's best player – but was forever traumatised by the hosts' surprise defeat to Uruguay that cost Brazil the title.

ZIZINHO

5

Four players have scored five goals in one *Copa América* game: Héctor Scarone was the first in Uruguay's 6-0 win over Bolivia in 1926.

OTHER COPA AMÉRICA RECORDS

Format changes, guest teams and a highly competitive field have meant that the *Copa América* rarely looks the same from one edition to the next. Nevertheless, a number of records have stood the test of time.

Uruguay's 1930 FIFA World Cup-winning captain **José Nasazzi** is the only footballer to be voted player of the tournament at two different *Copa América* tournaments. Even more impressively, he achieved the feat 12 years apart – first taking the prize in 1923, then again in 1935. He was a *Copa* winner in 1923, 1924, 1926 and 1935. Nasazzi also captained Uruguay to victory in the 1924 and 1928 Olympic Games.

NASAZZI

38

Uruguay have a unique record in remaining unbeaten in 38 *Copa América* games on home turf, all played in the country's capital Montevideo – comprising 31 wins and seven draws.

TROPHY-WINNING COACHES:

1 **Guillermo Stábile,** 6 (Argentina 1941, 1945, 1946, 1947, 1955, 1957)

2 **Alfio Basile,** 2 (Argentina 1991, 1993)

= **Juan Carlos Corazzo,** 2 (Uruguay 1959, 1967)

= **Ernesto Fígoli,** 2 (Uruguay 1920, 1926)

3 (35 coaches on 1 title each)

NATIONAL LEGEND
KEEP COMING BACK

Hérnan Dario Gómez is the only man to have coached three different nations at the *Copa América*. Gómez, who had been forced by injury to quit playing prematurely, led Colombia in the 1995, 1997 and 2011 tournaments. He also coached Ecuador at the *Copa América* in 2001, 2004 and 2019. Gómez achieved a hat-trick of countries as coach of Panama, who were guest invitees at the *Copa América Centenario* in the United States in 2016. Gómez shares the record of seven tournaments with Argentina's Guillermo Stábile and Uruguay's Óscar Washington Tabárez. He is also one of three coaches to have led at least three different national teams at a FIFA World Cup.

GÓMEZ

44

Guillermo Stábile solely holds the record for managing most *Copa América* matches (44), followed by Chile's Luis Tirado (35), Paraguay's Manuel Fleitas Solich (33), and Uruguay's Óscar Tabárez (30).

STÁBILE

NATIONAL LEGEND
MULTI-TASKING

Argentina's **Guillermo Stábile** coached Argentina from 1939 to 1960, having been appointed at the age of just 34. He was in charge for 123 games, winning 83 of them – and still managed to coach three clubs on the side at different times throughout his reign. He remained as Red Star Paris manager during his first year in the Argentina role, then led Argentine club Huracán for the next nine years – before leading domestic rivals Racing Club from 1949 to 1960. Stábile's Argentina missed out on *Copa América* success in 1949, but that year brought the first of three Argentina league championships in a row for Stábile's Racing Club.

SCORING RECORD
GOALS AT A PREMIUM

In terms of goals per game, the 2011 *Copa América* was the second tightest of all time – with only 54 strikes hitting the back of the net in 26 matches, at an average of 2.08 per game. The 1922 tournament, in Brazil, saw even fewer – 22 goals in 11 games, an average of two per game. Both competitions were a far cry from the prolific 1927 event in Peru, where 37 goals across six games averaged out at 6.17. The 91 goals in 2016 came at an average of 2.84 per match.

3

Argentina's *Copa América* success in 1957 was inspired by the inside-forward trio of Humberto Maschio, Antonio Valentín Angelillo and Omar Sívori. But they were dropped from the squad for the 1958 FIFA World Cup after being transferred to Italian clubs. Eventually Maschio and Sívori did play World Cup football in 1962 – but for Italy.

6

Six overseas "guests" were invited to play in the special *Copa América* Centenario tournament in 2016: Costa Rica, Haiti, Jamaica, Mexico, Panama and the USA, who were also the hosts.

VECINO

TOURNAMENT TRIVIA
SEEING RED

Brazil have the worst FIFA World Cup disciplinary record with 11 red cards ahead of Argentina on 10, but Uruguay hold the unwanted record in the *Copa América*. Uruguayan players have been sent off on 32 occasions, the most recent being **Matías Vecino** against Mexico in 2016. Following on are Argentina and Peru on 25 dismissals each, then Brazil (22) and Venezuela (21). Next come Chile (19), Paraguay (16), Bolivia and Ecuador (14 each) and Colombia (12). Guest nations complete the rankings with Mexico (10), United States (three), Costa Rica (two) and Honduras, Jamaica, Japan and Panama (one each).

TOURNAMENT TRIVIA
AWAY WINNERS

Only four men have coached a country other than their native one to *Copa América* glory. The first was Englishman Jack Greenwell, with Peru in 1939. Brazilian Danilo Alvim was the second to do it, with Bolivia in 1963 – against Brazil. History repeated itself in 2015 and 2016, when Argentina-born Jorge Sampaoli and then Juan Antonio Pizzi took Chile to *Copa* glory, both times beating Argentina in final penalty shoot-outs.

INVITED GUESTS:

1	Mexico,	10
2	Costa Rica,	5
3	USA,	4
4	Jamaica,	2
	= Japan,	2
	= Qatar,	2
7	Honduras,	1
	= Haiti,	1
	= Panama,	1
	= Australia,	1

21

It took 21 years, but Uruguay's Juan Emilio Píriz became the first *Copa América* player to be sent off, against Chile in 1937.

CAF AFRICA CUP OF NATIONS

The Confederation Africaine de Football (CAF) was set up in 1957 and immediately created the Cup of Nations. The finals are staged every two years. Ivory Coast was set to hold the finals in 2023, but concerns over the timing of the 2022 FIFA World Cup and the weather prompted a postponement until January and February 2024.

Founded: 1957

Current champions: Senegal

Most wins: Egypt, 7 titles

Next edition: Ivory Coast, 2024

6

Six different nations won titles from 1970 to 1980: Sudan, Congo Republic, Zaire, Morocco, Ghana, and Nigeria.

As of 2013, the CAF Africa Cup of Nations was switched to odd-numbered years to avoid clashing with the FIFA World Cup. The COVID-19 pandemic forced a delay to 2022 for the 2021 tournament.

11

The UNAF (North Africa) regional federation has won more titles than any other in Africa.

24

24 teams competed in the 2019 tournament, an increase from 16 in 2017.

The original CAF Africa Cup of Nations trophy was the Abdelaziz Abdallah Salem Trophy, named after the first CAF President, Egyptian Abdelaziz Abdallah Salem.

CAF AFRICA CUP OF NATIONS 2024 PREVIEW

The 2023 Africa Cup of Nations is being held between January 13 and February 11 in 2024, having been postponed by six months partly because of a fixture-crush created by the late staging of the 2022 FIFA World Cup. The African confederation also took into account the fact that the June and July would coincide with the rainy season.

TOURNAMENT TRIVIA
HOSTING COUNTDOWN

Ivory Coast has been aspiring to stage the finals again for the past six years. In 2017, plans were drawn up to redevelop two existing stadia and build three new ones. New training centres and hotels were also commissioned. The final will be played in the Stade Olympique d'Ebimpé in the north of Abidjan, which has a capacity of 60,000. Ground was broken on the site in 2016 and the stadium was completed three years later. Other matches will be played in the Stade Félix Houphouët-Boigny – also in Abidjan – as well as the western city of San Pedro, Korhogo in the north and Bouaké and Yamoussoukro in the central region.

2

The finals will be second staged under the CAF confederation presidency of South African Patrice Motsepe. The first African confederation leader from Southern Africa was elected president in March 2021. Motsepe, a mining billionaire, owns South Africa's Mamelodi Sundowns.

TOURNAMENT TRIVIA
IVORIAN PENALTIES

Ivory Coast will be welcoming the finals of the Africa Cup of Nations finals for only the second time. Local fans were disappointed at the first hosting in 1984. Eight teams competed in the finals, split into two first-round groups of four teams each. The Ivorians began in style with a 3–0 defeat of Togo in Abidjan then lost 2–1 to Egypt and 2–0 to Cameroon, and failed to make it to the semi-finals. In 1992, Ivory Coast won the cup for the first time, beating Ghana on penalties in Dakar, Senegal. Their winning margin of 11–10 was then the highest aggregate for a shootout in a major tournament. A second success was secured in 2015. Again they won in a shootout and again Ghana were their victims. This time a team starring **Yaya Touré** won 9–8 after 22 kicks.

TOURÉ

MOROCCO

10

Ten of CAF's FIFA member nations began the 2024 qualifying campaign of the Africa Cup of Nations having never reached the finals: Central African Republic, Chad, Djibouti, Eritrea, Eswatini, Lesotho, São Tomé and Príncipe, Seychelles, Somalia and South Sudan.

NATIONAL LEGEND
HISTORY MAN

Gérard Gabo is the longest-serving national coach in the history of the Ivory Coast. Gabo, who had played for ASEC Abidjan and the national team in the 1960s and early 1970s, spent six years in charge between 1974 and 1980. He was only the second Ivorian to hold the role after Bissouma Tapé in 1965. He was sacked after the Elephants' group stage exit at the 1980 Cup of Nations finals in Nigeria.

12

The status of defending champions can be a poisoned chalice at the finals of the Africa Cup of Nations. In 2021, Algeria became the 12th title-holders to exit the competition in the first round after a 3–1 defeat to Ivory Coast. The Algerians' captain, Riyad Mahrez, clipped a penalty against a post.

TOURNAMENT TRIVIA
MOROCCO QUICK OFF THE MARK

Morocco were the first nation to secure qualification for the finals, a full 10 months ahead of the party. The Atlas Lions had been drawn in qualifying Group K along with Liberia, South Africa and Zimbabwe. In May 2022, CAF announced that Zimbabwe had been disqualified following a suspension from the international game by FIFA. Victories at home to South Africa and away to Liberia meant Morocco were guaranteed one of the two qualifying positions in the group. They followed that success the following November and December by becoming the first African team to reach the semi-finals of the FIFA World Cup in Qatar.

STAR PLAYER
MANE MAGIC

In Ivory Coast, Senegal will be defending the crown they won for the first time in the 2021 tournament, which was staged in January and February 2022 after postponement because of the COVID-19 pandemic. The Lions of Teranga launched their title defence in the 2024 qualifying competition with a 3–1 home win over Benin in Group L in Dakar on 4 June 2022. All three goals were scored by **Sadio Mané**, who was about to leave Liverpool of the English Premier League to join German champions Bayern Munich. HIs first and third goals came from the penalty spot. Mané thus picked up where he had left off in the final of the 2021 tournament, where he converted the decisive spot-kick in the shootout as Senegal defeated Egypt 4–2. Six weeks later, history repeated itself in the FIFA World Cup. Mané again converted a decisive penalty as Senegal defeated Egypt in a shootout to win their African qualifying playoff for a place in the finals in Qatar.

MANÉ

CAF AFRICA CUP OF NATIONS TEAM RECORDS

Only three nations competed in the inaugural 1957 Africa Cup of Nations, while 51 vied for the 24 slots at the 2019 event. Egypt were late replacements as hosts, so participated in qualifying. The three countries not to play were Chad, Eritrea and Somalia.

9 Ghana have now reached nine finals in all – a tally Egypt matched in 2017. Egypt are also the most prolific hosts, having held the tournament five times, including in 2019.

TOURNAMENT TRIUMPHS:

1 **Egypt, 7** (1957, 1959, 1986, 1998, 2006, 2008, 2010)

2 **Cameroon, 5** (1984, 1988, 2000, 2002, 2017)

3 **Ghana, 4** (1963, 1965, 1978, 1982)

4 **Nigeria, 3** (1980, 1994, 2013)

5 **Côte d'Ivoire, 2** (1992, 2015)

= **Zaire/Congo DR, 2** (1968, 1974)

= **Algeria, 2** (1990, 2019)

TOURNAMENT TRIVIA
FROM TRAGEDY TO TRIUMPH

Zambia's unexpected glory at the 2012 CAF Africa Cup of Nations was fitting and poignant as the setting for their glory was just a few hundred metres from the scene of earlier tragedy. The 2012 players spent the day before the final against Côte d'Ivoire laying flowers in the sea in tribute to the 30 people who died when a plane crashed off the coast of Gabonese city Libreville on 27 April 1993. The victims that day included 18 Zambian internationals flying to Senegal for a FIFA World Cup qualifier. After the 2012 final, in which Zambia beat Côte d'Ivoire on penalties following a goalless draw after extra time, coach Hervé Renard dedicated the victory to those who lost their lives in 1993.

2

The 2012 event was only the second to be shared between two host nation – Equatorial Guinea and Gabon – after Ghana and Nigeria shared duties in 2000.

Ghana's *Black Stars* are still the only team to reach the final of four consecutive Africa Cup of Nations, lifting the trophy in 1963 and 1965 and finishing as runners-up in 1968 and 1970.

4

MOGNI

TOURNAMENT TRIVIA
REIGNING PHARAOHS

Egypt dominate the CAF Africa Cup of Nations records. They won the first tournament, in 1957, having been helped by a bye to the final when semi-final opponents South Africa were disqualified, and they have emerged as champions another six times since – more than any other country. Their victories in 2006, 2008 and 2010 make them the only country to have lifted the trophy three times in a row. They have also appeared in a record 25 tournaments, one more than Côte d'Ivoire and two more than Ghana.

TOURNAMENT TRIVIA
FOUR SHAME

Hosts Angola were responsible for perhaps the most dramatic collapse in Africa Cup of Nations history, when they threw away a four-goal lead in the opening match of the 2010 tournament. Even more embarrassingly, they were leading 4-0 against Mali with just 11 minutes left, in the capital Luanda's Estadio 11 de Novembro. Mali's final two goals, by Barcelona's Seydou Keita and Boulogne's Mustapha Yatabaré, were scored deep into stoppage time. Mali failed to make it past the first round, while Angola went out in the quarter-finals.

TOURNAMENT TRIVIA
THE WAITING IS THE HARDEST PART

Some 10 of the 54 full members of CAF have yet to appear in the finals of the Cup of Nations. The latest newcomers to join the party were Comoros and Gambia in the 2021 tournament. Comoros were drawn in Group C before losing 2-1 to hosts Cameroon in the round of 16. Comoros' tournament hero was French-born midfielder **Ahmed Mogni**, from Annecy. He scored twice in their surprise 3-2 victory over Ghana in the group games. Gambia went one better. They reached the quarter-finals on their tournament debut before also losing to hosts Cameroon. Still waiting to make their first appearance at the finals are Central African Republic, Chad, Djibouti, Eritrea, Lesotho, São Tomé and Príncipe, Seychelles, Somali, Eswatini (Swaziland) and South Sudan.

24

Côte d'Ivoire have won two of the highest-scoring penalty shoot-outs in full international history – they defeated Ghana 11-10 over 24 penalties in the 1992 Africa Cup of Nations final, and Cameroon 12-11, over the same number of kicks, in the quarter-finals of the 2006 Africa Cup of Nations.

In 2012, both Côte d'Ivoire and Zambia were competing in their third Africa Cup of Nations final, Côte d'Ivoire having won in 1992 and lost in 2006, while Zambia had finished as runners-up in 1974 and 1994.

CAF AFRICA CUP OF NATIONS PLAYER RECORDS

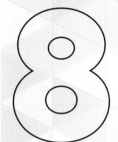

Ghana striker Asamoah Gyan became the third man to appear at eight different CAF Africa Cup of Nations tournaments when he captained the side in 2019, following Cameroon's Rigobert Song and Egypt's Ahmed Hassan.

The global prominence of the CAF Africa Cup of Nations has also grown, especially when the spotlight fell on major African stars taking time off from European club duties every other January. Now, more than ever, the tournament is a showcase for many of the most talented and successful players in the sport.

TOURNAMENT TRIVIA
SIBLING HARMONY

Both teams in the final of the 2015 CAF Africa Cup of Nations called upon a pair of brothers. Runners-up Ghana included Jordan and André Ayew, while Côte d'Ivoire's champions were spearheaded by captain **Yaya Touré** and his centre-back brother Kolo. . All four brothers took penalties in the 2015 final and scored, unlike in 2012, when Côte d'Ivoire were beaten in another penalty shoot-out, this time by Zambia. Yaya had been substituted in extra time, but Kolo missed in the 8-7 loss. Zambia's triumphant captain in 2012, player of the tournament Christian Katongo, had his brother Felix among his team-mates – he came off the bench – and they both scored in that shoot-out.

TOURÉ

ETO'O

NATIONAL LEGEND
SAM THE MAN

Cameroon's Samuel Eto'o, who made his full international debut – away to Costa Rica on 9 March 1997 – one day short of his 16th birthday, is the CAF Africa Cup of Nations' all-time leading goalscorer. He was part of Cameroon's victorious teams in 2000 and 2002, but had to wait until 2008 to pass Laurent Pokou's 14-goal CAF Africa Cup of Nations record. That year's competition took his overall tally to 16 goals – only for the former Real Madrid and Barcelona striker, to add another two in 2010. In 2005, Eto'o became the first player to be named African Footballer of the Year three years running. By 2022, Eto'o had risen to the presidency of the host Cameroon federation.

ALL-TIME TOP SCORERS:

1. **Samuel Eto'o** (Cameroon), 18
2. **Laurent Pokou** (Côte d'Ivoire), 14
3. **Rashidi Yekini** (Nigeria), 13
4. **Hassan El-Shazly** (Egypt), 12
5. **Didier Drogba** (Côte d'Ivoire), 11
   = **Hossam Hassan** (Egypt), 11
   = **Patrick Mboma** (Cameroon), 11

NATIONAL LEGEND
KEITA LEADS BY EXAMPLE

Salif Keita, who was five-goal top scorer in 1972, was a league title-winning striker in his native Mali with AS Real Bamako and Stade Malien but made his name in France with Saint-Étienne. Keita won three consecutive league titles, including the double in 1968 and 1970. His 1970 achievements earned him the African Footballer of the Year award. Subsequently Keita played for Marseille, Valencia and Sporting Clube de Portugal before winding down his career in the United States with New England Tea Men. Later he became president of the Mali football federation for a period of four years and then a senior government minister.

KEITA

NATIONAL LEGEND
NO HASSLE FOR HASSAN

Egypt's **Ahmed Hassan** not only became the first footballer to play in the final of four different CAF Africa Cup of Nations in 2010 – he also became the first to collect his fourth winners' medal. Earlier in the same tournament, his appearance in the quarter-final against Cameroon gave him his 170th cap – an Egyptian record. Hassan marked the game with three goals – one in his own net and two past Cameroon goalkeeper Carlos Kameni – although one appeared not to cross the line.

1957
The first CAF Africa Cup of Nations goal was a penalty scored by Egypt's Raafat Ateya in the 21st minute of their 2-1 semi-final win over Sudan in 1957.

POKOU

5

Côte d'Ivoire striker **Laurent Pokou** scored a record five goals in one CAF Africa Cup of Nations match as his side trounced Ethiopia 6-1 in the first round of the 1968 tournament. He finished top scorer at that tournament, and the following one – although he ended both without a winner's medal.

NATIONAL LEGEND
YO, YOBO

Nigeria's **Joseph Yobo** was brought on as a late substitute to the fans' acclaim in the closing minutes of the *Super Eagles'* victory over Burkina Faso in the 2013 CAF Africa Cup of Nations final in Johannesburg, South Africa. As captain, the one-time Marseille and Everton defender then had the honour of lifting the trophy. Yobo retired from international football in 2014, having made a record 101 appearances in his 13-year career.

YOBO

9

No player has scored more goals in one CAF Africa Cup of Nations than Zaire's Ndaye Mulamba's nine during the 1974 tournament.

OTHER CAF AFRICA CUP OF NATIONS RECORDS

Stephen Keshi – known to admiring fans as "Big Boss" – became only the second man to win the CAF Africa Cup of Nations as both player and manager when he led Nigeria to the title in 2013. He had previously lifted the trophy as captain in 1994. He tragically passed away in 2016, aged just 54.

KESHI

More different countries have won the Africa Cup of Nations than any other continental championship, with glory being shared among 14 separate nations – including Africa's three largest countries, Sudan, Algeria and Congo DR.

TOURNAMENT TRIVIA
ATAK ATTACKS

South Sudan won an international for the first time on 5 September 2015 when midfielder Atak Lual notched the only goal of a 2017 CAF Africa Cup of Nations qualifier against Equatorial Guinea. The game was played at South Sudan's national stadium in Juba. South Sudan had initially gained independence as a country in 2011, receiving CAF admission in February 2012 and FIFA status three months later. They drew their first official international, 2–2 against Uganda on 10 July 2012, but their winless run continued with one more draw and ten defeats before that success against Equatorial Guinea.

RENARD

1.96
The 2019 tournament in Egypt was the second-lowest-scoring Cup of Nations ever, with an average of a mere 1.96 goals per game.

NATIONAL LEGEND
RENARD REDEEMED

In 2015, Frenchman **Hervé Renard** became the first coach to win the CAF Africa Cup of Nations with two different countries. This time he was in charge of Côte d'Ivoire as they defeated Ghana on penalties. Three years earlier, Renard's Zambia had defeated the Ivorians, also on spot kicks, in what was his second spell as national coach. He had resigned in 2010 to become Angola's coach, and his return was not universally welcomed in Zambia. All was forgiven when his team won their first CAF Africa Cup of Nations though. Renard's celebrations included carrying on to the pitch injured defender Joseph Musonda, who had limped off after ten minutes of the final.

LAST FIVE CAF AFRICA CUP OF NATIONS-WINNING COACHES:

2020/21 Aliou Cissé (Senegal)

2019 – Djamel Belmadi (Algeria)

2017 – Hugo Broos (Cameroon)

2015 – Hervé Renard (Côte d'Ivoire)

2013 – Stephen Keshi (Nigeria)

TOURNAMENT TRIVIA
TOGO'S TRAGIC FATE

Togo were the victims of tragedy shortly before the 2010 CAF Africa Cup of Nations kicked off – followed by expulsion from the event. The team's bus was fired on by Angolan militants three days before their first scheduled match, killing three people: the team's assistant coach, press officer and bus driver. The team returned home to Togo for three days of national mourning, and were then thrown out of the competition by the CAF as punishment for missing their opening game against Ghana. Togo were later expelled from the 2012 and 2014 competitions, but this sanction was overturned on appeal in May 2010.

5

Mauritania made unwanted CAF Africa Cup of Nations history by having five players sent off during a qualifier away to Cabo Verde in June 2003, forcing the match to be abandoned. The hosts were leading 3–0 at the time and that stood as the final result.

LAST FIVE CAF AFRICA CUP OF NATIONS FINALS:

2022 – Senegal 0–0 Egypt
(aet, Senegal 7–6 on pens)

2019 – Algeria 1–0 Senegal

2017 – Cameroon 2–1 Egypt

2015 – Côte d'Ivoire 0–0 Ghana
(aet; Côte d'Ivoire 9–8 on pens)

2013 – Nigeria 1–0 Burkina Faso

The most recent CAF Africa Cup of Nations' 15 hat-tricks was scored back in 2008, by **Soufiane Alloudi** in the opening half-hour of Morocco's 5–1 first-round win over Namibia.

15

ALLOUDI

NAGY

NATIONAL LEGEND
GEDO BLASTER

Egypt's hero in 2010 was **Mohamed Nagy**, better known by his nickname "Gedo" – Egyptian Arabic for "Grandpa". He scored the only goal of the final, against Ghana, his fifth of the tournament, giving him the CAF Africa Cup of Nations Golden Boot. Yet he did all this without starting a single game. He had to settle for coming on as a substitute in all six of Egypt's matches, playing a total of 135 minutes. Gedo – born in Damanhur on 3 October 1984 – had made his international debut only two months earlier, and had played only two friendlies for Egypt before the tournament proper.

2

Only Egypt's Hassan El-Shazly has hit two CAF Africa Cup of Nations hat-tricks: his first came in a 6–3 victory over Nigeria in 1963, and he repeated the feat six years later in a 3–1 victory over Côte d'Ivoire.

TOURNAMENT TRIVIA
UNFINISHED BUSINESS

Beware – if you go to see Nigeria play Tunisia, you may not get the full 90 minutes. Nigeria were awarded third place at the 1978 CAF Africa Cup of Nations after Tunisia walked off after 42 minutes of their play-off, with the score at 1–1. . They were protesting about refereeing decisions, but Nigeria were thus granted a 2–0 victory by default. Oddly enough, it had been Nigeria who had walked off when the two teams met in the second leg of a qualifier for the 1962 tournament. Their action came when Tunisia equalised after 65 minutes. The punishment was a 2–0 win for Tunisia – putting them 3–2 ahead on aggregate.

TOURNAMENT TRIVIA
MISSING THE POINT

The absences of Cameroon, Nigeria and reigning champions Egypt from the 2012 Africa Cup of Nations were surprising – although each could at least comfort themselves on not missing out in quite such embarrassing circumstances as South Africa. They appeared happy to play out a goalless draw with Sierra Leone in their final qualifier, believing that would be enough to go through – and greeted the final whistle with celebrations on the pitch. But they were mistaken in thinking goal difference would be used to separate teams level on points in their group, with Niger qualifying instead thanks to a better head-to-head record.

OTHER FIFA TOURNAMENTS

More than three billion men and women, boys and girls happily invest hours, days, weeks and months indulging their passion for association football. The demand for opportunities to participate stretches from the smallest street to super-sized stadia. That, in turn, feeds the creation of more and more tournaments and competitions at local, national and international levels.

A new era for international competition is appearing over the horizon. New competitions and new scheduling are the order of the day. The peak of the world football pyramid remains the men's World Cup. Cementing a regained confidence in the power of national team football, Europe's successful delivery of the UEFA Nations League is being examined and mirrored in other regions. A World Series, using the springtime international break dates, is in the offing. This would offer greater intercontinental experience for national teams traditionally restricted to their own continents. World football federation FIFA is planning to stage its age group youth tournaments every year instead of every two years. FIFA is also embracing club football. An expanded Club World Cup is scheduled to kick off in 2025, while the original annual tournament will be maintained in a reshaped format. All this is to say nothing of the ever-more popular Beach Soccer sphere as well as the exploding electronic games market. Progress is also the watchword for the women's game. The expansion of the FIFA Women's World Cup has encouraged progress towards a Women's Club World Cup.

Real Madrid celebrate their FIFA Club World Cup victory in 2022.

FIFA U17s AND U20s WORLD CUP

FIFA has ambitious plans for its youth tournaments. Beyond 2025, the plan is for the U-17 World Cup to be contested annually, while the U-20 event is reverting to a biennial schedule. The U-17 World Cup was scheduled to resume in November 2023, having not been staged since 2019 when Brazil were both hosts and winners. The U-20 tournament missed its scheduled staging in 2019 but resumed in 2023, with Uruguay beating Italy in the final.

10

Nigeria's Victor Osimhen recorded an U-17 finals record 10-goal haul in 2015.

SEOUL WORLDCUP STADIUM

TOURNAMENT TRIVIA
HOPE AND GLORY

England won their first U-17 world title in the most thrilling way possible by hitting back from two goals down to beat Spain 5-2 in the 2017 final in Kolkata, India. They were the second successive England age-group team, after the U-20s' victory in Korea Republic, to become world champions. Liverpool's Rhian Brewster led the recovery with a goal just before half-time, after Spain had hit England twice on the break through Sergio Gómez. Brewster ended the tournament as the Golden Boot winner with hat-tricks in the quarter- and semi-finals.

HOST HISTORY
BRAZILIAN LATE SHOW

Hosts Brazil won the 2019 U-17 crown with one of the most dramatic recoveries in even their own illustrious history. Home fans in the central city of Gama, including legends Ronaldo and Cafu, were losing hope after seeing Mexico take a 66th-minute lead through Bryan González. But then Kaio Jorge equalised with an 84th-minute penalty before **Lázaro Vinicius Marques** volleyed Brazil's winning goal deep into stoppage time. Brazil have now won the title four times, one fewer than Nigeria. The young *Seleçao* had further success to celebrate when forward Gabriel Veron was hailed as the tournament's best player. Dutch teenager Sontje Hansen was its six-goal leading marksman.

LÁZARO

HOST HISTORY
SEOUL SURVIVOR

The final of the U-17 event in 2007 was the first to be hosted by a former FIFA World Cup venue – the 68,476-capacity Seoul FIFA World Cup Stadium in Korea Republic's capital, which had been built for the 2002 FIFA World Cup. The game was watched by a crowd of 36,125, a tournament record. The 2007 event was also the first to feature 24 teams instead of 16, and it was won by Nigeria – after Spain missed all three of their spot-kicks in a penalty shoot-out.

TOURNAMENT TRIVIA
LUCKY LUCIANO

Uruguay made it third time lucky in winning the 2023 FIFA U-20 World Cup in Argentina, having finished runners-up in 1997 and 2013. A 1–0 victory over Italy was delivered by an 84th-minute goal from **Luciano Rodríguez** in the Estadio Diego Maradona in La Plata. Italy's Cesare Casadei won the Golden Ball for best player and Golden Boot as seven-goal top scorer. Argentina staged the tournament at only seven weeks' notice after original host Indonesia was stripped of the event for refusing to admit the Israeli team. Israel finished third in Argentina. They beat favourites Brazil 3–2 after extra time in the quarter-finals before losing 1–0 to Uruguay.

RODRÍGUEZ

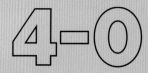

4–0

The most decisive win in an U-20 tournament final – West Germany beat Qatar 4-0 in 1981, and Spain beat Japan by the same margin in 1999.

12

Brazil have finished in the U-20 top three a record 12 times – five as winners, four as runners-up and three in third place.

RECENT HISTORY
ENGLAND'S GLORY

England celebrated their first world crown since 1966 in 2017 by winning the FIFA U-20 World Cup in Korea Republic. They defeated Venezuela 1–0 in the final in Suwon with a first half goal from Everton's Dominic Calvert-Lewin. Newcastle goalkeeper Freddie Woodman saved a late penalty from Watford's Adalberto Penaranda. Woodman was honoured as the tournament's top keeper, while teammate Dominic Solanke was voted best player.

MESSI

1991
In 1991, Portugal became the first hosts to win the U-20 title with a team that became known as the country's "Golden Generation", featuring Luís Figo, Rui Costa, João Pinto, Abel Xavier and Jorge Costa.

NATIONAL LEGEND
WHAT A MESSI

Lionel Messi made the world game sit up and take notice for the first time in 2005 when he was the star of the show as Argentina won the U-20 World Cup by defeating Nigeria 2–1 in Utrecht, Netherlands. Messi scored both of Argentina's goals in the final, from penalties, to secure the tournament's six-goal top scorer award. He also won the Golden Ball as the best player. Two years later, Sergio Agüero emulated Messi by finishing as six-goal top scorer in leading Argentina to a 2–1 cup victory over the Czech Republic in Toronto, Canada.

TOURNAMENT TRIVIA
DOMINANT DOMINIC

Ghana became the first African winners of the U-20 trophy in 2009 when they upset Brazil in the final – despite playing 83 of the 120 minutes with just ten men following Daniel Addo's red card. The final finished goalless, one of only two games in which **Dominic Adiyiah** failed to score. He still ended the tournament as top scorer with eight goals and also won the Golden Ball for best player. The Silver Ball went to Brazil's Alex Teixeira, even though it was his missed penalty, when the final shoot-out went to sudden death, which handed Ghana victory.

ADIYIAH

FIFA CLUB WORLD CUP

The world club prize has been contested in various formats since 1960, when Real Madrid defeated Peñarol over two legs. Since 2007, a seven-team system has been in operation, with further reorganisation on the way.

TOURNAMENT TRIVIA
ALL-CHANGE FOR A WIDER WORLD

In 2025, the FIFA Club World Cup will be replaced by a 32-team tournament to be played every four years. Europe will have 12 clubs: the UEFA Champions League winners between 2020–21 and 2023–24 plus eight clubs sorted by a ranking over the same four years. South America will have six clubs: the winners of the Copa Libertadores between 2021 and 2024 and two other top-ranked clubs. The four winners between 2021 and 2024 of each of the Champions Leagues in CONCACAF, Africa and Asia will enter, plus the top-ranking club from Oceania. The host country will enter one club. An annual tournament will see the UEFA Champions League winners play the winners of play-offs between the champion clubs from the other confederations.

INTERCONTINENTAL TITLE WINNERS BY COUNTRY:

1. 12 – Spain
2. 10 – Brazil
3. 9 – Argentina
   = 9 – Italy
5. 6 – Uruguay

36

European clubs hold a decisive advantage over their South American rivals down the years. UEFA's pride have taken the crown 36 times compared with CONMEBOL's 26.

4-0
The most one-sided FIFA Club World Cup final was played in 2011, when Barcelona defeated Santos of Brazil 4-0.

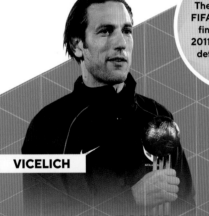

VICELICH

CLUB LEGEND
VETERAN IVAN

Auckland City were one of the surprises of the FIFA Club World Cup in 2014, spearheaded by 38-year-old **Ivan Vicelich** who won the Bronze Ball for the third best player of the tournament. Only Real Madrid's Sergio Ramos and Cristiano Ronaldo finished ahead of him. The New Zealanders finished third, the highest finish for a club from Oceania, after beating Cruz Azul on penalties following a 1-1 draw in the third-place play-off.

TOURNAMENT TRIVIA
THE REIGN OF SPAIN

Spain has dominated the FIFA Club World Cup since the world governing body's remodelling of the event. Between them, Real Madrid and Barcelona have won eight crowns. Barcelona launched the era of Spanish supremacy in 2009 by defeating Estudiantes de La Plata of Argentina 2-1 after extra time through goals from Pedro and Lionel Messi. They won again in 2011 before **Cristiano Ronaldo**'s Real Madrid triumphed three times in four years in 2014, 2016 and 2017. Real won yet again in 2018 after Ronaldo's departure. and also in 2022 to secure a record eighth all-formats success.

RONALDO

TOURNAMENT TRIVIA
HALA MADRID...AGAIN!

VALVERDE

Real Madrid added the world crown to their European title after beating Saudi Arabia's Al-Hilal 5–3 in Rabat to win the club prize for a record-extending eighth time. Vinícius Jr and **Federico Valverde** put European champions Real 2–0 up. Moussa Marega gave Al-Hilal hope before Vinícius set up a Madrid third for Karim Benzema. The teams went on swapping goals – Valverde for Madrid, Luciano Vietto for Al-Hilal then Vinícius again. Vietto, an Argentinian, who once played for Real's neighbours Atlético Madrid, struck back once more but in vain. Madrid's success was the tenth in a row for European teams. Rescheduling after the COVID-19 pandemic had seen delays in the staging of the tournament. Thus the 2022 finals were played in February 2023 in Morocco.

OVERALL FIFA CLUB WORLD CUP CHAMPIONS (2000-2021):

1 5 – **Real Madrid** (Spain)

2 3 – **Barcelona** (Spain)

3 2 – **Bayern Munich** (Germany)
  2 – **Corinthians** (Brazil)

5 1 – **Chelsea** (England)
  =1 – **AC Milan** (Italy)
  =1 – **Internacional** (Brazil)
  =1 – **Internazionale** (Italy)
  =1 – **Liverpool** (England)
  =1 – **Manchester United** (England)
  =1 – **São Paulo** (Brazil)

6
Barcelona's triumph in 2009 made them the first club to lift six different major trophies in one calendar year: the FIFA Club World Cup, the UEFA Champions League, the UEFA European Super Cup, and a Spanish hat-trick of La Liga, Copa del Rey and Super Cup.

6
Toni Kroos has won the FIFA Club World Cup six times between 2013 and 2022, a record.

7
With seven goals to his name since 2008, Cristiano Ronaldo is the top goalscorer in FIFA Club World Cup history.

TOURNAMENT TRIVIA
LONG-DISTANCE, LONG-RUNNING RIVALRY

The precursor to the modern FIFA Club World Cup was the Intercontinental Cup, also known informally as the World Club Cup or the European/South American Cup, which pitted the champions of Europe and South America against each other. Representatives of UEFA and CONMEBOL contested the event from 1960 to 2004, but now all continental confederations send at least one club to an expanded Club World Cup organised by the world governing body. The first final, in 1960, was between Spain's Real Madrid and Uruguay's Peñarol. After a goalless draw in the rain in Montevideo, Real triumphed 5–1 at their own stadium in Madrid – including three goals in the first eight minutes by Ferenc Puskás (two) and Alfredo di Stéfano.

TOURNAMENT TRIVIA
AFRICA AND ASIA STILL WAITING

Africa and Asia are still waiting to claim the Club World Cup. Only five teams from beyond Europe and Latin America have reached the final. The most recent, in 2022, were Saudi club **Al-Hilal** from Riyadh. Coached by Argentinian Ramón Díaz, Al-Hilal beat Wydad of Morocco on penalties and Brazilian giants Flamengo 3–2, before losing to Real Madrid. Previous Asian runners-up were Japan's Kashima Antlers, who lost to Real Madrid in extra time in 2016, and Al Ain of UAE, who fell to the Spanish giants 4–1 two years later. Two African clubs have reached the final. TP Mazembe from DR Congo were the first in 2010, losing 3–0 to Italy's Internazionale. Moroccan home favourites Raja Casablanca lost 2–0 to Bayern Munich in 2013.

AL-HILAL

MEN'S OLYMPIC FOOTBALL

Football first appeared at the Olympics in 1900 and became official in 1908. In 1996 in Atlanta, it evolved into an under-23 event with each team permitted three over-age players. Age limits were extended by 12 months in Tokyo in 2021 because of the Games' one-year delay after the COVID-19 pandemic.

NATIONAL LEGEND
LAPPING IT UP

Until London 2012, **Uruguay** had a perfect Olympic football record having won gold in both of their two previous appearances (1924 and 1928). Those Games were seen as an unofficial world championship and helped prompt FIFA into organising the first World Cup in 1930 – also won by Uruguay, who included 1924 and 1928 gold medallists José Nasazzi, José Andrade and Héctor Scarone in their squad. Uruguay's 1924 champions are also thought to have pioneered the lap of honour.

URUGUAY

13

Denmark's Sophus Nielsen is the top scorer in Olympic history with 13 goals to his name: 11 in 1908 and two in 2012.

23/27

Eastern European countries dominated Olympic football from 1948 to 1980, a period in which professional players were officially banned from taking part. Teams comprising so-called "state amateurs" from the Eastern Bloc took 23 of the 27 medals available during those years.

TOURNAMENT TRIVIA
CZECH OUT

The climax of the Antwerp 1920 Olympic Games tournament is the only time a major international football final has been abandoned. Czechoslovakia's players walked off the pitch minutes before half-time, in protest at the decisions made by 65-year-old English referee John Lewis – including the dismissal of Czech player Karel Steiner. Belgium, who were 2-0 up at the time, were awarded the victory, before Spain beat the Netherlands 3-1 in a play-off for silver.

PERALTA

TOURNAMENT TRIVIA
LONDON CALLING

Mexico were the unexpected winners when, in 2012, Wembley Stadium became the first venue to stage two Men's Olympic Football Tournament finals. The old stadium hosted the showpiece game when England's capital held the Olympics in 1948 and London is also now the only city to stage three separate summer Olympics, although the football final back in 1908 was played at White City. In 2012, **Oribe Peralta** scored both goals as Mexico defeated Brazil 2-1 in the final at the renovated Wembley. A late reply by Hulk was little consolation for the highly fancied South Americans, even though Leandro Damião did end as the tournament's six-goal top scorer.

MODERN-ERA OLYMPIC GOLD MEDALLISTS :

* 2020, Tokyo: Brazil

2016, Rio de Janeiro: Brazil

2012, London: Mexico

2008, Beijing: Argentina

2004, Athens: Argentina

2000, Sydney: Cameroon

1996, Atlanta: Nigeria

1992, Barcelona: Spain

1988, Seoul: USSR

1984, Los Angeles: France

1980, Moscow: Czechoslovakia

*Games staged in 2021 because of COVID-19 pandemic

NATIONAL LEGEND
BARCELONA-BOUND

Future Barcelona team-mates Samuel Eto'o and Xavi scored penalties for opposing sides in 2000 when Cameroon and Spain contested the first Olympic final to be settled by a shoot-out. Future FIFA World Cup or UEFA European Championship winners to have played at the Summer Olympics include Italy's Fabio Cannavaro, Gianluigi Buffon and Alessandro Nesta and Brazil's Roberto Carlos, Rivaldo and Ronaldo (Atlanta, 1996); Italy's Gianluca Zambrotta and Spain's Xavi, Carles Puyol and Joan Capdevila (Sydney, 2000); and Italy's Daniele De Rossi, Andrea Pirlo and Alberto Gilardino, and Portugal's Cristiano Ronaldo and Bruno Alves (Athens, 2004).

NATIONAL LEGEND
DOUBLING UP

Brazil successfully defended the men's Olympic football gold medal by beating Spain 2–1 in the year-delayed Tokyo tournament in 2021. The Brazilians had won Olympic gold for the first time on home ground in Rio de Janeiro in 2016. They topped their first-round group undefeated ahead of Ivory Coast, Germany and Saudi Arabia, and followed up with knockout round victories over Egypt 1–0 and Mexico 4–1 on penalties after a goalless extra time draw. In the final, Matheus Cunha opened the scoring against Spain in first-half stoppage time, but a Mikel Oyarzabal equaliser sent the clash into extra time. Winger Malcom scored the gold-medal winner in the 108th minute. Brazil forward **Richarlison** was the Games' five-goal leading scorer, including a hat-trick in the 4–2 opening victory over Germany.

RICHARLISON

3

Hungary are the most successful Olympic football team with three wins. Great Britain have also won three gold medals but those are their only medals, whereas Hungary also finished second and third in 1972 and 1960 respectively.

14 SECONDS
Neymar holds the record for the fastest goal in a men's Olympic football match: he netted after 14 seconds in the semi-final against Honduras in 2016.

6

Six Olympic finals have gone to extra time, with one decided by a replay and two by penalty shootouts.

TOURNAMENT TRIVIA
AFRICAN AMBITION

Ghana became the first African country to win an Olympic football medal when they picked up bronze in 1992, but Nigeria went even better four years later by claiming the continent's first Olympic football gold medal thanks to **Emmanuel Amunike**'s stoppage-time winner against Argentina. Nigeria's triumph came as a huge surprise to many – especially as their rival teams included future world stars such as Brazil's Ronaldo and Roberto Carlos, Argentina's Hernán Crespo and Roberto Ayala, Italy's Fabio Cannavaro and Gianluigi Buffon, and France's Robert Pires and Patrick Vieira.

AMUNIKE

FIFA BEACH SOCCER WORLD CUP

The Beach Soccer World Championships were launched in 1995 and brought into the FIFA World Cup family in 2005. Since 2009, the competition has been staged every two years. The popularity of the game in the Arab world was underlined by the award of hosting rights to the 2023 finals to United Arab Emirates.

NATIONAL LEGEND
ERIC THE KING

Eric Cantona – in turn footballer, actor, poet and philosopher – coached the France team who won the FIFA Beach Soccer World Cup in 2005. This was the first tournament staged under the FIFA World Cup banner, having previously been known as the Beach Soccer World Championship. The former Manchester United icon allowed himself only limited playing time but still ended the tournament with one goal to his credit – in a 7-4 quarter-final victory over Spain.

CANTONA

NATIONAL LEGEND
MAGIC ALEX

Alessandro Altobelli is the only player to score in both a FIFA World Cup final and a Beach World Cup. Altobelli struck Italy's third goal in their 3-1 victory over West Germany in the 1982 FIFA World Cup in Spain, and after abandoning grass for sand, he finished as the 1995 Beach Soccer World Championship's joint-top scorer with Zico on 12 goals. The next year, Altobelli was top scorer in his own right with 14. He notched a total of 30 World Cup goals on sand, all in the pre-FIFA era.

JORGINHO

NATIONAL LEGEND
TOP OF THE WORLD

Jorginho made history as the first player to win both the FIFA World Cup and the Beach Soccer World Cup. He helped Brazil to glory against Italy in Pasadena in 1994 but then went on to add the beach soccer prize to his career honours list in 1999 and 2004. He was voted player of the tournament on both occasions, having also been named in FIFA's All-Star squad for the senior tournament on grass in 1994.

2008
One of the most famous names in football made it onto the scoresheet in the FIFA Beach Soccer World Cup final in 2008: Diego Maradona. But this was not Argentina's 1986 World Cup-winning captain but his son Diego Maradona Jr, playing for Italy.

TOURNAMENT TRIVIA
BOSSING THE BEACH

Brazil established themselves early on as the kings of the beach, but they have struggled in recent tournaments, winning just one of the last six editions. The Brazilians hosted the opening 13 tournaments between 1995 and 2007, and won the first six titles. Their command was broken at last by Portugal in 2001, a success for Europe subsequently emulated by France and Russia. The tournament had been launched as the Beach Soccer World Championships before FIFA took over as the sport's governing body in 2005.

TOURNAMENT TOP SCORERS:

1 **Madjer** (Portugal) 88
2 **Dejen Stankovic** (Switzerland) 47
3 **Gabriele Gori** (Italy) 41
4 **Bruno** (Brazil) 39
  = **Belchor** (Portugal) 39
6 **Andre** (Brazil) 38
  = **Alan** (Portugal) 38
8 **Buru** (Brazil) 35
  = **Benjamin** (Brazil) 35
10 **Dmitry Shishin** (Russia) 33

NATIONAL LEGEND
MADJER FOR IT

Angolan-born Portuguese star **Madjer** set a record for goals scored in one tournament in 2006 when he put the ball in the net 21 times. He finished as sole or joint-top scorer in six tournaments and played a key role in all of Portugal's three victories in 2001, 2015 and 2019. His seven goals in one game, against Uruguay in 2009, broke his own record of six against Cameroon in 2006. Madjer retired after the 2019 triumph having notched no fewer than 140 World Cup goals – 65 more than his second-placed fellow countryman Alan (75).

286
The 2006 and 2019 tournaments, in Brazil and Paraguay respectively, were the most prolific in terms of goals, with the 16 teams recording 286 each time.

TOURNAMENT TRIVIA
FRENCH SELECTION

The 2008 tournament, on the southern coastal beaches of Marseille in France, was the first to take place outside of Brazil. The second was in the United Arab Emirates in 2009 and the third in Ravenna, Italy, in 2011. This was the first under a new system seeing the tournament staged every two years instead of annually. Altogether nine different nations have hosted the finals, with Africa the one confederation still awaiting its chance.

MADJER

NATIONAL LEGEND
ALL-ROUNDER ALONSO

Joaquín Alonso enjoyed a stellar career on both grass and sand. He won 18 caps for Spain's full national team, scoring once between 1978 and 1988, and was selected for both the 1980 Olympic Games and the 1982 FIFA World Cup on home soil. The midfielder spent most of his professional career with Sporting Gijón then, after retiring, coached his country on the beach. In 2013, Alonso's men finished as runners-up to Russia.

1
Tahiti became the first Oceanian country to reach the final of a FIFA tournament in 2015, when they lost 5-3 to hosts Portugal.

10
Seychelles will become the 11th nation to host the finals after being awarded the 2025 tournament by the FIFA Council in December 2022.

SHISHIN

TOURNAMENT TRIVIA
SHISHIN STRIKES

The FIFA Beach Soccer World Cup final in 2011 was the highest-scoring showdown in the competition's history as reigning champions Brazil lost 12-8 to a country not usually associated with balmy climatic conditions – Russia. The Russians went into the tournament as reigning European champions, however, and clinched their first world title with the help of a hat-trick in the final from **Dmitry Shishin** and the performances of player of the tournament Ilya Leonov. Russia beat Spain 5-1 in Tahiti in 2013 and Japan 5-2 on home sand in Moscow in 2021.

FIFAe WORLD CUP

The FIFAe World Cup had become, by 2023, the world's largest and most popular video game tournament. It had been launched in 2004 as the FIFA Interactive World Cup before being renamed the FIFA eWorld Cup in 2018. In 2020, it became the FIFAe World Cup as the world governing body expanded its tournaments. World Cup contestants won through worldwide qualifying events on the latest annual version of the FIFA video game.

TOURNAMENT TRIVIA
E-MPIRE BUILDER

Germany's Umut Gültekin (Umut) won the 2022 finals of the FIFAe World Cup after a two-year break in the competition enforced by the COVID-19 pandemic. In the final in Copenhagen, the 19-year-old beat Nicolas Villalba (nicolas99fc) 5-4 in a dramatic penalty shootout after a 0-0 aggregate draw. It was only the second time in 16 tournaments that a shootout had been needed.

TOURNAMENT TRIVIA
CASHING UP

The explosion in popularity of eSports has been demonstrated by the rise in World Cup prize money. The collective prize pool of USD 20,000 in 2004 had multiplied across the FIFAe series events to USD 1.2m by 2022. Challengers for the World Cup were chasing a top prize of USD 250,000 with USD 100,000 for the runner-up. The skills factor included adapting each year to the newly-upgraded FIFA game – just as professional footballers must adapt to annual law changes, interpretations and technological innovations such as VAR.

ESPORTS STAR
FIT OF PIQUÉ

In 2012, Real Madrid fan **Alfonso Ramos** became the first two-time FIFA Interactive World Cup champion. He also enjoyed another victory in a game played at the subsequent FIFA gala, this time with Barcelona centre-back **Gerard Piqué** at the controls as his opponent. Piqué predictably played as Barcelona against Alfonso's Real, and he not only lost 1-0 but saw the computer-game "Gerard Piqué" sent off. Ramos – nicknamed "Vamos Ramos" – celebrated both his 2012 triumphs with a dance inspired by Brazil striker Neymar. After retiring as a player, Ramos became coach of the Spanish eFootball national team.

RAMOS

FIFA
For the Game. For the World.

FIFA INTERACTIVE WORLD CUP 2012
CHAMPION
Alfonso Ramos (Spain)
Dubai, 28 MAY 2012

PIQUÉ

LET'S GO CLUBBING

The visibility and commercial potential of eSports has persuaded plenty of traditional clubs to dip their toes in the electronic waters across a variety of platforms. Major teams with officially contracted *FIFA* players include clubs such as Barcelona, Ajax, Borussia Mönchengladbach, Bayer Leverkusen, Manchester City and West Ham United. Players who started out as armchair amateurs now travel the world as eSports professionals.

ESPORTS STAR
MO's THE MAN

Mohammed "MoAuba" Harkous, the 2019 champion, was surprised by his reception at The Best FIFA Football Awards gala, where he rubbed shoulders with the likes of Cristiano Ronaldo and Lionel Messi. He found himself being asked for advice on how to improve video game skills by award winners such as France superstar Kylian Mbappé. Mo later said: "It was amazing because I considered myself a fan but they were asking me for tips." The first tournament Mo won as a teenager cost him a EUR 20 entry fee and his prize was a PlayStation console.

47 MILLION

The 2019 eWorld Cup Grand Final was streamed in six languages for the first time – Arabic, Chinese, English, German, Portuguese and Spanish – and broadcast to more than 75 territories around the world. The three-day tournament generated more than 47 million views across a multiplicity of online platforms.

HARKOUS

FIFAe WORLD CUP ROLL OF HONOUR:

Year	Venue	Final
2004	Zurich	Thiago Carrico de Azevedo (BRA) bt Matija Biljeskovic (SRB) 2-1
2005	London	Chris Bullard (ENG) bt Gabor Mokos (HUN) 5-2
2006	Amsterdam	Andries Smit (NED) bt Wolfgang Meier (AUT) 6-4
2008	Berlin	Alfonso Ramos (ESP) bt Michael Ribeiro (USA) 3-1
2009	Barcelona	Bruce Grannec (FRA) bt Ruben Morales Zerecero (MEX) 3-1
2010	Barcelona	Nenad Stojkovic (SRB) bt Ayhan Altundag (GER) 2-1
2011	Los Angeles	Francisco Cruz (POR) bt Javier Munoz (COL) 4-1
2012	Dubai	Alfonso Ramos (ESP) bt Bruce Grannec (FRA) 0-0 (4-3 on penalties)
2013	Madrid	Bruce Grannec (FRA) Andrei Torres Vivero (MEX) 1-0
2014	Rio de Janeiro	August Rosenmeier [Agge] (DEN) bt David Bytheway [Davebtw] (ENG) 3-1
2015	Munich	Abdulaziz Alshehri [Mr D0ne] (KSA) Julien Dassonville (FRA) 3-0
2016	New York	Mohamad Al-Bacha [Bacha] (DEN) bt Sean Allen [Dragonn] (ENG) 2-2, 3-3 (5-5 agg., Al-Bacha on away goals)
2017	London	Spencer Ealing [Gorilla] (ENG) bt Kai Wollin [Deto] (GER) 3-3, 4-0 (7-3 agg.)
2018	London	Mosaad Aldossary [Msdossary] (KSA) bt Stefano Pinna (BEL) 2-0, 2-0 (4-0 agg.)
2019	London	Mohammed Harkous [MoAuba] (GER) bt Mosaad Aldossary [Msdossary] (KSA) 1-1, 2-1 (3-2 agg.)
2022	Copenhagen	Umut Gültekin [Umut] (GER) bt Nicolas Villalba [nicolas99fc] (ARG) 0-0, 0-0 (0-0 agg. 5-4 on penalties)

WOMEN'S FOOTBALL

FIFA broke new ground with the decision to award hosting rights for the 2023 FIFA Women's World Cup to Australia and New Zealand. This was the first time that the event had been co-hosted, while the number of competing teams was raised from 24 to 32.

Such progress reflects a remarkable success story, which sees more than 30 million women now playing the game around the world – an impressive statistic considering that England's Football Association shut its doors on them for half a century in 1921. The FA dropped its restrictions only at the turn of the 1970s.

In the meantime, women's football had been racing ahead in other countries. This surge of interest ultimately led, in the early 1980s, to the first formal European Championships and, in 1988, to a FIFA invitational tournament in Chinese Taipei.

In 1991, FIFA launched an inaugural world championship. It was won by the USA, who subsequently established an enduring claim to primacy in the game. They have won both the FIFA Women's World Cup and Olympic Games gold on four occasions each. A gathering European enthusiasm for women's football was reflected by the rising profile of the UEFA Women's Euro. History came full circle with England's Euro victory in 2022. The Lionesses followed up by edging Brazil on penalties in a Finalissima against the women's champions of South America in April 2023.

WOMEN'S LISSIMA 2023

England's Lionesses lift the Finalissima trophy after their shootout victory over Brazil at Wembley on 6 April 2023.

FIFA WOMEN'S WORLD CUP 2023

Played in ten stadiums across two countries, the 2023 FIFA Women's World Cup was the most ambitious women's football competition ever, reflecting the amazing growth in the women's game. It kicked off in Auckland, New Zealand, on 20 July, with the final held one month and 64 games later in Sydney, Australia.

NATIONAL LEGENDS
TRIUMPHANT TRIO

A record 172 national teams, from FIFA's membership of 211, competed for 30 slots in the finals along with Australia and New Zealand, seeded directly as hosts. European federation UEFA commanded the largest number of places: 11. The final three qualifying places were taken by **Haiti**, Panama and Portugal after a 10-team inter-continental playoff event in New Zealand in February 2023.

TOURNAMENT TRIVIA
THE FOUR-YEAR ODYSSEY

In the spring of 2019, ten member associations registered an interest in hosting the 2023 FIFA Women's World Cup. They were Argentina, Australia, Belgium, Bolivia, Brazil, Colombia, Japan, Korea Republic, New Zealand and South Africa. By the time it came to Decision Day for the FIFA Council, Australia and New Zealand had developed a joint bid and most of the opposition had fallen away. Ultimately only one vote was needed, and they polled 22 votes compared with 13 for Colombia.

2

Australia is only the second association from the Asian Football Confederation to host the Women's World Cup, after China in 1991 and 2007.

HAITI NATIONAL TEAM

#BEYONDGREATNESS™

QUALIFIED

81.4

million Australian dollars were spent in upgrading the match day changing rooms and media facilities at Stadium Australia in anticipation of co-hosting the tournament.

TOURNAMENT TRIVIA
HISTORY, HISTORY, HISTORY

The 2023 finals of the FIFA Women's World Cup created history as the first edition to feature 32 teams, the first to be staged in the southern hemisphere and the first to be hosted by two nations: Australia and New Zealand. FIFA also accepted, for the first time for any of its World Cups, the principle of a dual-confederation event, since New Zealand is in Oceania while Australia switched to become a member of the Asian region almost two decades ago.

SCORING RECORD
TESSA THE TOPS

Belgium's **Tessa Wullaert** was the 17-goal leading scorer in the qualifying competition to reach the finals of the 2023 FIFA Women's World Cup. Her tally included five goals in a 19-0 defeat of Armenia, four in a 6-1 win away to Kosovo and a simple hat-trick in a 7-0 home win over the Kosovars. Wullaert has played her club football in Belgium, England, Germany and Netherlands. She first played for her country at the UEFA Women's U-19 Championship in 2011, and she made her debut for the seniors in the same year. Wullart has since achieved more than a century of international matches and become a double record-holder in both appearances (117) and goals (71).

WULLAERT

THE VENUES:

For the 2023 finals, FIFA selected five cities and six stadiums in Australia plus four cities and stadiums in New Zealand, with Stadium Australia, in the Sydney Olympic Park, hosting the final.

AUSTRALIA

STADIUM AUSTRALIA, SYDNEY
Capacity: 83,500

SYDNEY FOOTBALL STADIUM, SYDNEY
Capacity: 42,512

HINDMARSH STADIUM, ADELAIDE
Capacity: 18,400

LANG PARK, BRISBANE
Capacity: 52,263

MELBOURNE RECTANGULAR STADIUM, MELBOURNE
Capacity: 30,052

PERTH RECTANGULAR STADIUM, PERTH
Capacity: 22,225

NEW ZEALAND

EDEN PARK, AUCKLAND
Capacity: 48,276

FORSYTH BARR STADIUM, DUNEDIN
Capacity: 28,744

WAIKATO STADIUM, HAMILTON
Capacity: 25,111

WELLINGTON REGIONAL STADIUM, WELLINGTON
Capacity: 34,500

FIFA WOMEN'S WORLD CUP

The first FIFA Women's World Cup finals were held in China PR in 1991, and the tournament has since grown astronomically. It expanded to 24 teams in 2015, and featured 32 when Australia and New Zealand shared hosting in 2023.

ALL-TIME TOP SCORERS:

1. Marta, (BRA) – 17
2. Birgit Prinz, (GER) – 14
   = Abby Wambach, (USA) – 14
4. Michelle Akers, (USA) – 12
5. Cristiane, (BRA) – 11
   = Sun Wen, (CHN) – 11
   = Bettina Wiegmann, (GER) – 11

MARTA

FIFA WOMEN'S WORLD CUP FINAL RESULTS

1991 USA 2–1 Norway (China PR)

1995 Norway 2–0 Germany (Sweden)

1999 USA 0–0 China PR (USA) – USA won 5–4 on penalties

2003 Germany 2–1 Sweden (USA)

2007 Germany 2–0 Brazil (China PR)

2011 Japan 2–2 USA (Germany) – Japan won 3–1 on penalties

2015 USA 5–2 Japan (Canada)

2019 USA 2–0 Netherlands (France)

90,185
The highest-ever attendance for a FIFA Women's World Cup match remains the 90,185 fans who packed into the Rose Bowl to see the USA defeat China PR to win the 1999 tournament on home turf.

TOURNAMENT TRIVIA
CHINA PR ARE EVER PRESENT

The first game in the FIFA Women's World Cup finals saw hosts China PR defeat Norway 4–0 in front of 65,000 fans in Guangzhou on 16 November 1991. Together, China PR and Norway are among nine nations to have competed in all nine tournaments – along with Brazil, Germany, Japan, Nigeria, Sweden and the United States. Following the 2023 tournament, 44 nations have made at least one appearance at the FIFA Women's World Cup. Haiti, Morocco, Panama, Philippines, Portugal, the Republic of Ireland, Vietnam and Zambia all made their bow in Australia/New Zealand.

STAR PLAYER
GOAL MACHINE MARTA

Marta Vieira da Silva of Brazil has cemented her status as one of the greatest female players of all time with her goalscoring achievements in the FIFA Women's World Cup. Her total of 17 goals is three more than both Birgit Prinz (Germany) and Abby Wambach (United States). In 2007, Marta was awarded both the Golden Ball for best player and the Golden Boot for finishing as the seven-goal top scorer. She has also been hailed a record six times by FIFA as the world's No1 female player, and she extended her World Cup tally in the 2019 finals with penalties against Australia and Italy. She and team-mate Cristiane are the only two players to have scored goals in five successive finals tournaments.

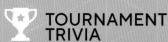

HAVELANGE'S DREAM COMES TRUE

The FIFA Women's World Cup was the brainchild of former FIFA President João Havelange. The tournament began as an experimental competition in 1991 and has expanded in size and importance ever since. The success of the 1999 finals in the United States was a turning point for the tournament, which now attracts huge crowds and worldwide TV coverage. The USA and Norway – countries in which football (or soccer) is one of the most popular girls' sports – dominated the early competitions.

In 2007, Germany became the first team to make a successful defence of the FIFA Women's World Cup. They also set another record by going through the tournament – six games and 540 minutes – without conceding a single goal. As a result, their goalkeeper Nadine Angerer overhauled Italy keeper Walter Zenga's record of 517 minutes unbeaten in the 1990 men's finals. The last player to score against the Germans had been Sweden's **Hanna Ljungberg** in the 41st minute of the 2003 final. Their run eventually ended when Christine Sinclair of Canada scored after 82 minutes of Germany's opening game in 2011.

LJUNGBERG

STAR PLAYER
MAGNIFICENT MEGAN

It is fair to say that United States captain **Megan Rapinoe** dominated the FIFA Women's World Cup 2019. Rapinoe, a 34-year-old from Redding, California, opened the scoring in the United States' 2-0 victory over Netherlands in the final, was voted player of the match and won the adidas Golden Ball as the tournament's best player. Rapinoe's penalty against the Dutch was her 50th goal in 158 appearances over 13 years for the USA. She has also made a name for her-self off the pitch. Rapinoe is an advocate for numerous LGBT organisations, and she famously knelt during the national anthem at an international match in support of American Football star Colin Kaepernick and his anti-racism protests.

7 Brazilian midfielder Formiga set a record in 2019 by appearing at her seventh FIFA Women's World Cup – more than any other player. She had first appeared as a 17-year-old at the 1995 tournament in Sweden.

RAPINOE

TERRIFIC TECH
VAR TO THE RESCUE

Stéphanie Frappart became the first referee to use video assistance in awarding a penalty at a major tournament in the FIFA Women's World Cup 2019 final. The 35-year-old French referee checked the touchline screen after Dutch defender Stefanie van der Gragt fouled American Alex Morgan early in the second half in Lyon. Megan Rapinoe duly converted the penalty. VAR made its tournament debut in France, and it was a constant feature throughout the finals, right from the opening match when hosts France beat Korea Republic 4-0. France, featuring seven players from European club champions Lyon, had a further "goal" by Griedge Mbock Bathy ruled out after a video review.

FRAPPART

UEFA WOMEN'S EUROPEAN CHAMPIONSHIP

18

Iceland midfielder Amanda Andradottir was the youngest player at the 2022 finals, having been born on 18 December 2003. Andradottir played for Sweden's Kristianstads. Father Andri Sigthorsson had also been an international player.

MEAD

Women's football has taken huge strides since it was banned in England in 1921. The resurgence continued in 2022 with the country's record-breaking hosting of the UEFA Women's EURO, which had been delayed for a year because of the COVID-19 pandemic.

DOUBLING UP
MEAD BOTH TOP PLAYER AND TOP SCORER

England forward **Beth Mead** was an award-winner twice-over at the 2022 finals. The 27-year-old Arsenal forward was hailed by European federation UEFA's technical experts as Player of the Tournament and also collected the Golden Boot for her goalscoring exploits. Mead scored six goals, including a hat-trick in the record-breaking 8-0 group stage victory over Norway. Germany's Alex Popp also scored six goals but the formal award was handed to Mead because she beat her rival 5-0 on assists. Popp scored in all Germany's five matches up to the final but missed the showdown after being injured in the warm-up.

TOURNAMENT TRIVIA
STANDING UP FOR UKRAINE

MONZUL

Kateryna Monzul was not only a deserving but also a poignant appointment as referee for the final. Ukraine's top female match official took charge at Wembley with her own country at war after the Russian military invasion five months earlier. Monzul, an international referee since 2004, had been in charge at three previous matches. Monzul refereed the finals of the 2014 UEFA Women's Champions League and 2015 FIFA Women's World Cup. One year later she became the first woman to referee matches in Ukraine's men's top tier. Ukraine did not qualify for the Euro finals while Russia were expelled by UEFA after the invasion and replaced by Portugal.

2

Sarina Wiegman is the only manager not only to lead two different teams into the final but also to win both: Netherlands in 2017 and England in 2022.

⚝ STAR PLAYER
NEW FOCUS FOR LUCKLESS PUTELLAS

Spain's dreams of a winning a first Women's European title faded when superstar captain **Alexia Putellas** suffered a serious knee ligament injury in training on the eve of the finals. Putellas had been hailed as The Best Women's Player by world federation FIFA in its annual awards and had hoped to lead Spain all the way to European glory. Instead, they finished second in their group behind Germany and were then beaten 2-1 in extra-time by hosts England in the quarter-finals. Next target for the Barcelona star is regaining fitness in time for the 2023 FIFA Women's World Cup in Australia and New Zealand.

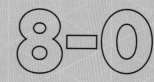

PUTELLAS

England set a European finals record with their 8-0 defeat of Norway in the group stage. Beth Mead scored a hat-trick and the other goals fell to Giorgia Stanway (penalty), Lauren Hemp, Ellen White (two) and Allesia Russo.

BIGGEST ATTENDANCES:

1 **87,192 – England 2-1 Germany**
(Wembley, 2022 final, aet)

2 **68,871 – England 1-0 Austria**
(Old Trafford, Manchester, 2022 group)

3 **41,301 – Germany 1-0 Norway**
(Stockholm, 2013 final)

4 **30,785 – N Ireland 0-5 England**
(Southampton, 2022 group)

5 **29,092 – England 3-2 Finland**
(City of Manchester Stadium, 2005 group)

FAN FEVER
The 2022 finals set a total attendance record of 574,875 with a single-match record of 87,192 for the Wembley final.

🏆 TOURNAMENT TRIVIA
GERMANY STILL THE ACT TO FOLLOW

Germany are tournament record holders with eight victories including an astonishing run featuring six successive titles from 1995. Title-winning specialist was Silvia Neid who was a European champion three times as a player and then twice as national team coach. Neid was FIFA's Women's Coach of the Year three times. She has proved an impossible act to follow. Germany lost 'their' crown in 2017 under Steffi Jones and lost a final for the first time in 2022 under Martina Voss-Tecklenburg.

🏆 TOURNAMENT TRIVIA
FOOTBALL COMES HOME AT LAST

One year after England's men fell a penalty kick short in their European Championship final, the women brought football home by defeating Germany 2-1 at Wembley. Match-winner was substitute Chloe Kelly in the second half of extra time. Earlier, England had taken the lead midway through the second half through Ella Toone, only to be pushed to the extra half hour by a Lina Magull equaliser. This was the first senior success by an England team since the men's FIFA World Cup victory in 1966 – also against German opposition and also in extra time.

WOMEN'S OLYMPIC FOOTBALL

Women's Olympic football has been dominated by North America since its introduction to the Games in Atlanta in 1996. The United States won four of the first six tournaments before Canada won the pandemic-delayed Games in Tokyo, where Team USA took bronze.

TOURNAMENT TRIVIA
SILVIA'S GOLDEN GOODBYE

Germany put the icing on their cake in 2016 by beating Sweden 2-1 to claim gold in Rio de Janeiro. After two FIFA Women's World Cup and eight UEFA European Championship victories, this was their first Olympic success and a perfect climax to coach **Silvia Neid**'s career in her last match after 11 years in charge. Without her, the Germans failed to qualify for the Games finals in Tokyo.

NEID

8

Germany hold the record for the most goals scored in a single Olympic finals match. The Germans beat China PR 8-0 in 2004, with five different players on the scoresheet, including a four-goal haul for Birgit Prinz.

NATIONAL LEGEND
MAGNIFICENT MARTA

Brazil superstar **Marta** finished with an Olympic silver medal in both 2004 and 2008 but missed out on home soil in 2016 when the *Canarinha* lost the bronze medal match against Canada. She would have found some consolation in becoming one of only five female players to have scored ten or more goals in Olympic football. With her three goals in the Tokyo tournament, Mart became the first player to score in five successive Games.

MARTA

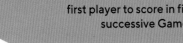

★ STAR PLAYER
SUPER SINCLAIR

Captain Christine Sinclair led by example as Canada followed up their bronze medals in 2012 and 2016 by winning gold for the first time in Tokyo. Sinclair had launched her tournament by memorably playing her 300th match for Canada and scoring their goal in a 1–1 draw with hosts Japan. In the gold medal final against Sweden, Sinclair won a penalty that secured a 1–1 draw and sent the tie to a shootout. Canada won 3–2 on penalties. Unhappily, Covid controls meant no fans could be present to see Sinclair and her team-mates make history.

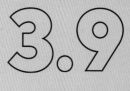

SINCLAIR

3.9

The number of matches in the Women's Olympic Football Tournament rose from 16 to 20 in 2004 and then 26 from 2008. The goals-per-game ratio slipped initially from 3.3 in Atlanta in 1996 to 2.5 in Rio de Janeiro in 2016, but then revived to a record 3.9 in Tokyo.

🏆 TOURNAMENT TRIVIA
THE POWER OF TEN

Netherlands striker Vivianne Miedema set a women's Olympic football record with her 10 goals in the pandemic-delayed Tokyo 2020 Games in 2021. This was the first time a player had reached double figures. Miedema had starred initially in the Netherlands' triumph at the Women's Euro in 2017 and at club level with Bayern Munich and Arsenal. In Tokyo, she scored four times in a 10–3 group stage victory over Zambia, then two more in both a 3–3 draw with Brazil and an 8–2 win over China PR. Miedema reached double figures with a brace against United States in the quarter-finals, but she missed her spot kick as the Netherlands lost 4–2 on penalties after a 2–2 draw.

🏆 TOURNAMENT TRIVIA
PIA AT THE PEAK

Pia Sundhage knows both sides of the Olympic women's football coin. The former international midfielder coached the United States to success in 2008 and 2012 and then returned to her native Sweden and led her own national team to silver at Rio 2016. Sundhage, who played for Sweden at the breakthrough 1996 Olympic Games in Atlanta, was voted the FIFA World Coach of the Year for Women's Football in 2012.

80,203

At London 2012, a tournament record 80,203 fans witnessed the USA defeat Japan in the final at Wembley. This remains the largest attendance for any women's football match in England.

WOMEN'S OLYMPIC FOOTBALL MEDALS:

1 **USA** (G:4, S:1, B:1)

2 **Germany** (G:1, S:0, B:3)

3 **Canada** (G:1, S:0, B:2)

4 **Norway** (G:1, S:0, B:1)

5 **Brazil** (G:0, S:2, B:0)

6 **Sweden** (G:0, S:2, B:0)

China PR (G:0, S:1, B:0)
= Japan (G:0, S:1, B:0)

LLOYD

2012

In 2012, Olympic hosts Great Britain fielded a team for the first time. Although they finished top of their first-round group with a perfect three wins from three, without conceding a goal, they were beaten 2–0 by Canada in the quarter-finals and missed out on a medal.

4

The USA have dominated the Olympics since women's football was introduced at the 1996 Games in Atlanta. They have won four gold medals as well as one silver and one bronze.

🏆 TOURNAMENT TRIVIA
BANK ON LLOYD

American **Carli Lloyd** is undoubtedly one of the greatest players in Olympic women's history. In 2008, she struck the winning goal for the USA against Brazil in the final in Beijing and then, four years later in London, claimed a decisive double in their 2–1 victory over Japan at Wembley.

OTHER WOMEN'S TOURNAMENTS

TOURNAMENT TRIVIA
SYDNEY TRANSPLANT

Sydney Leroux played in the FIFA U-20 Women's World Cup for two different nations. In 2004, when she was 14, she played two games without scoring for Canada. She then switched national allegiance in time to play for the USA in 2008, a tournament in which she finished as top scorer. Her five goals included the USA's opener in their 2-1 victory over Korea Republic in the final. Leroux would later claim another five-goal haul in the 2010 finals.

The demand for greater opportunities for women on the international stage sparked the creation of the FIFA U-20 and U-17 Women's World Cups. The tournaments offer an increasing number of countries the chance to play host. Pandemic issues disrupted the age-group schedules, but the return to action in 2022 saw Spain win the U-20 finals in Costa Rica and the U-17 finals in India.

LEROUX

TOURNAMENT TRIVIA
FRAPPART IN CHARGE

French official **Stéphanie Frappart** refereed the 2018 U-20 final in which Japan beat Spain 3-1 in Vannes, Brittany. One year later, she was appointed to referee the senior FIFA Women's World Cup final in Lyon in which the USA beat European champions Netherlands 2-0. Frappart was the first woman to oversee a major UEFA men's final, the UEFA Super Cup. In 2022 Frappart made a further breakthrough as the first woman to referee a men's FIFA World Cup finals tie (Costa Rica v Germany) in Qatar.

3

Germany and United States are the most successful nations in the FIFA U-20 Women's World Cup with three triumphs each.

FRAPPART

FIFA U-20 WOMEN'S WORLD CUP TOP SCORERS

1 **Christine Sinclair** (CAN, 2002) – 10
= **Alexandra Popp** (GER, 2010) – 10

3 **Inma Gabarro** (ESP, 2022) – 8

4 **Brittany Timko** (CAN, 2004) – 7
= **Kim Un-hwa** (PRK, 2012) – 7
= **Asisat Oshoala** (NIG, 2014) – 7

7 **Patricia Guijarro** (ESP, 2018) – 6

8 **Ma Xiaoxu** (CHN, 2006) – 5
= **Sydney Leroux** (USA, 2008) – 5
= **Mami Ueno** (JPN, 2016) – 5

STAR PLAYER
SUPER SINCLAIR

In 2002, Christine Sinclair of Canada became the first player to score ten goals in a single FIFA U-20 Women's World Cup. Her feat would be matched by Germany's Alexandra Popp eight years later. Sinclair was also the first player to score five times in one game, Canada's 6-2 quarter-final win over England in 2002. She later went on to become leading scorer at the Women's Olympic Football Tournament at London 2012.

TOURNAMENT TRIVIA
NIGERIAN BREAKTHROUGH

In 2014, Asisat Oshoala became the first African player to collect the Golden Ball for best player as well as the Golden Boot for leading scorer at the U-20 Women's World Cup in Canada. She and her Nigerian team-mates had to make do with the runners-up slot, however, after going down to Germany after extra time in the final. Oshoala's seven goals included four in Nigeria's 6-2 semi-final victory over Korea DPR.

113

In 2016, Papua New Guinea staged a FIFA tournament for the first time after original hosts South Africa withdrew. A total of 113 goals made this the equal highest-scoring tournament in the competition's history alongside Chile 2008.

FIFA U-17 WOMEN'S WORLD CUP TOP SCORERS

1 **Yeo Min-ji** (KOR, 2010) – 8
= **Ra Un-sim** (PRK, 2012) – 8
= **Lorena Navarro** (ESP, 2016) – 8

4 **Mukarama Abdulai** (GHA, 2018) – 7

5 **Dzsenifer Marozsán** (GER, 2008) – 6
= **Deyna Castellanos** (VEN, 2014) – 6
= **Gabriela García** (VEN, 2014) – 6

LÓPEZ

STAR PLAYER
DARING DEYNA

Venezuela's **Deyna Castellanos** shot to global fame at the 2016 finals after images of her audacious goal from the halfway line went viral. Castellanos struck four minutes into stoppage time to secure a 2-1 victory over Cameroon.

CASTELLANOS

TOURNAMENT TRIVIA
JORDANIAN LEGACY

The FIFA U-17 Women's World Cup 2016 in Jordan made history as it was the first FIFA women's tournament to be hosted in a Muslim country in the Middle East. Matches were played in the capital Amman as well as in Irbid and Al Zarqa. The tournament left a valuable legacy as the upgraded facilities enabled Jordan to host the Women's Asian Cup in 2018.

The 2022 tournament was the first FIFA women's event staged in India. It should have been played in 2020 but was postponed for two years because of the COVID-19 pandemic. Spain beat Colombia 1-0 in the final.

KOREAN JOY

Two years after Korea DPR won the inaugural FIFA U-17 Women's World Cup, southern neighbours Korea Republic lifted the trophy the next time round. The event's second final, in Trinidad & Tobago, was the first to go to penalties, with the South Koreans beating Japan 5-4 after a 3-3 draw.

TOURNAMENT TRIVIA
VICKY VICTORY

Vicky López (full name Victoria López Serrano Felix) lived up to her name at the 2022 finals in India. López won the Golden Ball for best player after Spain's 1-0 win over Colombia in the final in Mumbai. Her performances in inspiring Spain to their second U-17 crown included two goals in the last six minutes of a quarter-final in which Spain recovered from a goal down to overcome Japan 2-1. In January 2023, López became Barcelona's youngest top division goalscorer – men or women – in a defeat of Levante Las Planas. She was aged 16 years 5 months 27 days.

FIFA AWARDS

World football federation FIFA enjoyed a live show for The Best annual awards gala for 2022 after two years of online celebrations due to the COVID-19 pandemic. In February 2023, the world game brought the awards show to Paris to honour the outstanding achievements of winners who had commanded headlines all around the world over the previous 12 months and, most notably, in the FIFA World Cup finals in Qatar.

The annual FIFA gala saw pride of place taken by Argentina's Lionel Messi, some 32 years since Germany's Lothar Matthäus had been honoured at the original awards gala for 1991. Messi winning the men's prize had never been in doubt after his inspirational leadership and crucial goals for newly crowned FIFA World Cup-winners Argentina at the finals in Qatar in November and December 2022. He was hailed by FIFA for his achievements for the third time courtesy of a combined vote of national team coaches and captains, media and fans.

Messi's award marked a return to the status quo after two years interrupted by Robert Lewandowski. Poland's captain, in 2020 and 2021, had become only the second player in 12 years to break the stranglehold on the award, in its various guises, commanded by Messi and Portugal's Cristiano Ronaldo. A further notable 'establishment' success was achieved by Spain midfielder Alexia Putellas. She was again voted The Best women's player despite having been forced by injury to miss the UEFA Women's Euros.

The FIFA awards were devised and created in 1990–91 and were then, from 2010 to 2015, shared with the Ballon d'Or award. The latter had been created in the mid-1950s by the Paris magazine *France Football* and was originally awarded to the player hailed as European Footballer of the Year. Inaugural winner was the veteran England legend Sir Stanley Matthews. Later the reach of the Ballon d'Or was extended to players of all nationalities with European clubs and then to embrace all the world's footballers. This development prompted a five-year merger with the FIFA awards. In 2016, the two were uncoupled and FIFA, under the then newly-elected president Gianni Infantino, rebranded its own awards as The Best.

Hosts Samantha Johnson and Jermaine Jenas watch as Argentina fan Carlos Tula accepts the FIFA Fan Award for his country.

THE BEST FIFA MEN'S PLAYER

FIFA's award for the outstanding men's player over the previous 12 months is established as one of the greatest individual honours in the international game.

2022 WINNER
LIONEL MESSI

The name of Lionel Messi was effectively inscribed on The Best award in December 2022 in Lusail, Qatar, when he scored twice as Argentina won the FIFA World Cup. This was Messi's fourth major prize of the year, following the French league and domestic champions trophy with Paris Saint-Germain and the CONMEBOL/UEFA Cup with his country.

In the FIFA poll, Messi secured 52 points, well ahead of club-mate Kylian Mbappé (France and Paris Saint-Germain) and Karim Benzema (France and Real Madrid). Other nominees were Julián Alvárez (River Plate/Manchester City, Argentina), Jude Bellingham (Borussia Dortmund, England), Kevin De Bruyne (Manchester City, Belgium), Erling Haaland (Borussia Dortmund/Manchester City, Norway), Achraf Hakimi (Paris Saint-Germain, Morocco), Vinícius Junior (Real Madrid, Brazil), Robert Lewandowski (Bayern Munich/ Barcelona, Poland), Sadio Mané (Liverpool/Bayern Munich, Senegal), Luka Modrić (Real Madrid, Croatia), Neymar (Paris Saint-Germain, Brazil) and Mohamed Salah (Liverpool, Egypt).

Messi said: "I want to thank my teammates, [coach] Lionel Scaloni, [goalkeeper] Dibu [Emi Martínez]. We are representing them, without them we would not be here today ... The past year was crazy for me, I was able to achieve my dream after so much fighting, searching, insisting, it finally came and it is the most beautiful thing that happened to me in my career. I obviously want to thank my family, the people of Argentina, for having lived in a special way and it will remain in the memories for life."

PREVIOUS WINNERS :

2021	**Robert Lewandowski** (Poland)	
2020	**Robert Lewandowski** (Poland)	
2019	**Lionel Messi** (Argentina)	
2018	**Luka Modrić** (Croatia)	
2017	**Cristiano Ronaldo** (Portugal)	
2016	**Cristiano Ronaldo** (Portugal)	
2015	**Lionel Messi** (Argentina)	

1991
The year the award was first presented, to Germany's Lothar Matthäus.

1
Zinédine Zidane is the only man to have won the top FIFA award as both player and coach.

8
Brazilian players have won the award on eight occasions – more than any other nation.

France forward **Kylian Mbappé** was runner-up despite scoring only the second hat-trick in a men's FIFA World Cup Final, after Geoff Hurst in 1966

Votes for the award are divided equally between media representatives, national team coaches, national team captains, and the general public.

MBAPPÉ

THE BEST FIFA WOMEN'S PLAYER

This award acknowledges the ever-increasing popularity and success of the women's game, as was illustrated by the record global ratings achieved by the FIFA Women's World Cup in France in 2019.

2022 WINNER
ALEXIA PUTELLAS

Alexia Putellas was named The Best women's player for 2022, a repeat of the previous year when she became the first Spanish player to win a world women's player honour. The Spain and Barcelona midfielder was the first winner of the prize in two consecutive years. Putellas topped a poll ahead of United States' Alex Morgan and England's UEFA Women's Euro top scorer Beth Mead. Other nominees were Aitana Bonmati (Barcelona, Spain), Debinha (North Carolina Courage, Brazil), Jessie Fleming (Chelsea, Canada), Ada Hegerberg (Lyon, Norway), Sam Kerr (Chelsea, Australia), Vivianne Miedema (Arsenal, Netherlands), Lena Oberdorf (Wolfsburg, Germany), Alexandra Popp (Wolfsburg, Germany), Wendie Renard (Lyon, France), Keira Walsh (Manchester City/ Barcelona, England) and Leah Williamson (Arsenal, England).

Putellas enjoyed a remarkable year in which she captained Barcelona to a domestic treble and runners-up spot in the UEFA Women's Champions League final. She also made history as her country's first female player to reach 100 national team appearances. She celebrated the achievement with Spain's goal in a 1-1 draw against Italy. At club level, Putellas's leadership helped Barcelona win all 30 of their Primera División matches and she was also the 11-goal leading scorer in the UEFA Women's Champions League. Her only setback was an anterior cruciate ligament injury, which forced her to miss the UEFA Women's Euro finals in England.

PREVIOUS WINNERS :

2021	**Alexia Putellas**	(England)
2020	**Lucy Bronze**	(England)
2019	**Megan Rapinoe**	(USA)
2018	**Marta**	(Brazil)
2017	**Lieke Martens**	(Netherlands)
2016	**Carli Lloyd**	(USA)
2015	**Carli Lloyd**	(USA)

2001
The year that the inaugural Women's World Player of the Year award was given to Mia Hamm of the USA.

20
Marta's age when she became the youngest winner of the award in 2006.

Nadine Angerer is the only goalkeeper (male or female) to have won a FIFA Player of the Year award.

6
Brazilian legend Marta's six titles (including five in a row from 2006-10) are the most by any female player.

4
The number of winning individual players from the USA, more than any other nation.

ANGERER

215

OTHER FIFA AWARDS

Brilliance in football is measured mostly by achievements out on the pitch, but FIFA also recognises other outstanding contributions to the worldwide game over the past year. This ranges from the leadership and insight of coaches to respect for the principles of fair play.

2022 WINNERS:

The Best FIFA Men's Player: Lionel Messi (Paris Saint-Germain, Argentina)

The Best FIFA Women's Player: Alexia Putellas (FC Barcelona, Spain)

The Best FIFA Men's Coach: Lionel Scaloni (Argentina)

The Best FIFA Women's Coach: Sarina Wiegman (England)

The Best FIFA Men's Goalkeeper: Emiliano Martínez (Argentina, Aston Villa)

The Best FIFA Women's Goalkeeper: Mary Earps (England, Manchester United)

FIFA Puskás Award: Marcin Oleksy (Poland, Warta Poznań)

FIFA Fan Award: Argentina fans

FIFA Fair Play Award: Luka Lochoshvili (Georgia, Wolfsberger AC, US Cremonese)

FIFA FIFPRO Men's World 11: Thibaut Courtois (Belgium), **Achraf Hakimi** (Morocco), **Virgil Van Dijk** (Netherlands), **João Cancelo** (Portugal), **Kevin De Bruyne** (Belgium), **Luka Modrić** (Croatia), **Casemiro** (Brazil), **Lionel Messi** (Argentina), **Kylian Mbappé** (France), **Erling Haaland** (Norway), **Karim Benzema** (France)

FIFA FIFPRO Women's World 11: Christiane Endler (Chile), **Lucy Bronze** (England), **Mapi León (**Spain), **Leah Williamson** (England), **Wendie Renard** (France), **Alexia Putellas** (Spain), **Keira Walsh** (England), **Lena Oberdorf** (Germany), **Alex Morgan** (United States), **Sam Kerr** (Australia), **Beth Mead** (England)

Lionel Scaloni collected the award for The Best men's coach of 2022 after guiding Argentina to success in the 2022 FIFA World Cup. Scaloni was born 40 days before Argentina won their first World Cup in 1978. Later the defender was a team-mate of promising youngster Lionel Messi in the finals in Germany in 2006. Scaloni launched his club career with Newell's Old Boys then moved to Spain and Italy and had a brief loan spell at West Ham. He took over as manager of the under-20s in 2018. Within months, he was in charge of the senior team. He guided Argentina to victory at the *Copa América* in 2021. Victory over Italy in the 2022 South America/Europe Finalissima was the springboard for FIFA World Cup success – and The Best award.

Sarina Wiegman is no stranger to awards. The Dutch coach of England's 2022 European women's champions had already won The Best FIFA prize as top women's coach in 2020. Wiegman played for Dutch club Ter Leede, and made 99 official appearances for the Netherlands between 1987 to 2001. After retiring, she was the first woman to be appointed to the coaching staff of a Dutch professional club (Sparta Rotterdam). In 2017, she guided the Netherlands to victory in the UEFA Women's Euro and then to runners-up slot in the 2019 FIFA Women's World Cup. She took over England in September 2021 and led them to UEFA Women's Euro success in 2022.

EARPS

England's **Mary Earps** was crowned The Best FIFA Women's Goalkeeper after playing an outstanding role in England's victory at the 2022 UEFA Women's European Championship finals. Earps had also been a consistently impressive performer at club level for Manchester United. She topped the points poll ahead of Chelsea's Ann-Katrin Berger and Lyon's Christiane Endler. FIFA's testimonial acknowledged Earps' 'sharp reflexes, command of her penalty area and impressive distribution skills'. She played every minute of the tournament for the Lionesses, keeping four clean sheets and conceding only two goals. Her superb form was also recognised with a place in the Team of the Tournament.

The goal with which Polish amputee footballer **Marcin Oleksy** won the Puskás Award was possibly the most remarkable in the history of the prize. Oleksy was playing in the Polish amputees league championship for Warta Poznań against Stal Rzeszow when team-mate Dawid Novak crossed from the right wing. Oleksy threw his weight onto his prosthetic left leg and volleyed home acrobatically with his right foot. He said later: "I connected really cleanly and my eyes followed it all the way into the corner of the net." Runners-up were Richarlison's acrobatic effort for Brazil against Serbia at the FIFA World Cup and a strike by Dimitri Payet for Marseille against PAOK in the Europa Conference League.

OLEKSY

Georgian footballer **Luka Lochoshvili** received the FIFA Fair Play Award for a life-saving intervention during an Austrian league match. Lochoshvili, playing for Wolfsberger, reacted instantly after Austria Vienna's Georg Teigl was knocked unconscious in a collision. Teigl had swallowed his tongue and Lochoshvili cleared the defender's airways. Other contenders included Bayern Munich's Sadio Mané, for admitting to the referee that he scored a goal with his hand in a German league match, and Real Madrid's Eduardo Camavinga, for his encouragement to Ukraine players after playing against them for France in an under-21 international.

LOCHOSHVILI

PREVIOUS WINNERS:

2021

The Best Men's Player: Robert Lewandowski (Bayern Munich, Poland)

The Best Women's Player: Alexia Putellas (Barcelona, Spain)

The Best Men's Coach: Thomas Tuchel (Chelsea)

The Best Women's Coach: Emma Hayes (Chelsea)

The Best Men's Goalkeeper: Édouard Mendy (Chelsea, Senegal)

The Best Women's Goalkeeper: Christiane Endler (Lyon, Chile)

FIFA Puskás Award: Erik Lamela (Tottenham Hotspur)

FIFA Fan Award: Denmark and Finland fans

FIFA Fair Play Award: Denmark national team, medical and coaching staffs

FIFA The Best Special Awards: Christine Sinclair (Canada) and **Cristiano Ronaldo** (Portugal)

2020

The Best FIFA Men's Player: Robert Lewandowski (Poland, Bayern Munich)

The Best FIFA Women's Player: Lucy Bronze (England, Manchester City)

The Best FIFA Men's Coach: Jürgen Klopp (Liverpool)

The Best FIFA Women's Coach: Sarina Wiegmann (Netherlands)

The Best FIFA Men's Goalkeeper: Manuel Neuer (Bayern Munich, Germany)

The Best FIFA Women's Goalkeeper: Sarah Bouhaddi (Lyon, France)

FIFA Puskás Award: Heung-min Son (Tottenham Hotspur)

FIFA Fan Award: Marivaldo da Silva (Brazil)

FIFA Fair Play Award: Mattia Agnese (Italy)

FIFA Foundation Award: Marcus Rashford (Manchester United)

2019

The Best FIFA Men's Player: Lionel Messi (Barcelona, Argentina)

The Best FIFA Women's Player: Megan Rapinoe (Reign FC, USA)

The Best FIFA Men's Coach: Jürgen Klopp (Liverpool)

The Best FIFA Women's Coach: Jill Ellis (USA)

The Best FIFA Men's Goalkeeper: Alisson Becker (Liverpool, Brazil)

FIFA Puskás Award: Dániel Zsóri (Debrecen)

FIFA Fan Award: Silvia Grecco (Brazil)

FIFA Fair Play Award: Marcelo Bielsa and Leeds United

FIFA/
COCA-COLA
WORLD
RANKINGS

The FIFA/Coca-Cola Ranking has grown in importance year on year with its employment as the basis for tournament draws in competitions around the football world.

FIFA introduced a world ranking system in December 1992 to provide a monthly statistical analysis of the rise and fall of the fortunes of all the world game's national teams in men's football. Placings are computed on results in what are termed international "A" games and consider match results, goals scored, the strength of the opposition, regional balance and competition status. The women's world ranking, introduced in 2003, is published on a quarterly basis.

The rankings are important, not least because they have previously been used as a form guide by FIFA for draws for international competitions. A short break in publication accompanied the 2018 FIFA World Cup, when the system was refined to adjust anomalies concerning the assessment of friendly matches. This current iteration of FIFA's formula, named "SUM", relies on a system of addition and subtraction rather than averaging points over a given time period, as in previous versions.

Argentina took over top spot in the men's rankgings in spring 2023, ending Brazil's year-long reign as number one.

FIFA/COCA-COLA WORLD RANKING 2023

The FIFA World Cup in Qatar in November and December 2022 brought about a dramatic reset in the ranking after normal service had been resumed the previous year following the abrupt halt enforced by the worldwide COVID-19 pandemic. The international confederations all continue to look to the FIFA ranking in assessing their own comparative status.

Argentina did not take over at the top immediately after winning the World Cup, but they did not need long to secure top spot in the 211-nation table. Coach Lionel Scaloni's men won a number of celebratory friendly matches after the finals to overtake long-time ranking leaders Brazil, who slipped down to third behind France. Otherwise, little movement was evident among the major nations, with Belgium and England sitting just outside the top trio. Morocco and Senegal capitalised on their World Cup showings to take up slots in the top 20, while San Marino took up their customary position at the other end of the ranking.

The FIFA/Coca-Cola World Ranking has charted the ebb and flow of the men's national team game for three decades since it was devised and launched in December 1992. The fluctuating fortunes of countries at all levels are based on computer-based comparisons of match results, goals scored, the strength of the opposition, regional balance and competition status.

A more sensitive ranking model was launched in August 2018. The new version was named "SUM" because it relies on adding/subtracting points won or lost for a game to/from the previous point totals rather than averaging game points over a given time period, as was done before.

RANKING

Pos.	Country	Pts
1	**Argentina**	**1840.93**
2	**France**	**1838.45**
3	**Brazil**	**1834.21**
4	**Belgium**	**1792.53**
5	**England**	**1792.43**
6	**Netherlands**	**1731.23**
7	**Croatia**	**1730.02**
8	**Italy**	**1713.66**
9	**Portugal**	**1707.22**
10	**Spain**	**1682.85**
11	Morocco	1677.79
12	Switzerland	1664.24
13	United States	1653.77
14	Germany	1647.42
15	Mexico	1631.87
16	Uruguay	1631.29
17	Colombia	1617.08
18	Senegal	1613.21
19	Denmark	1594.53
20	Japan	1588.59
21	Peru	1561.2
22	Sweden	1558.7
23	Poland	1553.76
24	IR Iran	1553.23
25	Serbia	1541.52
26	Wales	1538.95
27	Korea Republic	1536.01
28	Tunisia	1535.76
29	Australia	1532.79
30	Ukraine	1530.04
31	Chile	1511.32
32	Austria	1508.24
33	Hungary	1504.24
34	Algeria	1504.19
35	Egypt	1500.67
36	Scotland	1500.52
37	Russia	1495.53
38	Czechia	1495.04
39	Costa Rica	1491.12
40	Nigeria	1480.8
41	Ecuador	1478.13
42	Cameroon	1470.21
43	Türkiye	1465.7
44	Norway	1463.77
45	Côte d'Ivoire	1449.95
46	Romania	1444.58
47	Canada	1442.66
48	Paraguay	1440.65
49	Rep. Ireland	1436.31
50	Burkina Faso	1433.91

51	Slovakia	1433.77	107	Kosovo	1186.26	163	South Sudan	993.36
52	Greece	1433.01	108	Estonia	1182.5	164	Vanuatu	986.65
53	Mali	1430.75	109	Tajikistan	1182.24	165	Cuba	986.2
54	Saudi Arabia	1421.46	110	Madagascar	1181.21	166	Puerto Rico	985.41
55	Venezuela	1410.47	111	Cyprus	1179.45	167	Barbados	984.05
56	Finland	1405.31	112	Kazakhstan	1177.05	168	Fiji	980.48
57	Bosnia/Herzegovina	1403.04	113	Guinea-Bissau	1172.3	169	St Lucia	978.91
58	Panama	1399.23	114	Thailand	1171.88	170	Guyana	975.81
59	Slovenia	1398.47	115	Korea DPR	1169.96	171	Moldova	972.91
60	Ghana	1396.01	116	Guatemala	1164.64	172	Malta	972.79
61	Qatar	1388.61	117	Sierra Leone	1161.79	173	Bermuda	966.27
62	Northern Ireland	1385.93	118	Angola	1158.57	174	Nepal	963.1
63	Jamaica	1381.87	119	Mozambique	1154.64	175	Grenada	960.4
64	Iceland	1369.03	120	The Gambia	1150.99	176	Cambodia	948.59
65	North Macedonia	1363.07	121	Libya	1145.82	177	Belize	939.96
66	South Africa	1350.08	122	Central African Rep.	1145.69	178	St Vincent/Grenadines	938.28
67	Iraq	1347.84	123	Niger	1142.57	179	Montserrat	938.02
68	Albania	1344.95	124	Azerbaijan	1142.25	180	Mauritius	932.02
69	Montenegro	1343.28	125	Faroe Islands	1138.98	181	Chad	930.22
70	Congo DR	1338.61	126	Zimbabwe	1138.56	182	Macau	917.93
71	Cabo Verde	1337.05	127	Malawi	1134.64	183	Mongolia	911.74
72	United Arab Emirates	1336.28	128	Sudan	1132.62	184	São Tomé & Príncipe	906.7
73	Oman	1333.54	129	Togo	1129.81	185	Bhutan	906.36
74	Uzbekistan	1318.36	130	Tanzania	1125.89	186	Dominica	904.88
75	El Salvador	1318.3	131	Comoros	1111.89	187	American Samoa	900.27
76	Bulgaria	1315.74	132	Latvia	1110.55	188	Laos	899.58
77	Georgia	1311.51	133	Antigua and Barbuda	1107.51	189	Cook Islands	899.33
78	Israel	1307.41	134	Solomon Islands	1103.61	190	Samoa	894.26
79	Guinea	1305.92	135	Rwanda	1100.67	191	Brunei Darussalam	891.12
80	Honduras	1300.38	136	Philippines	1097.67	192	Bangladesh	883.88
81	China PR	1297.98	137	Turkmenistan	1095.2	193	Djibouti	875.05
82	Gabon	1296.74	138	Malaysia	1082.13	194	Tonga	861.81
83	Bolivia	1296.42	139	St Kitts and Nevis	1081.4	195	Pakistan	861.18
84	Jordan	1293.26	140	Nicaragua	1079.17	196	Timor-Leste	860.45
85	Bahrain	1282.05	141	Suriname	1075.72	197	Seychelles	860.13
86	Zambia	1280.52	142	Ethiopia	1072.99	198	Cayman Islands	859.83
87	Haiti	1275.96	143	Kuwait	1071.92	199	Liechtenstein	855.77
88	Curaçao	1272.26	144	Eswatini	1069.89	200	Eritrea	855.56
89	Uganda	1257.3	145	Burundi	1069.71	201	Gibraltar	854.72
90	Syria	1246.75	146	Lithuania	1068.53	201	Somalia	854.72
91	Luxembourg	1245.78	147	Hong Kong, China	1057.03	203	Bahamas	852.87
92	Benin	1240.45	148	Liberia	1049.94	204	Aruba	850.88
93	Palestine	1239.19	149	Indonesia	1046.14	205	Turks and Caicos Is	839.39
94	Equatorial Guinea	1232.78	150	Lesotho	1046.02	206	Guam	838.33
95	Vietnam	1229.69	151	Dominican Republic	1038.13	207	Sri Lanka	825.25
96	Kyrgyz Republic	1225.44	152	Botswana	1037.31	208	US Virgin Islands	816.59
97	Armenia	1224.08	153	Andorra	1030.52	209	British Virgin Islands	804.11
98	Belarus	1210.17	154	Maldives	1024.72	210	Anguilla	785.69
99	Lebanon	1202.74	155	Afghanistan	1023.04	211	San Marino	759.12
100	New Zealand	1201.06	156	Chinese Taipei	1021.02			
101	India	1200.66	157	Yemen	1020.37			
102	Kenya	1200.18	158	Singapore	1014.04			
103	Congo	1197.89	159	Papua New Guinea	1007.46			
104	Trinidad & Tobago	1197.61	160	Myanmar	998.41			
105	Mauritania	1194.28	161	New Caledonia	995.58			
106	Namibia	1190.49	162	Tahiti	995.11			

FIFA/COCA-COLA WOMEN'S WORLD RANKING 2023

RANKING

A record-extending 188 nations featured in the FIFA/Coca-Cola Women's Ranking in the run-up to the FIFA Women's World Cup finals. The steady progress of women's football at both domestic and international levels continues. This has been reflected in a promise from European broadcasters to improve and extend their levels of coverage.

The United States have commanded top spot almost as long as the ranking has existed, with the main European powers competing to lead the pack of pursuers. These include the likes of European champions England, Germany, Sweden, France and Spain.

As with the men's ranking, the fluctuating fortunes of countries at all levels are based on computer-based comparisons of match results, goals scored, the strength of the opposition, regional balance and competition status. One difference, however, is that the women's ranking table is published only four times every year rather than monthly or bi-monthly. This reflects the less intense nature of the competitions schedule for women's national teams.

Pos.	Country	Pts
1	United States	2090.03
2	Germany	2061.56
3	Sweden	2049.71
4	England	2040.76
5	France	2026.65
6	Spain	2002.28
7	Canada	1996.34
8	Brazil	1995.3
9	Netherlands	1980.47
10	Australia	1919.69
11	Japan	1916.68
12	Norway	1908.25
13	Denmark	1866.25
14	China PR	1854.49
15	Iceland	1854.4
16	Italy	1846.5
17	Korea Republic	1840.27
18	Austria	1813.56
19	Belgium	1795.67
20	Switzerland	1765.9
21	Portugal	1745.13
22	Rep. Ireland	1743.59
23	Scotland	1735.87
24	Russia	1717.06
25	Colombia	1702.64
26	New Zealand	1699.7
27	Czechia	1690.16
28	Argentina	1682.45
29	Finland	1676.76
30	Wales	1665.82
31	Poland	1662.26
32	Vietnam	1648.89
33	Ukraine	1644.63
34	Serbia	1622.42
35	Mexico	1621.8
36	Costa Rica	1596.94
37	Chinese Taipei	1578.28
38	Romania	1564.03
39	Slovenia	1556.25
40	Nigeria	1554.94
41	Chile	1553.22
42	Hungary	1544.83
43	Jamaica	1536.81
44	Thailand	1530.56

45	N Ireland	1523.83
46	Philippines	1512.97
47	Slovakia	1512.7
48	Paraguay	1505.2
49	Uzbekistan	1498.55
50	Myanmar	1487.58
51	Venezuela	1486.32
52	Panama	1482.51
53	Haiti	1475.33
54	South Africa	1471.52
55	Papua New Guinea	1469.52
56	Cameroon	1445.75
57	Belarus	1443.08
58	Ghana	1419.63
59	Croatia	1416.26
60	India	1413.52
61	IR Iran	1409.89
62	Greece	1405.82
63	Türkiye	1388.37
64	Uruguay	1385.45
65	Bosnia/Herzegovina	1382.41
66	Côte d'Ivoire	1379.39
67	Ecuador	1376.11
68	Israel	1358.37
69	Fiji	1345.58
70	Equatorial Guinea	1344.47
71	Albania	1342.43
72	Morocco	1334.08
73	Jordan	1322.78
74	Peru	1318.61
75	Trinidad & Tobago	1318.11
76	Tunisia	1298.6
77	Zambia	1298.31
78	Hong Kong, China	1297.87
79	Azerbaijan	1290.24
80	Algeria	1288.27
81	Mali	1273.24
82	Senegal	1264.44
83	Guatemala	1259.69
84	Bahrain	1254.12
85	Guyana	1247.77
86	Malta	1245.35
87	Laos	1240.52
88	Egypt	1229.98
89	Malaysia	1228.66
90	Bulgaria	1228.25
91	Montenegro	1224.14
92	Tonga	1221.48
93	Guam	1218.07
94	Cuba	1217.56
95	Lithuania	1216.59
96	Bolivia	1213.1
97	Samoa	1212.01
98	Estonia	1211.02
99	Kazakhstan	1205.62
100	Faroe Islands	1201.16
101	Nepal	1199.88
102	Kosovo	1188.46
103	Puerto Rico	1186.72
104	Solomon Is	1181.11
105	Indonesia	1179.93
106	New Caledonia	1175.63
107	Tahiti	1175.09
108	Cook Islands	1174.93
109	Dominican Republic	1173.44
110	Congo	1161.46
111	Moldova	1161.34
112	Congo DR	1159
113	United Arab Emirates	1158.26
114	Nicaragua	1157.63
115	El Salvador	1148.88
116	Honduras	1145.7
117	Luxembourg	1145.65
118	Cambodia	1144.56
119	Latvia	1142.4
120	Togo	1138.33
121	Cyprus	1134.28
122	Vanuatu	1132.82
123	The Gambia	1129.72
124	Ethiopia	1117.66
125	Zimbabwe	1115.59
126	Georgia	1113.38
127	Mongolia	1108.79
128	Kyrgyz Republic	1099.57
129	North Macedonia	1093.35
130	Palestine	1091.95
131	Singapore	1090.86
132	St Kitts and Nevis	1090.74
133	Suriname	1089.15
134	Cabo Verde	1088.27
135	Gabon	1079.87
136	Guinea	1075.9
137	Turkmenistan	1075.41
138	Lebanon	1062.88
139	Sierra Leone	1059.98
140	Bangladesh	1054.55
141	Burkina Faso	1050.87
142	Armenia	1044.94
143	Angola	1037.32
144	American Samoa	1030
145	Benin	1020.94
146	Namibia	1011.92
147	Bermuda	1007.55
148	Kenya	991.78
149	Tajikistan	991.2
150	Botswana	984.32
151	St Lucia	982
152	Tanzania	980.17
153	Barbados	966.8
154	Sri Lanka	955.21
155	St Vincent/Grenadines	950.85
156	Timor-Leste	946.01
157	Pakistan	944.58
158	Syria	942.82
159	Malawi	941
160	Maldives	938.55
161	Uganda	924.09
162	Dominica	910.74
163	Rwanda	894.87
164	Liberia	891.31
165	Seychelles	884.64
166	Niger	877.93
167	Cayman Islands	854.05
168	Grenada	849.17
169	Lesotho	847.17
170	Saudi Arabia	844.3
171	Bhutan	841.86
172	Belize	839.85
173	Guinea-Bissau	834.73
174	Mozambique	820.17
175	Antigua and Barbuda	804.42
176	Burundi	799.08
177	Eswatini	798.94
178	US Virgin Islands	793.07
179	Curaçao	771.22
180	Andorra	751.46
181	British Virgin Islands	735.87
182	Aruba	728.86
183	Comoros	722.61
184	Madagascar	691
185	Anguilla	687.55
186	Turks and Caicos Is	664.95
187	South Sudan	649.69
188	Mauritius	375.59

PICTURE CREDITS

The publishers would like to thank the following sources for their kind permission to reproduce the pictures in this book. The page numbers for each of the photographs are listed below, giving the page on which they appear in the book and any location indicator (C-centre, T-top, B-bottom, L-left, R-right).

Getty Images: 88BR; /AFP: 21BL, 48B, 97TL, 105BL, 140BR, 155B, 174BL, 177T; /AMA/Corbis: 52C, 81T; /Mohammad Javad Abjoushak/SOPA Images/LightRocket: 168BL; /Robin Alam/Icon Sportswire: 130B; /Allsport: 57L, 159TR, 173TR; /Nelson Almeida/AFP: 91L; /Vanderlei Almeida/AFP: 173BL, 196TR; /Vincent Amalvy/AFP: 103BR; / Ashraf Amra/Anadolu Agency: 135R; /Anadolu Agency: 75BL; /Odd Andersen/AFP: 25BR; /ANP: 31BR; /Gabriele Aponte: 98; /Facundo Arrizabalaga: 24T; /Gonzalo Arroyo – UEFA: 55BR; /The Asashi Shimbun: 16T, 117TR; /Matthew Ashton/Corbis: 45BR, 65B; /Matthew Ashton/AMA: 37TR, 39C, 63T, 120, 121TR, 123BR, 126–127, 128BR, 142BL; /Frank Augstein: 12T; /Tnani Badreddine/Defodi Images: 86TR; /Naomi Baker: 209T; /Gokhan Balci/Anadolu Agency: 105TR, 107TL; /Marcel ter Bals/BSR Agency: 78TR; /Steve Bardens: 169T, 211TR; /Lars Baron: 31TL, 46T, 57CL, 68TR, 68B, 192L, 208BR; /Robbie Jay Barratt/AMA: 14BR, 43TR, 79L, 106B, 147C, 158; / Khalil Bashar/Jam Media: 105BR; /James Bayliss/AMA: 4BR; /Robyn Beck/AFP: 151TR; /Fethi Belaid/AFP: 106TL; /Daniel Beloumou Olomo/AFP: 110TR, 181L; /Bentley Archive/Popperfoto: 64R; /Martin Bernetti/AFP: 210T; /Bagu Blanco/Pressinphoto/Icon Sport: 101BR; /Bongarts: 28BL; /Shaun Botterill: 19TR, 23C, 47B, 157B, 149L, 157BL, 165TR; /Cris Bouroncle/AFP: 127BR, 191BR; /Gabriel Bouys/AFP: 32B, 108; /Rico Brouwer/Soccrates: 29bl, 119T, 148T; /Chris Brunskill: 11R, 41BR, 90TR, 95TL, 140T, 146BL; /Clive Brunskill: 94B; /Simon Bruty: 6, 99B, 134–135, 143T, 152, 161T, 214BR; /Rodrigo Buendia/AFP: 88T; /David S. Bustamante/Soccrates: 107B, 116BL, 139BL, 154; /Giuseppe Cacace/AFP: 123BL; /Richard Callis/Eurasia Sport Images: 131BL; /Michael Campanella: 52B; /David Cannon: 17L, 30T, 40TR, 61B; /Alex Caparros: 222; / David Catry/BELGA MAG/AFP: 203B; /Jean Catuffe: 48T, 49B, 89T; /Central Press: 63BL; /Central Press/Hulton Archive: 49TR; /Graham Chadwick: 61TC; /Matteo Ciambelli/NurPhoto: 44TR, 101T, 132TR; /Ciancaphoto Studio: 16B, 55BL; /Robert Cianflone: 67R, 69TL; /Fabrice Coffrini/AFP: 116TR; /Chris Cole: 146R; /Phil Cole: 43L; /Max Colin/Icon Sport: 13b; /Aitor Alcalde Colomer: 207T; /Annelie Cracchiolo/DeFodi Images: 53TR; /Carl de Souza/AFP: 99T, 109TR; / Mohammed Dabbous/Anadolu Agency: 137t; /DeFodi Images: 36BL, 45TL, 76TR; /Adrian Dennis/AFP: 56TR, 82B, 142, 164L; /Khaled Desouki/AFP: 180B, 182R, 183L, 193B; /Disney/Central Press/Hulton Archive: 15BR; /Kevork Djansezian: 131TR; /Stephen Dunn: 109BR; / Johannes Eisele/AFP: 5BL, 40BL; /Paul Ellis/AFP: 20TR; /Elsa: 146BL, 204; /Darren England: 115BR; /Eurasia Sport Images: 136TR; /Esteban Felix/AFP: 95TL; /Baptiste Fernandez/Icon Sport: 73BR; / Franck Fife/AFP: 19B, 166B; /Julian Finney: 11BL, 144–145, 148BL, 150B, 157TL; /Foto Olimpik/NurPhoto: 35C; /Stu Forster: 88BL; / David Fitzgerald/Sportsfile: 131BR; /Stuart Franklin: 29BR, 63BR, 95TR, 133BL, 208BR; /Sebastian Frej/MB Media: 14tl; /Romeo Gacad/AFP: 45TR; /Daniel Garcia/AFP: 96B, 146BC; /GES–Sportfoto: 10; /Paul Gilham: 111TR; /James Gill/Danehouse: 168TR; /Patrick Gorski/Icon Sportswire: 129BR; /El Grafico: 87B; /Laurence Griffiths: 63R, 64BL, 113TR, 156; /Alex Grimm: 23TL, 55TR, 136BL, 193T; /Jeff Gross: 133L; /Gianluigi Guercia/AFP: 185L; /Markus Gilliar: 153T, 157T; /Jack Guez/AFP: 84–85; /Norman Hall/LatinContent: 177B; /Lionel Hahn: 19tl; /Matthias Hangst: 22TL, 167C; /Etsuo Hara: 100R, 122B, 141T, 193BR; /Ronny Hartmann/AFP: 74TR; /Alexander Hassenstein: 21R, 22B, 147BR, 198; /Richard Heathcote: 97B, 150T, 205BL, 205BR; /Alexander Heimann/Bongarts: 132B; /Mike Hewitt: 90BL, 127TC; /Maja Hitij: 5TC; /Simon Hofmann: 156; /Hagen Hopkins: 125L; /Boris Horvat/AFP: 165B; /Harry How: 129TR; /Arif Hudaverdi Yaman/Anadolu Agency: 74BL; /Marvin Ibo Guengoer – GES Sportfoto: 54R, 147TR; /isifa: 69BR; /Dan Istitene: 25L; /Dimitri Iundt/Corbis/VC: 17TR; /Catherine Ivill: 45TR, 49CL, 80B, 200–201, 206TR; /Karim Jaafar/AFP: 117L; /Franklin Jacome: 99TL; /Raddad Jebarah/NurPhoto: 214T; /Petr Josek: 43BR; /Jasper Juinen: 13TR, 33TL, 34TL; /Sia Kambou/AFP: 110BL; /Sefa Karacan/Anadolu Agency: 32T; /Keystone: 17TC, 62R; /Keystone/Hulton Archive: 57BR; /Mike King: 146TR; /Glyn Kirk/AFP: 194BL; /Joe Klamar/AFP: 42BL; /Christof Koepsel/Bongarts: 92BR, 100TL; /Mark Kolbe: 115C; /Ozan Kose/AFP: 75T; /Patrick Kovarik/AFP: 82TR; /Jan Kruger: 169B; Kyodo News: 143B, 218–219; / Harry Langer/DeFodi Images: 1147BR; /David Leah/Mexsport: 128TR; /Christopher Lee: 69TR; / Fred Lee: 97TR; /Mark Leech/Offside: 51TR; / Sylvain Lefevre: 212–213; /Eddy Lemaistre/Corbis: 26BL; /Matthew Lewis: 55L, 211BL; /Christian Liewig/Corbis: 180, 183BR; /Sergio Lima/AFP: 91T; /Alex Livesey: 45C, 50BL, 51BL, 71T, 73C, 85R, 120; /Marcio Machado/Eurasia Sport Images: 191T, 217C; /Dale MacMillan/Soccrates:111BR; /Ian MacNicol: 41TR, 58BR; /David Maher/Sportsfile: 59C; /Joe Maher/FIFA: 215T, 216B; /Pierre-Philippe Marcou/AFP: 35T; /Hunter Martin/LatinContent: 94T; /Clive Mason: 140T; /Stephen McCarthy/Sportsfile: 58TR, 59BR; / Stephen McCarthy/FIFA: 155T; /Eamonn McCormack: 199C; /Jamie McDonald: 42T, 70B, 72TR; /Ross MacDonald/SNS Group: 65TR/Anatoliy

Medved/Icon Sportswire: 54C; /Stephanie Meek/CameraSport: 207B; /Marty Melville/AFP: 124B; MB Media: 141B, 171T; /Wagner Meier: 171B; /Martin Meissner/AFP: 33TR; /Buda Mendes: 170, 172B, 190R; /Craig Mercer/CameraSport: 36R; /Jeroen Meuwsen/BSR Agency:30BL; /Maddie Meyer: 125TR; /Vincent Michel/Icon Sport: 210BR; /Jiro Mochizuki/Icon Sport: 103TR; /Brendan Moran/Sportsfile: 79B; /Pablo Morano/BSR Agency: 151C; /Alex Morton: 166tr, 188BR; /Dean Mouhtaropoulos: 29T, 33B, 115TL, 197BL; /Peter Muhly/AFP: 82TL; /Dan Mullan: 56BL, 139T; /Marwan Naamani/AFP: 123TR; /Hoang Dinh Nam/AFP: 130TR; /Francois Nel: 95BR, 112–113, 114TR; /Mike Nelson/AFP: 127TR; /Adam Nurkiewicz: 164tr; /NurPhoto: 35BR; /Werner Otto/ullstein bild: 163TL; /Jeff Pachoud/AFP: 162; /Minas Panagiotakis: 215BR; /Ulrik Pedersen/NurPhoto: 104CR; /Hannah Peters: 124TR; /Serge Philippot/Onze/Icon Sport: 66TR; /Hrvoje Polan/AFP: 38BL; /Popperfoto: 18T, 20B, 38TR, 59BL, 91B, 92BL, 113TR, 122TR, 145TL 162B, 163BR, 175BR, 209B; /Joern Pollex: 96T; /Mike Powell: 153B; /Bruna Prado: 171C; /Savo Prelevic/AFP: 83C; /Pressefoto Ulmer/ullstein bild: 83B, 167TR; /Adam Pretty: 93R; /Gary M Prior: 39T; /Professional Sport/Popperfoto: 26TR; /Quality Sport Images: 57T; /Ben Radford: 58L, 71BR, 155C, 190BL; /David Ramos: 41BL, 73TR, 188–189; RDB/ullstein bild: 77T, 79TR, 216T, 217T; /Eric Renard/Icon Sport: 18BL; /Andreas Rentz/Bongarts: 47TL; /Alex Reyes/LatinContent: 100BL; /Chris Ricco: 15C; /Kyle Rivas: 131TC; /Rolls Press/Popperfoto: 12B; /Clive Rose: 5L, 67L, 77BL; /Martin Rose: 17R, 21TL; /Rouxel/AFP: 183R; /Alessandro Sabattini: 25BL, 118B; /Karim Sahib/AFP: 192BR; /Sampics/Corbis: 60TR; /Mark Sandten/Bongarts:133BR; /Fran Santiago: 34B; /Alexandre Schneider: 87T, 170B; /Rich Schultz: 95BL, ; /Antonio Scorza/AFP: 197C; /Richard Sellers/Soccrates: 119BL, 137B, 206BL, 220BL; /Abdelhak Senna/AFP: 184B, 185R; /Lefty Shivambu/Gallo Images: 111C, 181T, 182B; /Javier Soriano/AFP: 104, 163TR, 181T; /Cameron Spencer: 113B; /Michael Steele: 39BR, 70TR; /Srdjan Stevanovic: 62B, 67T; /Srdjan Stefanovic: 66B; /Laszlo Szirtesi – UEFA: 48TR; /Henri Szwarc/Icon Sport: 86B; /TF-Images: 81L; /Pier Marco Tacca: 76B; /Justin Tallis/Pool/AFP: 4TR; /Florencia Tan Jun/PxImages/Icon Sportswire: 92T; /Bob Thomas: 24BR, 27TL, 47C, 59T, 93L, 119BR, 138BL, 140BL, 147TL, 157R, 159BR, 195BL; /Mark Thompson: 82BR; / John Thys/AFP: 81B, 191BL; /Charly Triballeau/AFP: 109TL, 178, 181B; /Markus Tobisch/SEPA.Media: 217B; /Universal/Sygma: 183T; /VCG: 121BL; /VI Images: 5TL, 22R, 31B; /Robert van den Brugge/AFP: 37C; / Luis Veniegra/SOPA Images/LightRocket: 202B; /Joris Verwijst/BSR Agency: 37B; /Claudio Villa/Visionhaus: 25T, 102–103, 129C, 138T, 147TC; /Hector Vivas: 135BR; /Luke Walker: 199TL; /Ian Walton: 184TR; /Bernd Wende/ullstein bild: 23R; /Charlotte Wilson/Offside: 36B; /Craig Williamson/SNS Group: 76BL; /Zhizhao Wu: 195T, 145TR, 40BR.

PA Images: 67BR, 174TR, 194TR; /Matthew Ashton: 93TL; /Barry Coombs: 47TR; / DPA: 114BL; /Dominic Favre/AP: 72B; /Intime Sports/AP: 46BR; /Ross Kinnaird: 175TR; /Tony Marshall: 75R, 93TR; /Peter Robinson: 28T, 50R, 64T, 89B, 188T; /S&G and Barratts: 149BR; /SMG: 65L; /Scanpix Norway: 53TL; /Ariel Schalit/AP: 107C; / Sven Simon: 91TR; /Neal Simpson: 60B, 175BL; /Jon Super/AP: 205T.

Alamy: /Allstar Picture Library Ltd: 53tl; /AP: 161C; /PA Images: 61TR.

Shutterstock: /Anabela88: 171BL; /BOLDG: 85BR; /Colorsport: 44BL, 78B; / FMStox: 11L; /Khvost: 113TC; /Panatphong: 159TC; /Namig Rustamov: 11T; /Marcelo Savao/EPA: 196BL; /Wikrom Kitsamritchai: 8–9; /Tond Van Graphcraft: 11C.

Wikimedia Commons: 53BL, 160 (Martijn Mureau/CC Attribution Sharealike), 172TR, 180T (Yelika225), 203T (Adam.J.W.C.).

Every effort has been made to acknowledge correctly and contact the source and/or copyright holder of each picture. Any unintentional errors or omissions will be corrected in future editions of this book.

ABOUT THE AUTHOR

Keir Radnedge has been covering football for more than 50 years. He has written countless books on the subject, from tournament guides to comprehensive encyclopedias, aimed at all ages. His journalism career included the Daily Mail for 20 years, as well as the Guardian and other national newspapers and magazines in the UK and abroad. He is a former editor of World Soccer, generally recognised as the premier English-language magazine on global football. In addition to his writing, Keir has been a regular foreign football analyst for all UK broadcasters. He scripted official films of the early World Cups and is chairman of the football commission of AIPS, the international sports journalists' association.

ACKNOWLEDGEMENTS

Special thanks to **Aidan Radnedge** for support and assistance and an incomparable insight into the most intriguing corners of the world game.